KU-716-382

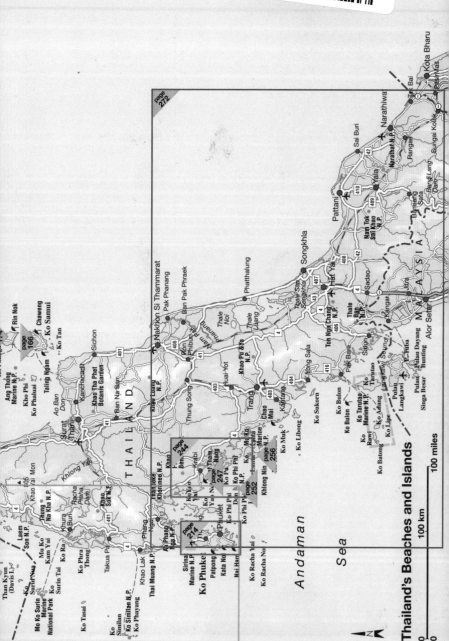

Thailand's Beaches and Islands

0   100 km

0   100 miles

N

Andaman Sea

M A L A Y S I A

T H A I L A N D

Gulf of Thailand

page 272

page 166

page 244

page 247

page 252

page 256

page 214

Than Kyun
(Davis I.)

Mo Ko Surin
Marine
National Park
Surin Tai

Ko
Similan

Ko Similan N.P.
Ko Phayang

Ko Racha Yai
Ko Racha Noi

Sirina
Marine N.F.
Ko Phuket
Patpong
Kata No.
Nai Harr

Laem
Son N.P.

Thai Muang N.P.
Khao Lak

Takua Pa

Khura
Buri

Ko Phra
Thong

Ko Phayang

Khao Sok N.P.

Racha
Prana
Dam

Ao Phang Nga
Nga N.P.

Ko Yao
Yai

Khao
Yai N.P.

Phuket

Krabi

Phanom
Bencha
N.P.

Khao
Lane
N.P.

Ko Pu

Ko Lanta
Marine
N.P.

Ko Phi Phi
Don

Ko Phi Phi
Le

Khlong Nin

Ko Muk

Ko Libong

Ko Sukorn

Ko Bulon

Ko
Tarutao
Marine N.P.

Ko Adang
Ko Lipe

Ko Batong

Ko Tarutao

Ko
Rawi

Pulau
Langkawi

Pulau
Singa Besar

Pulau Dayang
Bunting

Alor Setar

Jitra

Kangar

Thale Ban
N.P.

Sadao

Pak Bara

Satun

Langkawi Sound

Tuba

Perlis

Ko Tassai

Surat
Thani

Phang
Nga

Sichon

Ang Thong
Marine N.P.
Kho Phi
Ko Phalui
Taling Ngam

Ko Tan

Ko Samui
Chaweng

Rin Nok

Nakhon Si Thammarat

Thung Song

Trang

Kantang

Nam Phung

Khao Luang
N.P.

Pak Phanang

Ban Pak Phraek

Huai-Yot

Khao Pu/Ya
N.P.

Phatthalung

Thale
Noi

Thale
Luang

Kong Sala

Pho
Phibun

Ban Na San

Khao Tha Phet
Botanic Garden

Kanchanadit

Ao Ban
Don

Chawang

Phatthalung

Thale Sap
Songkhla

Songkhla

Hat Yai

Toh Nga Chang
N.P.

Sapon

Pattani

Yala

Betong

Nam Tok
Sai Khao
N.P.

Banang
Sata

Narathiwat N.P.

Narathiwat

Rangae

Sungai Kolok

Bang Lang
Dam

Waeng

Sai Buri

Kota Bharu

Pasir Mas

Tak Bai

401

401

401

41

4

4

4

44

44

4

4

4

42

42

43

43

410

409

407

408

408

408

404

403

403

416

406

005

009

Map Legend

═══╪═══	Motorway with Junction
══ ══	Motorway (under construction)
═══ ═══	Dual Carriageway
════════	Main Road
─────────	Secondary Road
════════	Minor Road
────────	Track
─ ─ ─ ─ ─	Footpath
▬ ▪ ▬ ▪	International Boundary
─ ─ ─ ─	Province Boundary
─ ▪ ─	National Park/Reserve
─ ─ ─ ─	Ferry Route
⊖	Border Crossing
✈ ✈	Airport
✝ ✝	Church (ruins)
✝	Monastery
▟ ▛	Castle (ruins)
⸫	Archaeological Site
∩	Cave
★	Place of Interest
✳	Viewpoint
⚐	Beach
════════	Motorway
════════	Dual Carriageway
─────── }	Main Roads
─────── }	Minor Roads
────────	Footpath
▬ ▬ ▬	Railway
▦	Pedestrian Area
▬	Important Building
▬	Park
❶	Numbered Sight
Ⓜ Ⓢ	Metro MRT/Skytrain BTS
🚌	Bus Station
❶	Tourist Information
✉	Post Office
✝	Cathedral/Church
☾	Mosque
✡	Synagogue
⚊	Statue/Monument
▯	Tower
♆	Lighthouse

☀ INSIGHT GUIDES

THAILAND'S
BEACHES AND ISLANDS

Discovery
CHANNEL

APA PUBLICATIONS
Part of the Langenscheidt Publishing Group
L

❋ INSIGHT GUIDE
THAILAND'S
Beaches and Islands

Editor
Francis Dorai
Art Director
Klaus Geisler
Picture Editor
Hilary Genin
Cartography Editor
Zoë Goodwin
Desktop Assistant
Carol Low
Production
Kenneth Chan
Editorial Director
Brian Bell

Distribution

UK & Ireland
GeoCenter International Ltd
Meridian House, Churchill Way West
Basingstoke, Hampshire RG21 6YR
Fax: (44 1256) 817 988

United States
Langenscheidt Publishers, Inc.
36–36 33rd Street, 4th Floor
Long Island City, NY 11106
Fax: (1) 718 784 0640

Australia
Universal Publishers
1 Waterloo Road
Macquarie Park, NSW 2113
Fax: (61) 2 9888 9074

New Zealand
Hema Maps New Zealand Ltd (HNZ)
Unit D, 24 Ra ORA Drive
East Tamaki, Auckland
Fax: (64) 9 273 6479

Worldwide
**Apa Publications GmbH & Co.
Verlag KG (Singapore branch)**
38 Joo Koon Road, Singapore 628990
Tel: (65) 6865 1600. Fax: (65) 6861 6438

Printing

Insight Print Services (Pte) Ltd
38 Joo Koon Road, Singapore 628990
Tel: (65) 6865 1600. Fax: (65) 6861 6438

©2006 Apa Publications GmbH & Co.
Verlag KG (Singapore branch)
All Rights Reserved

First Edition 2006

ABOUT THIS BOOK

The first Insight Guide pioneered the use of creative full-colour photography in travel guides in 1970. Since then, we have expanded our range to cater for our readers' need not only for reliable information about their chosen destination but also for a real understanding of that destination. Now, when the internet can supply inexhaustible – but not always reliable – facts, our books marry text and pictures to provide that much more elusive quality: knowledge. To achieve this, they rely heavily on the authority of locally based writers and photographers.

How to use this book

The book is carefully structured to convey an understanding of the capital, Bangkok, as well as Thailand's main beaches and islands:

◆ The Best of Thailand's Beaches & Islands at the front helps you to prioritise what you want to see: top family attractions, the most idyllic beaches, the best dive sites, the most exclusive resorts, must-see temples and national parks as well as the hottest restaurants and clubs.

◆ To understand this region better, you need to know about its past. The first section covers the region's history and culture in lively, authoritative essays written by specialist Thailand-based writers.

◆ The Places section provides a full rundown of all the attractions worth seeing. The main places of interest are coordinated by number with full-colour maps. In addition, a pull-out map at the back of the book gives details of Thailand's top beaches.

◆ Photo features illustrate various facets of Thailand, from temple architecture to festivals and marine life.

LEFT: the paradisiacal Similan Islands are a haven for divers and snorkellers.

◆ Photographs throughout the book are chosen not only to illustrate geography and landscape but also to convey the different moods of the region and the pulse of its people.

◆ Each Places chapter is accompanied by a Travel Tips section covering transport, restaurants, accommodation and activities in that specific region. At the end of the book is a A–Z listing of practical tips, plus language and further reading sections.

The contributors

This brand-new title was supervised and edited by **Francis Dorai**, Insight's Singapore-based managing editor, wth assistance from **Pasha Siraj**. Several writers were enlisted to research and write this book. British-born and Bangkok-based writer and artist **Steven Pettifor** wrote the chapters on Bangkok, Eastern Seaboard,

the Gulf of Thailand Coast, and Ko Samui, Ko Phangan & Ko Tao, including the respective Travel Tips sections and the A–Z listings. In addition, Pettifor also wrote the Outdoor Activities chapter.

Freelance writer **Lauren Smith**, who moved from the UK and made idyllic Phuket her home base, was well placed to write the Northern Andaman Coast, Phuket, and Krabi, Ko Phi Phi & Ko Lanta chapters, plus the relevant Travel Tips sections.

The final Places chapter, on Trang, Satun & Songkhla, was the work of Canadian freelance writer and photographer **Austin Bush**, who lives in Bangkok.

The bulk of the features section (including History, People & Culture, and Religion) and the photo features were written by **Dr Andrew Forbes**, a long-time Thailand expert who runs a press agency, CPA, in Chiang Mai, northern Thailand. The Nature & Environment chapter was written by fellow CPA associate writer/photographer **David Henley**.

Finally, the Cuisine chapter was the handiwork of **Rob McKeown**, who lives and breathes the varied cuisines of Asia as roving reporter for several international food and travel publications.

Among the talented photographers whose images bring Thailand's beaches and islands to life are **John W. Ishii**, **Austin Bush**, **Jock Montgomery**, **David Henley**, **Jason Lang** and **Marcus Wilson-Smith**.

This book was proofread by **Eliza Teoh** and indexed by **Pasha Siraj**.

CONTACTING THE EDITORS

We would appreciate it if readers would alert us to errors or outdated information by writing to:

**Insight Guides, P.O. Box 7910, London SE1 1WE, England.
Fax: (44) 20 7403 0290.
insight@apaguide.co.uk**

www.insightguides.com
In North America:
www.insighttravelguides.com

ABOVE: Aleenta resort, Pranburi, at dusk.

Contents

Travel Tips

Maps

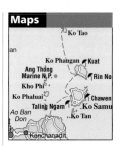

THE BEST OF THAILAND'S BEACHES AND ISLANDS

Setting priorities, making choices, unique attractions... here, at a glance, are our recommendations, plus some tips and tricks even the locals won't always know

THAILAND FOR FAMILIES

These attractions are popular with children, though not all will suit every age group.

LEFT: kitschy Dino Park.

- **Dino Park and Mini Golf: Phuket.** An 18-hole mini-golf course which trails over rocks and across rivers and waterfalls, past dinosaurs with smoking nostrils. *See page 224.*
- **Elephant trek: Ko Chang.** See elephants bathing and feeding at Ban Kwan Chang camp, then take a trek on elephant back into the forest. *See pages 131 and 145.*
- **Phuket Fantasea: Phuket.** A stage extravaganza combining dance, drama and acrobatics with pyrotechnics and performing elephants. *See pages 222 and 237.*

- **Siriacha Tiger Zoo: Si Racha.** The world's largest tiger zoo, with over 200 Bengal tigers. *See page 120.*
- **Siam Ocean World: Bangkok.** See over 30,000 marine animals in a giant Oceanarium, ride in a glass-bottomed boat and dive with the sharks. *See page 92.*
- **Snake Farm: Bangkok.** Learn all about tropical snakes and see a handler milking one for venom. *See page 93.*
- **Yellow Submarine: Pattaya.** Explore the briny depths without ever getting wet. *See page 139.*

RIGHT: elephant at the Phuket Fantasea.

ABOVE: a penitent at Phuket's annual Vegetarian Festival skewers himself with sharp objects after entering a trance.

ONLY IN THAILAND

- **Buffalo fighting: Ko Samui and Hat Yai.** This typically southern Thai pastime involves betting on the sidelines. *See pages 168 and 278.*
- **Cookery schools: Bangkok, Hua Hin and Ko Samui.** There's nothing like learning how to cook Thai food while you're in Thailand. *See pages 117, 163 and 188.*
- **Full Moon parties: Ko Phangan.** These wild all-night raves are Ko Phangan's main claim to fame. *See page 176.*
- **"Lady-boy" cabarets: Bangkok,** Pattaya, Ko Samui and Phuket. See men in drag who look better than women. *See pages 114, 137, 187 and 238.*
- **Monkey theatre: Ko Samui.** Watch monkeys clamber up trees at lighting speed to pluck coconuts. *See page 169.*
- **Night markets: Trang and Songkhla.** For local colour plus cheap shopping and food. *See pages 280 and 283.*
- **Vegetarian Festival: Phuket.** These acts of self-mutilation are only for the robust of heart. *See pages 43 and 217.*

MOST INTERESTING TEMPLES

- **Khao Luang cave: Petchaburi**. More than 100 Buddha images fill this cave temple. *See page 149.*
- **Wat Chalong: Phuket**. The island's largest and most important Buddhist temple. *See page 226.*
- **Wat Mahathat: Petchaburi**. 14th-century temple known for its fine carvings. *See page 149.*
- **Wat Matchimawat: Songkhla**. The town's most famous temple with paintings that are

over 200 years old. *See page 277.*
- **Wat Pho: Bangkok**. The capital's largest temple is best known for its gigantic statue of the reclining Buddha. *See page 80.*
- **Wat Phra Kaew: Bangkok**. No one visits the capital without seeing the Temple of the Emerald Buddha. *See page 74.*
- **Wat Tham Seua: Krabi**. Vast temple complex tucked amid forests and cliffs. *See page 244.*

ABOVE: monks offering prayers and incense at the Khao Luang cave in Petchaburi. **BELOW:** Phuket night lights.

TOP CULTURAL SIGHTS

- **Chinatown: Bangkok**. The sights and sounds of China along Sampeng Lane. *See page 88.*
- **Khao Wang: Petchaburi**. A vast hilltop complex of temples, pagodas and palace buildings. *See page 148.*
- **Maruekhathayawan Palace: Cha-am**. The seaside abode of a former Thai king. *See page 151.*

ABOVE: carvings at Pattaya's Sanctuary of Truth.

- **Orchid Garden and Thai Village: Phuket**. A showcase for Thai culture and dance, plus a vast orchid collection. *See page 215.*
- **Sanctuary of Truth: Pattaya**. This awe-

inspiring edifice pays homage to traditional Thai architecture. *See page 125.*
- **Thaksin Folklore Museum: Songkhla**. Highlights the culture, traditions and handicrafts of South Thailand. *See page 278.*
- **Vimanmek Mansion: Bangkok**. Billed as the world's largest golden teakwood structure. *See page 86.*

HOTTEST NIGHTSPOTS

- **Backyard Bar: Ko Phangan**. The hottest spot on this party island. *See page 191.*
- **Bed Supperclub: Bangkok**. Futuristic white oval pod with beds to lounge on. *See pages 97 and 113.*
- **Gecko Village: Ko Samui**. So hot it attracts DJs from the international circuit. *See page 187.*
- **Joe's Downstairs: Phuket**. The island's trendiest nightspot attracts a chi chi crowd. *See page 237.*
- **Mantra: Pattaya**. Sleek new bar that adds chic to this resort town. *See page 137.*
- **Pure: Ko Tao**. Island bar with a chilled-out vibe at the southern end of Sai Ree beach. *See page 193.*
- **Q Bar: Bangkok**. Seductive venue with Thailand's most

inventive drinks list. *See pages 97 and 113.*
- **Ratri Jazztaurant: Phuket**. Live jazz on Kata beach. *See page 238.*
- **Reggae Bar: Ko Phi Phi**. The island's biggest and best party venue. *See page 267.*
- **Sabay Bar: Ko Chang**. Hot and happening best describes this bar. *See page 145.*

8

TOP TABLES

- **Baan Khanitha: Bangkok**. Mouthwatering Thai food with just the right amount of spice. *See page 106.*
- **Baan Rim Pa: Phuket**. Exquisite Thai food on a cliff-top setting. *See page 232.*
- **Betelnut: Ko Samui**. It's California-meets-Thailand fusion fare at this stylish eatery. *See page 184.*
- **Biscotti: Bangkok**. Haute Italian cuisine at one of the city's top hotels. *See page 105.*
- **Casa Pascal: Pattaya**. This Continental fine-dining venue is a long-established Pattaya hotspot. *See page 135.*
- **Cy'an: Bangkok**. Mediterranean fare is given an Asian twist at this trendy place. *See page 106.*
- **La Mer: Hua Hin**. Dramatic views set the tone for the well-prepared seafood dishes. *See page 160.*
- **Red Snapper: Ko Lanta**. Right on the beach with a bold menu that fuses Thai and Western flavours. *See page 268.*
- **Salvatore's: Phuket**. One of Thailand's top Italian eateries is on an island. *See page 231.*
- **Supatra River House: Bangkok**. Riverside dining on a menu of Thai favourites. *See page 104.*

BEST NATURAL ATTRACTIONS

- **Ao Phang Nga: Northern Andaman Coast**. A surreal seascape of limestone pinnacles rising out of the water invite exploration. *See page 202.*
- **Hot Springs Waterfall: Krabi**. Bask in the warm waters of this waterfall before taking a cooling dip in the adjacent stream. *See page 246.*
- **Khao Sok National Park**. Thailand's most popular national park is unique in many ways, and has an amazing variety of flora and fauna. *See page 203.*
- **Khao Sam Roi Yot National Park**. Expect varied topography, with beaches, marshes, forests and mountains. *See page 155.*
- **Laem Phra Nang (Railay Bay): Krabi**. Hundreds of sheer-sided limestone cliffs attract rock climbers the world over. *See page 248.*
- **Tha Pom: Krabi**. Walk past mangroves to see an amazing stream with clear blue-green waters. *See page 245.*

BELOW: breathtaking Hat Tham Phra Nang, Krabi.

ABOVE: close encounter with a grouper at Chumphon Pinnacle.

BEST SNORKELLING AND DIVE SITES

- **Chumphon Pinnacle**. Famous for frequent sightings of grouper and other large fish. *See page 182.*
- **Hin Bai (Sail Rock)**. Rising like an iceberg out of the water, its highlight is a vertical chimney. *See page 178.*
- **Hin Daeng and Hin Muang**. World-class dive sites close to Ko Tao. *See page 259.*
- **Ko Rok**. Easily Thailand's best site for snorkelling, with colourful corals and fish found in shallow waters. *See page 258.*
- **Similan Islands**. Several dive sites within a compact area. *See page 201.*
- **Surin Islands**. Dive haven with the famous Richelieu Rock and the Burma Banks close by. *See page 200.*

ABOVE: Ao Maya (Maya Bay) on the island of Ko Phi Phi Ley was the main filming location for the movie *The Beach*.

BREATHTAKING VIEWS

- **Ao Maya**. From this vantage point on Ko Phi Phi Ley, the entire island seems encircled by towering limestone cliffs. *See page 253.*
- **Kata Hill** and **Laem Promthep**. Both points offers stunning views of Phuket. *See pages 224 and 225.*
- **Khao Wang**. Walk or take the cable car up to the summit for panoramas of this temple complex and the surrounding area. *See page 148.*
- **Ko Phi Phi Don**. Its famous viewpoint has incredible vistas of the beaches on Ao Lo Dalam and Ao Ton Sai. *See page 253.*
- **Ko Wua Talab**. Hike up the trail for a spectacular view of Ang Thong Marine National Park. *See page 172.*

MOST IDYLLIC BEACHES

- **Ao Kantiang: Ko Lanta**. No pressing crowds, only pure white sand and clear aquamarine waters. *See page 257.*
- **Hat Kuat: Ko Phangan**. It's easy to see to see why this lovely beach gets so many repeat visitors. *See page 175.*
- **Hat Nai Harn: Phuket**. Scant development and a broad stretch of white sand make this a clear winner. *See page 225.*
- **Hat Tham Phra Nang: Krabi**. Drop-dead gorgeous, possibly Thailand's most stunning. *See page 249.*
- **Ko Nang Yuan**. Three islets joined by mere wisps of the softest sand guarantees this beach top billing. *See page 181.*

MOST EXCLUSIVE RESORTS

- **Aleenta: Pranburi**. Stylish boutique-style resort frequented by Bangkok's smart set. *See page 162.*
- **Amanpuri: Phuket**. The ultimate in luxury resorts, and not surprisingly, Thailand's priciest. *See page 234.*
- **Chiva-Som: Hua Hin**. Spa, wellness centre and luxury resort in one stunning package. *See page 161.*
- **Evason Hideaway: Hua Hin**. Indulgent all-villa hotel with private pool and butler on call 24 hours a day. *See page 162.*
- **Pimalai: Ko Lanta**. Stylish luxury property that is almost upstaged by the stunning Ao Kantiang beach it rests on. *See page 269.*
- **The Racha: Ko Racha Yai**. Simple clean lines, chic furnishings and a dramatic glass-edged pool overlooking a turquoise bay. *See page 236.*
- **Rayavadee: Krabi**. Luxury Thai-style villas in the drop-dead gorgeous setting of Hat Tham Phra Nang beach. *See page 262.*
- **Sala Samui: Ko Samui**. Stylish all-villa resort, most with private pools, right on lovely Hat Choeng Mon. *See page 186.*
- **The Sarojin: Khao Lak**. Elegant Thai accents and modern styling makes this property stand out. Sits on its own private beach. *See page 209.*

BELOW: villa pool at The Racha resort on Ko Racha Yai.

LAZY DAYS AND ISLAND WAYS

With an ever-growing number of chic luxury resorts and spas, there is always something for those seeking style and sophistication. But for those who simply want to get away from it all, there are still remote islands and virtually deserted beaches to choose from

Famous for their welcoming smiles, the Thais have good reason for their contented grins – their country is ranked among the world's most popular tourist destinations. Holidaymakers now number a steady 10 million a year, making tourism the country's top industry earner. With a unique culture and a piquantly delicious cuisine, year-round balmy weather, palm-studded and powdery white sand beaches, forested mountains cloaked in dawn mists, time-honoured ancient ruins and old temples, and the excitement of a bustling megalopolis like Bangkok, it's easy to see why planeloads keep touching down on this exotic land.

For the majority of visitors, a Thai sojourn consists of a brief flirtation with the bright lights of Bangkok before escaping to the thousands of kilometres of sun-kissed coastline or to an island getaway. The clear azure waters that lap the shores of the Eastern Seaboard, Andaman Coast to the west and the Gulf of Thailand along the east, are among the world's best for scuba diving and snorkelling, sailing and fishing.

For those who find swimming with vibrant marine life among kaleidoscopic coral reefs or the exhilaration of kite-boarding along the windswept surf a little too exertive, Thailand's beaches and islands offer plenty of other attractions. Sharing borders with Burma to the west, Cambodia to the east and Malaysia to the south, this region has palace structures of the Thai royalty and the ever-present spires of Buddhist temple roofs contrasting with lush verdant jungle and forest topography.

Once the preserve of oversexed single men, cash-strapped backpackers and compliant tour groups, many of the country's beach areas now cater to a broader mix of discerning travellers, with stylish boutique resorts, spas and wellness centres, and fine dining restaurants. Holidaymakers will cross paths with hedonistic full moon party animals, starry-eyed honeymooning couples, spa aficionados looking for that ultimate massage, and new age junkies seeking spiritual awakening.

Thailand still has near desolate beaches and remote islands which the Hyatts and Hiltons haven't yet discovered – lest you think tranquil hideaways no longer exist. Despite the memory of the Asian tsunami and ongoing restlessness in the southernmost provinces, Thailand is a safe and carefree destination. No one needs an excuse for a beach holiday, really. ❏

PRECEDING PAGES: Ao Lo Dalam on Ko Phi Phi Don; a Ko Phangan beach bar at sunset.
LEFT: the colourful prows of Thai longtail boats along Ao Nang at Krabi.

HISTORY

Southern Thailand's sun-drenched beaches and islands were not always a bucolic playground for wintering tourists. In times past, the peninsula's central location in maritime Southeast Asia made it an important stopover for merchants along the region's lucrative trade routes

In the early 10th–14th centuries, before the consolidation of the Siamese kingdom, the peninsula was a fought-over staging ground for the shifting polities of the region, a vassal state to a succession of early thalassocracies and a confluence of diverse cultural and religious influences. Indeed, in the deep south today, one might discern in the communal unrest of the Muslim communities, a latter-day echo of the sociocultural, political and religious ambiguities of earlier times.

In the beginning

The earliest known civilisation in Thailand dates from around 3600 BC, when the people of Ban Chiang in the northeast developed bronze tools, fired pottery and began to cultivate rice. The Tai people, after whom the kingdom is named, did not even inhabit the region of present-day Thailand during this time, but are thought to have been living in looselyorganised groups in what is now regarded as southern China.

Little is known of the history of Thailand's coastal regions until around two millennia ago, by which time it seems certain that Malay peoples had settled in southern peninsular Thailand, along both the Andaman Sea and Gulf of Thailand coasts. Inland, in the wild hills and jungles of the central spine, small groups of negrito hunter-gatherers eked out a precarious living. Further to the north, Mon people had settled the Tenasserim region and

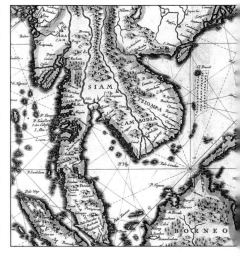

the southern Chao Phraya valley, while further east the Khmers had settled along the southeastern Gulf Coast and in the Mekong delta. Of the Tais, still living far to the north, there was as yet no sign.

Significantly, both the Indian and Chinese civilisations had by this time become formidable and advanced. Each group came to exercise powerful and distinct influences across Southeast Asia, becoming the cultural godfathers of the region. The first civilisations to develop among Thailand's coasts and islands were not Tai, therefore, but Malay, Mon and Khmer, each of which was influenced to a greater or lesser degree by both India and China.

LEFT: an artist's impression of Bangkok in 1846.
RIGHT: a 17th-century European map of Indochina.

The Golden Land and Srivijaya

As early as 300 BC, the Malay world, including peninsular Thailand, was already being Indianised by visiting traders in search of fragrant woods, pearls and especially gold, leading the Indians to name the region Suvarnabhumi or "Golden Land". These traders brought with them Hinduism as well as Buddhism, which became established in southern Thailand by the 1st century AD. By about AD 500, a loosely knit kingdom called Srivijaya had emerged, encompassing the coastal areas of Sumatra, peninsular Malaya and Thailand, as well as parts of Borneo. Ruled by *maharaja*s, or kings, its people practised both Hinduism and Buddhism.

THE KINGDOM OF PATTANI

Formerly a Malay sultanate comprising the present-day provinces of Pattani, Yala and Narathiwat, it became Muslim in the 11th century, but came under increasing Siamese influence until, in the mid-17th century, it became a tributary state of Ayutthaya. Pattani later rebelled against Thai control during the reign of King Rama I, and its ruler, Sultan Muhammad, was killed in battle. Then, a series of attempted rebellions prompted Bangkok to divide Pattani into seven smaller states. Despite a long association with Thailand, the Malays of Pattani were never culturally absorbed into mainstream Thai society, and the area remains fractious even today.

Sustained by brisk trade with India and China, Srivijaya flourished for almost 700 years.

From the 10th century, however, the power of the Srivijaya empire began to decline, weakened by a series of wars with the Javanese. As a maritime empire, Srivijaya was never a centralised state, so the wars were disruptive to trade. In the 11th century, a rival centre of power arose on the Sumatran coast, possibly in what is now Jambi Province. The power of the Hindu *maharaja*s was undermined by the arrival of Muslim traders and teachers, who began to spread Islam along the coast. Then, by the late 13th century, the Siamese kings of Sukhothai brought much of the Malay Peninsula under their control. Yet, despite this unrest, the region's rich resources of spices, resins and other products, so highly prized in China and India, kept Srivijaya prosperous until its final collapse in the 14th century.

The Mon kingdom of Dvaravati

At about the same time Srivijaya dominated the southern part of the Malay Peninsula, the Mon people established themselves as the rulers of the northern part of the peninsula and the Chao Phraya valley, centring on present-day Bangkok. The kingdom of Dvaravati flourished from the 6th to the 11th century, with Nakhon Pathom, U-Thong and Lopburi its major settlements. Much like Srivijaya, Dvaravati was strongly influenced by Indian culture and religion, and the Mons played a central role in the introduction of Buddhism to present-day Thailand and, in particular, the Andaman Coast. It is not clear whether Dvaravati was a single unitary state under the control of a powerful ruler, or a loose confederation of small principalities. Either way, the Mons succumbed to pressure from the north by the 12th–13th century. As the Tais moved south, conquering Nakhon Pathom and Lopburi, they absorbed much of Mon culture, including the Buddhist religion.

The Khmer empire

At the same time that the coastal regions of western Thailand were dominated by Srivijaya and Dvaravati, another major power was asserting its control over what is now eastern Thailand. This was the Khmer empire of Angkor, forerunner of present-day Cambodia.

Strongly influenced by Indian culture, Khmer civilisation reached its zenith under the reign of Suryavarman II (1113–50), during which time the temple of Angkor Wat in Cambodia was built. He united the kingdom, conquering Dvaravati and the area further west to the border with the kingdom of Pagan (modern Burma), expanding as far south into the Malay Peninsula as Nakhon Si Thammarat, and dominating the entire coast of the Gulf of Siam.

The next great Khmer ruler was Jayavarman VII (1181–1219), who defeated the Chams, unified the empire and initiated a series of astonishing building projects. Yet, this was to be the last flowering of Khmer inde-

of the modern Thai nation, although other less well-known Tai states, such as Chiang Saen and Lanna in north Thailand were established about the same time. Sukhothai expanded by forming alliances with the other Tai kingdoms. It adopted Theravada Buddhism as the state religion with the help of Sri Lankan monks. Under King Ramkhamhaeng (ruled 1279–98), Sukhothai enjoyed a golden age of prosperity. During his long reign, the Thai writing system evolved and the foundations of present-day Thailand were securely established. He expanded his control over the south, as far as the Andaman Sea and Nakhon Si Thammarat on the Gulf Coast, as well as over the Chao

pendence until modern times, as the Khmer empire fell victim to the emerging power that would later become known as Thailand.

Sukhothai, the first Thai kingdom

Sukhothai was part of the Khmer empire until 1238, when two Tai chieftains seceded and established the first independent Tai kingdom. This event is considered to mark the founding

Phraya valley and even southeast into what is within the borders of present-day Cambodia.

With the creation of the Sukhothai kingdom, a new political structure came into being across mainland Southeast Asia. At the same time, the Thai newcomers, an ethnically Sinitic people, intermarried with the inhabitants of the states they had supplanted and adopted their Indianised culture.

The kingdom of Ayutthaya

The glories of Sukhothai were short-lived, however. In the early 14th century, a rival Thai kingdom began to develop in the lower Chao Phraya valley, not far from present-day

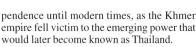

LEFT: terracotta figures from the 4th or 5th century found in U Thong show an Indian influence.
ABOVE: a bas relief at Angkor depicting Jayavarman's Khmer campaign against the Chams.
RIGHT: the Sukhothai King Ramkhamhaeng.

Much-loved Monarchy

Thai people take the institution of the monarchy very seriously. Since the first independent Thai kingdom was established some seven centuries ago, the Thais have been ruled over by kings. And though the monarchy has been constitutional since the revolution of 1932, the Thais continue to love and honour their royal family, especially its father figure, King Bhumibol Adulyadej, with a passion.

Thailand's first royal capital, Sukhothai, was succeeded by Ayutthaya in 1351, and

then by Bangkok in 1782. Perhaps as a consequence of this continuity, the Thai people are confirmed monarchists, with the throne making up one of the three central pillars of the national polity – in Thai *chat*, *sat* and *pramahakasat* – Thai Nation, Buddhist Religion and Chakri Dynasty. It would be hard to overestimate the affection and respect Thais feel for their kings, and this applies to non-Buddhist minorities as well. In many Muslim homes, for example, it is common to find a framed print of the king hanging next to a picture of the Kaaba at Mecca in a convincing statement of both spiritual and secular loyalty.

After the tragically early death of his brother King Ananda Mahidol (Rama VIII) in 1946, the succession passed to Thailand's present monarch, King Bhumibol Adulyadej. Born not in Thailand, but in distant Cambridge, Massachusetts, where his father Prince Mahidol Adulyadej was studying medicine at Harvard University, young Bhumibol soon proved a worthy successor to his grandfather King Chulalongkorn (Rama V). For a full six decades, often accompanied by his enduringly popular wife Queen Sirikit, he has travelled all over the kingdom, equally at home with peasants from the poor northeast or at high-tech research laboratories in the major cities. When not engaged in promoting ecological awareness or some major new agricultural project, he enjoys jazz music. Being an accomplished musician, he plays several instruments and has written many popular numbers. Perhaps because of this ability to reach out to the common man, he enjoys an extraordinary popularity shared in the past only by King Chulalongkorn.

Although he is a constitutional monarch, because of the esteem in which he is held by the Thai citizenry, King Bhumibol does play a political role, occasionally intervening when he feels politicians have got out of hand. In May 1992, when military strongman Suchinda Krapayoon seized power in a coup, the king intervened to end three days of riots and killings when soldiers opened fire on unarmed demonstrators gathered near the Democracy Monument. Suchinda was forced to resign in disgrace, and democracy was restored.

More recently, King Bhumibol has made it clear on a number of occasions that he disapproves of Prime Minister Thaksin Shinawatra's executive style of government. Thaksin, generally not a man who tolerates criticism, has been obliged to listen. So great is the moral authority of the king that no politician can afford to ignore him. He is the final bulwark against oppression and authoritarianism, yet he remains a modest, even diffident man, conscious of his position as *po luang*, the "royal father" of his people. ❑

LEFT: King Bhumibol and Queen Sirikit.

Bangkok. In 1350, the ambitious ruler U-Thong moved his capital from Lopburi to a nearby island on the river – a more defensible location – and gave the new city the name Ayutthaya, proclaiming himself King Ramathibodi (ruled 1351–69). He declared Theravada Buddhism the state religion, invited monks from Sri Lanka to help spread the faith, and compiled a legal code, based on the Indian Dharmashastra, which remained in force until the 19th century.

Ayutthaya soon eclipsed Sukhothai as the leading Thai polity. By the end of the 14th century, Ayutthaya was the strongest power in Southeast Asia. In the last year of his reign, Ramathibodi seized Angkor in what was the

Muslim early in the century, and Islam served as a unifying symbol of Malay solidarity against the Thais thereafter. Although Ayutthaya failed to make Malacca a vassal state, it established control over much of the peninsula.

The rise of Burma

The 16th century witnessed the rise of Burma, which, under a powerful and aggressive dynasty, waged war on the Thais. In 1569, Burmese forces captured the city of Ayutthaya. King Naresuan the Great (ruled 1590–1605) succeeded in restoring Siamese independence, but in 1765, the Burmese armies once again invaded Ayutthaya, destroying Siam's capital.

first of many successful Thai assaults on the Khmer capital. Forces were also sent to subdue Sukhothai, and the year after Ramathibodi died, his kingdom was recognised by China's Hongwu Emperor, of the newly-founded Ming dynasty, as Sukhothai's rightful successor.

During the 15th century, much of Ayutthaya's energies were directed southwards toward the Malay Peninsula, where its claims of sovereignty over the great trading port of Malacca were contested. The Malay states south of Nakhon Si Thammarat had become

Despite this, Siam made a rapid recovery. A noble of Chinese descent named Taksin led the resistance. From his base at Chanthaburi on the southeast coast, he defeated the Burmese and re-established the Siamese state. Taksin also set up the capital at Thonburi and was crowned king in 1768. He rapidly reunited the central Thai heartlands, then marched south and re-established Siamese rule over all southern Thailand and the Malay states as far south as Penang and Trengganu.

Although a brilliant military tactician, Taksin was, by 1779, in political trouble. He alienated the Buddhist establishment by claiming to have divine powers, and attacked the economically

ABOVE: a European impression of the royal capital of Ayutthaya during the time of King Narai.

powerful Chinese merchant class. In 1782, a rebellion broke out, and Taksin was deposed.

The Chakri dynasty of Bangkok

In 1782, General Chakri assumed the throne and took the title Phra Phutthayotfa (King Rama I). One of his first decisions was to move the capital across the Chao Phraya River from Thonburi to the small settlement of Bang Makok, the "place of olive plums", which would become the city of Bangkok. His new palace was located on Rattanakosin Island, protected from attack by the river to the west and by a series of canals to the north, east and south. Rama I restored much of the social and

political system of Ayutthaya, promulgating new law codes, reinstating court ceremonies and imposing discipline on the Buddhist monkhood. Six great ministries headed by royal princes administered the government, one of which – the Kalahom – controlled the south.

In 1785, underestimating the resilience and strength of the new king, the Burmese once again invaded, driving far to the south to attack Phuket, Chaiya and Phattalung before being defeated by Rama I near Kanchanaburi. By the time of his death in 1809, Rama I controlled the Malay Peninsula as far south as Kedah and Trengganu, as well as the Gulf Coast as far east as the Cambodian frontier with Vietnam. Siam had become an empire considerably larger than Thailand today.

Yet despite these amazing successes, Thailand's present frontiers were not yet fixed. In 1825, the British sent a mission to Bangkok. They had annexed southern Burma and were extending their control over Malaya. The king was reluctant to give in to British demands, but his advisors warned him that Siam would meet the same fate as Burma unless the British were accommodated. In 1826, therefore, Siam concluded its first commercial treaty with a Western power. Under the treaty, Siam agreed to establish a uniform taxation system, to reduce taxes on foreign trade and to abolish some of the royal monopolies. As a result, Siam's trade increased rapidly; many more foreigners settled in Bangkok and Western cultural influences began to spread. The kingdom became wealthier and its army better armed, but it now faced new challenges from Europe, not the old rivals Burma and Vietnam.

Under the threat of military pressure from France, a colonial power in Indochina since 1883, King Chulalongkorn (Rama V) was obliged to yield territory in the east, including western Cambodia, to the French. The British interceded to prevent further French aggression, but their price, in 1909, was British sov-

LEFT: Chakri monarchs in order of reign (left to right, from top), kings Mongkut (Rama IV), Chulalongkorn, Vajiravudh, Prajadhipok, Ananda and Bhumibol.
RIGHT: Thai leader Phibunsongkhram (bottom right) with US President Eisenhower in the 1950s.
FAR RIGHT: an early Thai mural depicting two scantily clad maidens and a foreigner lying with a woman.

ereignty over Thai-controlled Kedah, Kelantan, Perlis and Terengganu (part of present-day Malaysia) under the Anglo-Siamese Treaty of 1909. Only when this had been signed did Siam finally assume its present frontiers.

Military rule and modern times

In 1932, the Thai military staged a coup and ended the absolute power of the Chakri Dynasty. Three years later, in 1935, King Rama VII abdicated, and Ananda Mahidol (Rama VIII, 1935–46), who was then at school in Switzerland, was chosen to be the next monarch. For the next 15 years, Siam was without a resident monarch for the first time in its history, and power lay with the military. In 1939, military strongman Luang Phibunsongkhram ordered the name of the country changed from Siam to Thailand and adopted the current national flag.

In 1940, moving to align Thailand with the Japanese, Phibun launched a small-scale war against the Vichy French in Indochina, retaking western Cambodia, including Angkor and much of the coast. Subsequently, on 8 December 1941, Japan invaded Thailand as a springboard for its attack on the British in Malaya and Singapore. The Thai armed forces resisted for a few hours, but Phibun, now confident of a Japanese victory over the Allies, decided to

PATTAYA AND SEX TOURISM

Tourism really began to develop along Thailand's southeast coast in the 1970s, gradually transforming and enriching a region that had traditionally been dependent on farming and fishing. Perhaps the most infamous and uncontrolled transformation occurred in Pattaya.

Much has been written, not least by Thais, seeking to blame the country's infamous sex industry on foreigners, and particularly on US troops and the "rest and recreation" boom that accompanied Thailand's involvement in the Vietnam War. But prostitution isn't called the oldest profession in the world for nothing, and Thailand is no exception to the rule. Van Neck, a Dutchman who visited

Pattani in 1604, reported, "When foreigners come there from other lands to do their business, men come and ask whether they do not desire a woman".

They did, of course, as has been and generally still is the case in just about any port in the world. By the end of the Vietnam War, Pattaya was well on the way to becoming Asia's most infamous sex tourism destination. The pattern continued through the 1980s and 1990s, as American GIs were replaced by male tourists from Europe, Japan and China. The whole business is, of course, big money, and while some authorities have sought to clean up Pattaya, others have quietly profited from the growth of this lurid city.

enter a formal alliance with the Japanese. As a reward, he was permitted to occupy certain territories lost to the British, including northern Malaya. But in 1945, following the defeat of Japan, the new Thai government of Khuang Aphaiwong withdrew unilaterally from Malaya. Two years later, Thailand withdrew from western Cambodia as well.

A stable monarchy

In June 1946, King Bhumibol Adulyadej (Rama IX) ascended the throne, and remains king today, the longest reigning head of state in the world. During his long rule, democracy has become increasingly firmly established.

through the involvement of foreign Muslim fundamentalists from Malaysia and Indonesia.

The government of Thaksin Shinawatra, which was elected in 2001 and re-elected in 2005, had adopted carrot and stick policies in the deep south in an attempt to end the insurgency, but unrest and resentment continues, with frequent protests, bomb blasts and tough crackdowns by security forces. As a result, support for Thaksin in southern Thailand has dwindled almost to nothing, even though his swift and efficient response to the tragic tsunami that destroyed its southern beach resorts on 26 December 2004 *(see opposite)* boosted his popularity throughout the rest of the country.

In March 1992, he was instrumental in defusing the last attempted military coup. During his six decades as king, the entire country, including the southern peninsula and eastern seaboard, have prospered and developed.

Only in the very far south, at the extreme limits of Thailand's coastal belt, do the three Muslim majority provinces of Pattani, Yala and Narathiwat remain restive. For three decades, a low-scale insurgency with the aim of establishing an independent "Pattani Republic" has smouldered. Since the beginning of the 21st century, the situation has deteriorated, and the insurgency, once primarily political, has acquired a more religious nature

In January 2006, Thaksin faced another political crisis when his family was accused of evading taxes when they sold their stake in a family-owned telecommunications company. Thousands of protesters in Bangkok took to the streets and called for his resignation. Snap elections held in April were boycotted by opposition parties, and the Thaksin government was returned to power. In a rare intervention, King Bhumibol described the situation as undemocratic, prompting the Thai courts to annul the election results. ❑

ABOVE: Thaksin spearheaded a goodwill gesture in 2004 to airdrop paper cranes over the troubled south.

Tsunami Terror

On 26 December 2004, a massive underwater earthquake struck off the coast of Sumatra, Indonesia, at 7.58am local time. The force of the 9.0 magnitude quake was felt as far away as Thailand, where its intensity was noted but largely ignored – until hours later, when all hell broke loose. The earthquake triggered a series of deadly killer waves, some as high as 30 metres (98 ft), that travelled huge distances across the Indian Ocean and devastated parts of Thailand as well as Indonesia , India and Sri Lanka. The thousands killed globally as a result made it the deadliest tsunami in recorded history, with the furthest recorded death in Port Elizabeth, South Africa, some 8,000 km (5,000 miles) from the epicentre. The UN Office of the Envoy for Tsunami Recovery records the most recent official death toll as 186,983, with a further 42,883 still missing, bringing the total dead, or presumed dead, to 229,866.

As severe as the damage was in Thailand – with some 5,395 dead and another 2,845 people still certified missing – it was tame in comparison to other parts of Asia. Ko Phi Phi's exposed position in the open sea left it vulnerable and when the tsunami struck, it was all but destroyed. In Phuket, touristy Patong beach was ripped apart, with cars and boats swept inland, although the worst damage here was limited to the buildings immediately along the sea front. Quieter Kamala beach was also similarly affected. Although Phuket got the most media attention in the aftermath, it was neighbouring Khao Lak that suffered the worst damage. The flat, flood plain like terrain here allowed the waves to travel up to 3km (2 miles) inland, destroying virtually every structure in its path and leaving few survivors.

Phuket recovered quickly with beaches cleared in weeks, and buildings restored over the following months. Although some damage and reconstruction work can still be seen in Khao Lak, it too has moved on, with many hotels and restaurants having reopened or being rebuilt at time of press. The situation is much the same in Ko Phi Phi.

The underwater environment too has improved. While some coral in the shallow waters close to shore was damaged, the deeper reefs are showing better visibility and more species of marine life; the tsunami having effectively introduced a natural process of cleansing and re-generation.

Despite an initial drop in tourist numbers, Thailand's tourist industry is almost back on track again today. The likelihood of another tsunami of this scale is incredibly slim, and if the worst was to happen, an early warning

system, by way of tsunami towers erected along the beaches, has been put in place by the Thai government. A false alarm in Phuket on March 2005, resulting from an earthquake near Sumatra, proved just how effective these measures were. While fortunately nothing came of it, if a tsunami had occurred, the vast majority of people would have evacuated from the coast.

Today, a tsunami remembrance event takes place annually across Thailand. But as appropriate as these events are, in memory of the lives lost, ensuring that measures are in place to protect future generations is surely the most fitting memorial of all. ❏

RIGHT: a bonfire in memory of tsunami victims.

Decisive Dates

Beginnings

circa 250 BC: Maritime trade established between India and Southeast Asia; Hindu influences begin to filter into the region.

circa AD 200: Chen La culture established in lower Mekong region. Chinese cultural influences make an impact.

circa 500: Srivijaya kingdom encompasses parts of Sumatra and peninsular Thailand; Hindu-Buddhism now dominant in region.

circa 550: Mon kingdom of Dvaravati flourishes in the Chao Phraya River valley, giv-

ing a major boost to the Buddhist religion.

790: Khmer kingdom of Kambuja established by King Jayavarman I.

889–915: King Yasovarman I founds new Khmer capital, later to become Angkor.

1113–50: Surayavarman II oversees building of Angkor Wat; Khmer Empire reaches its apogee.

1181–1289: Jayavarman VII completes city of Angkor Thom, thought to have been the largest in the world at the time.

10th–12th centuries: A series of gradual migrations from southern China see the Tai-speaking peoples come to dominate mainland Southeast Asia.

Sukhothai and Ayutthaya

1238: Sukhothai, the first independent Thai state, is founded by King Indraditya.

1279–98: The Golden Era of Sukhothai under King Ramkhamhaeng. Thai culture becomes increasingly sophisticated. The Thai script is developed.

1296: Thai kingdom of Lanna founded by King Mengrai at Chiang Mai.

circa 1300: Thai political control extends as far south as the Andaman Sea, Nakhon Si Thammarat and the Gulf of Thailand.

1350: King Ramathibodi establishes a rival Thai kingdom at Ayutthaya; both Sukhothai and the Khmer kingdom of Angkor are in decline. Theravada Buddhism becomes the state religion of Ayutthaya; monks from Sri Lanka help spread the orthodox faith.

1393: Ayutthaya conquers Angkor.

1438: Ayutthaya eclipses Sukhothai and emerges as the most powerful state in mainland Southeast Asia.

circa 1540: The kingdom of Ayutthaya controls all peninsular Thailand and parts of northern Malaysia. In the east, Thai rule extends as far as Chanthaburi and Trat.

1569–90: Ayutthaya temporarily becomes a tributary to Burma.

circa 1600: The first significant economic and cultural ties with Europe – especially with Portuguese, French, Dutch and English traders – are established.

1656–88: Under King Narai, European (especially French) influence at the court of Ayutthaya reaches its zenith.

1760: Burmese King Alaungpaya seizes the Tenasserim Coast and besieges Ayutthaya; Alaungpaya is wounded and dies during retreat.

1763–66: Burmese King Hsinbyushin mounts new attacks, capturing much of the peninsula and besieging Ayutthaya.

1767: Burmese forces capture and sack Ayutthaya, killing or carrying into exile the Thai royal court. General Taksin organises resistance from his base at Chanthaburi.

1768: Taksin proclaims himself king and establishes a new capital at Thonburi, on the Chao Phraya, south of Ayutthaya.

1779: Taksin's main generals, brothers Chakri and Sarasin, drive back the Burmese and conquer Chiang Mai.

1782: Taksin is deposed for erratic behaviour and antagonising the Buddhist monkhood. Chao Phaya Chakri founds the current Chakri Dynasty (becoming King Rama I).

Founding of Bangkok to WWII

1782–1809: King Rama I moves the capital across the Chao Phraya River to Bangkok. He begins a massive building programme on Rattanakosin Island, site of the Grand Palace. The restored kingdom consolidates and expands its strength. A great cultural and religious revival begins.

1785: The last major Burmese invasion is beaten back, but not before Chumphon and Phattalung are sacked. Phuket is saved by the heroism of sisters Chan and Muk. King Rama I defeats the Burmese near Kanchanaburi. Thai authority is established as far south as Kedah and Terengganu in present-day Malaysia. Cambodia becomes a Thai tributary state.

1809–24: Reign of King Rama II. Wat Arun is built in Bangkok. Relations are reopened with the West, most notably Britain.

1824–51: Reign of King Rama III. Rebellion against Thai rule in the northern Malay states and fierce rivalry with Vietnam for control of Cambodia. Rama III resists Westernisation and promotes traditional values.

1851–68: Reign of King Mongkut (Rama IV), the Chakri Dynasty's first great reforming monarch.

1868–1910: Reign of King Chulalongkorn (Rama V), considered by many as the father of modern Thailand.

1932: A military coup ends absolutism and ushers in a constitutional monarchy.

1939: Siam's name is officially changed to Thailand.

1942: Invasion obliges Thailand to enter World War II as a Japanese ally. The south is a major invasion route, with Japanese naval landings at Nakhon Si Thammarat.

1945: After World War II, Thailand is treated lightly by the Allies under US pressure as a "forced ally" of Japan.

LEFT: a temple mural depicting a Thai-Burmese conflict during the Ayutthaya period.

RIGHT: an elephant at Khao Lak used in salvage efforts following the December 2004 tsunami.

Post-war and present-day

1946: King Bhumibol Adulyadej (Rama IX), the current monarch, ascends the throne.

1973–91: Series of coups and military governments with right-wing policies.

1975–85: Malay separatism brews in the southern provinces. After 1985, the situation quietens but does not die out.

1992: A coup attempt by General Suchinda is ended by royal intervention. Thailand enjoys increasing democratic progress.

1997: Thai economy suffers a serious setback in the Asian financial crisis.

2001: Billionaire Thaksin Shinawatra and his Thai Rak Thai Party win the elections

for the Lower House by a large majority.

2002: Separatist struggle in the far south reignites, but with a more Islamic and less Malay nationalist element.

2004: Indian Ocean tsunami devastates much of Thailand's Andaman Coast.

2005: Thaksin re-elected by a large majority despite accusations of corruption. Situation in the Muslim far south deteriorates sharply with rising communal violence and heavy-handed Thai military suppression.

2006: Results of snap election called by Thaksin to quell mass public demonstrations are annulled by Thai courts after the king declares it "undemocratic". ❑

PEOPLE AND CULTURE

The essence of "Thai-ness" has long been embodied by an adherence to Buddhism, a love for the monarchy and the use of the Thai language. But this notion is increasingly complemented by a recognition of the nation's diverse communities

The overwhelming majority of Thailand's population is ethnic Tai (or Thai), with the Central Tais predominating in the southeastern region between Bangkok and Cambodia, as well as down the peninsula about as far south as Prachuap Khiri Khan. Further to the south, their close cousins, the Southern Tais, gradually increase in numbers until by Ranong and Surat Thani, they are the majority.

Although the largest ethnic group, the Tais are relative newcomers to the region, having slowly migrated south from southern China in the 10th to 12th century. By about 1350, they had extended their control over all of present-day Thailand, as well as far into the Malay Peninsula, taking over territory previously controlled by the Khmers, Mons and Malays.

Living among the Tais today are a number of minorities who add considerably to the cultural, religious, linguistic and even culinary diversity of the region. These minorities include the Vietnamese in the southeast, Malays in the far south, ethnic Chinese, who have settled in urban areas throughout the entire region, as well as aboriginal groups like the Mani and the sea gypsies *(see page 35)*, the former living in isolated communities in the remoter parts of the mountainous interior and, the latter, along the Andaman Coast. Finally, there are smaller numbers of ethnic Khmer near the Cambodian border, as well as Mons, Burmans and Karens along the frontier with neighbouring Burma.

The present monarch, King Bhumibol Adulyadej *(see page 20)*, has made it a point to embrace all the citizens of Thailand – including non-Tais and non-Buddhists – within the remit of being Thai. During his long reign, cultural and linguistic diversity have increasingly been celebrated rather than discouraged.

Karens and Mons

West of Bangkok, in the mountainous interiors stretching from Ratchaburi to Chumphon and Ranong in the south, the Karen and Mon peoples, often seeking refuge from military persecution in Burma, or simply economic migrants seeking work and a better life (often

---

PRECEDING PAGES: a sea gypsy child at Ko Surin.
LEFT: young Thais on Ko Samet.
RIGHT: a Mon woman from western Thailand.

illegally), scratch a poor living from the soil. More prosperous descendants of the Mons – a people traditionally opposed to Thailand's old enemy, Burma, and therefore trusted by the Thais – live in Greater Bangkok, on the island of Ko Kret and further south in Phra Pradaeng, where in times past they served as loyal bulwarks against possible Burmese aggression.

The Muslim community

As one moves further south on the Isthmus of Kra, minarets begin to appear among the palm trees, a clear indication of the presence of Thai-speaking Muslims. Even further south, on the Malaysian frontier, are four provinces with a Malay-speaking Muslim majority. Here, Thai-speaking Buddhists are in a small minority, but control the administration and schools.

The farmers and fishermen of this region are overwhelmingly Malay, yet even among this apparently homogenous group there are differences. To the west, the Andaman Coast province of Satun has the highest Muslim population in Thailand, with more than 80 percent of the total. Yet the people here seem content to be Thai citizens, and have never become involved in the region's ongoing separatist movement. To the east, in the predominantly Malay provinces of Pattani, Narathiwat and Yala, disenchantment with rule from Bangkok is more widespread and Islamic practice more rigorous. This parallels the situation in the neighbouring Malaysian state of Kelantan, long the main power base of PAS, the conservative Islamic Party of Malaysia.

The Sino-Thais

In the Bight of Bangkok, just off the coast of Chonburi Province, the tiny island of Ko Si Chang was once the main disembarkation point for migrants arriving in Thailand from southern China. It is not surprising, therefore, that Bangkok's substantial Chinese community (around 14 percent of the population) trace their ancestry mainly to the Guangdong, Fujian and Guangxi provinces. The neighbouring coastal provinces, from Chanthaburi in the east to Petchaburi in the west, have a very Chinese feel to them too, as do the commercial sections of every provincial capital in the southern peninsular region and the small island towns of the Samui Archipelago.

The ethnic Chinese occupy a unique position in Thai society. Because they have excelled particularly at trading, the Chinese have come to dominate commerce throughout Southeast Asia, often causing resentment and hostility among the host populations. In countries such as Indonesia, Malaysia, Burma and Vietnam, this has sometimes led to anti-Chinese sentiments, ethnic tensions and occasional expulsions or even massacres of ethnic Chinese. Thailand happenns to be the exception. While the Tais are well aware of the commercial skills of the overseas Chinese, they have tended to intermarry with them rather than victimise or expel them. As a result, the two groups live side-by-side in almost complete harmony and, especially in urban centres, have intermarried to the extent that most "overseas Chinese" now consider themselves to be as much Thai as Chinese, if not more so. Making up an estimated 11 percent or more of the total population, these are called *luk chin*, or "children of China".

Today, few can read Chinese, though older

between the two. Indeed, Thailand's approach to its citizens of Chinese origin has been of inestimable value to the nation, and stands as an example to the rest of Southeast Asia.

Southern character

While the people of Thailand all share some common traits, there are interesting cultural distinctions between the southern Thais and those from other regions of the country.

The central and northern Thais often consider the southern Thais to be somewhat "hasty" – they can be quick-tempered and as fiery as their southern cuisine. They also speak faster, using a clipped dialect that while com-

people – especially men – can still converse in the southern Chinese dialects such as Chaozhou and Cantonese. They are very well integrated into Thai society, having adopted Theravada Buddhism and Thai names, cultural values and tastes. In return, the Thais have also absorbed much from the Chinese in matters linguistic, cultural and even culinary. Indeed, so well integrated have the two peoples become – especially in Bangkok and the provincial towns of the south – that it is often impossible to make an absolute distinction

LEFT: Muslim man outside a mosque in Khao Lak.
ABOVE: Bangkok's community of ethnic Chinese.

THE TAMILS OF PHUKET

Most of Phuket's Tamils migrated from neighbouring Malaysia in the 19th century, though some came directly from India. A number were prosperous money-lenders from the rich Chettiar class, while others found employment on rubber plantations. By the early 20th century, the island had a sizeable Tamil community, though it has since diminished significantly due to rem-igration. Today, the Tamils live mainly in or near Phuket Town, where community life centres on Thandayuda-pani Temple on Suthat Road, one of the few function-ing Hindu temples in Thailand. Here, the birthday of the god Ganesh is celebrated in August or September.

prehensible to other Thais, is distinctively southern. From a negative perspective, some southern Thai towns have acquired persistently shady reputations. Chonburi, southeast of Bangkok, has long been known for its *chao poh*, or "godfathers", gangsters who are often of ethnic Chinese origin. These Thai mafiosi made huge amounts of money from a mixture of legitimate, semi-legal and openly criminal businesses, running everything from transport companies and petrol stations to underground lotteries, prostitution and cigarette smuggling. These *chao poh* had their heyday in the 1990s, but many have since met violent ends.

The infamous Sia Yai of Angthong, for buri and Nakhon Si Thammarat may have to wait for some years before their reputations for lawlessness disappears.

Of course, not all Southern Thais are quick-tempered, and the great majority are law-abiding citizens. For their part, they sometimes see northern and northeastern Thais as too easy-going and unadventurous, lacking the southern drive and ambition.

National ethos

Yet despite these apparent differences, a shared reverence for the monarchy and a fervent belief in religion serve as the unifying glue that binds Thai society. A pride in the

instance, was blown apart by a claymore mine outside the provincial courthouse in 1989. Sa Jiew of Chonburi was killed in 1991 when his Mercedes was blown off the road by a rocket-propelled grenade. To counter the constant threat of assassination, many *chao poh* used bulletproof cars and employed Uzi-toting gunmen – many of whom came from Nakhon Si Thammarat, a southern town famed across Thailand for the ruthlessness of its gunmen.

In recent years the power of the *chao poh* has diminished considerably, partly through police action and partly because this kind of lawless behaviour has become unacceptable to many of today's urban Thais. Still, Chon-

country's long independence has also bred a quiet cultural confidence in Thais, whether southern or otherwise.

One of the nation's greatest treasures is one that is intangible – the famous Thai appreciation of *sanuk*, or "fun" – that is, enjoying life and having a good time. Perhaps less appreciated by outsiders but no less essential is the Thai trait of *supap*, or "politeness". If you are consistently smiling and polite, life in Thailand – even in Chonburi and Nakhon Si Thammarat – should be plain sailing. ❑

LEFT: a pacific sign in southern Thailand.
ABOVE: the Thais' friendly demeanour is well known.

Thailand's Sea Gypsies

The "sea gypsies" of southern Thailand, known in Thai as *chao lay*, or "people of the sea", are divided into three groups, though they sometimes intermarry and generally consider themselves as one kindred people. Numbering between 4,000 and 5,000, they live only along the Andaman Sea, either in huts by the shore, or on itinerant craft that ply the coastal waters south from Ranong to Ko Tarutao.

The Urak Lawoi people, numbering around 3,000, form the largest sea gypsy group. They live in simple shacks on beaches from Phuket to Ko Tarutao and make a living by fishing and beachcombing. Their two largest settlements are at Ko Sireh and Rawai in the southeast of Phuket.

Two other smaller groups also exist – the 1,000-strong Moklen community living between Ko Phra Tong near Takua Pa and Phuket, and the 500 or so Moken, living north from Ko Phra Thong to the Burmese frontier. Of the three groups, the Moken are the least adapted to modern life; they still use dugout canoes rather than motorised longtail boats, and avoid contact with settled people – especially local authorities – as much as possible. The Thais distinguish them from the other more assimilated groups by calling them *chao ko tae* or "real island folk". The Moken rarely build huts on dry land; they prefer living a completely nomadic existence on the waters of the Andaman Sea.

An indigenous people, it seems likely the *chao lay* people were among the earliest inhabitants of the region, predating the arrival of the Tais from the north by many centuries. They are shorter, stockier and darker than the Tais, are related to the *orang laut*, or "Sea People", of Malaysia, and perhaps also to the Mani or negrito peoples who inhabit the southern Thai interior. Little is known of the *chao lay*'s past as they have no written language or records. Their spoken languages are related to Malay, though the Moken, living furthest from

Malaysia, have borrowed a much larger vocabulary from the Thai and Burmese.

Chao lay religion is neither Buddhist nor Muslim, but rests on propitiating tutelary spirits, especially those associated with wind, wave and islands. The Moken are animists and venerate the sea. Every year during the full moon of the fifth lunar month, they stop working for three days and nights to feast, dance, sing and drink alcohol, often entering into a trance. The Moken say that their earliest ancestor was washed ashore, but on landing refused to become Muslim or Buddhist, choosing instead to return to the sea from where he

had come. Certainly, the sea gypsies remain a people apart, living on the fringes of southern Thai society. They are some of the poorest and least technologically sophisticated people in the entire country.

Yet, while they may be ill-equipped to deal with modern life, the *chao lay* have some natural advantages. During the December 2004 tsunami, although more than 1,000 sea gypsy households sustained damage and some loss of life, they seem to have instinctively understood the cataclysmic event better than their Thai neighbours, many saving themselves by moving early to higher ground. ❏

RIGHT: a sea gypsy on Ko Lanta mending nets.

A CALENDAR OF CELEBRATIONS

Whether religious or secular, national or local, festivals in Thailand are almost always an occasion for celebration

There can be no doubt that the Thais place great importance on their festivals. Some date back centuries, like Loy Krathong, which began in the 13th century. Others, like Lamphun's Lamyai Fruit Festival, are recent creations. In fact, new festivals are thought up every year, sometimes to promote tourism and often just for a bit of *sanuk* (fun). Some festivals are weighty matters upon which the future of the nation depends. Some are more spiritual, allowing one to make merit and ensure a better karmic rebirth, while others are purely secular celebrations of the joy of living. Note: As Buddhist festivals fall on the lunar calendar, their exact dates vary each year.

ABOVE: the King's Birthday is celebrated on 5 December nationwide, but most spectacularly at Rattanakosin in Bangkok. The Grand Palace is illuminated, and there is a fireworks display.

ABOVE: held in May at Sanam Luang in Bangkok, the Brahmin rituals of the Royal Ploughing Ceremony mark the start of the rice-growing season and divine whether the coming year's harvest will be plentiful.

LEFT: Visakha Puja, on the 15th day of the sixth lunar month, marks the birth, enlightenment and passing of the Buddha. It is Thailand's most important religious event, marked by candlelit processions at temples.

ABOVE: on 3 December is the Trooping of the Colours, held outside the old Thai Parliament in Bangkok. The King, Queen and members of the royal family review the elite Royal Guard, who are clad in elaborate, brightly coloured dress uniforms and tall plumed hats. The monarch himself arrives in style in his personal yellow Rolls Royce.

BELOW: every 13 April, Thais mark the traditional lunar new year – which coincides with the height of the hot season – with an extraordinary bout of good-humoured water throwing throughout the country. Don't expect to stay dry for long when in public. Songkran festivities may last as long as four or five days, and involve music, dancing and, very often, liberal amounts of alcohol.

BELOW: Makha Puja is observed on the full moon of the third lunar month, to mark one of the Buddha's most important sermons. Merit-making ceremonies are held at temples across Thailand. In a quiet and dignified tradition that goes back centuries, people strive to atone for past misdeeds and perform good deeds. Food and robes are offered to monks, candlelit processions wind around stupas, flowers and incense are offered to Buddha images, and caged animals are released.

BELOW: perhaps Thailand's loveliest festival, Loy Krathong is celebrated on the full moon night in November to pay respects to Mae Khongkha, goddess of the country's life-bringing rivers and lakes. The festival is supposed to have started at Sukhothai, the first Thai capital, during the time of King Ramkhamhaeng, when a court lady prepared a *krathong*, or float, for the king. Banana stem floats, beautifully decorated with flowers, incense, candles and small coins, are released on waterways across the country.

RELIGION

All over Thailand, the visitor will see saffron-clad Buddhist monks, and hear the soft chanting of Pali scriptures and the tinkling of temple bells. But look beyond the elaborate, brightly-coloured temples and you will see the influence of spirit worship on everyday life

Thailand is an overwhelmingly Buddhist nation. Around 95 percent of the population follows Buddhism, and its influence is apparent almost everywhere. Only in the very far south of the country, on the border with Malaysia, does Islam predominate.

The Way of the Elders

The main form of Buddhism practised is Theravada, or the "Way of the Elders", though in Chinese temples, the Mahayana, or "Greater Vehicle" tradition, may be found alongside Taoist and Confucian images. Both traditions teach that desire for worldly things leads to suffering, and that the only way to alleviate this suffering is to cast off desire. Theravada Buddhism emphasises personal salvation rather than the Mahayana way of the *bodhisattva*, which is the temporary renunciation of personal salvation in order to help humanity achieve enlightenment. The goal of the Theravadin is to become an *arhat*, or "worthy one".

In practice, most Thais hope that by making merit and honouring the *triratna*, or "Three Jewels" – the Buddha, the *sangha* (order of monks) and the *dharma* (sacred teachings) – they will attain a better rebirth and ultimately attain *nirvana*, or enlightenment. To do this, one should strive to build up positive *karma*. This may best be achieved by not taking life, abstaining from drinking alcohol and other intoxicants, avoiding gambling and sexual promiscuity, keeping calm and not becoming

angry, as well honouring the elderly, monks and the Thai monarchy. Most Thai Buddhist men will join the *sangha* and become monks at least once in their lives. Women too may become ordained as nuns, though fewer do so, and the act is usually delayed until old age, when the task of raising children has been completed.

Appeasing the spirits

Spirit worship plays a major, if informal role in Thai religious life, alongside the practice of Buddhism. It is widely accepted that there are spirits everywhere – spirits of the water, wind and woods, and both locality spirits and tutelary spirits. These spirits are not so much good

LEFT: Wat Yai Suwannaram, Petchaburi.
RIGHT: a Buddhist monk carrying an alms bowl.

or bad, but are powerful and unpredictable. Moreover, they have many of the foibles of humans, being capable of vindictiveness, lust, jealousy, greed and malice. To appease them, offerings must be made, and since they display many aspects of human nature, these offerings are often what people would value themselves.

To counteract the spirits and potential dangers in life, protective spells are cast and kept in small amulets mostly worn around the neck. Curiously, the amulets are not bought, but rather rented on an indefinite lease from "landlords", often monks considered to possess magical powers. Some monasteries have been turned into highly-profitable factories for

the production of amulets. There are amulets that offer protection against accidents while travelling or against bullet and knife wounds; some even boost sexual attraction. All this has no more to do with Buddhism than the protective blue-patterned tattoos sported by some rural Thais to ward off evil.

The city pillar

It is not known exactly when the Thai people first embraced a belief in spirits, but it was most probably long before their migration south into present-day Thailand, and certainly before their gradual conversion to Buddhism around 800–1200 AD. When the first Thai migrants established themselves in the plains around Sukhothai, their basic unit of organisation was the *muang*, a group of villages under the control and protection of a *wiang*, or fortified town. Of crucial importance to each *muang*, and located at the centre of each *wiang*, was the city pillar, or *lak muang*. Till today, it is a feature of towns in Thailand.

The *lak muang* – generally a rounded pole thought to represent a rice shoot – is the home of the guardian spirits of the city and surrounding district. It should be venerated on a regular basis, and an annual ceremony, with offerings of incense, flowers and candles, must also be held to ensure the continuing prosperity and safety of the *muang*. Long ago, during the region's animist past, the raising of city pillars was often associated with brutal rituals involving human sacrifice.

Fortunately, such rituals have long since disappeared from the scene, as gentler traditions

CONSECRATING A SPIRIT HOUSE

Setting up a spirit house is not a casual undertaking, but one that requires the good offices of an experienced professional. Usually this is a Brahmin priest called a *phram* (clad in white, in contrast to the Buddhist saffron robes), or at least someone schooled in Brahmin ritual.

The consecration ritual is commenced by scattering small coins around the site chosen for the new spirit house, and in the soil beneath the foundations. Then the spirit house is raised, and offerings are made. These include flowers (usually elegant garlands of jasmine), money, candles and incense – the latter often stuck into the crown of a pig's head.

The *phram*, together with the householder and his various relatives and friends, then pray to the spirits, beseeching the local *chao thii*, or Lord of the Locality, to take up residence in the new spirit house.

Spirit houses are often beautifully decorated, and to entice the *chao thii* into its new home, various inducements are generally added. These may include traditional offerings such as statues of dancers, ponies, servants and other necessities made of plaster or wood. In more recent times, contemporary offerings like cars and other modern consumer desirables have been offered as well, each carefully chosen to catch the spirit's fancy.

associated with Theravada Buddhism have modified spirit beliefs. Today, some *lak muang* are topped by a gilded image of the Buddha.

Spirit houses

For many centuries, offerings have been made when land had to be cleared for agriculture or building. After all, the spirits of a place are its original owners, and their feelings have to be taken into consideration. At some point, it was decided that an effective way of placating a locality spirit was to build it a small house of its own. That way, it would be comfortable, content, and above all, would not feel the urge to move in with its human neighbours!

worship has been a two-way process. There is hardly a Buddhist temple in the country that does not incorporate an elaborate spirit house in its grounds – built at the same time as the consecration of the temple in order to accommodate the displaced locality spirits.

As if this weren't enough, the Thais also feel obliged to consider the world outside the *muang*. If the *lak muang* is the centre of civilisation and safety, the jungled hills and inaccessible mountains are the opposite. It is no surprise that the Thais erect spirit houses along the roads linking their settlements, paying particular attention to threatening or ominous landscapes. Even today, every pass or steep section of road is

Thai Buddhists believe that every human house should have its own spirit house for the well-being of the locality spirit. These may be anywhere in the garden (even, in big cities, on the roof), with the important proviso that the shadow of human habitation should never fall on the spirit house, which is, after all, the home of the original and true owner of the land. Shops and commercial establishments have their own spirit houses as well.

The association of Buddhism with spirit

PHALLUS SHRINE

Certain spirit shrines, or their residents, are thought to have powers to redress specific problems. An example is the shrine of Chao Mae Thapthim, a female deity considered to reside in a venerable banyan tree in Nai Lert Park, just behind Bangkok's Swissôtel Nai Lert Park. Mae Thapthim has the power to induce fertility, and many young women seeking to become pregnant visit the shrine. They leave the usual presents of flowers and incense, as well as a less common type of offering – wooden phalluses that come in all sizes, from a few inches long to giant representations over a metre and a half in length, standing on legs or even wheels.

LEFT: the *lak muang*, or city pillar, of Trat.
ABOVE: a typical spirit shrine in Thailand.
RIGHT: altar at Bangkok's Chao Mae Thapthim shrine.

topped by a spirit house to accommodate the inconvenienced locality spirit. Passing drivers beep their horns in salutation, and many stop to make offerings. Spirit houses are also raised in fields to ensure the safety of the crop.

Islam in the south

It is only in the furthest south of peninsular Thailand, in Malay-speaking territory, that temples and spirit houses disappear, replaced by minarets and mosques. Islam first came to this region in the 8th century. Carried across the Indian Ocean by Arab and South Indian traders, it found fertile ground among the region's Malay-speaking people. The Muslim tradition of Thailand's deep south is, as in neighbouring Malaysia, Sunni Islam of the Shafi'i school.

When the first Muslims arrived, they settled and intermarried with the local Malay population, most of whom at the time practised a syncretic Hindu-Buddhist belief. By Islamic law, the children of such unions were raised as Muslims, and over the centuries a combination of intermarriage and proselytising led to the conversion of almost all the indigenous Malay population.

Comprising less than 5 percent of the population, Thai Muslims are a tiny minority, only dominant in the four southern provinces of Satun, Pattani, Yala and Narathiwat. In this

WITCH DOCTORS

There is an older spirit tradition practised by many Thai Muslims in the Malay-speaking south. Though widely believed in by most ordinary folk, it is officially condemned by orthodox Muslim teachers. This tradition is represented by the *bomoh*, or Malay "witch doctor", who can foretell future events, cure physical, mental and spiritual diseases, curse individuals or lift such curses. They rely on a fascinating mix of folk Islam overlaying a deep vein of other traditions that predated Islam in the region. Because of this syncretism, which is completely forbidden in orthodox Islam, much of *bomoh* practice is concealed from outsiders.

region, the people are conservative, generally working as farmers or fisherfolk, studying the faith in religious schools, and saving to go on the *haj*, or pilgrimage, to Mecca. The Shafi'i school is conservative and not overly rigorous, although in recent times, there has been growing fundamentalist influence from foreign Muslim radicals from Malaysia and Indonesia, giving rise to separatist movements and sporadic unrest in Pattani, Yala and Narathiwat provinces. Satun Province, although largely Muslim, has steered clear of such strife and unrest, and is safe to visit. ❑

ABOVE: worshippers at a mosque in Bang Thao, Phuket.

Vegetarian Festival

Phuket's most unusual religious event is the Vegetarian Festival, celebrated in the first nine days of the ninth month of the Chinese lunar calendar, usually in late September or early October.

This festival is somewhat like a Taoist version of the Christian Lent, when devout Chinese Thais abstain from eating meat of any kind. In Phuket Town, the festival's activities centre on six Chinese temples, with Jui Tui Temple *(see page 217)* on Thanon Ranong the most important, followed by Bang Niew Temple and Sui Boon Tong Temple. The festival is also observed in Kathu Town in Phuket (where the Vegetarian Festival is believed to have originated), and also at Trang Town in Trang Province.

As well as avoiding meat, devotees at the Vegetarian Festival organise processions, make temple offerings, stage cultural shows and consult with mediums. They also perform a series of bizarre and extraordinary acts of self-mortification that, to the uninitiated, seem scarcely credible. Devotees enter into a trance designed to bring the gods to earth to participate in the festival, then walk with bare soles on red-hot coals, climb ladders made of razor-sharp sword blades, stab themselves with all manner of sharp objects, and pierce their cheeks with sharpened stakes, swords, spears, daggers and even screwdrivers. It can be a bloody and disconcerting sight to the uninitiated. Miraculously, though, given that some devotees strike their heads repeatedly with axe blades, cut their tongues with knives, and may even throw themselves bodily into coffins filled with broken glass and blazing fuel, little permanent damage seems to be done.

The opening event is the raising of the lantern pole, an act that notifies the gods that the festival is about to begin. The pole is at least 10 metres (30 ft) tall and once erected, celebrants believe that the participating gods descend, bringing spiritual power to the event. Meanwhile, altars are

set up along major roads bearing offerings of fruit and flowers, incense, candles and nine tiny cups of tea. These are for the Nine Emperor Gods of the Taoist pantheon invited to participate in the festival and in whose honour the celebrations are held. Thousands of locals and visitors line the streets to observe the events, which are accompanied by loud music, frenzied dancing and the constant noise of exploding firecrackers.

Phuket's Chinese community claim that a visiting theatrical troupe from Fujian which performed in Kathu almost two centuries ago first began the festival. The story goes that the troupe was stricken with a strange

illness because its members had failed to propitiate the Nine Emperor Gods. In order to recover, they had to perform a nine-day penance, after which they became well. This supernatural incident eventually became the basis of the Vegetarian Festival.

During the festival, spectators and participants can enjoy specially-prepared vegetarian food at street stalls and markets all over the island. Strangely, these vegetarian dishes, in Thai or Chinese style, are made to resemble meat. Though made from soy or other vegetable substitutes, the food looks and often tastes very much like chicken, pork or duck. ❑

RIGHT: ritual self-mortification at the festival.

SOUTHERN THAI CUISINE

Southern Thai food is the stuff of poetry: "Mussaman curry
is like a lover. As peppery and fragrant as the cumin seed /
Its exciting allure arouses / I am urged to seek its source"

– *Boat Songs*, King Rama II

Among the many well-loved attractions found on the islands and beaches of Thailand, the dramatic limestone outcroppings, white sands and pellucid waters are familiar to most visitors. But many have very little knowledge of *aahaan pak tai*, the distinctive cuisine of the south and arguably the country's most dynamic style of cooking.

Even though the influence of cookbooks, international restaurants and travel shows (not to mention the Thai government's highly active efforts to promote the cuisine) has helped assure Thai food a place among the world's great cuisines, general awareness of Thailand's culinary traditions has yet to reach the level enjoyed by countries like Italy and France. While many foodies are aware of the distinct regional variations of Italian and French cooking, Thai cuisine is still often judged as a monolithic tradition, represented simplistically by a menu of dishes more characteristic of Bangkok's central cuisine.

Diverse influences

Of all the regional styles of cooking, that of southern Thailand bears all the hallmarks of substantial cross-cultural influence. History, trade, religion and empire are folded into the mix, whether due to the great Srivijaya rulers of Indonesia and their long-reaching influence, the 8th-century pilgrims of Islam who arrived before the Thai polity coalesced, the presence of Portuguese envoys, or the influ-

ence of Chinese festivals. The recurrent waves of spice trading that occurred from the 16th to 18th century contributed Persian spices like cardamom and cumin. In much the same way, the Portuguese trading ships introduced ingredients from the New World, like tomatoes, eggplants, cashews and chillies.

Aromatic curries can be almost Indian in their rich palette of spices and vibrant colours, and indeed much of the cuisine's character was influenced by the Tamil and Keralan workers who have since migrated to neighbouring Malaysia. The Chinese, on the other hand, in places like Phuket and Trang, brought with them their taste for coffee and dim sum.

LEFT: a spicy red curry and its many ingredients.
RIGHT: a 19th-century print of Siamese ladies dining.

Fierce and spicy flavours

So what does southern Thai food taste like? Along with Isaan cooking of the northeast, it wields the most aggressive flavours of all Thai food. Indeed, visitors unaccustomed to it will immediately notice the fiery hot flavour that southerners are so fond of – *rot phet*, imparted by sharp hits of the numerous types of chilli used. But like all Thai cuisine, this is balanced by sour, salty and sweet flavours. It is a richly woven meld of spices (which in some places can be so wide-ranging as to taste almost Persian) with a wondrous aroma hinting at its Indian influence, and pungent dashes of shrimp paste (a locally made speciality).

With technique at a premium, the artistry and complexity of preparation is almost jazz-like, with individual cooks improvising endlessly on old favourites, and occasionally yielding unlikely new combinations. The building blocks of flavour include *masala*-like curry blends, fermented vegetables and fish, various pickled bamboo shoots and greens, and an array of fruits which, like the versatile papaya, range from astringent when green and unripe to sugary sweet when ripened to maturity.

Bounteous ingredients

Natural bounty is a huge southern advantage. The Gulf of Thailand and the Andaman Sea

CHINESE FOOD IN TRANG TOWN

Though only a 10-minute ride from the limestone mountains of the coast, the sleepy trading town of Trang has something more than natural beauty: it is a little-known stronghold of Chinese food culture in the south. With a large population of second- and third-generation ethnic Chinese immigrants, the flavours here are Thai in influence, but also traditional enough to be heartily welcomed in China. Dim sum can be found on street corners in the morning, when blue-collar workers load up on noodles and tiny dumplings of shrimp, pork or crab. Come nightfall, the town's vaunted barbecued pork – an unctuous yet sweet creation permeated with just enough grill smoke

to qualify it as a savoury – takes centrestage. But the real drawcard here is black, heady and liquid. Trang, above all, is a coffee town. Shop owners of Hokkien Chinese descent roast their own beans and prepare coffee in a big, sock-like filter according to tradition. Every strip of shophouses has a coffee shop, so it is worth making the rounds. Some are rickety, the size of a pick-up truck, and made of wooden clapboards. Others are near mini temples and always full of monks. Near the train station are several coffee shops where the cups of traditional thick, black brews are replaced by sugar-laced iced coffees and plates of sweet *roti*, beloved by their youthful student clientele.

harbour troves of white snapper, horse mackerel, marbled goby (*soon hock*), squid, prawns and rock lobster. And because the Isthmus of Kra, which separates these bodies of water, is so thin, there is nary a catch that does not end up, often within a day, in both Ko Samui (in the Gulf) and Ko Lanta (in the Andaman).

Whether in the markets that spring up by the light of dawn, or at roadside stands under neon lights come nightfall, fruits are piled in abundance. Phuket has a luscious sweet pineapple with a taste that hints at vanilla, apricots and rose; it is so tender that the core can be eaten dipped in sugar. The spiky, stinky durian (especially the *kan yao* variety) is most prolific in the deep south province of Yala, while the cooling, purple-skinned mangosteen is excellent south of Nakhon Si Thammarat. Water greens, jungle ferns, ginger buds, snake beans, lemongrass, galangal shoots – there is an abundance of vegetables and herbs.

Of course, rice is still the staple. In the past, it sustained workers through the day with just small portions of chilli, curry or sauce added for flavour. Even now, rural Thais eat large helpings of rice with just morsels of dried or salted fish. Thankfully, long-grain jasmine-scented Thai rice is one of the most delicious to be found in Asia.

Representative dishes

The seafood of the south is so fresh that it warrants little fuss in preparation. The best of the catch, like Phuket's famed rock lobster or Trang's soft-shell crab, is simply grilled or stir-fried with assertive seasonings like lemongrass, black pepper and garlic. Squid is treated in the same way or, like many fish dishes, served with dipping sauces of chilli, lime and garlic. Deep-frying is a favourite too, whether served in a sweet-sour Chinese style or in a very southern way with turmeric and garlic.

The curries are fiercely spicy and leave their milder cousins of the central region looking a bit boring. One signature dish is *kaeng leuang*, a southern-style curry stained yellow-orange by turmeric and bristling with chillies, pickled bamboo shoots, shrimp paste, cucumber and syrupy sweet pineapple. Another,

LEFT: fresh bounty from Thailand's coastal waters.
RIGHT: pineapples grown on Phuket.

kaeng tai pla, is a vicious stew of chillies, pickled bamboo shoots, fermented fish and black pepper that broadcasts its scent in all directions. A gentler speciality to try is *khao yam*, a seemingly innocuous salad of rice, vegetables, slivers of green mango, kaffir lime leaves, coconut flakes, dried shrimp and a strong fish sauce called *budu*. The flavour is

floral and feminine, yet unmistakably southern in its lingering strength – all the more so if prepared with *sataw*, a large lima bean look-alike with a pungent flavour and aroma.

Muslim cooking

The Muslim cookery of the south eschews pork, of course, but goat, beef and chicken more than make up for it, as evidenced in the Indian *biryani*-like rice dishes eaten here. The fragrant spices of cumin, cardamom, turmeric, as well as black and white pepper are often at work, along with the different textures imparted by the use of yoghurt and ghee. Early morning and midday are the best times to find oxtail soup with torch ginger, shallots, chillies and coriander. *Roti*, the beloved Indian flatbread, is fun to watch being made, thanks to the often balletic slapping, pulling and whipping of the dough. It can be paired with a variety of curries and stuffed with egg or bananas according to preference. *Roti* stands often live or die by the quality of their curries, and are a good place to try the distinctive spice-rich *mussaman* curry, sometimes thickened with pulverised nuts.

Localised variations

The south of Thailand hosts some of the most highly localised strains of regional cooking in the country. The palate, the ingredients and the specialities vary with the town and whichever communities are dominant there. Locating any given speciality is as easy as locating where the people renowned for cooking it live.

A stronghold of culture and long a regional centre in earlier times, the mid-peninsula hub of Nakhon Si Thammarat is renowned for its balanced but vigorously hot delivery of *kaeng tai pla* and stir-fries like *kaeng khua kling*, a dry beef curry with bird's eye chillies, finger root and garlic. The booming border city of Hat Yai is known for its nightmarkets. Those in the know head straight for the fried chicken, crispy and redolent of lemongrass, shallots and garlic. Pattani and Yala boast old, wooden

HOW TO EAT THAI FOOD

Most Thai meals consist of several dishes placed in the centre of the table to be shared by all; the larger the group, the more dishes one can try. Except for dessert, there are no separate courses, as in a Western meal. Rather, the various dishes are enjoyed at the same time. Place a heap of rice onto your plate together with small portions of various dishes at the side (it's polite to take only a little at a time). Eat with a fork and spoon, using the fork in the left hand to push food onto the spoon. Chopsticks are only for Chinese and noodle dishes. In the far south, the traditional way of eating with the fingers is still practised by ethnic Malays.

Islamic architecture and a hot and salty cooking style of their own. Songkhla has a fine seafood tradition, and the border outpost of Satun, a sleepy ocean hamlet, is where the curries combine the characteristics of Thai and Indo-Malay food. Meanwhile, Ranong is an unsung star for its Chinese-style coffee houses, not unlike Trang *(see page 46)*.

Of course, the best thing about the culinary experience in southern Thailand is undoubtedly its stunning setting. A meal here is never too far from a picture-perfect beach. ❏

ABOVE: a food stall in Songkhla offering a wide selection of Thai curries.

Eating Out in Bangkok

Bangkok has always been one of the world's best places to eat. One could spend a month here slurping and spooning up the many varieties of Thai cuisine available – from Chinese-influenced foods like chicken rice and herbal soups, to done-in-a-flash dishes such as pork stir-fried with holy basil and chillies, a perennial favourite. Indeed, the spectrum of flavours ranges from the bold, as in the well-loved classic soup, *tom yam kung*, to the nuanced, with spices like cumin, cardamom and pepper. And that's just basic roadside sustenance. To find a good meal, simply follow one's instincts. Crowds are a good sign, and fresh produce and careful attention to food presentation are the probable indications of a good chef.

An experience not to be missed is the crowded stew and perfume of Bangkok's Chinatown, along Thanon Yaowarat, where car fumes mix with grill smoke, the spray of freshly-squeezed kaffir limes and the aroma of caramelising garlic and shallots. Located here are a legion of mango and durian sellers, roast duck specialists and vendors wielding cleavers to hack off slices of crispy pork. Of the many superb outdoor seafood set-ups, a pair of the most famous battle it out in almost "Iron Chef" style on opposite corners, one wearing a green outfit and the other red, but both dealing in the same swimming-fresh squid, prawns and mussels, simply grilled or steamed, then slathered with sauces (*naam jim*) of garlic, herbs, lime juice, fish sauce and everything from fermented bean to tamarind juice.

What has changed most of late, however, is the urban sophistication of dining – in the Western paradigm of indoor, air-conditioned service. Following in the trail blazed in large part by an American, Dan Ivarie of Bed Supperclub (who still consults on the menus), talented chefs like the Australian duo Daniel Moran and Amanda Gale of Cy'an (at the Metropolitan hotel) have shown a flair for homely platters that use

recognisable techniques but bold flavours based on local ingredients that Asians love. There is a fun, local café scene at places like Kalpapruek, Kuppa, Coffee Beans by Dao and Greyhound Café, where Thai-spiced pasta dishes, *roti* and curries reveal an East-West blend. Bangkok's large international community has birthed some fine Italian dining rooms, like the boisterous Zanotti and the sleek La Scala in The Sukhothai. A stunning Indo-Thai wooden structure houses what may be the city's sexiest spot, Hazara, and well-crafted vegetarian cooking with a global outlook can be enjoyed at Tamarind Café.

Want the best of both worlds? Ruen Mallika, housed in an atmospheric, traditional teak home, and whose owner is of royal lineage, not only has local flavour but also international polish. Mahanaga is a bit of a scene and while some of the more daring modern Thai dishes do not work, the Moorish-gone-Siamese decor actually does. Le Lys, run by a French-Thai couple, has a pétanque court as well as a bar which pours Provençal rose, pastis and hibiscus flower juice alike. But best of all, it features a menu that delivers southern-style curries and Isaan-style grilled meats with true local panache. ❑

RIGHT: chic dining establishment Cy'an.

NATURE AND ENVIRONMENT

Apart from its white sandy beaches, Thailand's natural
treasures include lush tropical rainforests teeming with
wildlife, stunning limestone karst formations and pristine
coral reefs. Sadly, preservation efforts cannot quite halt
their destruction by human activities and natural calamities

Thailand's biological treasures and diverse landforms derive from its geographical position at the crossroads of Southeast Asia. Just as the nation has accommodated many peoples and cultures, so has it served as a conduit dispersing varied plant and animal life.

Covering some 513,115 sq km (198,115 sq miles), Thailand's overall shape resembles the head of an elephant, with the southern peninsula forming the trunk. The vast valley called the Central Plain stretches about 450 km (280 miles) to the Gulf of Thailand. Over the years, rich silt that the overflowing tributaries habitually deposited have created an agricultural rice bowl, watered nowadays by intensive irrigation drawn from a network of large dams.

Endowed with heavy rainfall and humidity, Thailand's south encompasses the Isthmus of Kra right down to the Malay Peninsula. The coastal forests of the south were cleared to make way for rubber and palm plantations in the late 19th and early 20th centuries. The provinces of Petchaburi and Prachuap Khiri Khan form the narrow neck of land connecting the Central Plain with the peninsular south, where some of Thailand's most stunning white sand beaches are found. At its narrowest point, the slender strip of Thai territory from the Gulf of Thailand to Dan Singkhon on the Burmese border is a mere 12 km (7 miles) wide.

Flora

Up to the mid-20th century, forests covered about 70 percent of Thailand's land area. By 1960, the figure had dropped to 50 percent. Today, probably only about 15 percent of undisturbed forest remains, although perhaps another 15 percent of it has been replanted, often with non-indigenous species, or else turned into plantations growing palm oil trees, and, especially in the south, rubber and pineapple. In all of Southeast Asia, the scale and rate of deforestation in Thailand was once second only to that of Singapore. Following several fatal landslides, logging was outlawed in Thailand in 1989, and the situation is now more stable.

Healthy and thriving rainforests can still be found in the Khao Luang, Ko Surin, Ko Tarutao and Thale Ban national parks, all of which are in the south. Of special note too is Khao Sok National Park *(see page 204)*, the largest nature preserve in peninsular Thailand and dominated by thick forest-covered limestone peaks, some rising as high as 1,000 metres (3,280 ft).

Fauna

Of the world's 4,000 species of mammals, 287 are found in Thailand, including 18 hoofed species, 13 species of primates, nine types of wild cats (including tigers and clouded leopards), two species of bear, two of wild dogs

In the uplands of both the south and southeast, where rainfall is plentiful and the dry season brief, tropical rainforests are most abundant. These harbour the world's densest concentration of species, with herbs, shrubs, ferns and fungi forming the lowest layer of vegetation. Above ground level is a relatively open layer of palms, bamboos and shrubs. Mid-level trees, festooned with vines, mosses and orchids, create a 25-metre (82-ft) high canopy, with the more well-spaced trees of the uppermost canopy soaring as high as 60 metres (200 ft).

LEFT: Cheow Lan Lake at Khao Sok National Park.
ABOVE: tropical bloom and a gibbon.

KRABI'S MANGROVE FORESTS

Mangroves are considered the rainforests of the coast, and though many have been decimated by human activities, the mangrove forests of Krabi remain remarkably intact. They are home to many types of fish, shrimp and molluscs, provide shelter for dugongs, monkeys, lizards and sea turtles, and are also nesting grounds for hundreds of bird species, including the white-bellied sea eagle, ruddy kingfisher, mangrove pitta and the great knot. In mud and shallow waters, fiddler crabs and mudskippers abound. Fortunately, plans to further develop Krabi's Deep Water Port have been put on hold to protect this unique environment.

and eight varieties of dolphins. Bats are abundant, with 107 species identified so far. But tigers and the larger deer could soon join the list of mammals that have vanished since 1900: this includes rhinoceros, several species of deer, two otter species and the kouprey, a wild ox discovered in Thailand in the 1930s.

Declared the country's first protected species in 1921 and perilously close to extinction is the Asian elephant – Thailand's national symbol. From over 20,000 a century ago, fewer than 8,000 survive in Thailand today. Khao Yai National Park, north of Bangkok, offers the best chance of observing some of Thailand's remaining wild elephants.

Thailand also harbours four types of reptiles and three types of amphibians. Among the 175 species of snakes are deadly cobras, kraits and vipers. No doubt most of the insect species have yet to be identified, but there are 1,200 variegated butterflies. Beetle species may number in the tens of thousands, but have been so little studied that entomologists occasionally discover new ones.

Visitors to national parks may not see any large animals, but they will be rewarded with bird sightings. There are around 900 species permanently resident in the region, while about 240 non-breeding and wintering migratory species routinely pass through annually.

Coastal geography

With some 3,000 km (2,000 miles) of coastline and more than 30 islands washed by two seas, littoral geography is a significant drawcard of southern Thailand's environment. Tourists are continually drawn to the region's powdery sand beaches and clear waters rich in tropical marine life *(see pages 54–5 and 61)*. Geologically, the region is noted for its dramatic limestone karst formations jutting out of the sea. Soft and easily eroded, the limestone once formed the seabed. Spectacular caves carved out by underground streams and lagoons hidden within the limestine karsts make for fun-filled exploration on inflatable kayaks.

Ao Phang Nga National Park *(see page 202)* comprises an eye-popping series of crumbly cliffs, jutting islets and karst rocks. Though home to a variety of marine and coastal creatures, most people visit to marvel at and sail around the many looming karst towers.

Environment at risk

Thailand's environment is in danger of irreversible damage. With the destruction of habitats, many species of wildlife could disappear, not just from Thailand, but from the world.

The Forestry Department is underfunded and understaffed. In the past few decades, at least 40 rangers have been murdered in the line of duty. Earning less than a factory worker, many rangers also collude with loggers and poachers. The country's poorest people also inadvertently contribute to the environmental degradation by farming on protected lands. The endangered populations of tigers, bears and deer are further threatened by the demand for medicinal products among the Chinese, and for gourmet "jungle" dining.

The coastal environment too has not been spared. Illegal construction, surreptitious land grabs and poor sewage disposal remain a problem at some of the Eastern Seaboard resorts, notably Pattaya and Si Racha. Even national parkland is not sacrosanct. Ko Samet for instance is part of a marine national park, but unbridled development along its coast has progressed despite the law.

Elsewhere, new legislation, or existing legislation more rigorously applied, is slowly making a difference. But it is newer, or less developed islands like Ko Chang and Ko

SHELL FOSSIL CEMETERY

About 17 km (10 miles) west of Krabi is the unique and unusual Shell Fossil Beach. Here, fossilised shells dating back an estimated 75 million years have formed great stone slabs that project into the sea.

Lanta which stand to benefit most from the environmental lessons learned.

The situation is somewhat better on the western coast of the Gulf of Thailand and also along the Andaman Coast, although Phuket's Patong beach in particular suffers from over-building and has taken on some of the problems associated with Pattaya.

The coral reefs of southern Thailand's coastal waters are home to a diverse and spectacular range of marine life. Unfortunately, they are menaced by various human activities, including dynamite and poison fishing, both now strictly outlawed, anchor drag and over fishing. Perhaps surprisingly, the tsunami in 2004 caused relatively little damge, as coral thrives in oxygenated water and is intrinsically strong enough to withstand and even flourish in heavy seas. More damaging in the short to medium term is global warming, which is especially severe in the Indian Ocean. It causes coral bleaching, which in 1998 killed an estimated 90 percent of the inner reefs in

The disastrous tsunami of December 2004 had some positive spin-offs, though how well they will be exploited remains to be seen. Illegal buildings and ramshackle resorts were literally swept away by the gigantic waves, most notably at Ko Phi Phi, and the Thai authorities have made clear their determination to prevent illegal rebuilding. Understandably, this has met with forceful opposition by many displaced locals, and at the time of writing, even on a national park like Ko Phi Phi, illegal construction is once again underway.

LEFT: Thailand is home to the Asian elephant.
ABOVE: limestone cliffs seen from Railay Bay, Krabi.

the Seychelles. In a bid to counter this threat, "reef balls" of hollow, reinforced concrete are being sunk to rehabilitate reefs, notably in the Andaman Sea off Phuket and at Khao Lak, but also in the shallower Gulf of Thailand.

Tourism undoubtedly plays a part, most visibly when seaside hotels spew untreated sewage. Yet there are also encouraging signs that tourism may become a positive force in the preservation of what remains of Thailand's ecology. Some Thais – among them trekking guides, local green groups and even a few progressive politicians – are becoming aware that environmental caretaking will sustain tourism longer than continued destruction. ❑

UNDERWATER LANDSCAPE

Thailand's coral reefs are an outstanding wonderland of colour, home to a myriad species of fish and marine life

Off the west coast, the flora and fauna of the Andaman Sea are characteristic of the Indian Ocean. Off the east coast, in the Gulf of Thailand, they are characteristic of Indo-Pacific seas. Coral reefs off both coastlines have been little surveyed, but they support at least 400 species of fish and 30 kinds of sea snake. Bottlenose dolphins, and sometimes whales, are found in Thai waters. The gentle dugong, or "sea cow", is increasingly hard to find among the sea grasses of Phang Nga, Phuket, Trang and Satun provinces. Thailand's coral species number almost 300, with the Andaman Sea boasting an even greater diversity. Intact reefs, however, survive only in areas far from human habitation, such as the vicinity of the Surin and Similan islands.

ABOVE: vast gardens of cabbage patch coral share the reefs with outcrops of brain coral, organ pipe coral, soft corals, staghorns, sponges, sea fans, gorgonians and black coral – a plethora of beautiful but fragile life forms.

ABOVE: found in Thai waters are four species of turtle – green, leatherbacks, hawksbills and olive ridleys. All are endangered, and the hawksbill, found in the Andaman, is now very rare.

LEFT: the octopus inhabits many regions of the Andaman and South China seas, and is especially at home in coral reefs. Its soft bodies can squeeze through narrow gaps in the reef, providing refuge from predators and a hiding place from which to pounce on its prey.

BELOW: The cuttlefish makes a frequent appearance on Thai menus, and to support human consumption, they are now captively reared in large quantities. But species such as the *Sepia pharaonis* can, of course, still be observed in their natural habitat in the waters of the Gulf of Thailand. These creatures are among the most intelligent invertebrates in the animal kingdom. Like their close relatives the squid and octopus, they can expel "ink" when threatened.

ABOVE: The Andaman Sea is both deeper than the Gulf, as well as clearer and more saline. It has coral reefs that are more interesting and widely distributed, extending from Ko Tarutao Marine National Park on the frontiers with Malaysia to the reefs and shoals of Burma's Tenasserim region. Thankfully, the tsunami of December 2004 damaged only about 5 percent of the Andaman reefs.

ABOVE: clown fish are found throughout the warm waters of the Indian and Pacific Oceans. These colourful fish live in a symbiotic relationship with sea anemones or stony corals. Once an anemone or a coral has been selected as home, the clown fish will defend it spiritedly.

LEFT: The scorpionfish camouflages innocuously on the seabed, but can deliver an extremely poisonous sting if stepped on. Thailand's waters are estimated to support almost 2,000 fish species, including 600–700 freshwater fish. But data is incomplete, and the total number of both freshwater and saltwater fish may in fact be 30–40 percent higher.

BELOW: contrary to popular belief, only a few varieties of shark pose a threat to humans. Out of more than 350 species, only four have been confirmed to have killed appreciable numbers of humans in unprovoked attacks. These are the great white, oceanic whitetip, bull and tiger sharks. Fortunately, the first two species are not found in Thai waters, while the last two are rarely seen. Relatively common species found here include the nurse, leopard, silvertip, grey, blacktip and the gargantuan whale shark, none of which are known for their aggression towards humans.

OUTDOOR ACTIVITIES

From rocky limestone karsts and fecund tropical rainforests to extensive coastlines along the Gulf of Thailand and the Andaman Sea graced with some of the world's most idyllic beaches, bays and islands, the south's varied topography is a stunning backdrop for a host of outdoor activities

With such a diverse variety of natural settings to explore, visitors to the beaches and islands of Thailand are presented with an ever-growing number of land- and water-based activities to help them experience this incredible landscape. For the majority, outdoor activity still consists solely of lazy sunbathing on the beach with the occasional cooling dip in the sea. But with greater numbers of visitors seeking more vigorous activities, the local tourist industry is responding with novel leisure pursuits that range from kite-surfing to swimming with dolphins.

Responsible tourism

As with all tourist infrastructure, issues of environmental degradation often come under scrutiny. The local authorities are regularly accused of putting commercial interests ahead of natural preservation. The most recent activity to cause concern is sea walking off Pattaya and Phuket, where coral beds are partially cleared so that tourists can don scuba gear and stomp in abandon along the ocean floor.

While activity-based tour operators will rarely admit to causing environmental damage, more proactive companies realise that long-term profits depend on the sustainability of the environment. Responsible tourism practices can range from using reusable containers on nature tours to training and hiring local guides. If you are concerned about potential damage to the environment, ask about the preservation measures an operator takes before signing up for an outdoor adventure.

On water

Thailand's mild, clear, aquamarine waters are ideal for waterborne activities. The more populous beach resorts of Phuket, Pattaya, Ko Samui, Hua Hin and Ko Chang are typically enlivened (or plagued, depending on how you see it) by noisy jet skis. The family-friendly inflatable banana boat rides are always a hoot as well, but be sure to don a life jacket for those inevitable bouncing spills.

Thailand's relatively calm seas are well suited to waterskiing and the trendier wake-

LEFT: perched on a cliff face at Railay Bay, Krabi.
RIGHT: parasailing at Ko Hae, off Phuket.

JET SKIING ALERT

Considering there were two jet-ski linked fatalities to swimmers off Phuket's beaches in 2005 alone, it is no surprise that some beaches ban them. If you hire a jet ski, be careful where and how you ride it.

boarding, though novices may first prefer to refine their technique at a cable ski lake in Phuket, Pattaya, or on the outskirts of Bangkok. More environmentally sound (minus the speedboat), and even more "in" than wakeboarding is the relatively new sport of kite-surfing. Costing around B4,000 for a day, surfing behind a wind-propelled kite is a serious sport

that has only recently started appearing at beaches along Hua Hin, Phuket and Ko Samui.

For a unique and lofty perspective of Thai beach life, a 15-minute parasailing ride, floating high above the sea strapped to a parachute, is exciting yet safe. Back at sea level, windsurfing equipment and instruction is widely available.

Deep-sea fishing trips can be as laidback or as rod-pumping as the fish decide to make it. Most major resorts can arrange charters, where the evening meal depends on how well you do battle with a resistant giant tuna or a powerful barracuda or marlin.

Less conventional forms of aquatic entertainment are also appearing along the Thai

coast. If you have ever dreamt about venturing into the briny depths but are unsure about scuba diving, hop aboard Pattaya's Yellow Submarine. For the unique opportunity to interact with the ocean's most developed species, then Oasis Sea World in Chanthaburi Province offers the family the chance to swim with dolphins.

Sailing

Even though chartering a yacht or catamaran is beyond the means of most holidaymakers, prices for sailing in Thailand are still reasonable compared to other more established sailing centres. With relatively low boat traffic (apart from the noisy longtail boats that plague the shores of some of the more popular beaches) and favourable weather conditions, you can still enjoy solitude sailing in Thai waters. What better way to experience the south's dramatic scenery than by dropping anchor in the silvery bay of an uninhabited isle?

The recreational boating industry has been slow to develop in Thailand, but since the government dropped its hefty import tax on yachts, the outlook has been brighter. Marinas have been built in Phuket and Pattaya, and soon, one will be in Ko Samui. With more charter companies emerging, a greater variety of boats are available. Increased interest has brought greater publicity for Phuket King's Cup Regatta, Asia's leading sailing event held annually in December, as well as the younger Ko Samui International Regatta in May.

Kayaking and white-water rafting

Blessed with thousands of kilometres of pristine waterways and shoreline, a kayaking tour is the most rewarding, eco-friendly and scenic way to explore the many limestone crags, secluded lagoons and tidal caves (known as *hong*) that are scattered in the waters around Ao Phang Nga and Trang in the Andaman Sea, or Ang Thong Marine National Park near Ko Samui in the Gulf of Thailand.

Embark on a day-long or several-day adventure at a gliding pace that even the least physically fit will find comfortable. A great way to view undisturbed wildlife and meet new friends, the large bulky kayaks are very

LEFT: jet-skiing and wind-surfing off Pattaya.
RIGHT: sea-canoeing around Krabi's limestone karsts.

stable and rarely capsize. Paddle from the coast and listen to the cacophony of sounds made by small animals and birdlife that permeate the dense growth as you negotiate the kayak through sinewy mangrove swamps.

If an organised tour sounds too ambitious, then sea kayaks are also available for hourly rental on the beaches of Ko Chang, Ko Samui, Ko Phangan, Phuket, Krabi, and Ko Phi Phi. For those who regard kayaking as too tame, then tumble over bumpy rapids on a dramatic knuckle-clenching white-water rafting expedition along the rivers that flow through wildlife sanctuaries and national parks in Phang Nga Province and elsewhere.

On land

Energetic, exercise-minded visitors may lean towards more physical activities in the wilderness such as hiking, rock climbing or mountain biking. Allowing for more intimate opportunities for contact with nature, these activities will allow you to help preserve the fragile terrain as well as enjoy the lively landscape – whatever the season, you will get a chance to absorb a real slice of life in the wilderness.

Thailand's rock climbing sites are fast becoming known the world over. The towering limestone karsts that have made the Krabi coast so famous are the perfect challenge for novices and experts alike. There are several

NATIONAL PARKS OF SOUTH THAILAND

Thailand has over 110 national parks, sanctuaries and marine parks to investigate. Most are sparse on accommodation, but organised bird-watching and hiking tours, as well as boat trips to deserted islands, are a sustainable way to explore these protected areas.

Apart from Khao Sok National Park *(see page 203)*, the following are worth highlighting. Located some 60 km (40 miles) from Petchaburi, Thailand's largest park, Kaeng Krachan *(see page 150)*, is a haven for numerous species of large mammals, including tigers, elephants, leopards, bears, deer, gibbons and monkeys.

Khao Sam Roi Yot National Park *(see page 155)* trans-

lates as "Three Hundred Mountain Peaks", in reference to the limestone pinnacles jutting up from the park's mangrove swamps to heights above 600 metres (2,000 ft). Wildlife include crab-eating macaques and the rare serow – a mountain goat-antelope. Bird-watchers shouldn't miss a trip to Thailand's largest wetland bird reserve, Thale Noi Waterfowl Park. At the tip of Songkhla Lake, it is home to nearly 200 species of waterfowl.

Mu Ko Lanta National Park *(see page 258)* as well as Ko Tarutao Marine National Park *(see page 275)* are island chains whose waters teem with marine life such as sharks, whales and the rare dugong.

climbing schools now operating along the Andaman coast, especially at Krabi. Though less known for its rocky attributes, Ko Tao has also begun to offer climbing and bouldering.

If teetering against the rock face by means of a rope sounds too nerve-wracking, then a steady hike though forest trails will present an up close and personal way of experiencing Thailand's wealth of wildlife. The best hikes are undertaken in national park land *(see pages 51 and 59)* and should only be embarked upon in the company of an experienced guide. Park rangers offer their services for a fee, although most do not speak more than a word or two of English. Several tour companies organise

day and overnight treks into the bigger parks.

When most people picture Thailand, they think of romantic jungle rides atop majestic elephants. Capitalising on this exotic image, elephant rides are widely available at all major beach destinations. The reality, however, is somewhat less romantic, with elephant camps or villages conducting hour-long to half-day tours around well-worn vegetated trails.

In the shadow of the mighty pachyderm, horse riding has been slow to catch on in Thailand and is still largely a pursuit for the wealthy. However, the most accessible spot to saddle up is on Hua Hin beach, where a stable of old nags are led up and down the sands. Riding clubs in Pattaya and Phuket are open to non-members with reasonable hourly and daily rates.

For those who prefer horsepower of a different kind, try out the All Terrain Vehicle (ATV) tours which are becoming more common at the major resort areas. Unfortunately, some ATV operators restrict their rides to unexciting fenced off circuits. More thrilling tours venture through thick muddy forest. Alternatively, mountain biking is another great way of navigating the dense undergrowth behind Thailand's beaches.

Golf

Golf has fast become a popular pastime for Thailand's middle and upper classes, with a significant number of internationally-designed championship courses having opened since the early 1990s. The history of the sport in Thailand dates back to the 1920s, when King Rama VI and members of the aristocracy played their first rounds at the country's first ever golf club, the Royal Hua Hin Golf Course. Aside from being a relaxing way to bronze up while on vacation, the attraction of Thailand's fairways are the incredible locations and lush backdrops, reasonable course fees for visitors and the novelty of female caddies.

Most of the country's fairways are located in the central region around Bangkok and along the Eastern Seaboard towards Pattaya. Hua Hin also has several courses, as does Phuket, while Ko Samui recently opened its first 18-hole course. ❑

ECO-FRIENDLY TOURS

While Thailand is only just waking up to the impact of ecotourism and environmental conservation, more and more people visit the country to espressly participate in conservation activities. Many see the sustaining of fragile ecosystems and endangered species as a worthy cause, more rewarding than a beach holiday getaway.

In Phang Nga Province, one can volunteer to monitor sea turtle breeding grounds, or help restore local mangroves (www.losthorizonsasia.com). On Phuket, the Gibbon Rehabilitation Project prepares rescued and abused gibbons for reintroduction to the wild, and is in constant need of volunteers (www.gibbonproject.org).

LEFT: elephant riding along Nai Yang beach, Phuket.

Diving and Snorkelling

With long coastlines skirting either side of the Isthmus of Kra, Thailand is a major diving and snorkelling destination. The waters are clear and warm year-round, and a plethora of colourful coral reefs attract a huge variety of marine life, including turtles, sharks and rays *(see pages 54–5)*. With dive shops and live-aboard tours accessing more remote dive sites as far as Malaysia to the south, Burma to the west and Cambodia to the east, Thailand is one of the most affordable places in the world to discover subaquatic vistas.

The Thai coast is split into three shores. Sharing the waters of the Gulf of Thailand, the Eastern Seaboard stretches from Bangkok to Ko Chang, while the Gulf Coast runs down from Bangkok to the deep south. To the west, the Andaman Sea is a part of the expansive Indian Ocean, licking the shores of Ranong near Burma all the way down to Satun on the Malaysian border.

Certain popular spots for diving have emerged from these two distinct seas. The Andaman Sea is generally considered better in terms of reef and marine diversity, water clarity and a wealth of idyllic islands to drop anchor at. Reached primarily by live-aboard trips from Phuket, the remote Similan and Surin island chains are considered the country's premier sites, while the waters off Phuket, Krabi, Ko Phi Phi and Ko Lanta are also popular drop points. For an even greater sense of adventure, live-aboard trips sail into Burmese waters to dive the lesser explored reefs of the Mergui Archipelago and the deep, shark-abundant Burma Banks – all off the Andaman Sea coast.

Many overseas visitors learn how to dive while holidaying in Thailand. Allthough both sides of the Thai coast provide ample opportunities for good diving, a good number of people head to Thailand's dive capital at Ko Tao, which has a large number of dive schools. There are around 50 dive schools currently and plenty of employment opportunities for wannabe dive instructors.

Most dive trips from the neighbouring islands of Ko Samui and Ko Phangan head to Ko Tao for the better sites, which unfortunately make for frequent sightings of other dive groups as well as fish. Pattaya's waters offer little in terms of coral and water clarity, although this is compensated by a number of interesting wreck dives. Fast gaining in popularity, the Ko Chang archipelago, with over 50 islands, is still being mapped out as a dive destination.

The majority of dive schools offer PADI Open Water certification with rates averaging B6,000–9,000, and B800 fun dives for qualified divers, which are discounted if you bring your own equipment. Before embarking on any dive trip, ask the operator a few key questions, such as if they operate their own boats, insurance, hotel pick-ups, and if there is an instructor or dive master who speaks your native language. If studying a PADI Open Water course, ask how many people will be in your class at the same time.

And remember, the cheapest dive shops are not always the safest. If you should get into trouble while submerged, there are emergency hyperbaric chambers situated in or around all the major dive centres. ❑

● *See respective Places chapters for details of dive sites, and Travel Tips for dive school listings.*

RIGHT: face to fish in the Andaman Sea.

PLACES

A detailed guide to Bangkok and the country's
beaches and islands, with the principal sites clearly
cross-referenced by number to the maps

Blessed with some 3,000 km (2,000 miles) of stunning coastline and more than 30 paradisiacal islands washed by two seas – the Gulf of Thailand and the Andaman Sea – Thailand attracts a wide range of visitors, from gregarious party animals to reclusive honeymooners.

Barely 90 minutes from the capital, the brash and saucy coastal resort of Pattaya, with its golf courses and the energy of a cosmopolitan playground, has been dubbed the "Riviera of the Eastern Seaboard". Further east, the small pretty island of Ko Samet is a favourite weekend escape for young Bangkokians, while Ko Chang, Thailand's second largest island, is part of an extensive marine national park only just waking up to tourism's potential.

Heading south, the winding Gulf of Thailand Coast boasts shores fringed with powdery white sand beaches and backed by mountains. The most accessible and popular is family-friendly Hua Hin, which has an air of exclusivity due to its patronage by Thai royalty, but Pranburi is fast making a name for itself too, with its clutch of cutting-edge and design-conscious resorts. Out at sea, Ko Samui, the biggest of some 80 islands comprising the Samui Archipelago, is a significant drawcard and can be combined with visits to neighbouring Ko Phangan, notorious for its any-thing-goes full moon raves, and Ko Tao, a renowned mecca for diving.

Licked by the blue-green waters of Andaman Sea along the west coast is Thailand's largest island, Phuket, the kingdom's premier island holiday spot. It has some of the world's most luxurious hotels, but it's still possible to explore rustic fishing villages and fragile mangrove forests.

Further south are Ao Phang Nga and Krabi, and islands like Ko Phi Phi and Ko Lanta, literally lands that time forgot. With their prehistoric-like landscape and craggy limestone towers teetering skyward from clear azure waters, this is the preserve of intrepid rock climbers. At sea, kayakers are drawn by caves carved out by underground streams and lagoons hidden within limestone cliffs. Still further out in the sea are renowned dive sites, near Similan and Surin islands, that beckon the world's diving fraternity.

Heading south are Trang, Satun and Songkhla, all breathtakingly beauti-ful but still relatively untouched by tourism. Wisely, this book leaves out the restive Muslim-dominated provinces – Pattani, Yala and Narathiwat – in the deep south of Thailand. Everything else, as they say, is fair game.   ❏

PRECEDING PAGES: aerial view of Ko Nang Yuan; early morning on Hat Lamai, Ko Samui.
LEFT: drinking in the scene at Ao Maya (Maya Bay), Ko Phi Phi Ley.

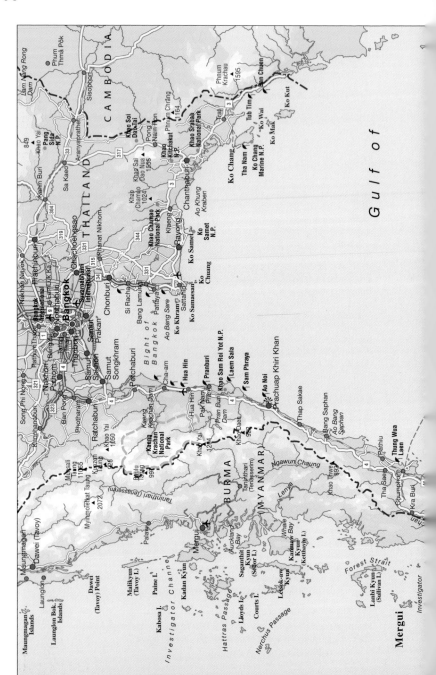

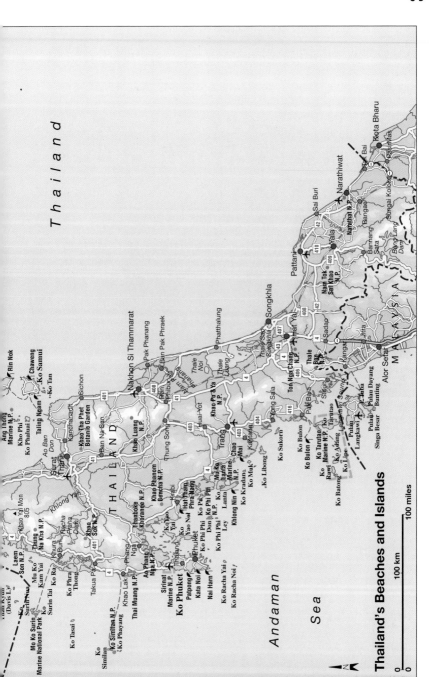

Thailand's Beaches and Islands

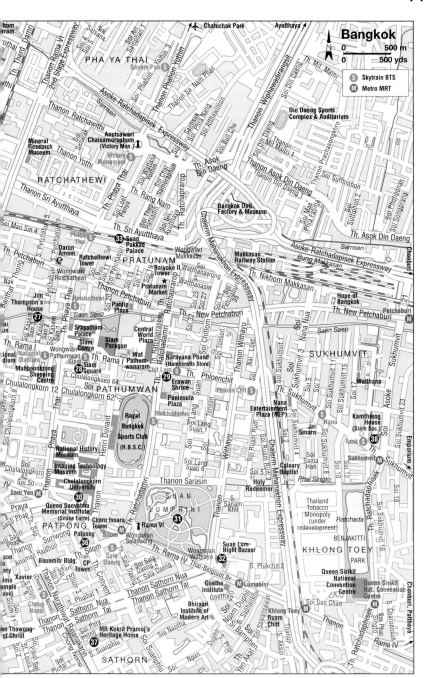

BANGKOK

Thailand's steamy capital offers a mind-blowing array of
experiences: royal architecture at Rattanakosin,
spirituality at centuries-old Buddhist temples, and
unparalleled shopping at raucous street markets
and hip mega malls. Come evening, there's
a vast array of eateries and nightlife

Bangkok

A t first glance, this metropolis of
nearly 10 million seems a
bewildering melding of new,
old and indeterminate, as well as
exotic, commonplace and indescrib-
able, all tossed together into a gigantic
urban maze. It's hardly surprising
considering only 60 to 70 years ago,
much of what makes up Bangkok was
empty land. More so than with most
large cities, the traveller's mental map
of Bangkok needs a few anchors.

The Chao Phraya River is the
most obvious anchor; Bangkok's
founding king dug a canal between
two of the river's bends and sliced
off a parcel of land into an artificial
island called Rattanakosin. An
essential part of any city tour, its glit-
tering highlights include the Grand
Palace and Wat Phra Kaew. South of
Rattanakosin are the enclaves where
foreigners originally settled, such as
Chinatown, Little India (or Pahurat),
and Thanon Silom, where the European riverfront community resided.
Today, Silom, together with Thanon
Sathorn and Thanon Sukhumvit further east, have become important
business and commercial centres.

On the other side of the Chao
Phraya is Thonburi, with canals still
threading through its colourful
neighbourhoods and where life has
not changed much since the time it
briefly functioned as the capital.

RATTANAKOSIN

The establishment of the royal district
of **Phra Nakorn**, centred on the
island of **Rattanakosin**, marked
Bangkok's rise in 1782 as the new
capital of Thailand. Rattanakosin's
foundations were based on the former
capital of Ayutthaya, which was abandoned after the Burmese ransacked it
in 1767. With the majestic Grand
Palace as its epicentre, the defensive
moats and walls formed a stronghold,
while canals were dug to transport
people across marsh and swampland.

Maps
on pages
70–71

LEFT: rooftop dining at
Sirocco restaurant,
State Tower building.
BELOW: Bangkok's
motorcycle taxis wait
for customers.

TIP

The dress code for Wat Phra Kaew and the Grand Palace is strict. Visitors must be dressed smartly – no shorts, short skirts or revealing tops, sandals or flip-flops. Suitable clothing may be borrowed from an office near the Gate of Victory, so unless you want to don stale rubber slip-ons and a gaudy sarong, dress conservatively and behave accordingly.

BELOW: the striking Phra Si Rattana Chedi. **RIGHT:** a supplicant outside Wat Phra Kaew.

Rattanakosin brims with architectural grandeur; it contains many government offices and two of Thailand's most respected universities – Thammasat and Silpakorn – in addition to being the religious and ceremonial nucleus of the nation.

Rattanakosin is best explored on foot. The area's proximity to the river means that it can be conveniently accessed by water transport.

Wat Phra Kaew and the Grand Palace complex

Jostling among throngs of tourists may not engender the most romantic vision of exotic Thailand, but the dignified splendour of two of Bangkok's principal attractions – Wat Phra Kaew and the Grand Palace – is breathtaking in spite of the heaving crowds. These structures are an arresting spectacle of form and colour: glistening golden *chedi*, glass mosaic-studded pillars, towering mythological gods, and fabulously ornate temple and palace edifices.

The site originally spread over 160 hectares (65 acres) around this strategic locale by the banks of the Chao Phraya River. It was begun by King Rama I in 1782, who ordered a new residence built to house the Emerald Buddha, the country's most revered religious image, as well as a palace befitting the new capital of Bangkok. The entire compound is surrounded by high crenellated walls, securing a self-sufficient city within a city.

The only entrance (and exit) to the **Wat Phra Kaew and Grand Palace ❶** complex is along Thanon Na Phra Lan to the north (daily 8.30am–3.30pm; admission charge includes entry to Vimanmek and several other sights in Dusit; tel: 0-222 2818; www.palaces.thai.net). Make sure you are dressed appropriately *(see margin tip)* and disregard touts who linger outside the complex telling you that it is closed.

The complex is loosely divided into two, with the Wat Phra Kaew encountered first to the left, and the Grand Palace and its peripheral buildings to the right. Most of the Grand Palace's interiors are inaccessible to public view, but the exteriors are still awesome to witness.

Wat Phra Kaew

Wat Phra Kaew (Temple of the Emerald Buddha) serves as the royal chapel of the Grand Palace. The magnificent temple compound is modelled after palace chapels in the former capitals of Sukhothai and Ayutthaya, and contains typical monastic structures, except living quarters for monks, a feature found in most other Thai temples.

At the main entrance to the temple compound is the statue of Shivaka Kumar Baccha, reputed to be the Buddha's private physician. First to capture the eye on the upper terrace on the left are the gleaming gold mosaic tiles encrusting the Sri Lankan-style **Phra Si Rattana Chedi Ⓐ** – said to enshrine a piece of the Buddha's breastbone.

In the centre is **Phra Mondop Ⓑ** (Library of Buddhist Scriptures), a delicate building, studded with blue and green glass mosaic, and topped by a multi-tiered roof fashioned like the crown of a Thai king. The library is surrounded by statues of sacred white elephants.

Adjacent to it is the **Prasat Phra Thep Bidom Ⓒ** (Royal Pantheon). This contains life-sized statues of the Chakri kings and is open to the public only on Chakri Day, 6 April. Around the building stand marvellous gilded statues of mythological creatures, including the half-female, half-lion *aponsi*. The original pantheon was built in 1855, but was destroyed by fire and rebuilt in 1903. Flanking the entrance of the Prasat Phra Thep Bidom are two towering gilded *chedi*.

Behind Phra Mondop is a large sandstone model of the famous Khmer temple of Angkor Wat in Cambodia. The model was built during King Rama IV's reign when Cambodia was a vassal Thai state.

The walls of the cloister enclosing the temple courtyard are painted with a picture book of murals telling

The resplendently decorated exterior of the Phra Mondop at the Temple of the Emerald Buddha.

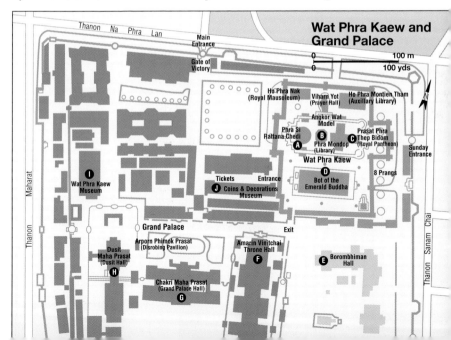

Wat Phra Kaew and Grand Palace

Thanon Na Phra Lan

Main Entrance

Gate of Victory

0 — 100 m
0 — 100 yds

Ho Phra Nak (Royal Mausoleum)
Viharn Yot (Prayer Hall)
Ho Phra Montien Tham (Auxiliary Library)
Angkor Wat Model
Phra Si Rattana Chedi Ⓐ
Phra Mondop (Library) Ⓑ
Prasat Phra Thep Bidom Ⓒ (Royal Pantheon)
Sunday Entrance

Wat Phra Kaew

Tickets   Entrance
Coins & Decorations Museum Ⓙ
Bot of the Emerald Buddha Ⓓ
8 Prangs

Wat Phra Kaew Museum Ⓘ

Maharat
Thanon
Thanon Sanam Chai

Grand Palace

Exit

Arporn Phimok Prasat (Disrobing Pavilion)
Dusit Maha Prasat (Dusit Hall) Ⓗ
Amarin Vinitchai Throne Hall Ⓕ
Borombhiman Hall Ⓔ
Chakri Maha Prasat (Grand Palace Hall) Ⓖ

Map below

Three times a year, the Thai king presides over the changing of the Emerald Buddha's robes: a golden, diamond-studded tunic is used for the hot season; a gilded robe flecked with blue for the rainy season; and a robe of enamel-coated solid gold for the cool season.

BELOW: gilded *garuda* encircle the main hall of Wat Phra Kaew.

the *Ramakien* epic, the Thai version of the Indian *Ramayana*. Originally painted during the reign of King Rama III (1824–50), they have been meticulously restored.

Around the cloisters, six pairs of towering stone *yaksha* (demons), again characters from the *Ramakien*, stand guard, armed with clubs, protecting the Emerald Buddha. At the complex's eastern edge are eight *prang* structures, which represent Buddhism's Eightfold Path.

The Emerald Buddha

Finally, you come to the Wat Phra Kaew's most sacred structure, the **Bot of the Emerald Buddha D**. Outside this main hall, at the open-air shrine, the air is always alive with the supplicants' murmured prayers and heavy with the scent of floral offerings and joss sticks.

At the top of the elaborate golden 11-metre (36-ft) altar, in a glass case and protected by a nine-tiered umbrella, sits the country's most celebrated image, the diminutive 75-cm (30-inch) tall Emerald Buddha, which, surprisingly, is not made of emerald but carved from a solid block of green jade. Many non-Buddhists are invariably disappointed by the size of the statue (it's hard to get a clear view of it from ground level), but its power and importance should be instantly apparent from the demeanour of the pilgrims inside the hall.

Of unknown origin – legend claims the Emerald Buddha image was carved in India, but stylistically, its design is 13th or 14th century Thai – the statue was found in Chiang Rai in 1434. Kept hidden in a *chedi* there for some reason, the image was revealed when the *chedi* was struck by lighting during a storm. The Lao army took the figure back to Vientiane, Laos, in the mid-16th century where it stayed put until 1779 when it was seized by the Thais. When Bangkok was established as the new capital, King Rama I brought the statue back with him in 1784. The statue is claimed to bestow good fortune on the kingdom that possesses it.

The Grand Palace

Adjoining Wat Phra Kaew is the **Grand Palace**. Embodying Thailand's characteristic blend of temporal and spiritual elements, the Grand Palace has been added to or modified by every Thai king. The result is a mélange of architectural styles, from traditional Thai, Khmer and Chinese to British, French and Italian Renaissance. In the early 20th century, the royal abode shifted to the more private Chitralada Palace in Dusit district *(see page 86)*, with the Grand Palace now reserved only for special ceremonies and state visits.

Palace buildings

Exit from Wat Phra Kaew. On your left and tucked behind a closed gate guarded by sentry is the French-inspired **Borombhiman Hall E**. It was built in 1903 as a residence for

King Rama VI but is now reserved as a state guesthouse for dignitaries.

To the right lies the **Amarin Vinitchai Throne Hall F**, part of the three-building Phra Maha Montien complex. Originally a royal residence, it contained the bedchamber of King Rama 1.

Next to it in a large courtyard stands the triple-spired royal residence – and the grandest building in the complex – the **Chakri Maha Prasat G** (Grand Palace Hall). This two-storey hall was constructed during King Chulalongkorn's reign (1868–1910) to commemorate the 100th anniversary of the Chakri dynasty in 1882. An impressive mixture of Thai and Western architecture, it was designed by British architects. The Thai spires, however, were added at the last moment, following protests that it was improper for a hallowed Thai site to be dominated by a European-style building.

The top floor contains golden urns with ashes of the Chakri kings; the first floor still functions as an audience chamber for royal banquets and state visits, while the

ground floor is now a **Weapons Museum**. Outside, the courtyard is dotted with ornamental ebony trees pruned in the Chinese *bonsai* style.

The next building of interest is the **Dusit Maha Prasat H** (Dusit Hall), built in 1789 by King Chakri (Rama I) to replace an earlier wooden structure. A splendid example of classical Thai architecture, its four-tiered roof supports an elegant nine-level spire. To its left stands the exquisite **Arporn Phimok Prasat** (Disrobing Pavilion). It was built to the height of the king's palanquin so that he could alight from his elephant and don his ceremonial hat and gown before proceeding to the audience hall.

Opposite, don't miss the collection of small Buddha images made of silver, ivory, crystal and other materials at the **Wat Phra Kaew Museum I**. On the way out, next to the ticket office, is the **Coins and Decorations Museum J**. It has a collection of coins dating from the 11th century and also royal regalia, decorations and medals made of gold and precious stones.

Map on page 75

A Chinese-style statue outside the Dusit Maha Prasat.

BELOW: Chakri Maha Prasat, a mix of Thai and Western styles.

A Mythical Zoo

A stroll round any Thai temple compound *(see also pages 98–99)* is like exploring a bestial forest of the imagination. Fantastical gilded creatures born from folklore and literature stand as guardians of the sacred, each with its own characteristic features and powers. Many of these creatures were born in the Himaphan Forest, the mythical Himalayan forest that surrounds the heavenly Mount Meru in Hindu and Buddhist scripture. Though Himaphan is invisible to human eyes, Thai artisans have spent centuries refining their imaginative depictions of its denizens. Here's a quick safari ride through some of the more common beasts you may encounter.

Garuda: Considered the most powerful creature of the Himaphan Forest, this half-eagle, half-man demigod is the mount of the Hindu god Vishnu. *Garuda* is the sworn enemy of the magical water serpent *naga*. *Garuda* is often depicted with *naga* caught in his talons. Since Ayutthayan times, the *garuda* has been a symbol for the Royal Seal, and today, brightly-coloured representations are emblazoned across official documents as well as building facades of royally-approved banks and corporations.

Naga: Brother and nemesis of *garuda*, the *naga* is a semi-divine creature with multiple human heads and serpent tails. The snake has special symbolism to most of the world's faiths and cultures, and in Buddhism, a great *naga* is said to have provided shelter to the meditating Buddha. A resident of the watery underworld, the *naga* is associated with water's life-giving force, as well as acting as a bridge between the earthly and divine realms. *Naga* are typically represented along steps leading into temples.

Erawan: The magical elephant *erawan* was the elephant steed for Indra, the Hindu king of the gods. The gigantic pachyderm has 33 heads, each with seven tusks so long that thousands of angels live inside them. Obviously, with such a gargantuan beast, a more modest three-headed version is usually represented. For proof of *erawan's* importance to Thais, head to Erawan Shrine *(see page 92)* at one of Bangkok's busiest intersections, where wooden elephants are presented as offerings.

Kinnaree and **Aponsi:** This exotic looking belle has the head and body of a woman with the tail and legs of a swan. Known for her talent in song and dance, beautifully crafted *kinnaree* sculptures can be seen at the Wat Phra Kaew. Perhaps a distant relative, *aponsi* is similarly portrayed as half-female, half-lion. The Golden Kinnaree is the Thai film industry equivalent of the Oscar.

Hongsa: This bird-like creature has similarities to the swan and goose, and is a prevalent motif in traditional arts and crafts. In Hindu mythology, the *hongsa* is the mount of Brahma, the god of creation. Take a drive along Utthayan Avenue in Bangkok's southern suburb of Puttha Monthon; some 1,000 golden *hongsa* birds decorate the tops of lampposts along this stretch of road.

Yaksha: Although these giant half-demon, half-god creatures appear forbidding as they guard the entrances to the temple structures at Wat Phra Kaew and Wat Arun, they are actually protectors of earthbound wealth. Led by Kuvera, they are worshipped as symbols of fertility and are also believed to protect newborn infants. ❑

LEFT: a fearsome *yaksha* statue at Wat Phra Kaew.

Lak Muang

Every Thai city has a foundation stone *(see page 40)*, around which the city's guardian spirits gravitate, protecting and bringing good fortune to worshippers. Bangkok was officially founded in 1782, when King Rama I erected the **Lak Muang ❷** or City Pillar (daily 5am–7pm; free), to mark the official centre of the capital. Located across Thanon Sanam Chai from the eastern wall of the Grand Palace, the gilded wooden pillar resembles the Hindu Shiva *lingam*, which represents potency. The pillar accompanies the taller Lak Muang of Thonburi, which was moved here when the district (and former capital) became part of Bangkok.

Sanam Luang

North of the Wat Phra Kaew and Grand Palace, the large oval turf of **Sanam Luang ❸** (Royal Field) is where royal cremations as well as important ceremonies are held. The field is particularly lively on the Thai King's and Queen's birthdays, Songkran festival and the Ploughing Ceremony in May. The often dusty field is filled with sleeping vagrants and evening soothsayers foretelling your destiny, and from February to April, kite flyers.

National Museum

To the west of Sanam Luang at Thanon Na Phra That is the city's **National Museum ❹** (Wed–Sun 9am–4pm; admission charge; guided tours at 9.30am Wed and Thur; tel: 0-2224 1333; www.thailandmuseum.com). Besides housing a vast collection of antiquities from all over Southeast Asia, the museum has an interesting history of its own. Its grounds and some of the principal rooms were part of the former Wang Na (Front Palace) of the king's second-in-line, called the Prince Successor, a feature of the Thai monarchy until 1870.

The oldest buildings in the compound date from 1782, including the splendid **Buddhaisawan Chapel**. Built by the Prince Successor as his private place of worship within the palace, it contains some of Thailand's most beautiful and best-preserved murals dating from the 1790s

Maps on pages 70–71

The Lak Muang is a good place to catch performances of Thai dance. People who have their prayers answered sometimes hire the resident dance troupe here to perform.

BELOW: the murals of Buddhaisawan Chapel.

as well as Thailand's second most sacred Buddha image, the famous **Phra Buddha Sihing** – which dates back to 13th-century Sukhothai.

To the left of the entrance is the **Sivamokhaphiman Hall**, originally an open-sided audience hall that now houses a prehistoric art collection. The front of the building is devoted to the **Thai History Gallery**, documenting the country's history from the Sukhothai period (13th century) to the present Rattanakosin period (1782 onwards).

Also on site is the **Red House** (Tamnak Daeng), an old golden teak dwelling that once belonged to King Rama I's elder sister. Built in the Ayutthaya style, the house has an ornate wood finish and elegant early Bangkok-style furnishings.

The central audience hall of the Wang Na is divided into rooms (No. 4–15) containing various ethnological exhibits like elephant *howdah*, wood carvings, ceramics, palanquins, royal furnishings, weapons, *khon* masks, musical instruments and other treasures. Temporary exhibits are displayed in the Throne Hall.

Located outside Wat Mahathat is one of Bangkok's more popular amulet markets. Thais use these amulets to ward off evil and attract good fortune. The amulets are mostly worn as pendants on heavy neck chains.

BELOW: Wat Pho's giant reclining Buddha.

Wat Mahathat

Nestled between Silpakorn and Thammasat universities is the **Wat Mahathat** ❺ (daily 7am–8pm; free), best accessed from Sanam Luang. Founded in the 1700s, the temple houses the **Maha Chulalongkorn Rajavidyalaya University**, one of the two highest seats of Buddhist learning in the country, and where King Rama IV spent almost 25 years studying as a monk before taking the throne in 1851.

Wat Mahathat exudes a more genuine, working temple atmosphere compared to the more ceremonial temples in the area, with locals swarming here to receive spiritual tutelage. Apart from an outdoor herbal medicine market, an **amulet market** *(see margin picture)* pitches along Trok Silpakorn alley between the temple and Silpakorn University. You might also be able to get in tune with your inner self at the temple's **International Buddhist Meditation Centre** (tel: 0-2623 6326; www.mcu.ac.th), which conducts regular classes in English.

Wat Pho

South of the Grand Palace and Wat Phra Kaew complex, on Thanon Thai Wang, is **Wat Pho** ❻ (daily 8am–5pm; admission charge), Bangkok's largest and oldest surviving temple. Apart from its historic significance, visitors come to Wat Pho for two things – to pay homage to the monumental Reclining Buddha, and to unwind at the city's best traditional massage centre.

Also known to Thais as Wat Phra Chetuphon, the temple dates back to the 16th century. However, it did not achieve real importance until the establishment of Bangkok as the capital. Wat Pho was a particular favourite of the first four Bangkok kings, all of whom added to its treasures. The four towering coloured *chedi* to the west of the *bot* (ordina-

tion hall) are memorials to the past monarchs, and around the hall are 90-plus other *chedi*. The temple cloisters contain 394 bronze Buddha images, retrieved from ancient ruins in Sukhothai and Ayutthaya. One of the most important additions was the Reclining Buddha by King Rama III in 1832, who also converted the temple into the country's earliest place of public learning. The monarch instructed that the walls be inscribed with lessons on astrology, history, morality and archaeology.

Wat Pho's giant Reclining Buddha, 46 metres (150 ft) long and 15 metres (50 ft) high, depicts the resting Buddha passing into nirvana. The flat soles of the Buddha's feet are inlaid with mother-of-pearl designs, illustrating the 108 auspicious signs for recognising Buddha. Also numbering 108 are the metallic bowls that span the wall; a coin dropped in each supposedly brings goodwill to the devotee.

Wat Pho massage school

Wat Pho became, and still is, the place to learn about traditional medicine, particularly massage and meditation. The temple's medicine pavilion displays stone tablets indicating beneficial body points for massage. Skirting the temple grounds are several small rock gardens which contain statues of hermits striking poses; these were used as diagnostic aids. The **Wat Pho Thai Traditional Massage School** (daily 10am–5pm; tel: 0-2221 2974) offers cheap hour-long massages, and also offers courses for those wanting to learn the art of Thai massage.

Wat Ratchabophit

Located on the opposite bank of Khlong Lord canal on Thanon Fuang Nakhon is **Wat Ratchabophit ⑦** (daily 5am–8pm, chapel 9–9.30am and 5.30–6pm; free), recognisable for its characteristic amalgamation of Thai temple architecture and period European style, an unusual design fusion that places the main circular *chedi* and its circular cloister in the centre. Started in 1869 by King Chulalongkorn (Rama V), the complex took well over two decades to complete.

Maps on pages 70–71

TIP

When having a Thai massage, try to relax completely and believe that you're in safe hands. The massage will involve some contortionist-like poses and the natural inclination is to resist when you are sometimes bent into awkward positions. Don't fight it; just relax and go with the flow. You'll avoid injuries this way.

BELOW:
Wat Ratchabophit marries Thai and European styles of architecture.

TIP

One of the best times
to visit Wat Arun is late
afternoon, when there
are fewer visitors.
When you are done,
take the ferry across
the river to Tha Tien
pier where you will
enjoy great sunset
views of Wat Arun
from the popular but
rundown bar-shack
called Boh on the
wooden pier.

BELOW: longtail
boats on the Chao
Phraya River.

The ordination hall is covered in brightly patterned Chinese ceramic tiles, known as *bencharong*, while the windows and entrance doors to the hall are exquisite works of art, with tiny pieces of mother-of-pearl inlaid in lacquer. The doors open into one of the most surprising temple interiors in Thailand – a Gothic-inspired chapel of solid columns that looks more like a medieval cathedral than a Thai temple.

THONBURI

Established by King Taksin after the fall of Ayutthaya in 1767, Thonburi served as Thailand's third capital for 15 years prior to Bangkok's establishment in 1782. Taksin spent most of his reign conquering factions of rebels after his throne, leaving time only late in his reign to embellish his city. While Thonburi, which can be reached by numerous bridges, is short on major tourist attractions and only has a number of high-end hotels, it has a more easy-going atmosphere than frenetic Bangkok across the Chao Phraya River. Bereft of the gleaming tower blocks

of downtown Bangkok, life in this residential half of the capital primarily revolves around the network of canals and the river.

The canals worth exploring include **Khlong Bangkok Noi**, which winds into **Khlong Bangkok Yai** downstream, as well as connecting to **Khlong Om** upstream. Once a source of fresh daily produce, the floating markets at **Wat Sai** and **Taling Chan** have become little more than tourist souvenir stops these days. With rickety teak houses, vendors selling produce from boats, fishermen dangling rods out of windows and kids frolicking in the water, the sights along Thonburi's canals are reminiscent of a more peaceful bygone era.

Canal and river cruising

The major canals are serviced by public longtail boats. But as services can be erratic at certain times of the day, it is better to hire your own private longtail boat for a more leisurely exploration of the canals *(see page 103)*.

Getting from pier to pier along the Chao Phraya River is best served by the **Chao Phraya Express** boats, which operate from the southern outskirts up to Nonthaburi in the north. For shuttling from one side of the river to the other, make use of the cheap cross-river ferries; these can be boarded at the many jetties that also service the Chao Phraya Express boats *(see page 103)*.

Wat Arun

When King Taksin first moored at the Thonburi bank of the Chao Phraya River at sunrise after sailing down from the sacked capital of Ayutthaya in 1768, he found an old temple shrine and felt compelled to build a fitting holding place for the sacred Emerald Buddha. Eventually known as **Wat Arun** ❽ or the Temple of Dawn (daily 8.30am–5.30pm;

admission charge), the temple was originally attached to Taksin's new palace (Wang Derm).

After Taksin's demise, the new King Chakri (Rama I) moved the capital (and the Emerald Buddha) to Bangkok, but the temple kept the interest of the first five kings. Over the years, the temple grew in size and ornamentation. In the early 19th century King Rama II enlarged the structure and raised the central *prang* (Khmer-style tower) to 104 metres (345 ft), making it the country's tallest religious structure.

Recycling piles of broken ceramic that was leftover ballast from Chinese merchant ships, Rama III introduced the colourful fragments of porcelain that cover most of the temple's exterior. The great *prang* represents the Hindu-Buddhist Mount Meru, home of the gods with its 33 heavens. There are four smaller *prang* standing at each corner of the temple with niches containing statues of Nayu, the god of wind, on horseback. The entire complex is guarded by mythical giants called *yaksha*, similar to those that protect Wat Phra Kaew.

Museum of Royal Barges

On the north bank of the Khlong Bangkok Noi canal, a major waterway during King Taksin's reign, is the **National Museum of Royal Barges** ❾ (daily 9am–5pm; admission charge, photo fee extra; tel: 0-2424 0004). The dry-dock displays eight vessels from a fleet of over 50 that are rarely put to sail except on auspicious occasions. On such a day, a flotilla of 52 barges, manned by 2,082 oarsmen from the Thai navy, will carry the King along the Chao Phraya River to Wat Arun, where the monarch offers new robes to monks in a ceremony known as *kathin*.

The Royal Barges date back to 14th-century Ayutthaya, with the present fleet constructed in the early 20th century. In the old days, the royal family, like everyone else, would travel by boat. The king would sit in the largest of the barges, the magnificent *Suphannahongse*, which was made from a single trunk of teak stretching over 46 metres (151 ft). The model on display was built in 1911 and based on the design of its 18th-century predecessor.

Maps on pages 70–71

An ornate garuda decorates the prow of a royal barge, seen at the National Museum of Royal Barges. This one is called the Narai Song Subhan.

LEFT: a young monk.
BELOW: Wat Arun, the Temple of the Dawn.

Located near Wat Suthat is the Giant Swing. In former days, young men would rock themselves back and forth to set the swing in motion, while trying to grab a bag of gold coins suspended on a nearby pole.

BELOW: seated Buddha images at Wat Suthat.

OLD CITY & DUSIT

Dominated by the wide boulevard of Thanon Ratchadamnoen, this section of the "Old City" contains all the peripheral buildings and temples that lie just outside Rattanakosin island. The area once marked the outskirts of the city, with the canals of Khlong Banglamphu and Khlong Ong Ang ferrying in supplies from the surrounding countryside. Time has drastically altered the area's visual appeal, yet there is still a strong sense of the past, making this is one of the city's most pleasant areas to explore.

Wat Suthat

Standing tall behind the Giant Swing, once the venue for a now-outlawed Brahmin ceremony, is **Wat Suthat** ❿ (daily 8.30am–9pm; admission charge), considered one of the country's six principal temples. Begun by Rama I in 1807, it took three reigns to complete. The temple is noted for its enormous *bot*, or ordination hall, said to be the tallest in Bangkok, and for its equally large *viharn* (sermon hall), both of them surrounded by cloisters of gilded

Buddha images. The 8-metre (26-ft) tall Phra Sri Sakyamuni Buddha is one of the largest surviving bronze images from Sukhothai, and was transported by boat all the way from the northern kingdom. The temple courtyard is a virtual museum of statuary, with stone figures of Chinese generals and scholars. They came as ballast in rice ships returning from deliveries to China and were donated to temples.

Democracy Monument

Behind City Hall, north along Thanon Dinso, is a roundabout anchored by the **Democracy Monument** ⓫. Designed by Italian sculptor Corrado Feroci (also known as Silpa Bhirasri), the 1939 monument is a celebration of Thailand's transition from absolute to constitutional monarchy in 1932. Marked by four elongated wings, the central metal tray contains a copy of the constitution. A rallying point for civil discontent in May 1992, the monument became the scene of a bloodbath after the army violently surpressed peaceful demonstrations against the military dictatorship.

14 October Monument

Just a short walk from the Democracy Monument along Thanon Ratchadamneon Klang towards the corner of Thanon Tanao brings you to another chiselled edifice to the democratic struggle, the **14 October Monument**. While it is not as grandiose as the Democracy Monument, this granite memorial remembers the victims of the 1973 mass demonstrations against authoritarian rule in Thailand's chequered history.

Wat Bowonniwet

Due north of the 14 October Monument along Thanon Tanao is **Wat Bowonniwet** ⓬ (daily 8am–5pm; free), a modest looking monastery with strong royal bonds. Built in 1826 during the reign of Rama III,

King Mongkut (Rama IV) served as abbot of the temple for a small portion of his 27 years as a monk. More recently, the present King Bhumibol (Rama IX) donned saffron robes here after his coronation in 1946. Home to Thailand's second Buddhist university, the temple is known for its extraordinary murals painted by monk-artist Khrua In Khong.

Thanon Ratchadamnoen

Stretching all the way from the Grand Palace to the Dusit Park area, the wide **Thanon Ratchadamnoen** (Royal Passage) splits into three sections and is modelled after Paris' famous boulevards. Built at the turn of the 20th century, the tree-lined avenue has some of the city's widest and least cluttered pavements. On royal birthdays, the area is turned into a sea of decorative lights, flags and royal portraits.

Loha Prasat and Wat Ratchanatda

Just at the point where Thanon Ratchadamnoen Klang crosses the Pan Fah canal bridge, veering left into Ratchadamnoen Nok, are several noticeable structures on both sides of the busy intersection. More evocative of Burmese temple structures, the **Loha Prasat** ⓭ (Metal Palace) shares the same grounds as **Wat Ratchanadda** (sometimes spelt as Rajanadda) and is the main attraction here (both daily 8am–5pm; free).

Originally meant to be the temple's *chedi*, Loha Prasat's unusual architecture is said to draw from an Indian design dating back some 2,500 years ago. Built by Rama III in 1846, two tiers square the central tower, peaked by 37 iron spires which symbolise the virtues needed to attain enlightenment. Just behind the temple is a thriving amulet market, similar to the one found at Wat Mahathat *(see page 80)*.

Golden Mount

Standing tall south of Mahakan Fort, the elevated spire of the **Golden Mount** ⓮ (Phu Khao Thong) was for many years Bangkok's highest point (daily 7.30am–5.30pm; admission charge). Started by Rama III as a huge *chedi*, the city's soft earth

During World War II, the Golden Mount served as a watch tower, with guards armed with signal flags to warn if the enemy invaders were drawing close.

Maps on pages 70–71

LEFT: the Democracy Monument.
BELOW: metal spires of the Loha Prasat.

made it impossible to build on and the site soon became an artificial hill overgrown with trees and shrubbery. King Mongkut added a more modest *chedi* to the abandoned hill, and later King Chulalongkorn completed work on the 78-metre (256-ft) high plot. The summit is reached by a stairway that curves around the side of the hill, and is shaded by trees and dotted with small shrines along the way. A part of **Wat Saket** located at the bottom of the Golden Mount, the gilded *chedi* is said to contain a Buddha relic from India.

Ananta Samakhom Throne Hall, which dates back to 1907, is more European than Thai in character.

Thanon Khao San

Since the early 1980s, **Thanon Khao San** (or Khao San Road as it's popularly referred to) has been a self-contained ghetto for the backpacking globetrotter. Once a rather seedy gathering of cheap guesthouses, rice shops and pokey bars, as portrayed in Alex Garland's novel *The Beach*, Banglamphu's nerve centre has undergone a significant upgrade in recent years. The arrival of boutique hotels along with new bars and international chains like Starbucks have taken some of its edge away, but this neon-lit street is still full of character.

Dusit area

Crossing Khlong Banglamphu, Thanon Ratchadamnoen Klang turns into Ratchadamnoen Nok, with the pleasant, tree-lined boulevard leading down to a broad square in front of the old National Assembly building. Known as **Royal Plaza**, the square is watched over by a bronze **Statue of King Chulalongkorn** (Rama V) on horseback. Chulalongkorn was responsible for the construction of much of this part of Bangkok, which was once a rustic royal retreat from the city and the Grand Place. With the present king residing in nearby **Chitralada Palace** and the day-to-day governance taking place in Parliament House, this area is still the heartbeat of the nation.

Ananta Samakhom

As you head down the broad boulevard of Thanon Ratchadamnoen Nok, in the distance you will see the monumental edifice of the **Ananta Samakhom Throne Hall** ⑯, an Italian-Renaissance style hall of grey marble crowned by a huge dome (daily 9.30am–3.15pm; admission charge, or free with Grand Palace entrance ticket). It is the tallest building within the manicured gardens of **Dusit Park**, a royal oasis livened up by canals, bridges and fountains. Built in 1907 by King Chulalongkorn as a grandiose hall for receiving visiting dignitaries and other state ceremonies, the highlight of the hall's rich interior is the dome ceiling frescoes depicting the Chakri monarchs from Rama I to Rama VI.

Vimanmek Mansion

Behind Ananta Samakhom Throne Hall is the **Vimanmek Mansion** ⑰, billed as the world's largest golden

BELOW:
backpacker haven, Thanon Khao San.

teak building (daily 9.30am–3.15pm; admission charge, or free with Grand Palace entrance ticket; tel: 0-2628 6300; www.thai.palaces.net; compulsory guided tours every 30 minutes; visitors dressed in shorts must wear sarongs that are provided at the door; shoes and bags have to be stowed in lockers).

Originally built in 1868 as a summer house for King Chulalongkorn on the east coast island of Ko Si Chang *(see page 120)*, the king ordered the three-storey mansion dismantled and reassembled on the Dusit grounds in 1901. Made entirely from golden teak and without a single nail used in the construction, the gingerbread fretwork and octagonal tower of this 72-room lodge looks more Victorian than period Thai. The king and his large family lived here for only five years, during which time no males were allowed entry. The mansion eventually fell out of favour, lying abandoned until restored for the Bangkok bicentennial 50 years later.

Vimanmek (meaning Palace in the Clouds) offers an interesting glimpse into how the royal family of the day lived. In the pavilion on the south side of the mansion are free performances of Thai dance and martial arts every day at 10.30am and 2pm.

Abhisek Dusit Throne Hall

To the right of Vimanmek is the **Abhisek Dusit Throne Hall** (daily 9.30am–3.15pm; admission charge, or free with Grand Palace entrance ticket). Constructed in 1903 for King Chulalongkorn as an accompanying throne hall to Vimanmek, the ornate building is another sumptuous melding of Victorian and Moorish styles, but still retaining its distinctly Thai sheen. The main hall is now used as a showroom-cum-museum for the SUPPORT foundation, a charitable organisation headed by Queen Sirikit which helps preserve traditional arts and crafts.

Dusit Zoo

To the east is the **Dusit Zoo** (daily 8am–6pm; admission charge; tel: 0-2281 2000). The grounds were originally part of the Royal Dusit Garden Palace, where King Chula-

Maps on pages 70–71

TIP

Be sure to keep your admission ticket to the Wat Phra Kaew and Grand Palace *(see page 74)*. This allows you access to many of Dusit's sights for free, like the Ananta Samakhom Throne Hall, Vimanmek Mansion, Abhisek Dusit Throne Hall, and the Royal Elephant Museum.

LEFT: the Abhisek Dusit Throne Hall. **BELOW:** Vimanmek Mansion, the world's largest teak building.

longkorn had his private botanical garden. The 19-hectare (47-acre) site became a public zoo in 1938. The zoo has around 300 different species of mammals, almost 1,000 bird species and around 300 different kinds of reptiles, but conditions at some of the animal enclosures are less than adequate.

Wat Benjamabophit

To the south of the Chulalongkorn statue is **Wat Benjamabophit** , more popularly known as the Marble Temple (daily 8am–5.30pm; admission charge). Located along Thanon Rama V, this is the last major temple built in central Bangkok and the best example of modern Thai religious architecture.

Started by King Chulalongkorn at the turn of the century, the *wat* was designed by the king's half-brother Prince Naris together with Italian architect Hercules Manfredi. Completed in 1911, these two collaborators fused elements of East and West to dramatic effect. The most obvious of these must be the walls of Carrara marble from Italy, the cruciform shape and the unique European-crafted stained-glass windows depicting Thai mythological scenes. The *bot*'s principal Buddha image is a replica of the famous Phra Buddha Chinarat of Phitsanulok, with the base containing the ashes of King Chulalongkorn.

Behind the *bot* is a gallery holding 53 original and copied significant Buddha images from all over Buddhist Asia, providing a useful educational display. The temple is most interesting in the early morning, when merit-makers gather before its gates to donate food and offerings to the line of bowl-wielding monks – unlike elsewhere where monks walk the streets searching for alms.

CHINATOWN

Chinatown was settled by Chinese merchants in the 1780s, after being asked to relocate here so that the Grand Palace could be built. In 1863, King Mongkut built Thanon Charoen Krung (New Road), the first paved street in Bangkok, and Chinatown soon began mushrooming outwards from the original dirt track of Sampeng (now officially Soi Wanit 1). Other adjacent plots of land were given to the Indian and Muslim communities.

With narrow roads and lanes teeming with commercial bustle, this is one of the capital's most traffic-clogged districts. Exploring on foot allows you to soak up the mercantile atmosphere. Away from downtown's plush mega-malls, Chinatown is a raw experience of Bangkok past and present: old shophouses, godowns (warehouses), temples and shrines, all swelling with activity.

Sampeng Lane

The **Sampeng** area is considered the old pulse of Chinatown and has had a rowdy history. What began as a mercantile pursuit soon degenerated into a raunchy entertainment area.

An Ayutthaya-style Buddha image in the "abhaya mudra" (reassurance) posture at a gallery in Wat Benjamabophit.

BELOW: ceremony at Wat Benjamabophit.

By 1900, it had a reputation as "Sin Alley", with lanes leading to opium dens, gambling houses and brothels. Eventually, however, Sampeng lost its sleaze and became a bustling lane of small shops selling goods imported from China. The stretch of **Sampeng Lane** ⑳ that lies between Thanon Ratchawong and Thanon Mangkon sells everything from cheap clothing and footwear to sticky confectionary, cosmetics and costume jewellery.

Pahurat Market

West of Sampeng Lane is Bangkok's Little India at **Pahurat Market** ㉑, a two-level bazaar (daily 9am–6pm). It is filled with Hindu and Sikh people selling all manner of fabrics including saris, as well as Hindu deities and wedding regalia, together with traditional Thai dance costumes. On Thanon Pahurat and parts of Thanon Chakraphet are cheap curry eateries and Indian tea and spice stalls. Indian migrants from the late 19th century converged here, and today, their presence is still strongly felt. Nearby at Thanon

Chakraphet is the golden-domed **Sri Guru Singh Sabha** temple, the focal point of Bangkok's Sikh community.

Pak Khlong Talad

With floral garland offerings at temples and shrines all over the city, Bangkok needs a constant supply of fresh blooms. West of the Pahurat Market to the riverfront, at the mouth of Khlong Lord on Thanon Chakraphet, **Pak Khlong Talad** ㉒ (Flower Market) serves as the capital's flower and vegetable garden (daily 24 hours). The bunches of bargain-priced exotic as well as familiar flowers are a riot of fragrance and colour.

Thanon Yaowarat and Nakhon Kasem

Parallel to Sampeng Lane is **Thanon Yaowarat**, which gives its name to Chinatown and in parts looks much like a Hong Kong street with its forest of neon signs. The street is best known for its gold shops.

Between Thanon Yaowarat and Thanon Charoen Krung, at the corner with Thanon Chakrawat, is

Maps on pages 70–71

The flowers at Pak Khlong Talad may be unceremoniously wrapped in newsprint, but prices are extremely low.

BELOW: bustling Thanon Yaowarat.

The solid gold Buddha image at Wat Traimit was found purely by accident.

Nakhon Kasem ㉓ or Thieves' Market (daily 8am–8pm). A few decades ago, this was a black market for stolen goods. It later developed into an antiques dealers' area, but today, most antiques stalls have gone. If you search hard enough among the piles of run of the mill goods, you may chance upon a few old treasures.

Wat Mangkon Kamalawat

On Thanon Charoen Krung near Soi Itsaranuphap is the towering gateway of ornate **Wat Mangkon Kamalawat** ㉔ or Leng Noi Yee (Dragon Flower Temple) as it's also known (daily 8.30am–3.30pm; free). The most revered temple in Chinatown, the place is a constant swirl of activity and incense smoke. Built in 1871, it is one of the most important centres for Mahayana Buddhism (most Thais practice Theravada Buddhism) in Thailand. Elements of Taoist and Confucianist worship are also prevalent here.

Soi Itsaranuphap

Chinatown's most interesting lane is **Soi Itsaranuphap** (Soi 16), which runs south from Thanon Phlab Phla Chai and and passes a 19th-century Thai temple called **Wat Kanikaphon** (daily 6am–4pm; free). Around the entrance to Soi Itsaranuphap are shops selling "hell money" and miniature houses, Mercedes cars, and other items made of paper for the Chinese *kong tek* ceremony. The items are taken to the temple and burnt as offerings to deceased relatives.

Talad Kao and Talad Mai

Soi Itsaranuphap has two of the city's best-known markets. Closer to the corner with Sampeng Lane is the two-century old **Talad Kao** ㉕ (Old Market) while a little off Soi Itsaranuphap (closer to Thanon Charoen Krung) is the newer **Talad Mai** (New Market), which has been plying its wares for over a century. The old market wraps up by late morning, while the newer one keeps trading until sundown. These fresh markets have a reputation for high-quality meat, fish and vegetables, and overflow during Chinese New Year.

Wat Traimit

Just east of the point where Thanon Yaowarat meets Thanon Charoen Krung, across from the Odeon Circle China Gate, is the unremarkable looking **Wat Traimit** ㉖ (daily 8am–5pm; admission charge).

The real treasure lies within – the famous **Golden Buddha**. According to history, it was found by accident in the 1950s. The 3-metre (10-ft) tall stucco figure was being transported to its present site when the crane lifting it snapped and sent the statue smashing to the ground. A crack in the stucco revealed a solid gold image weighing some 5.5 tonnes. The gleaming image is said to date from 13th-century Sukhothai, and was probably encased in stucco during the Ayutthayan period to conceal its true worth from the Burmese invaders.

PATHUMWAN & PRATUNAM

The commercial heart of downtown Bangkok, **Pathumwan** is a sprawl of shopping malls, all connected by the Skytrain. It's mainly a consumerist's paradise, yet there are still plenty of sights more reminiscent of an older and more traditional Bangkok. Cleaved in the early 19th century, the man-made canal **Khlong Saen Saep** enabled the capital to spread north to **Pratunam** and beyond.

Jim Thompson's Museum

Just a short walk to the end of Soi Kasemsan 2 from the National Stadium Skytrain station, the protected oasis of **Jim Thompson's House Museum** ㉗ is the principal downtown attraction on most tourist itineraries (daily 9am–5pm; admission charge includes compulsory guided tours of the museum; tel: 0-2216 7368; www.jimthompsonhouse.com).

Jim Thompson was the American silk entrepreneur responsible for the revival of Thai silk. Thompson, an architect by training, first arrived in Thailand at the end of World War II, serving as a military officer. After the war, he returned to Bangkok to live, and soon became interested in the almost redundant craft of silk weaving and design.

Thompson mysteriously disappeared in the jungles of Malaysia's Cameron Highlands in 1967, but his well-preserved house still stands today by the banks of the Khlong Saen Saep canal. Thompson was an enthusiastic collector of Asian arts and antiquities, many of which adorn his traditional house-turned-museum.

The museum comprises six teak structures, which were transported from Ayutthaya and elsewhere to the silk weaving enclave of Ban Khrua, just across Khlong Saen Saep, before being reassembled at its present site in 1959. From the windows of the house, it's easy to imagine how scenic the view would have been some 40 years ago, looking across the lush gardens, or "jungle" as Thompson called it.

Next to the old house is a pondside café, while opposite is **Art Centre at Jim Thompson House**, a contemporary gallery holds regular exhibitions of local and international art and crafts.

Maps on pages 70–71

TIP

Resist the urge to shop at the rather pricey gift shop of Jim Thompson's House Museum. Better deals are available at the Jim Thompson Factory Outlet along 153 Th. Sukuhmvit Soi 93 (tel: 0-2332 6530).

BELOW: interior and garden of Jim Thompson's House.

BELOW: Erawan Shrine attracts worshippers all day long.
RIGHT: tranquil lake at Lumpini Park.

Shopping along Th. Rama 1

As downtown Bangkok loses character to a growing conglomeration of faceless air-conditioned malls, **Siam Square** ㉘, along Thanon Rama I, retains its maverick air as one of the city's few remaining street-side shopping enclaves. This maze of teen-friendly low-rise shops, cafés and restaurants is a favourite hangout for students.

Cross the footbridge over Thanon Phaya Thai from Siam Square and head into the bewildering mayhem of **Mahboonkrong**, better known as MBK. A monster mall, MBK is always busy with youngsters, especially at weekends when they crowd around shops selling a cluttered variety of teen-friendly merchandise.

Across from Siam Square along Thanon Rama 1 are the inter-connecting malls of **Siam Centre** and **Siam Discovery Centre**. The former is the turf of Bangkok's younger set, with its local designer wear and sports and surf clothing shops, while the latter stocks international brand names and elegant home accessories.

New on the scene is the swanky retail haven of **Siam Paragon**. As well as a slew of chi chi brand name shops, the mall houses Southeast Asia's largest aquarium at **Siam Ocean World** (daily 9am-10pm, tel: 0-2687 2000; admission charge; www.siamoceanworld.com). Located in the basement, the aquarium is divided into seven zones and has a giant Oceanarium filled with over 30,000 marine creatures. Visitors can also ride in a glass-bottomed boat and dive with sharks.

Erawan Shrine

At the end of Thanon Rama I is the chaotic junction where the street intersects with Thanon Ratchadamri and changes its name to Thanon Ploenchit. At the corner of Thanon Ratchadamri and Thanon Ploenchit stands the **Erawan Shrine** ㉙ (daily 8am–10pm). The aromatic haze of incense hits you before you actually see the shrine. Attracting locals and Asian tourists in droves, the shrine is dedicated to the four-headed Hindu god of creation, Brahma. Originally erected on the site of the former Erawan Hotel, rebuilt as the present

Grand Hyatt Erawan, the initial spirit house *(see page 41)* was deemed ineffective after a spate of unfortunate events (including deaths) slowed the hotel's construction. After astrological advice, this plaster-gilded 1956 replacement halted the unlucky run, and ever since then the shrine has been revered for its strong talismanic powers.

In early 2006, the shrine was hacked to pieces by a madman, who was subsequently lynched by an angry mob (such is the devotion that Thais accord to this shrine). The shrine has since been rebuilt.

Thanon Ploenchit malls

Behind the shrine, along Thanon Ploenchit, is the **Erawan Bangkok**, a boutique mall connected to the Grand Hyatt Erawan. Across the street is the **Gaysorn**, a designer mall that is relatively quiet save for the trickle of "hi-so" spenders and wannabe window shoppers. North along Thanon Ratchadamri, just opposite the large **Central World Plaza** mall, is **Narayana Phand**, a large treasure trove of Thai arts and crafts. The three-floor emporia is your one-stop shop for Thai handicrafts.

Snake Farm

For an encounter with dangerous reptiles, visit the **Queen Saovabha Memorial Institute** ❸⓿, popularly called the **Snake Farm** (Mon–Fri 8.30am–4.30pm, Sat–Sun 8.30am–noon; admission charge; tel: 0-2520 1614). Located on Thanon Rama IV, it was founded in 1923 as the Pasteur Institute. The institute's principal work lies in the research and treatment of snakebites and the extraction of antivenins. Venom-milking sessions (Mon–Fri 11am and 2.30pm, Sat–Sun 11am; slide show 30 mins before) are the best times to visit, when snakes are pulled from the pit and mercilessly goaded for a squealing audience.

Lumphini Park

Green spots are few and far between in Bangkok, but in the heart of downtown at the intersection of Thanon Rama IV and Thanon Ratchadamri is **Lumphini Park** ❸❶ (daily 4.30am–9pm; free), Bangkok's premier green lung. The park was given to the public in 1925 by King Vajiravudh (Rama VI), whose memorial statue stands in front of the main gates. Embellished with lakes (with pedal boats for hire) and a Chinese-style clock tower, sunrise or sunset sees elderly Chinese practising tai chi, sweaty joggers and mass aerobics.

Suan Lum Night Bazaar

Across from Lumphini's Thanon Withayu (Wireless Road) gates, the **Suan Lum Night Bazaar** ❸❷ (daily 3pm–midnight) is a more sanitised and cooler alternative to the frenzied Chatuchak Weekend Market *(see page 97)*. Geared for tourists, the open-air bazaar offers souvenirs, clothing, handicrafts, antiques, jewellery and home decor. Also found at Suan Lum Night Bazaar is **Joe Louis Theatre** (one show nightly at

Maps on pages 70–71

A young volunteer at the Snake Farm gingerly handles a python as he poses for a photograph.

BELOW: Joe Louis Theatre at Suan Lum Night Bazaar.

The Sala Rim Naam restaurant at the Oriental Hotel puts on a nightly show of traditional Thai dance-drama accompanied by a Thai set dinner.

BELOW: the Authors' Lounge at the Oriental.

7.30pm; admission charge; tel: 0-2252 9683; www.joelouis-theater. com). Sakorn Yangkeawsot, who goes by the moniker Joe Louis, is responsible for reviving the fading art of *hun lakhon lek*, a unique form of traditional Thai puppetry.

Pratunam area

Northwards, over the Khlong Saen Saep canal and Thanon Petchaburi, is **Pratunam Market**. This bustling warren of stalls is more a lure for residents than tourists, with piles of cheap clothing, fabrics and assorted fashion accessories. The area is shadowed by Thailand's tallest building, **Baiyoke II Tower**, whose 84th floor observation deck (daily 10am–10pm; admission charge) offers eye-popping views of the city and beyond. Across Thanon Petchaburi from Pratunam is a mall entirely devoted to IT, **Panthip Plaza** (daily 10am–9pm).

Suan Pakkad Palace

Most tourists make a beeline for Jim Thompson's House, missing out on an equally-delightful abode, the **Suan Pakkad Palace ㉝** (daily 9am–4pm; admission charge includes a guided tour; tel: 0-2245 4934; www.suan pakkad.com). Located a short walk along Thanon Sri Ayutthaya from Phaya Thai Skytrain station, the name Suan Pakkad or "Cabbage Patch", refers to its former use as farmland before the palace was constructed in 1952. The former residence of the late Prince and Princess Chumbhot, who were prolific art collectors and gardeners, Suan Pakkad comprises five teak houses sitting amid a lush garden and lotus pond. Converted into a museum, the wooden houses display an eclectic collection of antiques and artefacts.

BANGRAK & SILOM

Gravitating eastwards from some of the Chao Phraya River's premier riverfront real estate, Thanon Silom is the principal route that intersects the business district, ending at Thanon Rama IV with Lumphini Park beyond. Parallel to Silom are Sathorn, Surawong and Si Phraya roads, all of which make up the district of **Bangrak**.

Thanon Silom along with Thanon Sathorn are considered the city's main business arteries, but come dusk, the shift from day to night trade becomes apparent when the office workers depart and a bevy of attractive females and males (and those of indeterminate sex) begin to converge in the area.

But it's not all starchy office blocks and unbridled sleaze that make up Bangrak. Between the River City shopping centre and Shangri-La hotel is what is regarded as the old *farang* (foreigner) district. Easily navigable, the lanes in this pocket still hold a few buildings from its days as a 19th-century port settlement.

Oriental Hotel

Founded back in the 1870s, the **Oriental Hotel**'s ㉞ reputation is well known; it has consistently been

rated as one of the world's best. A riverside retreat for the influential and wealthy, the Oriental's grandeur has endured through the years. To best imbibe its old world atmosphere, have afternoon tea in the elegant **Authors' Lounge** and muse over the literary greats that have passed through its doors, such as Somerset Maugham, Noel Coward and Graham Greene.

Assumption Cathedral

Turn right outside the Oriental Hotel, along Oriental Avenue, towards the river where a side road on the left leads to a small square dominated by the **Assumption Cathedral** (daily 6am–9pm; free). Built in 1910, the red-brick cathedral is surrounded by a Catholic mission. Its ornate interior is topped with a beautiful domed ceiling hovering over a large sacristy with gilded pillars. Take a breather here and have a mull over Bangkok's secluded architectural delights.

Maha Uma Devi Temple

Looming behind the Assumption Cathedral at the corner of Silom and Charoen Krung is the faux-classical **State Tower**, worth mentioning for its fashionable rooftop drink and dine venue called The Dome.

Continuing further along Thanon Silom on the right, on the corner of Soi Pan, is the vibrant Hindu **Maha Uma Devi Temple** ❸❺ (daily 6am–8pm; free). Named after Shiva's consort, Uma Devi, the temple was established in the 1860s by the city's Tamil community, whose presence is still prevalent in the area. It is known to Thais as Wat Khaek, meaning "guests' temple" (*khaek* is also a less welcoming term used by locals for anyone from the Asian subcontinent).

Patpong

Come nightfall, the upper end of Thanon Silom transforms into a pleasure haven to entertain customers of all persuasions. Stall vendors set up a **night market** along Thanon Silom from Soi 2–Soi 8, commandeering the narrow pavements in either direction, including the fleshpot of **Patpong** ❸❻ (Soi 1 and Soi 2). The market plies mainly tourist tat, including counterfeit

Maps on pages 70–71

The towering entrance facade of the Maha Uma Devi Temple.

BELOW: seamy streets and sights of Patpong.

watches, fake name-brand bags and clothes, and bootleg CDs and DVDs.

With its slew of trashy go-go bars and anything-goes strip clubs, Patpong's sleazy reputation is still deserved, although government clampdowns on nightlife over the years have almost reduced this slice of vice to little more than amusing eye candy. Despite touts claiming a freakish assortment of sex shows, today's tamer experience is a blitz of neon, relentless techno beats and gyrating bikini-clad dancers on bar tops.

A few lanes east from Patpong, pumping **Silom Soi 4** attracts throngs of beautiful and young (both straight and gay) revellers to its compact dance clubs and bars. Nearby **Silom Soi 2** is similar in appeal, though designated for gay partygoers. And further on still, the hostess bars along **Soi Thaniya** cater for an exclusively Japanese clientele.

Kukrit Pramoj's Home

Halfway down Thanon Sathorn, tucked away on Soi Phra Phinij, is **MR Kukrit Pramoj's Heritage Home ③⑦** (Sat and Sun 10am–5pm;

admission charge; tel: 0-2286 8185). Born of royal descent (signified by the title Mom Ratchawong – MR), the late Kukrit Pramoj had a brief stint as prime minister during the disruptive 1970s, but is better remembered as a prolific author and cultural preservationist.

Surrounded by an ornate Khmer-style garden, this splendid wooden home, now a museum, comprises five stilt buildings that recalls the traditional architecture of the Central Plains. The *bonsai* garden adds a sense of serenity, and the home is livened up with displays of beautiful *objets d'art*, antique pottery and an ornate bed that belonged to Rama II.

SUKHUMVIT

Thanon **Sukhumvit**, a bustling, traffic-clogged artery, pushes the urban sprawl eastwards, continuing all the way to the Cambodian border. The efficient Skytrain provides the fastest means of transport between the plethora of upmarket shops, restaurants and entertainment venues that line this major artery.

Although thin on key tourist

BELOW: Bangkok's hip Bed Supperclub.

attractions, Thanon Sukhumvit is where most of the city's growing expatriate community nests.

Sukhumvit's early blocks burst with a profusion of tailors, pool halls, beer bars, inns and hotels. A **night market** crowds the pavements from Soi 3–19, replaced later at night by makeshift food and drink stalls. The area has a lascivious veneer, anchored by the three-storey mall of go-go bars, **Nana Entertainment Plaza** (NEP), on Soi 4. Working girls soliciting for customers can be found along street corners from Soi 5 to Soi 19. Further along across the Asoke intersection (Soi 21) is Sukhumvit's other notorious neon strip devoted to pole dancing, **Soi Cowboy**.

However' Sukhumvit's overall character is far from sleazy, with many of the city's best nightspots dotted along the winding side streets. Leading the charge is **Soi 11**, where both **Q Bar** and the hip **Bed Supperclub** sit nearby one another.

Kamthieng House

One of Sukhumvit's oldest buildings is the headquarters of the **Siam Society** at Sukhumvit Soi 21 (Soi Asoke), founded in 1904 to promote the study of Thai culture (Tues–Sat 9am–5pm; tel: 0-2661 6470-77; www.siam-society.org). There's an excellent library full of rare books on Thai history, old manuscripts and maps. On the same grounds is the **Kamthieng House** ❸, a 150-year-old wooden home transplanted from Chiang Mai and carefully reassembled here as an ethnological museum.

Emporium area

On the corner of Soi 24, near Phrom Phong Skytrain station, is Sukhumvit's premier shopping magnet, **Emporium**. This is a great place to watch Bangkok's affluent parade in their finest togs and splash out at its many designer stores. The side lanes around Emporium are cluttered with a number of upmarket furniture and decor shops, coffee bars, galleries and restaurants. Further east, just off Thong Lo Skytrain station is **Soi 55** (Soi Thonglor), lined with garish wedding studios and boutique shopping arcades like the über-stylish **H1** and **Playground**. ❑

Kamthieng House was literally moved from its former home in Chiang Mai to Bangkok.

BELOW: a fabric stall at Chatuchak Market.

Chatuchak Market

The final stop (Mo Chit) on the Skytrain's northern line drops you at the **Chatuchak Weekend Market** (Sat–Sun 7am–6pm). Reputed to be the world's biggest flea market, Chatuchak is a must-see for any visitor; even the least enthusiastic shopper will be overawed by the sheer scale and variety of goods. With an estimated 400,000 visitors weaving through the market's maze-like interior every weekend, Chatuchak is a heady assault on the senses; an early start (by 9am) is essential to beat the heat and ensuing claustrophobia. The fun is in stumbling across hidden pockets of culture or kitsch as you meander through the alleyways.

TEMPLE ART AND ARCHITECTURE

The temple (*wat*) plays a vital role in every community, large and small; for many visitors Thailand's temples are the country's most enduring sights

A typical Thai *wat* (or temple) has two enclosing walls that divide it from the secular world. The monks' quarters are situated between the outer and inner walls. In larger temples the inner walls may be lined with Buddha images and serve as cloisters for meditation. This part of the temple is called *buddhavasa* or *phutthawat*. Inside the inner walls is the *bot* or *ubosot* (ordination hall) surrounded by eight stone tablets and set on consecrated ground. This is the most sacred part of the temple and only monks can enter it. The *bot* contains a Buddha image, but it is the *viharn* (sermon hall) that contains the principal Buddha images. Also in the inner courtyard are the bell-shaped *chedi* (relic chambers), which contain the relics of pious or distinguished people. *Salas* (pavilions) can be found all around the temple; the largest of these areas is the *sala kan prian* (study hall), used for saying afternoon prayers. Apart from Buddha images, various mythological creatures *(see page 78)* are found within the temple compound.

ABOVE: a double gallery enclosing the *bot* of Wat Pho houses 394 seat bronze Buddha images. These were brought from Sukothai and Ayutthaya during the reign of Rama I, and are of assorted periods and style. The base of the main image contains the ashes of Rama I.

BELOW: gilded *chofa* (bird-like decorations), intricately carved gables, and green and ochre coloured tiles are common features of Thai temple roofs.

ABOVE: temple exteriors are often very ornate, such as that of the Bot of the Emerald Buddha at Wat Phra Kaew. Gold tiles, glass mosaic, lacquer and mother-of-pearl are some of the materials used.

BELOW: Thai temple murals are created on a background that has been prepared and dried before the artist paints on it using coloured pigments mixed with glue. Often featured on the interior of temple walls, such murals depict the classic subjects of Thai painting, including tales from the *Jataka* (Buddha's birth and previous lives) and other Buddhist themes, and also vignettes of local life. During the reign of Rama III (1824–51), mural painting reached its peak, with artists not only following the principles of traditional Thai art, but also introducing new elements, like Western perspective. The mural below, from Wat Suthat in Bangkok, is an example of the late 18th-century art style (better known as the Rattanakosin Period).

BELOW: the gleaming Phra Si Rattana Chedi at Wat Phra Kaew is bell-shaped with a ringed spire and a three-tiered base, a feature of Sri Lankan reliquary towers. Close-up inspection will reveal a surface made up of thousands of tiny gold mosaic pieces.

BELOW: these towering *chedi* at Wat Pho sit on square bases and have graceful and elegant proportions, remininscent of the Lanna-style architecture of north Thailand. Decorated with coloured tiles, the *chedi* are memorials to the first four Chakri kings.

BELOW: Wat Arun features five rounded *prang* – reflecting Cambodian-Khmer influence – encrusted with thousands of broken porcelain pieces. These porcelain shards were leftover ballast from Chinese ships which visited Bangkok in its early days.

B ANGKOK

TRANSPORT

GETTING THERE

By Air

Bangkok International Airport (tel: 0-2535 1111; www.airportthai. co.th), known locally as **Don Muang**, is located about 30 km (19 miles) north of the city centre. Serving over 80 airlines and 25 million passengers annually, the airport is running well above capacity, leading to frequent delays at immigration.

Completion of the **New Bangkok International Airport** (NBIA) or **Suvarnabhumi Airport** (www.suvarnabhumiairport.com) has been delayed; it is now re-scheduled to open in late 2006 or early 2007. The new airport is located on the eastern outskirts of the city in Samut Prakan province, about 30 km (19 miles) from the city.

Don Muang has two terminals that serve international carriers; internal flights are handled by the domestic terminal. **Terminal 1:** arrivals, tel: 0-2535 1149 or 2535 1310; departures, tel: 0-2535 1254 or 2535 1123; **Terminal 2:** arrivals, tel: 0-2535 1301; departures, tel: 0-2535 1386; **Domestic**

Terminal: arrivals, tel: 0-2535 1253; departures, tel: 0-2535 1192 or 2535 1277.

All the terminals are linked by a free shuttle bus that runs every 15 minutes between 5am and 11pm. Terminals 1 and 2 are also joined by an elevated walkway.

Although nowhere near the standards of other Asian super airports like Changi in Singapore or Chek Lap Kok in Hong Kong, Don Muang airport is still a clean and fairly pleasant place to while away the time before boarding your flight. It has several bars, restaurants, shops, a duty-free shop and a unique golf course located between the runways.

Note: When taking an international flight out of Don Muang, keep B500 for the Passenger Service Charge (airport tax). There is no airport tax for domestic flights.

By Rail

The **State Railway of Thailand** (www.railway.co.th) operates trains that are clean, cheap and reliable. There are two entry points by rail into Thailand, both from Malaysia. The more popular service is the daily train that leaves Butterworth near Penang in northwest

Malaysia at 2.10pm for Hat Yai (south Thailand) and arrives in Bangkok's Hualamphong Station at 10.05am the next day. Trains leave Hualamphong Station daily at 2.45pm for the return journey to Malaysia.

By Road

Malaysia provides the main road access into Thailand, with crossings near Betong and Sungai Kolok. From Laos, it is possible to cross from Vientiane into Nong Khai in northeast Thailand by using the Friendship Bridge across the Mekong River. From Cambodia, the most commonly used border crossing is from Poipet which connects to Aranyaprathet, east of Bangkok.

GETTING AROUND

From the Airport

The journey from Bangkok International Airport to the city centre takes between 30 and 45 minutes, depending on traffic conditions (the worst period is between 4pm and 9pm). In the Arrival Hall, you may be harangued by touts. Never volunteer your name or destination to these people. If you already have a reservation at a hotel, a representative will have your name written on a sign, or at least a sign bearing the name of your hotel. If you haven't made prior arrangements, take a taxi, limousine or the airport bus into the city.

By Taxi

Operating 24 hours daily, all taxis officially serving the airport are air-conditioned and metered. The taxi stand is located just outside the Arrival Hall of all terminals. Join the queue and tell the person at the desk where you want to go to. A receipt will be issued, with the licence plate number of the taxi and your destination in Thai written on it. Make sure the driver turns on the meter. At the end of your trip, pay what is on the meter plus a B50 airport surcharge. If the driver uses the expressway to speed up the journey, he will ask for your approval first. If you agree, you have to pay the toll fee of B60, comprising B20 for the first toll booth and B40 for the second. Depending on traffic, an average fare from the airport to the city centre is around B200–250 (excluding toll fees and the airport surcharge).

By Limousine

There are two limousine companies operating at the airport. **Airport Associate Co Ltd** (the counter sign reads **Airport Taxi**; tel: 0-2982 4900; www.airporttaxi thai.com) in Terminal 1 and 2 operates a service (using Mercedes Benz sedans) to the city for B800, an 8-seater van for B1,100; limousine to Pattaya for B2,400 and 8-seater van for B2,700.

Thai Airways Limousines (tel:

0-2535 2801; www.thaiairways.com) in Terminal 1 and 2 has a premium service (using Mercedes Benz E220) to downtown for B1,500, or a regular service (Mercedes Benz 180) for B1,000.

By Airport Bus

If you don't have much luggage, consider using the Airport Bus, which passes the main hotel locations in downtown Bangkok. Tickets can be bought on the bus or at the booths outside the Arrival Hall of all terminals. Buses depart every 15 minutes from 5.30am to 12.30am, and the fare is B100 per person.
Airport Bus Routes:
A-1 to Thanon Charoen Krung (New Road) via Pratunam, Thanon Ratchadamri, Thanon Silom and Thanon Surawong.
A-2 to Sanam Luang (Banglamphu) via Thanon Phayathai and Thanon Lan Luang.
A-3 to Soi Thonglor (Sukhumvit 55) via Thanon Petchaburi and Thanon Sukhumvit.
A-4 to Hualamphong Railway Station via Thanon Ploenchit, Thanon Rama, Thanon Phayathai and Thanon Rama IV.

By Train

Another fast and cheap way into the city is to take the train. **Don Muang Station** is just across the street from the airport (look for the Amari Hotel entrance sign in the Arrival Hall of Terminal 1). It takes roughly 40 minutes to **Hualamphong Station**, not far from Chinatown. There are trains at 15 to 30 minute intervals from 5am to 8pm. The fare is B5 for ordinary trains and B21 for express trains. The drawback is having to drag luggage over the pedestrian bridge and onto the train.

Public Transport

Skytrain (BTS)

BTS Tourist Information Centre: tel: 0-2617 7340; Hotline tel: 0-2617 6000; www.bts.co.th.

The Bangkok Transit System's (BTS) elevated train service, better known as Skytrain, which started operations in December 1999, is the perfect way of beating the city's traffic-congested streets.

It consists of two lines. The **Sukhumvit Line** runs from Mo Chit station in the north to On Nut in the southeast. The **Silom Line** runs from National Stadium, near Siam Square, south to Saphan Taksin station near Tha Sathorn (or Central Pier). Both lines intersect at Siam station.

The Skytrain is fast, frequent and clean, but suffers from overcrowding during peak hours. Accessibility too is a problem for the disabled and aged as there aren't enough escalators or lifts.

Trains operate from 6am to midnight (3 minutes peak; 5 minutes off-peak). Single-trip fares vary according to distance, starting at B10 and rising to B40. Self-service ticket machines are available at all station concourses. Tourists may find it more useful to buy the unlimited ride 1-Day Pass (B100) or the 30-Day Adult Pass (which comes in three types: B250, 10 rides; B300, 15 rides; and B540, 30 rides) – all available at station counters.

Metro (MRT or Subway)

Customer Relations Centre: tel: 0-2624 5200; www.mrta.co.th or www.bangkokmetro.co.th.

Bangkok's metro line, variously referred to as the MRT, metro or subway – was launched in July 2004 by the Mass Rapid Transit Authority (MRTA). The line has 18 stations, stretching 20 km (12 miles) between Bang Sue in the northern suburbs of Bangkok to the city's main railway station, Hualamphong, near Chinatown.

Three of its stations – Silom, Sukhumvit and Chatuchak Park – are interchanges, and passengers can transfer to the Skytrain network at these points. More lines and extensions to both rail networks are planned.

Operating from 6am to midnight, the air-conditioned trains are frequent (2–4 minutes peak, 4–6 minutes off-peak). Fares start at B14, increasing B2 for every station, with a maximum of B36.

Unlike the Skytrain, coin-sized plastic tokens are used instead of cards. These are dispensed by self-service ticket machines at all stations. Also available at station counters are the unlimited ride 1-Day Pass (B150), 3-Day Pass (B300) and the stored-value Adult Card (B200; includes B50 deposit).

Taxis

Taxis are abundant in Bangkok. They are metered, air-conditioned, inexpensive, and comfortably seat 3 to 4 persons.

Taxis can be hailed anywhere along the streets; there are no taxi stands on the streets but you can expect to find them outside hotels and shopping centres. Metered taxis are recognisable by the sign on their roofs with an illuminated red light above the dashboard indicating whether it's free or not. Taxis mostly come in bold colour combinations of red and blue, or green and yellow, with some newer ones completely bright orange or green.

The flag fall charge is B35; after the first 2 km (1 mile), the meter goes up by B4–5.50 every kilometre, depending on distance travelled. If stuck in traffic, a small per

minute surcharge kicks in. If your journey crosses town, ask the driver to take the expressway. Using the network of elevated two-lane roads can reduce travel time by half. The toll fare of B20 to B50 is given to the driver at the payment booth, not at the end of the trip. A 10 percent tip on top of the fare is suggested; it's not a must.

Before starting any journey, check whether the meter has been reset and turned on; many drivers conveniently "forget" to do so and charge a lump sum at the end of the journey. On seeing a foreign face, some drivers may quote a flat fee instead of using the meter. Unless you're desperate, don't use these. Fares, however, can be negotiated for longer distances outside Bangkok: for instance, Pattaya (B1,200), Ko Samet (B1,500) or Hua Hin (B1,500 to B2,500).

Drivers don't speak much English, but all know the locations of major hotels. Foreigners frequently mangle Thai pronunciation, so it's a good idea to have a destination written on a piece of paper. Thai drivers can usually understand street addresses written in capital Roman letters. Or else, get someone to write the destination in Thai.

If you arrange for a pick up, there is a B20 surcharge.
Siam Taxi: tel: 1661 (hotline)
Julie Taxi: tel: 01-846 2014; www.julietaxi.com. Slightly more expensive than metered taxis, Julie's drivers are polite and speak some English. Also provides sightseeing tours.

Tuk-Tuk

Tuk-tuk are the brightly coloured three-wheeled taxis whose name comes from the incessant noise their two-stroke engines make. Although synonymous with Bangkok, tuk-tuks have been

increasingly losing favour with both locals and visitors. The heat, pollution and noise have become too overwhelming for most passengers. Few tuk-tuk drivers speak English, so make sure your destination is written down in Thai. Unless you bargain hard, tuk-tuk fares are rarely lower than metered taxi fares.

Expect to pay B30 to B50 for short journeys of a few blocks or around 15 minutes or less, and B50 to B100 for longer journeys. A B100 ride should get you a half-hour ride across most parts of downtown. Be sure to negotiate the fare beforehand.

Motorcycle Taxis

Motorcycle taxi stands (with young men in fluorescent orange vests) are clustered at the entrance of most *soi* (small sidestreets) and beside any busy intersection or building entrance. The drivers are experts at weaving through Bangkok's heavy traffic and may cut travel time in half, but they they can be reckless.

Hire only a driver who provides a passenger helmet. Fares must be negotiated beforehand, and they are rarely lower than taxi fares for the same distance travelled. Hold on tight and keep your knees tucked in because drivers tend to weave precariously in and out of traffic.

A short distance, like the length of a street, will cost B10 to B20, with longer rides at B50 to B100. During rush hours (8–10am and 4–6pm), prices are higher.

Buses

Bus transport in Bangkok is very cheap but can also be equally arduous, time-consuming and confusing. Municipal and private operators all come under the charge of the **Bangkok Mass Transit**

Authority (tel: 0-2246 0973; www.bmta.co.th). With little English signage and few conductors or drivers speaking English, boarding the right bus is an exercise in frustration. Most bus maps are out of date, so stick to Bangkok's other transport options.

Boats

The most common waterborne transport is the **Chao Phraya River Express Boat** (tel: 0-2623 6001/3), which travels from Tha Nonthaburi pier in the north and ends at Tha Wat Rachasingkhon near Krungthep Bridge in the south. Boats run every 15 minutes from 6am to 6.40pm, and they stop at different piers according to the coloured flag on top of the boat. Yellow flag boats are fastest and do not stop at many piers, while the orange flag and no-flag boats stop at most of the marked river piers. If unsure, check before boarding. Fares cost from B6 to B15 and are paid to the conductor on board or at some pier counters.

The **Chao Phraya Tourist Boat** (www.chaophrayaboat.co.th) operates daily from 9.30am to 3pm and costs B100. After 3pm, you can use the ticket on the regular express boats. A useful commentary is provided on board, along with a small guidebook and a bottle of water. The route begins at Tha Sathorn (Central Pier) and travels upriver to Tha Phra Arthit, stopping at 10 major piers along the way. Boats leave every 30 minutes and you can get off at any pier and pick up another boat later on this hop-on-and-off service.

Cross-river ferries are used for getting from one side of the river to the other. They can be boarded at the jetties that also service the Chao Phraya River Express. Costing B2 per journey, the cross-river

RENTING LONGTAIL BOATS

If you wish to explore the canals of Thonburi, private longtail boat rentals can be negotiated from most of the river's main piers. A 90-minute to 2-hour tour will take you into the quieter canal communities. Ask to pull up and get out if anything interests you. Negotiate rates beforehand; an hour-long trip will cost B400 to B500, rising to B900 for 2 hours. The price is for the entire boat, which seats up to 16 people, not per person.

ferries operate daily from 5am to 10pm or later.

The **longtail canal boat taxis** ply the narrow inner canals of Bangkok and are used for carrying passengers from the centre of town to the outlying districts. Many of the piers are located near traffic bridges and tickets cost B5 to B15, depending on distance, with services operating roughly every 10 minutes until 6 to 7pm.

Rental Cars

Driving in Bangkok is not recommended. Road surfaces can be appalling, signs are confusing and, apart from the main roads, most side streets (soi) are very narrow and difficult to negotiate. Traffic flow on main arteries often changes direction at certain times of the day, with little indication as to when. Local drivers can be inconsiderate and aggressive, and drink driving and road rage incidents are on the rise. If still intent on hiring a car, then an international driver's licence is necessary. A small car can be hired for around B1,500 a day including insurance.
Avis, 2/12 Th. Withayu, tel: 0-2255 5300/4; and Bangkok

International Airport Bldg 2, tel: 0-2535 4031/2; www.avisthailand.com. **Hertz**, Soi 71, Th. Sukhumvit, tel: 0-2711 0574/8; www.hertz.com.

TRIPS OUT OF BANGKOK

By Road

Thailand has a good road system with over 50,000 km (31,000 miles) of motorways and more being built every year. Road signs are in both Thai and English and you should have no difficulty following a map. An international driver's licence is required.

Unfortunately, driving on a narrow but busy road can be a terrifying experience with right-of-way determined by size. It is not unusual for a bus to overtake a truck despite the fact that the oncoming lane is filled with vehicles. A safer option is to hire a car or a van with driver for trips outside of Bangkok. The rates probably won't be more than B1,500 per day. Try **Highway Car Rent**, tel: 0-2266 9393; www.highway.co.th, or **Krungthai Car Rent**, tel: 0-2291 8888; www.krungthai.co.th.

You can get to several places outside the city, like Pattaya and Hua Hin, by simply flagging a taxi along a Bangkok street or booking one beforehand (see page 102). Be sure to negotiate a flat rate before boarding; don't use the meter.

By Air

Thai Airways International (THAI) services a domestic network, with as many as 14 daily services to the more popular destinations like Chiang Mai and Phuket. **Bangkok Airways** is the second-largest domestic operator. In recent years, a number of low-cost airlines have

entered the market, flying to the main tourism centres in Thailand.
Air Asia: Bangkok International Airport, tel: 0-2215 9999; www.airasia.com.
Bangkok Airways: 99 Th. Vibhavadi Rangsit, tel: 0-2265 5555; www.bangkokair.com.
Nok Air: Bangkok International Airport, tel: 1318 (Call Centre); www.nokair.com.
Orient Thai Airlines: 17th Floor, 138/70 Jewellery Centre, Th. Nares, tel: 1126 (Call Centre); www.orient-thai.com.
PB Air: 16th Floor, UBC II Building, 591 Th. Sukhumvit, Soi 33, tel: 0-2261 0220; www.pbair.com.
Phuket Air: Lumpini Tower, 1168 Th. Rama IV, tel: 0-2679 8999; www.phuketairlines.com.

Thai Airways International: 89 Th. Vibhavadi Rangsit, tel: 0-2628 2000; www.thaiairways.com.

By Bus

Air-conditioned buses service many destinations in Thailand. VIP coaches with extra leg room are the best for overnight journeys. All buses are operated by **Transport Company Ltd** (www.transport.co.th), with terminals at these locations:
Eastern (Ekamai) Bus Terminal: Th. Sukhumvit opposite Soi 63, tel: 0-2391 8907.
Southern Bus Terminal: Th. Boromrat Chonnani, Thonburi, tel: 0-2435 5605.
Northern (Mo Chit) and Northeastern Bus Terminal: Th.

Khampaengphet 2, Northern: tel: 0-2936 2852/66 ext. 311; Northeastern: tel: 0-2936 2852/66 ext. 611.

By Train

State Railway of Thailand (tel: 1690; www.railway.co.th) operates three principal routes – north, northeast and south – from **Hualamphong Railway Station** at Th. Rama 4, tel: 0-2225 6964. Express and rapid services on the main lines offer first-class air-conditioned or second-class fan-cooled carriages with sleeping cabins or berths. In addition to the above, some trains depart from **Bangkok Noi Station**, tel: 0-2411 3102, in Thonburi.

RESTAURANTS

RATTANAKOSIN

Thai

Coconut Palm
394/3-5 Th. Maharaj. Mobile tel: 0-1827 2394. Open: daily 10am–7pm. $.
Family-style restaurant serving far better meals than its Western-style fast food interior suggests. The small range of soups and curries (red, green, tom yam and the coconut soup, or tom kha gai) disappear by lunchtime.
Rub Ar-roon
310 Th. Maharaj. Tel: 0-2622 2312. Open: daily 8am –6.30pm. $.
Chinese shophouse with coffees, toasted sandwiches and not-too-spicy

local food (although you can ask for it to be spicy). This was a pharmacy over 80 years ago, and the herbal display cabinets are still in place, adding to the nice bar/bistro atmosphere (although the only alcohol served is beer).

THONBURI

Thai

Supatra River House
266 Soi Wat Rakhang, Th. Arun-Amarin, Sirirat. Tel: 0-2411 0305. Open: daily L & D. $$.
www.supatrariverhouse.com
Former home of owners Patravadi Mechudhon (of Patravadi Theatre fame) and her sister. Excellent Thai cuisine is served on

the riverbank terrace. On Fri and Sat, traditional music and dance accompanies your dinner. Take the express boat to Tha Maharaj pier and transfer to the opposite bank on Supatra's free shuttle boat.

OLD CITY & DUSIT

Middle Eastern

Chabad House
108/1 Soi Rambutri. Tel: 0-2282 6388. Open: Sun–Thur noon–9pm, Fri noon–4.30pm. $.
Run as a charitable business by the synagogue in the same building, this Israeli-run café offers nicer (and cleaner) surroundings than most other Middle

Eastern-style eateries in the neighbourhood. And all the food is kosher of course. Good falafel, salads, hummus and the usual tahini-based dips accompany a wide choice of mains.

Thai

May Kaidee
117/1 Th. Tanao. Tel: 0-2281 7137. Open: daily 8am–11pm. $.
www.maykaidee.com
Owner May has a reputation for her vegetarian cuisine. Second outlet at nearby 111/1-3 Th. Tanee. Isaan-style (from northeast Thailand) vegetarian dishes with mushrooms, tofu and soya beans, and massaman curry with tofu, potatoes and peanuts are good

options. May also gives cooking lessons. To find this place, take the *soi* next to Burger King, and turn left.

Roti-Mataba

136 Th. Phra Arthit. Tel: 0-2282 2119. Open: Tues–Sun 7am–10pm. $.

A whole army of women here make the Muslim-style breads – like flat unleavened *roti* and meat-stuffed *mataba* – by the hundreds in this incredibly busy shophouse. Dip the crisp *roti* into their delicious *massaman* and *korma* curries of fish, vegetable or meat. There are only a few tables inside and on the pavement, so be prepared to wait.

Tom Yum Kung

Th. Khao San. Tel: 0-2629 2772. Open: daily 3pm–2am. $.
www.tomyumkungkhaosan.com

This restaurant is proof that Khao San attracts more than just backpackers. Perennially packed with young Thais. Soup, stir fries and sizzling seafood hot plates are popular choices at this townhouse set back from the main street.

CHINATOWN

Chinese

Hua Seng Hong Yaowaraj

438 Th. Charoen Krung Soi 14. Tel: 0-2627 5030. Open: daily 9am–9pm. $–$$.

A former shophouse turned restaurant with marble top tables, wooden chairs and air-conditioning. A raucous Chinese lunch venue selling all-day *dim sum* from an outside counter and all manner of congee, hot and sour soup, barbecued pork, fish maw and braised goose dishes inside.

Shangrila Yaowarat

306 Th. Yaowarat. Tel: 0-2224 5933. Open: daily 10am–10pm. $$.

Busy Cantonese place dishes out casual café-style *dim sum* lunches, then brings out the table-cloths and napkins for dinner. Menu includes drunken chicken with jel-lyfish, smoked pigeon, and live seafood from the tanks on the ground floor. Or choose from the displays of roasted duck, steaming *dim sum* and freshly baked pastries.

Indian

Punjab Sweets and Restaurant

436/5 Th. Chakraphet. Tel: 0-2623 7606. Open: daily 8am–9pm. $.

Bangkok's Little India (Pahurat) sits at the western edge of China-town. Its alleyways are crowded with tailors and tiny Indian cafés, of which this is one of the best. Its meat- and dairy-free food includes a good choice of curries and *dosa* (rice-flour pancakes) from South India, and Punjabi sweets wrapped in edible silver foil.

PATHUMWAN & PRATUNAM

French

Cáfe Le Notre

Gnd Fl Natural Ville Executive Residences, 61 Soi Lang Suan. Tel: 0-2250 7050/1. Open: daily 6am–10.30pm. $–$$.

Inheriting the Parisian panache of its main operation, this stylish café has a mini menu of starters, salads and mains to supplement its wonderful cakes and pastries. Great quality (despite being in a serviced apartment block) at the price.

Italian

Biscotti

Four Seasons Hotel, 155 Th. Ratchadamri. Tel: 0-2255 5443. Open: daily L & D. $$$.

A power dining mecca of terracotta, marble and wood in another stylish Tony Chi-designed outlet. The large and busy open kitchen sets the tone for its excellent Italian cuisine, while the open space is ideal for being seen. Packed with business people for lunch and a who's who list of Thai society for dinner.

Calderazzo

59 Soi Lang Suan. Tel: 0-2252 8108/9. Open: daily L & D. $$–$$$.

Clever lighting and wood, stone, metal and glass create a warm and stylish atmosphere for good homey southern Italian food such as grilled vegetables in hazelnut pesto, hand-rolled rag pasta with goat cheese sauce, lamb loin in red wine, and heavenly profiteroles drenched in warm chocolate sauce.

Thai

Curries & More

63/3 Soi Ruam Rudee. Tel: 0-2253 5405/7. Open: daily 11am–11.30pm. $$.
www.curriesandmore.com

Serves tasty Thai food with the spices toned down to suit international palates. Charming townhouse setting with sculptures, paintings and ceramics. The *kaeng leuang* (yellow curry) is excellent. It also has some Western dishes (pasta, pies, crepes and excellent apple crumble).

Le Lys

75/2 Langsuan Soi 3. Tel: 0-2652 2401. Open: daily noon–10.30pm. $.

Charming wooden house with large windows and a homey interior of silk fabrics, and Thai and Chinese pottery. The Thai-French owners favour tamarind-flavoured soups (*tom som* with stuffed squid) and delicious baby clams in curry sauce. Terrace and garden seating available.

PRICE CATEGORIES

Price per person for a three-course meal without drinks:

$ = under US$10
$$ = US$10–$25
$$$ = US$25–$50
$$$$ = over US$50

BANGRAK & SILOM

Chinese

China House
Oriental Hotel, 48 Oriental Ave.
Tel: 0-2236 0400. Open: daily
L & D. $$$.
Elegant Sino-Portuguese colonial townhouse set apart from the hotel – and small enough to believe you're dining at home. Great *dim sum* lunch and dinner specials like "Monk Jumped Over the Wall," supposedly named after Chinese monks, who – seduced by the beautiful aroma – jumped over a temple wall to try this dish.

French

Le Bouchon
37/17 Patpong Soi 2.
Tel: 0-2234 9109. Open:
Mon–Sat L & D, Sun D. $$–$$$.
This lovely seven-table bistro gains a certain frisson from its location in Patpong – very French and slightly naughty, like a Marseille dockyard diner. Very popular with local French expats for its simple home cooking and friendly banter at the small bar where diners wait for seats while sipping aperitifs.

Le Normandie
Oriental Hotel, 48 Oriental Ave.
Tel: 0-2236 0400. Open:
Mon–Sat L & D, Sun D. $$$$.
Formal French dining with jacket and tie required for the men. Concoctions like goose liver with Perigord truffles, and

sole fillets with Oscietra caviar cream sauce verge on brilliance. In the stately, marmalade-coloured interior, crystal chandeliers hang from a quilted silk ceiling while the floor to ceiling windows overlook the Chao Phraya River.

International/Fusion

Cy'an
Metropolitan Hotel, 27 Th.
Sathorn Tai. Tel: 0-2625 3333.
Open: daily B, L & D. $$$–$$$$.
Serves inspired Mediterranean-Asian seafood amid the cutting-edge minimalism of this hip hotel. Spanish and Moroccan flourishes bring sweet and spicy flavours to dishes like seared tiger prawns, and tortellini with pine nuts, raisins and parmesan. Amazing 22 types of wine available by the glass.

Eat Me
Fl 1, 1/6 Piphat Soi 2, off Th.
Convent. Tel: 0-2238 0931.
Open: daily D. $$$.
Popular restaurant with art exhibitions often featuring edgy young artists promoted by the nearby H Gallery. The food is modern Australian, featuring dishes such as charred scallops with mango, herb salad, pickled onion and citrus dressing. Low lighting and a fragmented layout lend intimacy. On cool nights ask for a table on the terrace. Excellent wine list of mainly Australian varietals.

Sirocco
Fl 63 State Tower Bangkok,
1055 Th. Silom. Tel: 0-2624
9555. Open: daily D. $$$.
www.thedomebkk.com
Spectacular 200-metre (656-ft) high rooftop restaurant with magnificent views over the river. Greco-Roman architecture and a jazz band add to the sense of occasion. The Italian and Mediterranean food is inconsistent, but who cares? This is a must-visit, if only for the views. In the same complex, there's good seafood in the classy **Distil Bar**, and an expensive Italian eatery called **Mezzaluna**.

Italian

Zanotti
Gnd fl, Saladaeng Colonnade,
21/2 Soi Saladaeng. Tel: 0-2636
0002. Open: daily L & D. $$$.
www.zanotti-ristorante.com
Chef-owner Gianmaria Zanotti has created a restaurant that people visit for the buzz as much as for the food. The homey Italian fare from the Piedmont and Tuscany regions includes over 20 pasta dishes and seafood and steaks charcoal-grilled over orange wood from Chiang Mai. Good selection of wines by the glass.

Japanese

Aoi
132/10-11 Silom Soi 6.
Tel: 0-2235 2321/2. Open: daily
L & D. $$.
Black stone walkways

invoke a cool calm in this unfussy restaurant serving well-prepared Japanese food. Downstairs is a sushi bar. Set meals are much cheaper than the à la carte options.

Thai

Baan Khanitha
69 Th. Sathorn Tai. Tel: 0-2675
4200. Open: daily L & D. $$.
www.baan-khanitha.com
Having outgrown its home on Soi Ruam Rudee, this well-known place (with a second outlet at 36/1 Sukhumvit Soi 23; tel: 0-2258 4181) moved to a much larger location in Sathorn. Busy with mainly Japanese and Western customers dining on tasty foreigner-friendly flavours ranging from Chiang Mai sausage and spicy salads to various curries, like red duck with grapes.

The Blue Elephant
233 Th. Sathorn Tai. Tel: 0-2673
9353. Open: daily L & D. $$–$$$.
www.blueelephant.com/bangkok
One of a few very upmarket Thai restaurants located outside hotels, this is part of a Belgian-owned international chain. The menu mixes Thai standards with a few fusion dishes like foie gras in tamarind sauce. The food is excellent, but the flavours are slightly toned down to suit Western palates. Housed in a beautiful century-old restored building that was the former Thai-Chinese Chamber of Commerce.

SUKHUMVIT

American

New York Steakhouse
JW Marriott Hotel, 4 Sukhumvit
Soi 2. Tel: 0-2656 7700. Open:
daily D. $$$$.
Top-notch restaurant
with a relaxed atmos-
phere despite the formal
trappings of club-like
dark woods and high-
backed leather chairs.
Start with the rich
Manhattan clam chowder
before sinking your teeth
into the grain-fed Angus
beef. The beef is
imported chilled, not
frozen – which accounts
for the high prices.

French

Le Banyan
59 Sukhumvit Soi 8. Tel: 0-2253
5556. Open: Mon–Sat D. $$$.
Great little French restau-
rant with a formal but
appealingly eccentric air.
Maitre d' Bruno Bischoff
is the perfect foil to
diminutive Michel Bin-
aux, who prepares many
dishes tableside often
looking very amused. Try
the speciality of pressed
duck or pan-fried foie
gras with apple and fresh
morel mushrooms.

Indian

Hazara
29 Sukhumvit Soi 38. Tel: 0-
2713 6048/9. Open: daily D. $$.
www.facebars.com
Tasty north Indian fare,
such as peppery *khadai
kheenga* (shrimps stir-

fried with bell peppers),
in a glorious setting
embellished with Asian
antiques and artefacts.
It is housed in a tradi-
tional Thai cluster
complex and comprises
the trendy Face Bar, a
Thai restaurant, a patis-
serie and even a spa.

International

Bed Supperclub
26 Sukhumvit Soi 11. Tel:
0-2651 3537. Open: Sun–Thur
7.30pm–midnight, Fri–Sat
7.30pm–1am. $$$.
www.bedsupperclub.com
Extraordinary tubular
construction with an
all-white interior where
diners lie on beds and
cushions to eat the
brilliant fusion cuisine
whipped up by chef Dan
Ivarie. Select from multi-
choice three-course set
menus. Also has mixed
media shows including
dance, theatre and
video. Next door is Bed
Bar, one of the city's top
clubs and popular with
Bangkok's trendy.

Crepes & Co
18 Sukhumvit Soi 12.
Tel: 0-2251 2895. Open:
Mon–Sat 9am–midnight,
Sun 8am–midnight. $$.
Creperie that specialises
in unusual fillings along
with the expected crepe
suzette. Also has *tajine*
stews and other Moroc-
can dishes, and Greek
favourites like *kotopolou*
(tomato and chicken
casserole) and eggplant
melizana. The tasteful
wooden interior with
Berber-style tented ceil-

ing and world music on
CD gives it a cosmopoli-
tan atmosphere.

Greyhound
Fl 2 Emporium, Th. Sukhumvit.
Tel: 0-2664 8663. Open: daily
11am–9.15pm. $$.
www.greyhound.co.th
Trendy modern Thai café
serving Western-
accented dishes like
Thai anchovy spaghetti
with chilli. Meals are
chalked up on giant
blackboards and there
are glass-fronted
displays of mouth-
watering cakes.

Italian

Rossini's
Sheraton Grande Sukhumvit,
250 Th. Sukhumvit. Tel: 0-2649
8888. Open: daily L & D.
$$–$$$.
A faux mediaeval castle
interior with cobbled
floor and domed ceiling
gives a relaxed formality
to this excellent restau-
rant. Start with timbale
of blue crab and lobster
tartar with scented
avocado and move on to
lobster and watercress-
stuffed tortellini.

Japanese

Shin Daikoku
32/8 Soi Wattana, Sukhumvit
Soi 19. Tel: 0-2254 9980/3.
Open: daily L & D. $$.
A peaceful ambience
amid bamboo partitions
and private rooms around
a Japanese garden-style
fishpond. Standard *sushi*
and *sashimi* options plus
a traditional 9-course
kaiseki set meal.

Thai

Cabbages & Condoms
10 Sukhumvit Soi 12.
Tel: 0-2229 4610. Open: daily
11am–10pm. $–$$.
Renowned for its family
planning promotion (its
owner is former senator
Mechai "Mr Condom"
Viravaidhya, who has
done much for AIDS
awareness in Thailand).
The two-storey restau-
rant, with mainly outdoor
seating, has a pleasant
ambience and decent
Thai standards. Free
condoms as you leave.

Mahanaga
2 Sukhumvit Soi 29. Tel: 0-2662
3060. Open: daily L & D. $$$.
www.mahanaga.com
With its beautiful and
spacious interior of Thai
statuary, North African
accents and Indian glass
mosaics, this is one of
the finest examples yet
of modern international-
ism in Bangkok dining.
The less inspired fusion
dishes such as lamb
chop in *massaman* curry
don't ruin the overall
splendour of the interior.

Ruen Mallika
189 Sukhumvit Soi 22.
Tel: 0-2663 3211/2. Open: daily
11am–11pm. $$.
www.ruenmallika.com
Rama I period wooden
house with garden tables
and traditional floor-
cushion seating inside.
Opt for *kaeng tai pla* (fish
stomach curry), which
tastes better than it
sounds, *mee krob*
(sweet and herby crispy
noodles) or battered and
deep-fried fresh flowers.

ACCOMMODATION

Choosing a Hotel

Hotels in Bangkok, with their first-rate service and range of facilities, are among the best in the world. Many moderately-priced hotels in Bangkok would be considered first class in Europe, and even budget hotels will invariably have a swimming pool and at least one decent food outlet.

Those on a tight budget will find numerous guesthouses offering decent accommodation. Once of primary interest only to backpackers because of their sparse facilities, many have been upgraded to include air-conditioning and en-suite bathrooms.

Prices & Bookings

Many mid- and top-end hotels charge a standard 7 percent VAT and 10 percent service to the bill, so check to see if the rate includes this or not. Increasingly, internet bookings are cheaper than the walk-in or call-up rate. Either check the hotel website directly or online hotel sites, like **Thailand Hotels Association** (www.thaihotels.org).

Be sure to book a room in advance during Christmas, New Year and Chinese New Year holidays, and if travelling outside Bangkok, during Songkran in mid-April.

THONBURI

Luxury

Peninsula
333 Th. Charoennakorn. Tel: 0-2861 2888. www.peninsula.com
Standing proud on the opposite bank of the Chao Phraya River, this distinguished hotel has the city's nicest river views. It has earned the reputation of being one of the world's best hotels. Stylishly contemporary but still Asian in character, it has some of the best dining options in the city, plus impeccable service. Free shuttle boats (6am–midnight) take you to Tha Sathorn pier opposite and the Sapha Taksin Skytrain station. (370 rooms)

Expensive

Bangkok Marriott Resort & Spa
257 Th. Charoennakorn. Tel: 0-2476 0022.
www.marriotthotels.com
With verdant grounds and a wonderfully landscaped pool that fronts the river, this resort truly feels like an escape from the frenetic city. Located on the Thonburi side, it is quite far down the river almost to the edge of town, but the free 15-minute boat shuttle to Tha Sathorn pier is part of the novelty of staying here. Self-contained,

with six restaurants, three bars, a Mandara spa and a full-service business centre, the hotel is also part of a shopping complex. Its Riverside Terrace hosts nightly Thai dance performances along with dinner. (413 rooms)

OLD CITY & DUSIT

Expensive

Chakrabongse Villa
396 Th. Maharaj. Tel: 0-2225 0139. www.thaivillas.com
This is a wonderfully unique find in this area, and indeed the city. A beautiful early 20th-century historic residence with tropical gardens, a swimming pool and superb views of Wat Arun directly opposite. There are only three ambience-filled villas here, each decked out in traditional Thai style: Garden Suite, Riverview Suite and Thai House. (3 rooms)

Moderate

Old Bangkok Inn
609 Th. Phra Sumen. Tel: 0-2629 1785. www.oldbangkokinn.com
One of Bangkok's newest boutique hotels, this lovely eco-friendly inn exudes an old world charm. With just eight rooms decorated in antique dark wood furniture and named after local herbs and flowers,

this family-run place has all the mod cons and yet situated in the heart of the historic district. (8 rooms)

Budget

D&D Inn
68-70 Th. Khao San. Tel: 0-2629 0526/8. www.khaosanby.com
Right in the middle of Khao San, this is more of a hotel than guesthouse, with a rooftop swimming pool, bar and an open pavilion for traditional massage. Rooms are well equipped with bathrooms, air-conditioning, TV, fridge and IDD phone. (200 rooms)

Peachy Guest House
10 Th. Phra Athit. Tel: 0-2281 6659.
This guesthouse occupies a converted school with a bit more old world charm than most of Khao San's concrete box digs. The rooms are basic but clean and comfortable with most rooms facing the garden. A short walk to Khao San, but still removed from all the mayhem. (57 rooms)

PRICE CATEGORIES

Price categories are for a double room without breakfast and taxes:
Luxury = over US$200
Expensive = US$100–200
Moderate = US$50–100
Budget = under US$50

CHINATOWN

Budget

Riverview Guesthouse
768 Soi Phanurangsi,
Th. Songwad. Tel: 0-2235 8501,
Fax: 0-2237 5428.
Few places offer cheap
accommodation in the
city that have river views,
but this one does. While
basic inside, its location
and the ambience of
Chinatown are the main
draws. The better rooms
have air-con, fridge and
TV, and there's a top-
floor restaurant. Finding
this place is an adven-
ture in itself. (45 rooms)

PATHUMWAN & PRATUNAM

Luxury

Conrad Bangkok
All Seasons Place, 87 Th.
Withayu. Tel: 0-2690 9999.
www.conradhotels.com
Oozing class, this top-
notch hotel is located
near embassies and
next door to the All Sea-
sons Place shopping
centre. Spacious and
contemporary rooms are
furnished with Thai silk
and woods, with data
ports for high-speed
internet access and
large bathrooms with
rainshowers. Excellent
choice of eateries, as
well as chic Plus 87
nightclub/restaurant and
jazzy Diplomat Bar. The
serviced apartments
here are a better deal for

longer stays. Ploenchit
Skytrain station is a 6-
minute walk away.
(392 rooms)

Four Seasons
155 Th. Ratchadamri.
Tel: 0-2251 6127.
www.fourseasons.com/bangkok
From the magnificent
lobby decorated with
Thai murals by renowned
local artists and hand-
painted silk ceilings, to
the city's best hotel
swimming pool and
highest staff-to-guest
ratio, the Four Seasons
is consistently excellent.
And it has the accolades
and awards to prove it.
Located right in the
heart of downtown, a few
minutes' walk from
Ratchadamri Skytrain
station. The staff's
attention to detail helps
set it apart from other
luxury establishments.
Some of the city's best
dining outlets are found
here. (256 rooms)

Grand Hyatt Erawan
494 Th. Ratchadamri.
Tel: 0-2254 1234.
www.bangkok.grand.hyatt.com
It's all about location,
and the Hyatt is smack in
the middle of downtown
shopping and beside the
Erawan Shrine. Refur-
bished a few years ago
to a tasteful contempo-
rary style, and still looking good. The basement
restaurant-nightclub
Spasso is a fave nightlife
spot. Connected to the
Erawan Bangkok mall
and a short walk to Chit
Lom Skytrain station.
Excellent range of
eateries. (387 rooms)

Expensive

Amari Watergate
847 Th. Petchaburi.
Tel: 0-2653 9000/19.
www.amari.com/watergate
This large tower isn't
very attractive on the
outside but has been
refurbished within. Excellent facilities, including a
great gym and the base-
ment Americana pub
Henry J. Beans. Located
just across from Pratu-
nam Market and the
main shopping district
around Central World
Plaza. The closest
Skytrain station is Chit
Lom but unfortunately
not within walking
distance. (563 rooms)

Nai Lert Park Bangkok
2 Th. Withayu. Tel: 0-2253
0123. www.swissotel.com
Set within beautiful
gardens with a land-
scaped pool and jogging
track, this hotel is
located in Bangkok's
central business and
diplomatic district.
Recently upgraded by its
new owners, the Raffles
International group, it
now sports a more
contemporary edge; the
hip lounge bar, Syn,
affirms its new look. The
curious should check out
the mass of phallic
totems at Nai Lert
Shrine, located at the
hotel's rear beside the
canal. (338 rooms)

Moderate

Reflections Rooms
81 Soi Phaholyothin 7.
Tel: 0-2270 3343.

www.reflections-thai.com
Located north of Pratu-
nam beside Aree Skytrain
station, this is Bangkok's
most unique art hotel,
designed by a Czech and
with a bright pink façade.
Each room was themati-
cally designed by local
and international design-
ers and artists. Has a
pool, small spa, and
lively restaurant. Both
weird and wonderful.
(28 rooms)

Novotel Bangkok
Siam Square Soi 6. Tel: 0-2255
6888. www.accorhotels-asia.com
Tailored toward the
business traveller, this
hotel is tucked among
the maze of shopping
alleys in Siam Square
and is a short walk to
the main Siam Skytrain
station. At least four
cinemas are nearby, and
its massive basement
entertainment complex,
Concept CM2, is
frequently packed.
(429 rooms)

Budget

A-One Inn
13–15 Soi Kasemsan 1,
Th. Rama I. Tel: 0-2215 3029.
www.aoneinn.com
Located beside Siam
Square and with easy
access to the National
Stadium Skytrain
station, the narrow lane
it's located on has
become a downtown
bargain hotel area, with
lots of options nearby.
Offers fair-sized rooms
with all the mod cons
plus friendly service.
(20 rooms)

BANGRAK & SILOM

Luxury

Banyan Tree Bangkok
21/100 Th. Sathorn Tai.
Tel: 0-2679 1200.
www.banyantree.com
Located in the precariously narrow Thai Wah II Tower, Bangkok's second-tallest hotel features large and stylishly appointed luxury suites with separate living and working areas, plus in-room fax and high-speed internet connection. The Vertigo restaurant on the roof of the tower and the pampering Banyan Tree Spa (the highest in the city) offer spectacular views of the capital. (216 suites)

Dusit Thani
946 Th. Rama IV. Tel: 0-2236 9999. www.dusit.com
The first high-rise hotel in Bangkok, this classic example of fashionably retro 1950s architecture is located across Lumphini Park, near Silom's many corporate headquarters and the nightlife of Patpong, with both the Skytrain and

metro stations right outside its doors. It has lost out a little to younger and more stylish hotels, but recent refurbishments will ensure its place among Bangkok's top digs. Enjoy a pampering massage at its exquisite Devarana Spa and then float on to its top-floor D'Sens restaurant for impeccable French dining. Its Thai and Vietnamese restaurants are highly rated too. (532 rooms)

The Metropolitan
27 Th. Sathorn Tai.
Tel: 0-2625 3333.
www.metropolitan.como.bz
Sister to the famous Metropolitan in London, Bangkok's younger twin is set among a row of top-end hotels on Thanon Sathorn. Its drink and dine outlets, Cy'an and Met Bar, are among the city's top nightspots. This designer hotel is cool and contemporary, blending East and West minimalist chic in equal measures. 10-minute walk to Saladaeng Skytrain and Lumphini metro stations. (171 rooms)

The Oriental
48 Oriental Avenue. Tel: 0-2659 9000. www.mandarinoriental.com
Part of the history of East meeting West, the Oriental, established in 1876, is the most famous hotel in Bangkok, and well known for its attention to detail and grand setting along the Chao Phraya River. The Authors' Wing is the only original surviving structure and its lounge is a delight to sit in and enjoy afternoon tea, while Le Normandie French restaurant is the only place in town that requires a tie for dinner. (395 rooms)

The Sukhothai
13/3 Th. South Sathorn. Tel: 0-2344 8888. www.sukhothai.com
This stunning contemporary Asian hotel draws architectural inspiration from the ancient Thai kingdom of the same name. One of the top five hotels in Bangkok, this class act has well appointed rooms, the excellent La Scala Italian restaurant and chic Zuk Bar, tropical gardens and a reflecting pool. An 8-minute walk to Lumphini metro station. (219 rooms)

Expensive

Le Bua at State Tower
State Tower, 1055/111
Th. Silom. Tel: 0-2624 9999.
www.lebua.com
Located on the corner of Thanon Silom and Thanon Charoen Krung, these are deluxe serviced apartments within the gigantic State Tower. Just a 10-minute walk to Saphan Taksin Skytrain station, State Tower has established itself as a Bangkok landmark, with its opulent 64th-floor rooftop dine and drink outlets collectively called The Dome. The contemporary Asian-style apartments have 1–3 bedrooms with kitchenettes. (462 suites)

Montien
54 Th. Surawong. Tel: 0-2233 7060/69. www.montien.com
This 1960s throwback is one of the city's oldest modern hotels, and located just a stone's throw from the naughty nightlife of Patpong and Soi Thaniya. A short walk to Saladaeng Skytrain station, this grand airy hotel with three restaurants retains a strong Thai atmosphere. (475 rooms)

Moderate

Holiday Inn Silom
981 Th. Silom. Tel: 0-2238 4300. www.bangkok-silom.holiday-inn.com
Located right next to the Jewellery Trade Centre towards the river end of Thanon Silom, this large

BELOW: dine at dizzing heights on roof-top Vertigo restaurant, Banyan Tree Bangkok.

comfortable hotel is of much higher quality than its Holiday Inn branding would suggest. Only an 8-minute walk to Surasak Skytrain station. (725 rooms)

Sofitel Silom

188 Th. Silom. Tel: 0-2238 1991. www.accorhotels-asia.com

This 38-storey hotel located in the quieter part of busy Thanon Silom is only a short walk to Chong Nonsi Skytrain station. Stylishly refurbished to a chic modern style, it caters to both business and leisure travellers. Wine bar V9 has stunning city views from its 37th-floor perch while one floor above is the excellent Shanghai 38 Chinese restaurant. (454 rooms)

Budget

La Residence

173/8-9 Th. Surawong. Tel: 0-2266 5400.

e-mail: residence@loxinfo.co.th

A small boutique hotel a short distance yet far enough away from the pulse of Patpong, with funky individually decorated rooms of different sizes. All the expected room amenities and a friendly vibe, though short on trimmings like a swimming pool. (26 rooms)

Tower Inn

533 Th. Silom. Tel: 0-2237 8300. www.towerinn.com

Halfway down Thanon Silom towards the river and within walking distance of Chong Nonsi

Skytrain station, this well located high-rise hotel has large executive rooms, a swimming pool and a great rooftop terrace with views. There is also a business centre and function rooms, a lobby bar and restaurant. Sees a lot of repeat visitors, and offers monthly rates too. (175 rooms)

SUKHUMVIT

Luxury

Sheraton Grande Sukhumvit

250 Th. Sukhumvit. Tel: 0-2653 0333. www.starwood.com/bangkok

Great location on Thanon Sukhumvit, not far from Benjakitti Park and walking distance to Asok Skytrain and Sukhumvit metro stations. First-rate facilities and services, with extra large rooms containing all the bells and whistles you expect from a five-star property. Beautifully landscaped swimming pool and excellent spa, plus three good restaurants, nightclub and the highly-rated Living Room live jazz bar. (445 rooms)

Expensive

Davis

88 Th. Sukhumvit Soi 24. Tel: 0-2260 8000. www.davisbangkok.net

Boutique hotel with a melange of style influences. There are different theme rooms all with the latest mod

cons, plus 10 large villas with their own swimming pools. There is a rooftop pool with bar, and Club 88, a live music joint. Adjoining Camp Davis is a complex of more bars and restaurants. Phrom Pong Skytrain station is a 12-minute walk away. (164 rooms and 10 villas)

JW Marriott

4 Th. Sukhumvit Soi 2. Tel: 0-2656 7700.

www.marriotthotels.com

This classy five-star hotel is just around the corner from Bangkok's risque Nana Entertainment Plaza, but don't let that deter you. All the usual amenities, plus Bangkok's largest fitness centre, efficient business facilities and spacious well-appointed rooms make this one of the best hotels in the city. It has some of the city's best dining in the New York Steakhouse. Convenient location between the Nana and Ploenchit Skytrain stations. (441 rooms)

Moderate

Landmark

138 Th. Sukhumvit. Tel: 0-2254 0404. www.landmarkbangkok.com

Good location on Thanon Sukhumvit, with easy access to Nana Skytrain station and the girly bar enclave of Nana Entertainment Plaza. Geared toward the business traveller with a busy business centre. (415 rooms)

President Park

95 Th. Sukhumvit Soi 24. Tel: 0-2661 1000.

www.presidentpark.com

Great for families or business executives, this modern apartment complex is tastefully designed. Spacious studios come with kitchenettes. Three large pools and full leisure facilities in its Capitol Club. Daily, weekly and monthly rates available, with breakfast included. Short walk to Phrom Phong Skytrain station. (228 rooms)

Budget

Atlanta

78 Th. Sukhumvit Soi 2. Tel: 0-2252 1650.

www.theatlantahotel.bizland.com

A Sukhumvit legend, this 1950s throwback is rich in character and is a real treasure among faceless modern structures. The first hotel along Sukhumvit, it has a pool set in landscaped gardens and a great Thai restaurant. Quirky extras include Thai dancing on weekends, and classic roll-top desks in the rooms. Closest Skytrain station is Ploenchit. (49 rooms)

Sukhumvit 11

1/33 Th. Sukhumvit Soi 11. Tel: 0-2253 5927. www.suk11.com

Located in the heart of the Sukhumvit area and within walking distance of Nana Skytrain station this personable, family-run Thai-style guesthouse is a gem of a find, and often full. (67 rooms, ensuite and with shared facilities)

ACTIVITIES

THE ARTS

While Thailand's traditional arts and crafts heritage is well identified, there are surprisingly few venues in the capital to appreciate it fully. The contemporary art scene on the other hand is simmering away with numerous art galleries. There is no distinct cultural enclave in Bangkok; events and sites are found throughout the city.

Performing Arts Venues

Joe Louis Theatre: Suan Lum Night Bazaar, 1875 Th. Rama IV, tel: 0-2252 9683; www.joelouis-theater.com. Stages the fading art of *hun lakhon lek*, a unique form of puppetry inspired by local folk tales and the *Ramakien*. Three puppeteers move on stage manipulating expressive marionettes. Nightly show at 7.30pm.

National Theatre: Th. Ratchini, tel: 0-2224 1342. Grand old theatre that hosts traditional music and dance performances every month.

Patravadi Theatre: 69/1 Soi Wat Rakhang, Thonburi, tel: 0-2412 7287; www.patravaditheatre.com. The nucelus of the Thai contemporary arts scene, led by Patravadi Medchudhon, who artfully blends traditional and modern dance and drama. Performance on Sat only at 7.30pm.

Thailand Cultural Centre: Th. Ratchada Phisek, tel: 0-2247 0028; www.thaiculturalcenter.com. Stages everything from loud pop concerts to sophisticated high-brow works by the Bangkok Opera (www.bangkokopera.com). This is also where the Bangkok Symphony Orchestra performs.

Dinner Dance & Drama

Apart from Siam Niramit *(see below)*, Bangkok has almost nowhere else to view dance-drama spectacles except in a condensed form at a few restaurants. Catering to the average guest's short attention span, they present an hour-long show of bite-sized dance and drama after a Thai dinner. The **Erawan Shrine** *(see page 92)* has free performances of Thai dance-drama.

Ruen Thep Room: Silom Village, 286 Th. Silom, tel: 0-2234 4581. A large hall of dark wood and Thai paintings and sculptures creates the right ambience for the nightly hour-long dance and drama performance at 8.30pm.

Sala Rim Nam: opposite Oriental Hotel, 48 Oriental Avenue, tel: 0-2437 6211. Set on the opposite riverbank, the Oriental's riverside restaurant offers a set dinner menu accompanied by an entertaining dance and drama performance at 8.30pm nightly.

Siam Niramit: 19 Th. Tiamruammit, Huaykwang, tel: 0-2649 9222; www.siamniramit.com. A beautifully costumed extravaganza that traverses the country's history and diverse cultures in three acts. Nightly performance at 8pm. Pre-show buffet dinner available at its restaurant.

Art Galleries

Most contemporary art on view in Bangkok is created by home-grown artists. There is also an increasing number of regional Asian artists who display their works here. Check the monthly free cultural map *Art Connection*, the *Bangkok Post, The Nation* and local magazines for details.

H Gallery: 201 Soi 12 Th. Sathorn, tel: 0-1310 4428; www.hgallerybkk.com. Run by an American, it's located in an old converted wooden school building. Promotes a stable of young and eclectic commercially viable artists.

100 Tonson Gallery: 100 Soi Tonson, Th. Ploenchit, tel: 0-2684 1527; www.100tonsongallery.com. Attracts some of the country's best artists and holds high-profile exhibitions that create a lot of media buzz.

Queen's Gallery: 101 Th. Ratchadamnoen Klang, tel: 0-2281 5360; www.queengallery.org. Five-floor gallery with a steady exhibition schedule of modern and contemporary art, predominantly locally produced works.

Silpakorn University Gallery: 31 Th. Na Phra Lan, opposite the Grand Palace, tel: 0-623 6120 ext 1418. Thailand's oldest and most prestigious arts university; three galleries display works by students, teachers and visiting artists.

Cinema

Bangkok's cinemas are comfortable and tickets are cheap; they mainly screen mainstream Hollywood pulp. Thai movies have improved dramatically in the last few years. There are numerous large and modern multiplexes but only one independent art cinema called the House.

EGV Multiplexes: 6th Floor, Siam Discovery Centre, Th. Rama I, tel: 0-2812 9999 (all branches); www.egv.com.

House Boutique Cinema: RCA Plaza, Royal City Avenue, tel: 0-2641 5177/8; www.houserama.com.

Major Cineplex: Central World Plaza, 7th Floor, Th. Ratchadamri; Sukhumvit Ekkamai, Soi 61

Sukhumvit; and Ratchayothin, 1839 Th. Pahonyothin, tel: 0-2515 5555 (all branches); www.majorcineplex.com.

SF Cinema City: 7th Floor, Mahboonkrong Centre, 444 Th. Phayathai, tel: 0-2611 6444; and 6th Floor, Emporium, Sukhumvit Soi 24, tel: 0-2260 9333; www.sfcinemacity.com.

NIGHTLIFE

Bangkok's reputation as a centre for sex of every persuasion frequently overshadows its other nighttime offerings. While there has been no reduction in the number of massage parlours and bars, there has been an upsurge in other activities to meet the needs of the new breed of travellers. Jazz clubs, cool bars and chic clubs are aplenty, attracting young Thais and visitors in droves.

The only damper in Bangkok's nightlife scene is the intrusive Social Order Campaign introduced in 2001, which forces nightlife spots to close early and allows the police to raid bars and clubs to conduct random urine tests on patrons for drugs. Be sure to bring along your passport (even a photocopy will do) to be allowed entry at some nightspots.

For more sleazy nightlife, head to the fleshpots at Patpong (see pages 95–96) and Sukhumvit (see pages 96–97).

Dance Bars & Clubs

Entry fees for clubs in Bangkok were almost unheard of a decade ago, but in order to keep out the riff-raff (particularly working girls) and keep the crowd chic and trendy, several spots now impose a cover charge.

Sukhumvit

Bed Supperclub: 26 Sukhumvit Soi 11, tel: 0-2651 3537; www.bedsupperclub.com. This striking, elliptically shaped eatery and lounge bar has diners literally eating off from beds. Laid-back vibes are played by resident DJs while diners mull over their meal. The other half of the venue operates as a bar/club.

Mystique: 71/8 Sukhumvit Soi 31, tel: 0-2662 2374; www.mystique bangkok.com. Grotto to hedonism that combines kitsch with retro chic. The ground floor is a club with a bar counter framed by a massive fish tank. Level 2 is the Purple Room (where Dracula would be at home) while the chill-out bar on the rooftop looks like a transplant from Morocco.

Q Bar: 34 Sukhumvit Soi 11, tel: 0-2252 3274; www.qbarbangkok.com. Modelled after a New York lounge bar, this stylishly dark and seductive two-floored venue hosts some of the city's coolest dance music. The nightly line-up of mix maestros at the bar is legendary and the drinks list is impressive, with 50 brands of vodka alone.

Silom

Tapas Café & Tapas Room: Soi 4 Th. Silom, tel: 0-2632 0920/1. A true survivor in the city's party scene, this compact two-floored stylish dance bar is packed with beautiful twentysomething locals and expats downing jugs of icy margaritas. Choice of two music genres with different DJs on the downstairs deck and above.

Bars & Pubs

Old City & Dusit

Café Democ: 78 Th. Ratchadamnoen, tel: 0-2622 2571. Progressive drum 'n' bass, and hip and

trip hop is the music of choice here, mixed by local celebrity DJs with the occasional international guest spinner.

Pathumwan & Pratunam

Bacchus: 20/6-7 Soi Ruam Rudee, tel: 0-2650 8986. Located in the pleasant restaurant enclave of Ruam Rudee Village, this elegant four-storey wine bar sees a steady flow of creative and media types.

Syn Bar: Nai Lert Park Hotel, 2 Th. Withayu, tel: 0-2253 0123. This former hotel lobby bar has been dramatically transformed into a retro-chic cocktail lounge by a New York designer. The stunning all-female bartenders mix up some devilishly tasty cocktails and flavoured martinis.

Silom & Bangrak

Distil: State Tower, Th. Silom, tel: 0-2624 9555; www.thedomebkk.com. Located higher than any of the city's other nightspots, Distil is part of the opulent Dome complex on the 64th floor of State Tower building. Choose your poison from the 2,000-bottle wine cellar, lie back on the comfy outdoor balcony sofa cushions and enjoy the spectacular panorama from this lofty perch.

Met Bar: Metropolitan Hotel, Th. Sathorn, tel: 0-2625 3399. Equalling the panache of London's trendy Met Bar, Bangkok's younger sister at the Metropolitan is one of the capital's most exclusive yet friendly nightspots. The dark, intimate members-only bar has resident and visiting international DJs.

V9: Sofitel Silom Hotel, Th. Silom, tel: 0-2238 1991. With awesome views from the 37th floor, this stylish wine bar and restaurant is a fine spot to sip great-value wines. There's a wine shop in front, while inside, fusion cuisine is served.

Sukhumvit

Bull's Head: Soi 33/1 Th. Sukhumvit, tel: 0-2259 4444; www.greatbritishpub.com. Tucked away on a street predominated by Japanese eateries, this is as English and authentic as a pub can be. Attracts a loyal group of regular expats who enjoy monthly visits by international comedians at the hugely popular Punchline Comedy Club.

Face: Soi 38 Th. Sukhumvit, tel: 0-2713 6048/9; www.facebars.com. Part of a small exclusive chain of restaurants and bars (branches in Shanghai and Jakarta), Face Bar is located in a Thai villa housing Indian and Thai restaurants. Expect a mellow vibe in this beautiful antique-filled lounge bar.

Live Jazz Venues

Bamboo Bar: Oriental Hotel, 48 Oriental Avenue, tel: 0-2236 0400. The perfect place to soak up jazz, this cosy, intimate bar with its wicker furnishings evokes a bygone era. The band is almost on your lap as they play laidback jazz classics and back up distinguished guest singers.

Diplomat: Conrad Hotel, 87 Th. Withayu, tel: 0-2690 9999. One of the city's best bars, this is a great warm-up spot for the hotel's other hip hang out spot, the **87 Plus**

BELOW: live jazz at the Saxophone.

Two good sources of information about what's going on are the *Bangkok Post* and *The Nation*, both of which have daily listing sections and weekend entertainment supplements. Other sources of information include magazines like *BK*, *Metro* and *Bangkok Dining & Entertainment*.

club. Sit at the circular bartop in the middle and be mesmerised by seductive jazz singers.

Saxophone Pub & Restaurant: 3/8 Th. Phayathai, Victory Monument, tel: 0-2246 5472. As much a monument as its neighbouring war memorial, this lively venue has been packing them in for close to two decades. This two-floor bar hosts great resident bands (at least two a night), who get the whole place jumping and jiving to excellent jazz as well as R&B, soul and funk.

Kathoey Cabaret

For a night of campy fun, see a Vegas-style lip-synching show performed by transsexuals known as "lady-boys" or *kathoey*.

Calypso: Asia Hotel, Th. Phayathai, tel: 0-2216 8937/8; www.calypso cabaret.com. One of the city's best

cabarets is staged twice nightly at 8.15pm and 9.45pm. Tickets cost B1,000, including one free drink.

Gay Venues

Balcony: 86-88 Soi 4 Th. Silom, tel: 0-2235 5891, www.balconypub. com. Longstanding lively bar with a mixed party crowd that spills out onto the street.

DJ Station: 8/6-8 Silom Soi 2, tel: 0-2266 4029; www.dj-station.com. Bangkok's most popular gay club, packed throughout the night. The atmosphere is electric and patrons often dress outrageously.

Dick's Café: 894/7-8 Soi Pratuchai, Duangthawee Plaza, tel: 0-2637 0078; www.dickscafe.com. Taped jazz music and paintings by local artists create a mellow mood. A great place to unwind.

Freemans: 60/18-21 Th. Silom, tel: 0-2632 8033. A three-storey club with an industrial-like setting where techno-pop rules. A trendy crowd arrives by midnight to catch the *kathoey* (transsexual) cabaret.

SHOPPING

General

Shopping has become an obsessive leisure activity for many Bangkokians. Teenagers, young couples and families love meandering through the new mega malls and department stores. These air-conditioned sanitised environments provide an escape from the city's heat and smog. On weekends, the human traffic at the most popular places can become almost unbearable.

Most malls and department stores open daily from 10am–10pm. Every Jun–July and Dec–Jan, major department stores

and malls take part in the Thailand Grand Sales, though many also offer a 5 percent tourist discount year round – simply show your passport at the point of purchase. Alternatively, you can claim the 7 percent VAT refund at the airport (see page 294).

Shopping Malls

Central World Plaza: Th. Ratchadamri, tel: 0-2255 9400. Mammoth mall with spacious walkways propped either end by the Zen and Isetan department stores.

Emporium: 622 Th. Sukhumvit, tel: 0-2664 8000/9. Mainly brand-name stores, as well as more practical electronics shops. Thai section on the 4th floor has handicrafts and jewellery.

Erawan Bangkok: 494 Th. Ploenchit, tel: 0-2250 7777; www.erawan bangkok.com. Connected to the Grand Hyatt Erawan, this boutique mall has chic shops and eateries.

Gaysorn: 999 Th. Ploenchit, tel: 0-2656 1149. Another glitzy mall for high fashion labels; go to the third floor for home decor shops.

H1: 998 Soi Thonglor, Sukhumvit 55, tel: 0-2714 9578. A clutch of low-rise trendy shops, restaurants and bars on the road that is becoming Bangkok's home to boutique malls.

Mahboonkrong (MBK): 444 Th. Phayathai, tel: 0-2217 9119. This is one of Bangkok's most popular malls, hence the heaving crowds. In general, most goods and services are aimed at Thai youth or bargain-hunting tourists.

Playground: 818 Soi Thonglor, Sukhumvit 55, tel: 0-2714 7888; www.playgroundstore.co.th. Bangkok's newest boutique mall combines art installations with home decor and fashion shops and trendy cafés.

Siam Centre: 989 Th. Rama I, tel: 0-2658 1000. Several tailors and numerous clothing stores, a video games arcade for kids and home decor stores. Restaurants and sports zone on the top floor.

Siam Discovery Centre: 989 Th. Rama I, tel: 0-2658 1000. Packed with imported brands with prices to match. Fifth floor is Kids World, devoted to youngsters.

Siam Paragon: Th. Rama I, tel: 0-2610 9000; www.siamparagon.co.th. Massive new mall next to Siam Centre. All the big brand names are found here. Houses Siam Ocean World in its basement.

Markets

Despite the proliferation of air-conditioned shopping malls in the city, markets (both day and night) and street vendors still cater to the majority of Bangkok's ordinary people with their cheaply goods and basic necessities. They are also colourful places to observe the more visceral aspects of Bangkok. The following places covered in the Bangkok chapter are worth seeking out: **Pratunam Market** (page 94); **Khao San** (page 86); Chinatown's **Sampeng Lane** and **Pahurat Market** (pages 88–89); **Suan Lum Night Bazaar** (page 93); **Patpong** (page 95); **Sukhumvit** (page 97) and **Chatuchak Weekend Market** (page 97).

What To Buy

Antiques

River City: 23 Trok Rongnamkaeng, tel: 0-2237 0077/8. Bangkok's art and antiques centre, with the second to fourth floors selling art and antiques goods. Antique auctions are held monthly in the Auction House, but beware of pilfered artefacts from historical sites.

Electronics

Panthip Plaza: 604/3 Th. Petchaburi, tel: 0-2251 9724/8. The biggest marketplace for computer gear in Thailand, plus virtually every PC software in existence (although much of it pirated). 150 shops spread over five floors selling hardware and software.

Fashion & Clothes

Thais follow fashion trends closely and are quick to copy the latest collections from foreign design houses – and flog them at a fraction of the cost. The only downside is they fit the Thai physique – small and slim. There aren't any international Thai fashion houses but **Fly Now** and **Greyhound** are making major inroads.

Fly Now: 2nd Floor, Gaysorn, Th. Ploenchit, tel: 0-2656 1359; www.flynow.co.th. One of the country's few home-grown fashion labels to grace the world's catwalks.

Greyhound: 2nd Floor, Emporium, Soi 24 Th. Sukhumvit, tel: 0-2664 8664; www.greyhound.co.th. This trendy domestic fashion brand can sometimes be hit or miss, with branches and great cafés in several malls.

Jaspal: 2nd Floor, Siam Centre, Th. Rama I, tel: 0-2251 5918; www.jaspal.com. Local fashion chain with branches in most shopping malls. Influenced by British and European style trends. Unlike most Thai labels, sizes go up to XL.

Tailors

There are nearly as many tailors as noodle shops in the capital, and while the craftsmanship isn't a stitch near to Saville Row, prices are a bargain. There is a proliferation of cheap tailors around Sukhumvit's early soi and also at Thanon Khao San.

Embassy Fashion House: Th.

Withayu, tel: 0-2251 2620. Most tailors give you the hard sell, but this place stands out for its relaxed service. Wide range of local and imported fabrics. Nearby embassy staff patronise this shop, and many big name hotels recommend it too.

Textiles

Almeta Silk: 20/3 Th. Sukhumvit Soi 23, tel: 0-2258 4227. Made-to-order handwoven silk in stunning colour combinations that can be turned into home furnishings.
Jim Thompson Thai Silk: 9 Th. Surawong, tel: 0-2632 8100/4; and **Jim Thompson Factory Outlet:** 153 Th. Sukhumvit Soi 93; www.jimthompson.com. With several branches around the city, this famous silk company has had a contemporary makeover in recent years. Clothing, accessories and home furnishings.
Mae Fah Luang Foundation: 4th Floor, Siam Discovery Centre, Th. Rama I, tel: 02-658 0424/5; www.doitung.org. This royally initiated craft foundation has been credited for its traditional weaves infused with a funky sense of the contemporary.

Gems & Jewellery

Bangkok is well known for its gemstone scams. Buy only from reputable shops endorsed by the Tourism Authority of Thailand and the Thai Gem and Jewellery Traders Association. These shops carry the Jewel Fest (www.jewelfest.com) logo and issue a certificate of authenticity that comes with a money-back guarantee.

Handicrafts/Home Decor

Apart from Chatuchak Weekend Market and Suan Lum Night Bazaar, the shops below are worth a browse. Expect prices to be higher though.
Cocoon: 3rd Floor, Gaysorn, Th.

Ploenchit, tel: 0-2656 1006. Exciting modern twists to Thai and Asian fabrics and home decor.
Narayana Phand: 127 Th. Ratchadamri, tel: 0-2252 4670. One-stop shop for all things Thai. Spread over several floors, there's everything from traditional musical instruments to ornamental headpieces.
Rasi Sayam: 82, Sukhumvit Soi 33, tel: 0-2262 0729. Sells fine traditional Thai handicrafts and *objet d'art*, with many one-of-a-kind pieces.
Propaganda: 4th Floor, Siam Discovery Centre Th. Rama 1, tel: 0-2658 0430; www.propagandaonline.com. Quirkily designed home decor items (think of a Thai version of Alessi) like funky tableware and molar-shaped toothbrush holders. Second outlet at Emporium.

OUTDOOR ACTIVITIES

Participant Sports

Bowling

RCA Bowl: 3rd Floor, RCA Plaza, tel: 0-2641 5870/3. Teenagers come here to rock 'n' bowl to the modern music and disco-like lights. There are 42 lanes open from 10am to 1am.
SF Strike Bowl: 7th Floor MBK Centre, tel: 0-2611 4555. A 28-lane bowling alley, and a Game Zone with pool, table football and air hockey.

Golf

Thais are big golfing buffs, going so far as to employ some of the golfing world's stellar architects to design international-class courses. At around B500 to B2,000, green fees are considerably lower than abroad and clubs are not sticky

about letting guests play.
Green Valley Country Club: 92 Moo 3, Th. Bangna-Trad, tel: 0-2316 5883/9. Beautifully landscaped with a grand clubhouse, this 18-hole course was designed by Robert Trent Jones Jr.
Panya Indra Golf Course: 99 Moo 6, Km 9 Kannayao, Th. Ramindra, tel: 0-2943 0000; www.panyagolf.com. About 30 minutes from downtown, this well-kept course has a challenging 27-hole course.
Thana City Golf & Country Club: Th. Bangna-Trad Km 14, tel: 0-2336 1971/8. The Greg Norman-designed 18-hole course frequently hosts competitions.

Go-Karting

PTT Speedway Karting Stadium: 2nd Floor, RCA Plaza, Royal City Ave, Th. Rama IX, tel: 0-2203 1205; www.kartingstadium.com. This facility with a 600-metre (1,968-ft) long race circuit is a well-managed outfit. The karts are extremely fast and light, reaching a top speed of around 60 kph (37 mph). The stadium has a hi-tech computerised time clock, highlighting individual fastest laps.

Spectator Sports

Muay Thai

Bangkok has two principal places to view Thai boxing, or *muay thai*.
Lumpini Boxing Stadium: Th. Rama IV, tel: 0-2251 4303. Matches at 6pm on Tues and Fri and Sat. Tickets at B500, B800 and B1,500. Note: this stadium is scheduled to relocate in the near future to Soi Nang Linchi 3.
Ratchadamnoen Boxing Stadium: 1 Th. Ratchadamnoen Nok, tel: 0-2281 4205. Matches at 6pm on Mon, Wed and Thur, and 5pm on Sun. Tickets: B500, B800 and B1,500.

SIGHTSEEING TOURS

Unfortunately Bangkok has very little in the way of organised sightseeing tours. The few existing tours are often targeted at the domestic market with guides speaking only Thai. However, all the major hotels have tour desks that can arrange visits (with private guide and car with driver) to the major tourist sites.

The **Chao Phraya Tourist Boat** (see page 103) is more of a shuttle service than a tour proper but you do get a running commentary on board of the sights along the Chao Phraya River. For those wishing to explore the canals of Thonburi or Nonthaburi, **private longtail boats** (see page 103) can be rented from most of the river's main piers.

Dinner cruises (or evening cocktails) on board an authentic teakwood barge is a nice way of spending the evening and soaking up the sights along the river.
Loy Nava Dinner Cruise: tel: 0-2437 4932; www.loynava.com. A teakwood barge was refurbished and converted into the *Tahsaneeya Nava*. Its 2-hour dinner cruise (daily 6pm and 8pm) starts with a traditional welcome by hostesses. Dinner is a Thai set menu accompanied by live traditional music. Cost: B1,150 per person.
Manohra Cruises: tel : 0-2477 0770; www.manohracruises.com. This company uses either the *Manohra* or *Manohra Moon*, both rice barges restored for dining and cocktail cruises. Dinner cruises from 7.30pm to 10pm costs B1,500 per person while cocktail cruises (a drink and light snacks) cost B640. Departs daily from the pier at the Bangkok Marriot Resort but can also pick up from Tha Sathorn or Tha Oriental piers.

The following special-interest tour agencies are recommended:
Real Asia: tel: 0-2712 9301/2; www.realasia.net. Offers 1-day cycling tours (including a ride on a longtail boat) into the capital's more scenic and traffic-free countryside (B1,500 per person). Also has walking and canal boat tours plus an interesting train tour into the countryside at Samut Sakhon.
Tamarind Tours: tel: 0-2238 3227; www.tamarindtours.com. This creative regional tour company offers trips all over Southeast Asia, as well as interesting 1-day trips (like Bangkok X Files for instance) around the city. Informed guides lead unique thematic tours to some of the city's lesser-visited attractions.

SPAS

Banyan Tree Spa: 21st Floor, Thai Wah Tower II, Th. Sathorn, tel: 0-2679 1052; www.banyantreespa.com. The highest and one of the largest in Bangkok with spectacular city panoramas and 23 treatment rooms, plus saunas, steam bath and jet pools.
Being Spa: 88 Sukhumvit Soi 51, tel: 0-2662 6171; www.beingspa.com. One of the first independent spas in the city, this place has a classic Asian feel. 12 treatment rooms with some featuring hydrotherapy shower beds.
Bua Spa: 81 Sukhumvit Soi 53, tel: 0-2260 7304; www.buaspa.com. Offering a Balinese-Asian experience, this independent spa has prices that reflect its wealthy expat clientele, but is still lower than hotel spa prices.
Devarana Spa: The Dusit Thani, 946 Th. Rama IV, tel: 0-2636 3600; www.devarana.com. One of Bangkok's most stylish and evocative havens to health. Flowing with natural light, this spa has a very calming Zen mood.
Divana Spa: 7 Sukhumvit Soi 25, tel: 0-2661 6784; www.divanaspa.com. A hidden garden oasis in the heart of the city, this independent spa formulates many of the spa products from its own organic garden.
Oriental Spa: The Oriental. 48 Oriental Ave, tel: 0-2439 7613; www.mandarinoriental.com. This spa is one of the capital's first and also one of the best temples to well-being. Situated in a century-old teakwood house on the banks of the Chao Phraya River.
Rasayana Retreat: 57 Soi Sukhumvit 39, tel: 0-2662 4803; www.rasayanaretreat.com. Independant spa with all the usual facilties and treatments plus Bangkok's only raw food restaurant.

COOKERY SCHOOLS

Blue Elephant Cookery School: Blue Elephant Restaurant, 233 Th. Sathorn, tel: 0-2673 9353; www.blueelephant.com. Located in an old mansion, the school offers half-day classes that begin with a trip to a Thai produce market. Up to four dishes are taught in the hands-on classes.
Oriental Cookery School: Oriental Hotel, 48 Oriental Avenue, tel: 0-2659 0000; www.mandarinoriental.com. The legendary hotel runs pricey cooking demonstrations rather than hands-on classes, but even this is a fascinating gastronomic experience.
Thai House: Nonthaburi, tel: 0-2903 9611, 2997 5161; www.thaihouse.co.th. Combines Thai cookery lessons with a stay in a rustic Thai-style house in the suburbs of Nonthaburi; 1-, 2- and 3-day courses with meals and lodging included.

EASTERN SEABOARD

Miles of sandy beaches, dozens of tiny offshore islands waiting to be explored, wildlife centres and treks through jungled forest to hidden waterfalls... you can find these and more on Thailand's most developed and easily accessible shore

Map on page 120

The Eastern Seaboard is Thailand's most commercially and industrially developed shore, with the length from Bangkok to Rayong holding numerous factories and oil refineries. Thankfully, the development has done little to deter tourism's potential, and with miles of sandy beaches and dozens of islands lying just offshore, plus relatively calm seas all year through (*see margin tip page 121*), it's easy to find your own private oasis.

This section of the Thai coast has just about something for everyone; the beaches around Pattaya and Rayong, along with the islands of Ko Samet and Ko Chang abound with activities. Speckled with fruit orchards and several national parks, the region is also a golfer's paradise, with over 20 international-standard fairways in the proximity of Pattaya.

Highway 3 is the principal road that trails its way through the provinces of Chonburi, Rayong, Chantaburi and Trat, all the way to Cambodia. There is a rail line as far as Pattaya, but services are limited and slow. Two small airports serve the vicinity, the closest is U-Tapao near Pattaya and there is a new airport in Trat province, which flies in passengers from Bangkok en route to Ko Chang.

After several protracted delays,

the new **Suvarnabhumi International Airport** in the eastern suburbs of Bangkok will open in late 2006 or early 2007, bringing with it an anticipated influx of new hotels, increased residential space and other peripheral facilities. As the location will significantly shorten journey time to destinations like Pattaya, luxury international hotel brands have recently been opening up new hotels along the coast. It is likely that this region will see further growth and transformation in the coming years.

LEFT: a laid-back beach bar on Ko Chang.
BELOW: tigers at play at Sriracha Tiger Zoo.

BANG SAEN

Considered the gateway to the Eastern Seaboard, the elevated highway that leads out of Bangkok ends at **Chonburi**. Just south of Chonburi municipality, the 2-km (1-mile) long beach at **Bang Saen ❶** springs to life each weekend as hordes of middle-class Bangkokians arrive in cars and buses. The nearest stretch of beach from the capital, you will find it covered with a profusion of beach umbrellas and inflatable inner tubes, the surf filled with bobbing bodies fully dressed to avoid a tan (many Thais associate tanned skin with working folk who toil in the sun).

SI RACHA

The run-of-the-mill coastal town of **Si Racha ❷**, about 100 km (62 miles) from Bangkok, nestles between two hill ranges with a busy harbour extending beyond its piers. Its famous hot sauce – *nam prik si racha* – can be enjoyed at waterfront restaurants, where fresh shrimp and crab are dipped into the thick, tangy red sauce. The offshore islet of **Ko Loi**, connected by a bridge, is home to the tree-shrouded **Wat Ko Loi**. Fusing Thai and Chinese elements, it sits on top of a rocky outcrop.

The **Sriracha Tiger Zoo** (daily 8am–6pm; tel: 0-3829 6556/8; admission charge; www.tigerzoo.com) claims to be the largest tiger zoo in the world, with over 200 Bengal tigers; you can visit the nursery to hold and feed the young cubs. The tigers star in the daily circus shows, which also features thousands of crocodiles. There is also an elephant show, a bear show, pig racing, ostrich riding, and plenty of other entertaining animals and birds.

KO SI CHANG

A 45-minute boat ride from Si Racha is the island of **Ko Si Chang ❸**, known primarily as a coastal retreat for King Chulalongkorn (Rama V).

Statue of a gilded fat Buddha at Wat Ko Loi, on the island of Ko Loi.

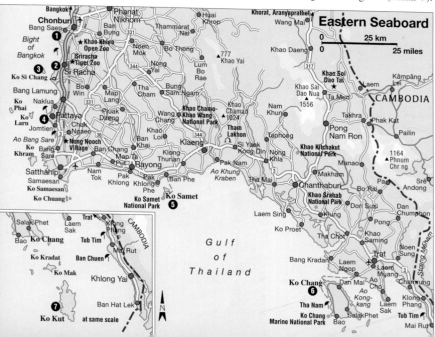

Map on page 120

The king built his summer palace here in the 1890s only to abandon it after the French briefly occupied the island a few years later. Once a customs point for cargo ships unloading onto smaller vessels to sail up the Chao Phraya River, the sea is always crowded with large freighters and rows of flat barges waiting to be supplied. Busy at weekends with Thai daytrippers, the island has a few passable beaches, though certainly not Thailand's best nor cleanest.

Ko Si Chang provides an interesting slice of island living minus the typical tourism onslaught. It can be visited as a day or overnight trip from the capital or as a stop off en route east to Pattaya or beyond. Daytrippers are approached as soon as they step off the ferry by drivers of motorcycle trishaws, who offer 3–4 hour long tours around the island for B250.

Sights and activities

Once off the pier and after exploring **Tha Bon**, the island's main fishing town, most visitors head straight for the grounds of **Judhadhut Palace** (daily 8am–6pm; free).

Undergoing restoration, the grounds double up as an ocean front public park, with a small pebbly beach beside the rebuilt **Atsadang Bridge**. Once a colonnaded wooden pier used as Chulalongkorn's landing stage, this is now a popular spot for kids to leap off from and swim around moored fishing boats.

While the main teak palace itself was dismantled and rebuilt in Bangkok as the Vimanmek Mansion (see *page 86*), several of the palace's other structures have been remodelled, including the green wooden house **Ruen Mai Rim Talay**, which was used as a convalescence home for infirm Western visitors. The pretty gardens that extend up the hill are worthy of exploring; at the top is the white spire of **Wat Atsadang Nimit**. As with palace buildings of the day, the temple's design was a fusion of Thai and European architecture, with the circular *chedi* featuring unique stained glass panels.

Strange as it may sound, ask any trishaw driver to take you to the **Dracula's Castle** and they will pull up in the middle of nowhere beside a

TIP

The best months of the year along the Eastern Seaboard are from Nov to Feb. Expect scorching temperatures from Mar to May, and rain from June to Oct. But even then, the wet season is not as intense at the west coast, making for relatively calm seas even during the rainy months.

BELOW: Wat Atsadang Nimit (left) and Atsadang Bridge (right).

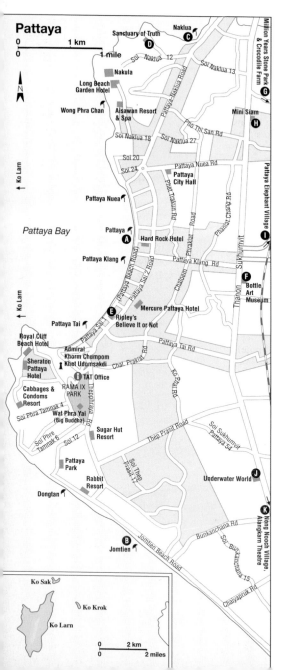

Pattaya

bizarre-looking house that eerily towers above the tree line. The abode is a labour of love for a professor of architecture and isn't open to the public, but it provides a creepy photo opportunity before continuing on to the island's principal beach of **Hat Tham Pang** (Fallen Cave) on the west coast. Depending on the tide, the 1-km (½-mile) long beach can shrink in size, and is usually crowded with lines of beach umbrellas and food shacks located behind.

Religious retreats on the island include the meditation centre at **Wat Tham Yai Prik** (daily 8am–6pm; free), where monks and nuns meditate in caves that reach deep into the rocky hill that the temple rests against. Foreigners often come to stay here and find their spiritual centre. There is no charge to stay at the temple, but donations are welcomed.

Over on steep Kayasira hill is **Sanjao Pho Khao Yai** (daily 8am–6pm; free), the Shrine of the Father Spirit of the Great Hill, a gaudy Chinese temple perched high on the rock with great views overlooking the town and port below. Said to date back to China's Ming Dynasty, the colourful temple is a popular stop for Chinese visitors who pay homage at the damp cave shrines before hiking up further to a *sala* containing Buddha's footprint.

There aren't many restaurants of note but **Pan & David's**, a simple street side eatery is recommended *(see page 131).* Run by an American and his Thai wife, the restaurant is a good source of tourist tips. The couple can also help arrange fishing, scuba diving and boat trips to nearby islands like **Ko Khang Khao**, which has the nicest beach in the area.

PATTAYA

Good and bad, **Pattaya**'s ❹ reputation precedes itself, with most people having formed their own opinion of this resort area even before they step foot here. This notoriety dates back to the Vietnam War when boatloads of American GIs flocked to the then quiet beaches and bars for R&R. With the Thai Navy still operating from the nearby port at Satthahip, battalions of visiting US marines occasionally descend on Pattaya – to the delight of the resort's entertainment spots.

Located 147 km (91 miles) from Bangkok, or just under two hours by road, the seaside town has long been popular with Thai youth and families. In recent years, Europeans have been outnumbered by visitors from Asia and the Middle East, along with significant numbers from Russia.

The once-polluted beaches have been cleaned up but they are nowhere near as pristine as the southern islands. However, what Pattaya lacks, it more than compensates for in other areas. There is a plethora of good-value accommodation and restaurants, a wide range of outdoor and indoor activities, as well as several cultural attractions. Beyond that, Pattaya's buzzing, if salacious, nightlife scene is some-thing to be experienced, or avoided, depending on your sensibility.

Although Pattaya tries hard to create the ambience of a cosmopolitan playground, with glitzy malls and hotels, a pedestrianised shopping street and tree-lined paths, it still retains a provincial character.

Pattaya is also a popular spot for foreigners owning beach condos and houses, used as weekend getaways for Bangkok expats and as winter homes for retirees from Europe. Property is being built at an astonishing rate. There are some swanky residences on the market, and improvements to infrastructure, especially international schools, is drawing in more respectable residents. But its seedy reputation also attracts a strong criminal element. Thankfully, the underworld is rarely visible to the average tourist and Pattaya feels as safe as anywhere else in Thailand.

Pattaya's beaches

On the beach front is the 3-km (2-mile) long crescent-shaped **Hat Pattaya Ⓐ**, the least attractive of the three beaches with only a narrow

Maps on pages 120 & 122

Dragon statue at Wat Tham Yai Prik on the island of Ko Si Chang

LEFT: snooze time at Pattaya.
RIGHT: a sweeping view of Jomtien beach.

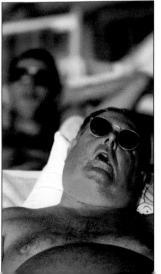

umbrella-crammed wisp of yellow sands. It is backed by a palm-lined promenade that has unfortunately become a pitching point for working girls. The Phra Tamnak hill area separates the main resort splay from a nestle of mid- and high-end hotels (like the Sheraton and Royal Cliff) that front several small but pleasant beaches.

Just a short ride south is the 6-km (4-mile) long **Hat Jomtien B**, with a long stretch of beach that is only marginally cleaner and better than Hat Pattaya. The nicest looking (ie fewer umbrellas) and least populated bays are found in north Pattaya, rounding the **Hat Naklua C** headland towards the fishing village. Accessed from Naklua Soi 16, is **Hat Wongamart**, a pleasant stretch of sand backed by several condo towers and small hotels.

Beach activities

Pattaya and Jomtien are good locations for watersports, with windsurfing and sailing equipment available for rent, along with jet skis, waterscooters and waterskiing equipment. The brave could try parasailing,

strapped into a parachute and towed aloft by a speedboat.

Off shore, **Ko Larn** – identified in brochures as **Coral Island** but whose name actually translates as Bald Island – is one of Pattaya's most popular day trip locations. Its once pristine coral reefs have been destroyed by fishermen using dynamite to stun fish. Yet, glass-bottomed boats still ferry visitors around its waters, the passengers peering in vain at the dead grey coral in the hope of seeing something alive. Ko Larn has the wide, soft sand beaches that Pattaya lacks and is a great place to spend a leisurely day. The shore is lined with seafood restaurants, and there are watersports facilities for those who manage to get off their beach chairs.

Several scuba schools run dive trips to Pattaya's outlying islands; the surrounding waters harbour one of Thailand's best wreck dive sites with no less than four sunken vessels scattered between Pattaya and Satthahip port. Ko Larn and the surrounding islands like **Ko Sak** and **Ko Krok** see more tourist activity – visibility isn't crystal clear but the waters are fairly

Keep an eye out for jet skiers when swimming at Pattaya or Jomtien beaches. Accidents have happened in the past.

BELOW: Ko Larn, also known as Coral Island.

protected from currents which make them suitable for beginners. The further islands of **Ko Rin** and **Ko Man Wichai** are better dive spots with clearer visibility and abundant marine life, including sharks and turtles. The **Hardeep Wreck**, **Bremen Wreck**, and the recently-scuttled **HMS Kram Wreck**, are frequently explored by more experienced divers.

Land attractions

On land, a must-see is the intricate wood-carved edifice **Sanctuary of Truth** ➍ in Naklua Soi 12 (daily 8am–5pm; admission charge; tel: 0-3836 7229; www.sanctuaryoftruth. com). This awe-inspiring structure made of teak is intended to revive traditional artisan techniques as well as act as a spiritual beacon. Dramatically perched on the seafront and protected by fortification, the fantastical tower blends ancient religious iconography from Thailand and Cambodia. Work began in 1981 and is still ongoing. Aside from the cathedral-like structure filled with chiselled figures, there is also a lagoon with dolphins who perform twice daily and willingly shake fins with visitors for a bucket of fish.

Rather more kitschy is the branch of **Ripley's Believe It or Not** ➎ (daily 11am–11pm; tel: 0-3871 0294; admission charge; www.ripleysthai land.com) at the Royal Garden Plaza. Its collection of oddities from around the world may appeal to some.

While many of Pattaya's visitors prefer to quaff bottles of cold beer, others can opt to view a unique collection of delicate miniatures displayed inside some 300 bottles at the **Bottle Art Museum** ➏ on Thanon Sukhumvit (daily 8.30am–8pm; admission charge; tel: 0-3842 2957; www.bottlemuseum.com). All the items have been patiently assembled over a period of 15 years by a Dutchman, Pieter Bij De Leij and a Thai woman, Prapaisi Thaipanich.

Another of Pattaya's touristy stops is the **Million Years Stone Park & Crocodile Farm** ➐ (daily 8am–6.30pm; admission charge; tel: 0-3824 9347; www.thaistonepark.org). This is a collection of weirdly-shaped boulders set among a landscape of rare and exotic flora. Situated off Thanon Chaiyaphruek, there are also beasts aplenty at the park, like crocodiles, bears, tigers, camels and even giant freshwater catfish.

Feel like a giant at **Mini Siam** ➑ as you step around tiny scale models of many of the world's architectural landmarks (daily 7am–10pm; admission charge; tel: 0-3872 7333; www.minisiam.net). This Lilliputian world is on Thanon Sukhumvit in North Pattaya.

Families with young children will enjoy **Pattaya Elephant Village** ➒ on Thanon Sukhumvit (daily 8.30am–7pm; admission charge; tel: 0-3824 9818; www.elephant-village-pattaya.com). It offers a daily elephant show as well as fun rides into the surrounding countryside.

A land-based view of marine wonders can be had at **Underwater**

Map on page 122

TIP

For those who do not want to get wet, book a trip with the **Yellow Submarine** (tel: 0-3841 5234; www.thaisubmarine. com). The 2-hour trip involves a boat ride to Ko Sak, southwest of Pattaya, where the submarine is moored. Climb aboard and the vessel will sink up to 30 metres (98 ft) for a close-up view of marine life; visibility will vary depending on the time of year.

BELOW: the Sanctuary of Truth in Pattaya.

Up close and personal with an elephant at Pattaya's Nong Nooch Village.

World ❿ (daily 9am–6pm; admission charge; tel: 0-3875 6879), just after the Thanon Thep Prasit junction with Thanon Sukhumvit. The large aquarium has a 100-metre (328-ft) long fibreglass viewing tunnel along with a touch pool for hands-on interaction with small marine animals, and a shark and ray tank. For an extra fee, you can also scuba dive with sharks.

South of Pattaya at km 163 of Thanon Sukhumvit is **Nong Nooch Village ⓚ**, a 243-ha (600-acre) landscaped parkland enclosing two manmade lakes (daily 8am–6pm; admission charge; tel: 0-3842 9321; www.nongnoochtropicalgarden.com). Apart from one of the biggest collections of orchids and palms in the world, the park features a butterfly garden, mini-zoo and a daily cultural show with traditional dancing, boxing and an elephant circus.

Pattaya's nightlife

The town's main nightlife clusters along or off Thanon Hat Pattaya (Beach Road) and Walking Street in **South Pattaya**. There is a staggering range of bars, Irish pubs, German brew houses, live music venues, nightclubs, as well as an overwhelming saturation of go-go bars, open air "beer bars" and massage parlours. The international mix here also has a Russian edge, so much so that one place, **Las Vegas** off Walking Street, features Eastern European go-go dancers. The strip called **Boyz Town** (Pattayaland Soi 3) has go go bars and strip clubs that cater to gay men.

Pattaya has at least three lip-synching Vegas-style cabaret shows that feature a pageant of stunning *kathoey* or "lady-boys" (transsexuals). It's all good clean fun and the best is **Tiffany's** (tel: 0-3842 1700; www.tiffany-show.com).

More family oriented is the multi-media cultural extravaganza called **Alangkarn Theatre** (Tue–Sun shows at 7pm & 8.45pm; admission charge; tel: 0-3825 6000; www.alangkarnthailand.com) at km 155 along Thanon Sukhumvit. The show combines traditional dance and theatre to present a spectacle of historic Thailand, complete with elephant battles, lasers and pyrotechnics.

KO SAMET

Located 200 km (124 miles) or three hours by road from Bangkok and a short boat trip across from the fishing harbour of **Ban Phe**, the postcard perfect island of **Ko Samet** ❺ is a popular weekend getaway for Bangkokians. The island is well known among Thais as the place where Sunthorn Phu (1786–1855), a flamboyantly romantic court poet, retired to compose some of his works. Born in nearby Klaeng on the mainland, Sunthorn called the island Ko Kaew Phisadan, or "island with sand like crushed crystal", and it was here that his best-known poem *Phra Aphaimani* was set – a tale about a prince and a mermaid.

From a quiet poetic retreat, the island has gained popularity as a laid-back resort, helped by the fine white sand beaches and clear turquoise blue waters. The island was declared part of a national marine park in 1981 (entry fee on arrival at Na Dan pier; park rangers also stop passengers getting off the ferries at Ao Wong Deuan), so technically, most of the resort and bungalow operations are illegal. However, development along the coast has progressed despite the law, though as yet it remains fairly unobtrusive with single-storey huts and bungalows. But as a sign of things to come, a few new boutique resorts have opened on the quieter beaches, while other establishments are upgrading their facilities.

Ko Samet's beaches

Almost all the island's sandy beaches run down the east coast, starting near the larger northern tip with Hat Sai Kaew, and gradually getting more isolated as the island narrows to the southern bay of Ao Karang. Most of the island's infrastructure – school, clinic, temple, market and few shops – are located near **Na Dan** ❶ pier and along the paved road to Hat Sai Kaew.

The island is relatively small at only 6 km (4 miles) long and 3 km (2 miles) wide, and a hike from top-to-bottom, passing by all the east coast beaches, can be done in a few hours, though the coastal track cuts across several rocky headlands. There is a single road running down the centre of the island, which turns to bumpy dirt track on its outer reaches.

The west coast's only beach, **Ao Phrao** ❸, is the most exclusive, with two upmarket hotels nestled into this small scenic bay. On the east, **Hat Sai Kaew** ❸ (Diamond Sand), a short walk from Na Dan pier, is the most developed spot on the island. Blessed with powdery white sands, this is also one of the most congested. This is where most Thais and package tour visitors stay as there is a bigger selection of air-conditioned hotels, bars and seafood restaurants.

Further down the coast is the bay of **Ao Hin Khok** ❹, separated from Hat Sai Kaew by a rocky promontory on which perches a weathered statue of a mermaid – inspired by Sunthorn Phu's famous poem. Here and at the next bay – **Ao Phai** ❺ which has an

Maps on pages 120 & 128

TIP

While the regular fishing boat ferries are much cheaper, taking a speedboat across to Ko Samet (around B800) from the mainland port is much faster, drops you on the bay of your choice, and usually means you escape the National Park entry fee of B200 per foreign person, which is pretty steep compared to the B20 that Thais are charged.

BELOW: Hat Sai Kaew on Ko Samet.

equally nice white sandy beach – are where foreigners tend to nest. Hotels like **Naga Bungalows** (Ao Hin Khok) and **Silver Sand** (Ao Phai) frequently host late night parties.

The next white sand bay is small and intimate **Ao Tub Tim** . There are only two places to stay here but the noisier attractions of Ao Phai are only a short walk away. There are two more quiet bays, **Ao Nuan** and **Ao Chao**, until you hit the picturesque, crescent-shaped **Ao Wong Deuan** Ⓖ, which is becoming increasingly spoiled by boats, noisy jet skis and the cram of bars and resorts (mostly middle- to upper-end price range). The facilities are good, with minimarts, motorcycle rental and Internet cafés, but the scene is more akin to Pattaya with older Western men being pampered by their hired female "guides".

After Ao Wong Deuan, the bays become very peaceful, like scenic **Ao Thian** Ⓗ (Candlelight Beach),

Banana boat rides on Ao Wong Deuan. This beach has ample facilities but can get noisy as a result.

BELOW: lounging at Ao Thian, Ko Samet.

which is actually a series of small beaches separated by rocky outcrops, and the southern **Ao Kui** Ⓘ, which is little more than a quiet beach with one basic bungalow outfit.

Sights and activities

Most activity at Ko Samet is relaxed and beach bound – sunbathing, beach strolls, swimming and snorkelling – though jet skis and inflatable banana boats do occasionally interrupt the peace. Vendors hawk fruit, beer, ice-cream, snacks and sarongs, and there's an army of women offering massage and hair braiding on the busier beaches. There isn't much in the way of reef around the shoreline and what few spots there are have been badly damaged, but you will still encounter colourful varieties of tropical fish. Several resorts offer snorkelling trips by speedboat around Ko Samet and to nearby islets.

A few places offer scuba diving off the beach at Ao Phrao, while

boat trips head out to nearby islands such as **Ko Talu**, where visibility is clearer but abandoned commercial fishing debris is an eyesore. Further east is **Hin Ploeng**, and off the island's southern tip is **Shark Point**, which can have strong currents and is best suited for experienced divers.

Ko Samet is best avoided on public holidays, when visitors outnumber beds, and tents are pitched on any spare patch of land. Evenings are relatively low-key; restaurants set up fresh seafood beach barbeques, while some eateries entertain the purse-tight backpacker crowd with the latest pirated Hollywood flicks. With local tourists making the bulk of arrivals, Samet's service staff can be rather curt to the needs of foreign visitors.

KO CHANG

Thailand's second largest island at 492 sq km (190 sq miles) after Phuket, **Ko Chang** ❻ (Elephant Island) is part of a national marine park that includes some 52 islands. Around a five-hour drive from Bangkok (or 45 minutes by plane to

Trat on the mainland, then transfer by boat), the verdant island is often compared to Hawaii and Tahiti, and is part of Trat province close to the Cambodian border. Located 20 km (12 miles) southwest of Trat town, the mainland pier of **Laem Ngop** is the main jumping off point to the island.

For years the island had managed to escape rapid development the likes of Phuket and Ko Samui, remaining a firm favourite with backpackers, until recently, when Prime Minister Thaksin Shinawatra began to actively promote Ko Chang as a playground for the rich. This has meant a rapid increase in resort construction and infrastructure, including an upgrade in the road that runs around (and will eventually loop) the island, and the opening of a domestic airport in Trat. The current building boom means that in certain areas, the tranquillity is pierced by the noise of construction. Although temporary, it's still worth asking if there's any work being conducted at or near your hotel.

While the upsurge in construction may detract from the island's untouched appeal, it does mean that

Maps on pages 120 & 130

Seashells from the beach at Ko Chang.

BELOW: sunset viewed from Ko Chang.

Hat Sai Khao has the best infrastructure on Ko Chang, including bars, cafes, restaurants and even ATM machines.

BELOW: Than Mayom Waterfall, Ko Chang.

there is quality, and in some instances stylish, accommodation available. This is drawing in a greater number of wealthy Thai vacationers, who with the increase of car ferries from the mainland, seem intent on bringing their vehicles over to explore the island's one road. The road has several hazardous hill passes with sharp bends, and exploring on a rented motorcycle should be attempted only by experienced riders.

Ko Chang's beaches

Still, don't be put off by the changes taking place; the island still has a relatively untouched hilly interior, mangrove forest and some lovely beaches. The main beaches line up along the west coast, with **Hat Sai Khao Ⓐ** (White Sand Beach), the most developed (and longest) stretch with its swathe of powdery sands framed by a backdrop of casuarina trees.

South is **Hat Khlong Phrao Ⓑ**, one of the nicest yet quietest beaches on the island. It is effectively divided into the northern, central and southern sections by canals. Beyond that lies **Hat Kai Bae Ⓒ**, which has seen much recent development. Unfortunately, parts of its beach disappear when the tide is high. Next up is the last vestige of Ko Chang's hippie traveller scene, the lovely stretch of **Hat Tha Nam Ⓓ**, or Lonely Beach; it's no longer such a haven of solitude with plush resorts starting to edge in. Just over 1-km (½-mile) long, this fine sand beach gets a little coarser towards the south. It's the island's best beach for swimming, although there is a steep shelf at the northern tip. Next is **Ao Bai Lan Ⓔ**, a bay with rocks and reef but no beach.

At the bottom of the west coast is the stilted fishing village of **Ban Bang Bao Ⓕ**, which has become little more than a narrow concrete pier devoted to tourism, with seafood restaurants, dive shops, souvenir shops and a guesthouse. This is also

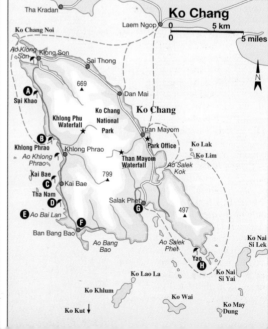

Map
on page
130

the departure point for dive and snorkel trips to surrounding islands.

The coastal road continues east but eventually arrives at a gate which claims private access to Ko Chang Grand Lagoona resort. Until the island loop is completed, this is where the journey ends.

Accessed from the east coast, the next bay along the south coast nestles **Salak Phet** ⓖ fishing village, which has a more authentic and less developed feel than Ban Bang Bao.

Compared to the west coast, the eastern shoreline has little in the way of beaches and is largely ignored by most visitors. This makes a leisurely drive along the plantation- and hill-backed road a real pleasure, with few vehicles and the reward of a seafood lunch at Salak Phet. An alternative route runs along the east of Salak Phet where a newly-built winding road continues all the way to **Hat Yao** ⓗ, or Long Beach, on the southern tip.

Sights and activities

Most island hoppers understandably confine themselves to the west coast beaches, but just as appealing is the lush vegetated mountainous backbone that few bother to venture into. The island's ecosystem includes many avian species (including hornbills), macaques, pythons and cobras, monitor lizards, deer and boar, as well as striking wild flora. Day-long as well as overnight treks are conducted by the reputable **Trekkers of Ko Chang** (tel: 0-3952 5029), and many hotels organise trips with **Mr Anong** (mobile tel: 0-6152 5271).

With the island named after the noble pachyderm, it is no surprise that there are at least three elephant camps conducting treks into the interior. The best one, located deep in the forest, is the elephant camp of **Ban Kwan Chang** (book treks with Jungleway, mobile tel: 0-9223 4795, www.jungleway.com), which con-

ducts well-organised half-day treks and feeding sessions with the gentle pachyderms.

Other popular activities include kayaking and treks to the island's numerous waterfalls. The two most well trodden are **Khlong Phu Waterfall** and **Than Mayom Waterfall**, both of which have park offices that charge foreigners an inflated B200 for each fall, while Thais pay B20.

Snorkelling and scuba diving trips usually head to the smaller outlying islands (*see page 132*) off the southern end of Ko Chang, going as far as **Ko Kut**, the second largest island in the archipelago. There is fine diving at reasonably shallow depths, and is best done from November to March when the sea is calmer and visibility clearer. Some of the best sites include the pinnacles off **Ko Rang**, the reefs around **Ko Wai**, where sharks frequently hover, shallow dives off **Ko Khlum** and **Hin Luk Bat**, a rock pinnacle 30 minutes south by boat from Ban Bang Bao, and the **Thonburi Wreck** off Ko Chang's southeastern tip, where the warship *Thonburi* was sunk by the French in 1941.

TIP

Hat Tha Nam (also known as Lonely Beach) is one of Ko Chang's nicest beaches but beware of the strong undertow and currents at its northern end. A good number of drownings have occured in these treacherous waters.

BELOW:
exploring Ko Chang on elephant back.

Maps
on pages
120 & 130

*Glowing sunset over
the Ko Chang coast.*

BELOW: the tiny island
of Ko Wai, off Ko Chang.

Nightlife

Ko Chang's nightlife is subdued compared to Ko Samui or Phuket, with each beach having its own preferred watering holes. **Hat Sai Khao** is where the main energy is, where the large **Sabay Bar** sees the most action. Lying on cushioned beach mats is the typical set up, and live music is a feature at many bars. As a sign of things to come, there is a block of raucous "beer bars" (nicknamed Mini Pattaya by residents) on the road at the southern end of Hat Sai Khao, with scantily-clad bar girls to lure in customers.

Further down the west coast, **Hat Kai Bae** has a small nightlife scene with a couple of unassuming bars within walking distance along the road. **Hat Tha Nam** has its own pocket of entertainment with a couple of bars that close by midnight.

Ko Chang Archipelago

If Ko Chang feels a little too well trodden, head for the string of isolated islands off the southern tip. Many of Ko Chang's best snorkel and dive sites are found in the waters surrounding these islands. Around 10 km (6 miles) off Ko Chang, the tiny island of **Ko Wai** has limited and basic accommodation, but the vibe here is very relaxed, the views of surrounding islands are spectacular, and there's a lovely coral reef just a short swim from the main beach.

An hour by speedboat from the mainland pier of Laem Ngop, the flat island of **Ko Mak** is dense with coconut trees and has two lovely beaches that are sparse of tourists, but unfortunately abundant with sand flies; be sure to bring insect repellent. While the beaches are relatively unspoilt, the lack of development means that stretches of sand on **Ao Kao**, on Ko Mak's southwest coast, are littered with unsightly flotsam from fishing craft – a possible danger to bare-footed walkers. **Ao Suan Yai**, on the opposite side of Ko Mak, is the island's prettiest bay. Both places have some basic accommodation and restaurants.

The southernmost island in the archipelago and the closest to Cambodia is **Ko Kut** ❼, Thailand's fourth largest island and 2½ hours away by speedboat. Some 25-km (16-mile) long and 12-km (7-mile) wide, some of the island's populace is of Khmer origin, with most inhabitants earning a living off fishing or agriculture. Aside from several beaches and clear seas, attractions include **Khlong Chao Waterfall** and the fishing village at **Ao Sa Lad**. Due to its remote location, the island's development has been fairly low-key, attracting mainly organised tour groups.

Seasonal boats to Ko Wai, Ko Mak and Ko Kut leave from Laem Ngop pier on mainland Trat. From Ko Chang's Bang Bao pier, there are boats that organise tours to the more popular islands; resorts can also arrange for you to hitch a ride on a sightseeing tour boat. Speed boats can be arranged, but are expensive and are best done in a group. ❑

EASTERN SEABOARD

KO SI CHANG

TRANSPORT

GETTING THERE

By Taxi

In Bangkok, a taxi can be booked to make the 100-km (62-mile) journey to Si Racha, the jump-off point for the island of Ko Si Chang. The ride should take about 1–1½ hours. Make sure to negotiate a flat rate before boarding; it should cost no more than B800 to B1,000. *Songthaew* (pick-up trucks) on the pier can be negotiated for the return journey to Bangkok or for the onward journey to Pattaya (costing roughly B300–400).

By Bus

Air-conditioned buses leave every hour, from 6.50am to 9pm daily, from Bangkok's **Ekamai Bus Terminal** for Si Racha bus station (B81). The journey takes around 1½ hours. Take a *tuk-tuk* (B30) from the bus station to Jarin pier.

By Boat

Ferries to Ko Si Chang leave from Jarin pier every hour from 7am to 8pm daily. The journey takes around 40 minutes and costs B40 one way. Ferries return to the mainland every hour from 7am to 6pm. Alternatively, private speed-boats can also be hired at the pier for around B1,000 one way.

GETTING AROUND

The easiest way to explore the island is on the local three-wheel motorcycle called *samlor*. Drivers can be hired to do a 3- to 4-hour tour of the island for about B250, but agree beforehand on the number of places you want to stop at first. A single journey to anywhere on the island costs around B30.

Motorcycles can also be rented (B250–300 per day) if you wish to explore on your own.

RESTAURANTS

Thai & Western

Pan & David
167 Moo 3, Th. Makhaamthaew. Tel: 0-3821 6075. Open: Wed–Mon L & D. $.
www.ko-sichang.com/eat.html
Situated beside the quiet road that leads to the summer palace, this ever-popular restaurant is run by American expat David and his Thai wife Pan. The simple open-sided eatery has garden seating and is backed by the sea-view Rim Talay resort. The wide menu here includes breakfast options as well as fresh seafood, Italian, French and Thai as well as vegetarian dishes. Has a small wine selection.

Thai

Sichang View Resort
91 Moo 6. Tel: 0-3821 6210/1. Open: daily L & D. $–$$.
Set on a clifftop with lofty views out to sea, the only downside to this restaurant is the rather leisurely service. Serves good Thai and Chinese food. The seafood dishes are especially excellent; try the delicious white snapper and crabs.

PRICE CATEGORIES

Price per person for a three-course meal without drinks:
$ = under US$10
$$ = US$10–$25

ACCOMMODATION

Budget

Sichang Palace
81 Moo 1, Th. Asdang.
Tel: 0-3821 6276/9.
Slightly over-the-top appearance, this is as upmarket as it gets on the island. Near the pier in town. All rooms have air-conditioning, TV and hot water, and there's also a swimming pool, coffee shop, nightclub and billiards room. (60 rooms)

Sichang View Resort
91 Moo 6. Tel: 0-3821 6210/1.
On a hilltop with great sunset and sea views, this well-kept resort in a lovely tropical garden has rooms with TVs and air-conditioning or fans; more expensive rooms have hot water. The restaurant serves good seafood. (10 rooms)

Tiewpai Park Resort
8 Moo 2. Tel: 0-3821 6084.
www.tiewpai.com
Popular with backpackers, this friendly place in the heart of the island has a variety of room types, from dormitory beds to Thai-style air-conditioned rooms with en suite bathrooms. Island tours by boat and motorcycles for hire. (17 bungalows)

PRICE CATEGORIES

Price categories are for a double room without breakfast and taxes:
Budget = under US$50

PATTAYA

TRANSPORT

GETTING THERE

By Air

U-Tapao Airport in Sattahip, about 1 hour east of Pattaya, caters largely to chartered flights from Europe as well as domestic flights. **Bangkok Airways** connects Pattaya with Phuket (once daily) and Ko Samui (twice daily).

By Taxi

Most hotels in Pattaya can arrange private transfers from Bangkok. Or you can book a taxi in Bangkok for the 147-km (91-mile) trip to Pattaya. The ride takes 1½–2 hours and costs B1,000–1,200 (including toll fees). Be sure to agree on the rate before boarding the taxi.

By Bus

Air-conditioned buses leave every 30 minutes daily (5am–11pm) from Bangkok's **Ekamai Bus Terminal** to Pattaya (B110). The journey takes around 2 hours.

By Minivan

In Bangkok's Don Muang Airport, **Thai Airways Limousines** (tel: 0-2535 2801) at Terminals 1 and 2 operates minivans (B200 per person) to Pattaya (9am, noon, 7pm) daily. Return trips are at 6.30am, 2pm and 6.30pm.

GETTING AROUND

The easiest way to get around Pattaya is by *songthaew* trucks that run along Thanon Pattaya 2 and Thanon Hat Pattaya (Beach Road). The fare is B10. For longer rides to Naklua and Jomtien, the fare goes up to B20–30. Motorcycle taxis are common, but be sure to agree on the rate first. Motorcycles (B200–700 per day) or cars (B1,200–2,000 per day) can be rented from private operators or **Avis** at the Dusit hotel (tel: 0-3836 1627). There is also the **Pattaya Beach Bus** with three routes: Naklua, Pattaya and Jomtien. A single trip is B30; a one-day pass costs B90.

RESTAURANTS

International

Art Café
285/3 Moo 5, Th. Naklua Soi 16. Tel: 0-3836 7652. Open: daily L & D. $$–$$$.
www.artcafe-thailand.com
Tucked behind the beachfront condos of Naklua, this French-Mediterranean restaurant occupies a wooden colonial-style house surrounded by a garden. With lovely al fresco seating at the front, this is the perfect setting to indulge in a fine meal.

Bruno's
306/63 Chateau Dale Plaza, Th. Thappraya. Tel: 0-3836 4600. Open: daily L & D. $$–$$$.
www.brunos-pattaya.com
One of Pattaya's most

popular expat-friendly bistros, Bruno's offers fine dining at affordable prices. Warm welcoming vibe. Expect well presented French-European dishes and an extensive wine list.

Casa Pascal

Th. Pattaya 2, South Pattaya. Tel: 0-3872 3660. Open: daily L & D; Sun brunch. $$$–$$$$.
www.restaurant-pattaya.com

Smack in the centre of Pattaya's main drag opposite the Royal Garden Plaza. This Swiss-run place is one of the best places for fine dining in Pattaya. The European menu is mainly French-influenced with some Italian selections thrown in.

Paradise

215/62–3 Th. Pattaya 2. Tel: 0-3872 3177. Open: daily L & D. $$–$$$.

On a busy thoroughfare, Paradise is run by a Swiss-trained chef and has plenty of European specialities. Thai food is also represented, but the restaurant is mainly known for its selection of exotic meats, including crocodile, ostrich, emu and kangaroo.

Sportsman Pub & Restaurant

482 Moo 10, Soi 13, Th. Pattaya 2. Tel: 0-3871 0609. Open: daily B, L & D. $$–$$$.
www.thesportsmanspub.com

This busy British-style alehouse is just as well known for its hearty menu of *farang*-friendly favourites as its range of imported beers. Fill up on bulging breakfasts,

pies, burgers, steaks and the all-you-can-eat Sunday roast beef lunch.

Thai

Cabbages & Condoms

366/11, Th. Phra Tamnak Soi 4. Tel: 0-3825 0556/8. Open: daily B, L & D. $–$$.
www.cabbagesandcondoms.co.th

Its curious name comes from its owner, former Senator Mechai, whose work on birth control has earned him the nickname "Mr Condom". Building on the fine reputation of its older sister outlet in Bangkok, this eatery – which looks out to the ocean – serves excellent Thai standards.

Lobster Pot

228 Th. Hat Pattaya (Walking St). Tel: 0-3842 6083. Open: daily L & D. $$. www.lobsterpotpattaya.com

Its central location and incessant advertising ensures a busy flow of custom. With a large wooden terrace jutting into the ocean and fresh seafood hauled from the markets, this is a safe bet for quality seafood.

Nang Nual

Two branches: Th. Hat Pattaya (Walking St) & Jomtien. Tel: 0-3842 8708 (Walking St); tel: 0-3823 1548 (Jomtien). Open: B, L & D. $$–$$$.

With two prime waterfront locations on Pattaya Bay and Jomtien beach, this established seafood restaurant is well known. It certainly isn't glam, but for freshly caught fish and shellfish cooked Thai style, it's unbeatable. The branch

on Walking St has a sea view, while the Jomtien eatery is beside the main beach road.

PIC Kitchen

Fl 2, 255 Th. Pattaya 2, Soi 5. Tel: 0-3842 8374. Open: daily B, L & D. $$–$$$.
www.pic-kitchen.com

Under the same ownership as Sugar Hut, this longtime favourite in Pattaya offers a real Thai experience with floor seating in a garden-facing *sala* (pavilion), or regular table dining in air-conditioned comfort. Excellent Thai and the odd international dish, like British Raj Curry.

Sugar Hut

391/18 Moo 10, Th. Thappraya. Tel: 0-3825 1686. Open: daily B, L & D. $$–$$$.
www.sugar-hut.com

One of Pattaya's most famous Thai restaurants, the tropical garden setting is the main draw here, but the food is equally good. Surrounded by stilted wooden villas and with wandering peacocks and squawking parrots, this outdoor resort restaurant has a lovely ambience.

Other Asian

Le Saigon Bayview

Fl 23, Pattaya Hill Resort, 329/245 Moo 12, Th. Phra Tamnak Soi 2. Tel: 0-3825 0329. Open: daily D. $$–$$$.

This is Pattaya's only independent rooftop restaurant offering views of Pattaya Bay and Jomtien. Open from late afternoon for drinks,

choose from the extensive wine list before getting a table on the terrace. Serves authentic Vietnamese as well as innovative fusion dishes.

Mantra Restaurant & Bar

240 Moo 5, Th. Hat Pattaya. Tel: 0-3842 9591. Open: daily 6pm–1am. $$$–$$$$.
www.mantra-pattaya.com

Hot new restaurant that serves an interesting mix of Asian (Thai, Japanese, Chinese, Indian) and Mediterranean dishes. Wide ranging and eclectic menu allows you to pick and match your food. The decor is equally dramatic with seating on two levels. Later in the evening, it turns into a pulsating nightspot that plays chill-out music.

Vientiane

Fl 1, Julie Complex, Th. Hat Pattaya (Walking St). Tel: 0-3841 1298. Open: daily L & D. $–$$.

Long-standing café-style eatery that recently relocated to a better-placed setting overlooking Pattaya Bay. Well-loved by foreign residents, this reasonably priced restaurant serves some of Pattaya's most authentic Thai, Laotian and Chinese dishes.

PRICE CATEGORIES

Price per person for a three-course meal without drinks:

$ = under US$10
$$ = US$10–$25
$$$ = US$25–$50
$$$$ = over US$50

ACCOMMODATION

Expensive

Hard Rock Hotel Pattaya
Th. Hat Pattaya (Beach Rd).
Tel: 0-3842 8755.
www.hardrockhotelpattaya.com
For beachside fun in a contemporary setting, Hard Rock is the place. The rooms are fairly standard, with the flashy pop colours and music memorabilia typical of all Hard Rock outlets. The vast hotel pool comes complete with boulders and thatched *sala* for you to lie under, while Hard Rock's health club is the perfect foil to Pattaya's entertainment scene. (320 rooms)

Long Beach Garden Hotel & Spa
499/7 Moo 5, Wongamart, Naklua Soi 16. Tel: 0-3841 4616.
www.longbeachgardenhotel.com
Located on a prime stretch of beach in Naklua Soi 16, this towering four-star hotel has rooms and suites evoking Thai, Balinese and colonial decor. Geared toward European and Asian package tours, there are five eating options, both indoor and out, and the pool is backed by a waterfall. (670 rooms)

Sheraton Pattaya
437 Th. Phra Tamnak.
Tel: 0-3825 9888.
www.sheraton.com/pattaya
This newly-opened hotel is in a secluded spot on the Phra Tamnak headland looking directly out to Ko Larn. More like a private country club than a typical hotel, the beautifully-landscaped resort has calming water elements and even its own beach. Many of the rooms have their own ocean-facing *sala* (pavilion), and the Amburaya Spa is there for body tuning. (156 rooms)

Sugar Hut
391/18 Moo 10, Th. Thappraya.
Tel: 0-3825 1686.
www.sugar-hut.com
While its location off a main road away from any beach isn't ideal, this verdant tropical resort makes you forget where you are as soon as you enter. The traditional 1- or 2-bedroom Thai bungalows are very rustic, with indoor garden bathrooms. There's an excellent Thai restaurant that is busy with residents and visiting diners and a lovely pool. (28 villas)

Moderate

Aisawan Resort & Spa
445/3 Moo 5, Wongamart, Th. Naklua. Tel: 0-3841 1940.
www.aisawan.com
Set right on Wongamart beach at Naklua Bay, this large, modern-looking hotel is popular with well-heeled Asian travellers. A stylish blend of traditional and contemporary Asian design, the well-equipped hotel features two swimming pools and three restaurants plus conference facilities. (374 rooms)

Cabbages & Condoms
366/11 Th. Phra Tamnak Soi 4.
Tel: 0-3825 0556-8.
www.cabbagesandcondoms.co.th
Taking its name from owner, former Senator Mechai, whose campaigning on AIDS awareness has earned him the title "Mr Condom", this rustic retreat feels far removed from Pattaya's notorious nightlife. The ocean and treetop suites all have teak decks and private jacuzzis, and there's a large sea-view pool surrounded by a pretty garden. Staying here means you also contribute money to help Thailand's less fortunate.

Rabbit Resort
Dongtan, Jomtien. Tel: 0-3830 3303/4. www.rabbitresort.com
Set slightly back from Dongtan beach in Jomtien, Rabbit is a Thai-style resort set among pretty gardens. Popular with Bangkok weekenders, the rooms are decorated with traditional local furniture and fabrics, giving the place a homely feel. There are two swimming pools, a restaurant and a beach grill. (45 rooms)

Budget

Dynasty Resort Pattaya
378/3–11 Moo 12, Th. Phra Tamnak. Tel: 0-3825 0721.
www.dynastyinn.com
This resort on a quiet street in the pleasant Phra Tamnak hill area has no sea view but is good value, with a secluded stretch of beach just a short walk away. Rooms are spacious, though a little characterless. There's a large pool and friendly staff. Ask about their shuttle pick-ups from Bangkok. (69 rooms)

Mercure Pattaya
484 Soi 15, Moo 10, Th. Pattaya 2. Tel: 0-3842 5050.
www.mercurepattaya.com
Part of a reputable chain known for its reliable quality, this large, brand-new outlet in the heart of downtown Pattaya is elegant considering its low rates. The rooms are equipped with modern conveniences. Large swimming pool and four dining outlets.
(245 rooms)

Sunshine Garden Hotel
240/3 Moo 5, Th. Naklua.
Tel: 0-3842 1300.
www.sunshinegardenhotel.com
While not on the beach, this good-value garden hideaway is within walking distance of both Pattaya and Naklua beaches. Garden and pool-facing rooms, suites and bungalows, all with their own balconies. (132 rooms)

PRICE CATEGORIES

Price categories are for a double room without breakfast and taxes:
Expensive = US$100–200
Moderate = US$50–100
Budget = under US$50

ACTIVITIES

THE ARTS

Art Galleries

Thailand has few contemporary art galleries outside Bangkok, but as the number of long-term residents in resort towns grows, exhibitions of local and international art are beginning to find a stage. The Royal Garden Plaza in Pattaya hosts occasional displays of painting and sculpture, and the newly-opened Liam's Gallery is probably the Eastern Seaboard's first independent gallery space.

Liam's Gallery: 352/107 Th. Phra Tamnak Soi 4, Moo 12, tel: 0-3825 1808; www.liamsgallery.com. This gallery is owned by Irish businessman and cultural philanthropist Liam O'Keefe, an avid collector of local art for over four decades. Displays works by some of the country's brightest talents.

NIGHTLIFE

Dance Bars & Clubs

Classroom: Pattayaland Soi 2, tel: 0-3842 0185; www.classroom1.com. A tame go-go bar sans nudity, where girls dress in kinky schoolgirl uniforms. Has a less in-your-face ambience that approaches normality in this town.

Lucifer: Th. Hat Pattaya (Walking St), tel: 0-3871 0216. A fresh-faced sister establishment to the Bangkok club on Patpong. Opens onto Walking Street with a Latin bar in front drawing a slightly older clientele, while in the back is the pumped up, hell-themed club playing mainstream R&B and hip-hop.

Marine: Th. Hat Pattaya (Walking St), tel: 0-3842 8583. Trashy and loud, this is where everyone gravitates to once Pattaya's girlie bars start winding down. The music is mainly Euro-dance and techno.

Bars & Pubs

Hopf Brew House: 219 Th. Hat Pattaya (Beach Rd), tel: 0-3871 0653. Popular microbrewery that sees a steady flow of Pattaya's more respectable types who come for the wood-fired pizzas and Italian and European dishes. In-house band livens things up.

The Kilkenny: Th. Hat Pattaya (Walking St), tel: 0-3871 1094; e-mail: Kilkenny@loxinfo.co.th. Another of Pattaya's Gaelic watering holes, this pub has a lively atmosphere with quality beers on tap, a daily specials board of pub grub, and all the latest sports on TV.

Mantra Restaurant & Bar: 240 Moo 5, Th. Hat Pattaya, tel: 0-3842 9591. Sleek new spot that functions both as an eatery *(see page 135)* and a nightspot. The ambience is evocative of a Bedouin tented camp with day beds and cozy nooks where you can chill out and order cocktails from its innovative drinks list.

Live Music Venues

The Blues Factory: 131/3 Moo 10, Soi Lucky Star (off Walking St), www.thebluesfactorypattaya.com. One of Pattaya's best music venues and suitable for all, including families. Features live blues and rock nightly by resident guitarist Lam Morrison, and the house band, the Blues Machine. Happy Hour 8–10pm.

The Jazz Pit: Fl 2, 255 Th. Pattaya 2 Soi 5, tel: 0-3842 8374; www.pic-kitchen.com. With a logo

claiming "it's not for everybody", this music bar with a cool, laid-back vibe adjoins the popular PIC Kitchen restaurant. Live bands and jam sessions feature resident ensembles and overseas acts.

Hard Rock Café: Th. Hat Pattaya (Beach Rd), tel: 0-3842 8755; www.hardrockhotelpattaya.com. This global brand differs little from place to place except on Saturdays when the foam party puts a soapy sheen on the merriment. House bands play from 10pm.

Kathoey Cabaret

For a night full of campy fun, Pattaya is well known for its Vegas-style lip-synching shows at Tiffany's, Alcazar and Simon Cabaret. As you gawk at the svelte and attractive troupe of females parading on stage, just remember that they were all (and some still are) men.

Tiffany's: 464 Moo 9, Th. Pattaya 2, tel: 0-3842 1700/5; www.tiffany-show.co.th. Probably Thailand's most famous *kathoey* or "lady-boy" (transsexual) cabaret routine with three nightly shows (6pm, 7.30pm, 9pm; B500–600) in the 1,000-seat auditorium. Presents dance extravaganzas inspired by Broadway, historic Thailand and China.

Alcazar: 78/14 Th. Pattaya 2, tel: 0-3841 0225; www.alcazar-pattaya.com. Pattaya's second most recognised drag cabaret offers a spectacular show in a 1,200-seat venue. Three nightly shows at 6.30pm, 8pm and 9.30pm.

Gay Venues

It's hard to miss Pattaya's main concentration of gay activity, with a big neon sign across the width of Pattayaland Soi 3 flashing

"Boyz Town". For more information, visit www.pattayagay.com.

Le Café Royale's Piano Bar: 325/102–9 Pattayaland Soi 3, tel: 0-3842 3515; www.caferoyale-pattaya.com. Smack in the heart of Pattaya's gay nightlife, this piano bar is attached to the hotel of the same name.

Splash Show Bar: 327/108 Pattayaland Soi 3, tel: 0-3842 3515; www.throbsplash.com. By the same owners as Throb Go Go Bar next door, Splash's shows of dancers trying to perform in a large water tank is actually more hilarious than titillating.

SHOPPING

Pattaya is the Eastern Seaboard's best shopping option, with several malls and a couple of outdoor tourist markets. Beyond the usual high-street brands, choices are basically limited to market stall counterfeits and tacky tourist bric-a-brac, though there are replica antiques and collectable shops and several recently opened galleries.

Shopping Malls

Royal Garden Plaza: Th. Hat Pattaya (Beach Rd), tel: 0-3871 0294. As close to an urban mall as you can get in Pattaya, this place may not have exclusive brand names but there is a good range of shops selling both imported and local goods. Also has eateries and a cinema.

Mike Shopping Mall: Th. Hat Pattaya (Beach Rd), tel: 0-3842 9019. Aimed at the Chinese tourist market but thronged by all. Mike's shops carry goods of a more bargain basement quality than Royal Garden's, but it is still good for essentials.

Factory Outlet Malls

Fly Now: Th. Sukhumvit, tel: 0-3822 1744; www.flynow.co.th. Located next to Cholchan Resort, Thailand's principal fashion house Fly Now offers discounted export-quality clothing, household items, bedding and baskets.

Outlet Mall Pattaya: Cnr of Th. Thepprasit & Th. Sukhumvit, tel: 0-3842 7764. American-style shopping with discounts on legitimate name brands. Nothing too fancy but good basics from the likes of Lacoste, Levis, Adidas, Diesel and such.

Markets

Night Square Night Market: Th. Pattaya 2 (btw Th. Pattaya North and Soi 0). Cheap clothing, handicrafts and the like. A good place to stock up on mementos before heading home.

World Gems Collection: 98 Moo 6, Th. North Pattaya, tel: 0-3841 2333; www.worldgemscollection.com. Claiming to be Asia's largest jewellery outlet, this monster showroom has a museum and a factory where you can see pieces being made. Thousands of stones and jewellery pieces to choose from.

OUTDOOR ACTIVITIES

Diving

Aquanauts Dive Centre: 437/17 Moo 9, Th. Hat Pattaya (Beach Rd) Soi 6, tel: 0-3836 1724; www.aquanautsdive.com. A British-owned operation with over a decade of experience in Pattaya. In addition to its basic courses, it offers several speciality courses, as well as wreck dives and cave dives for more experienced divers.

Mermaid's Scuba Diving Centre: 75/124 Moo 12, Th. Hat Jomtien (Jomtien Beach Rd), tel: 0-3823 2219; www.mermaiddive.com. A large, well-managed dive centre with three boats offering regular courses and fun dives, as well as speciality courses such as the PADI National Geographic Diver Course.

Bungee Jumping

Jungle Bungy Jump: Th. Boonkanjana Soi 5, Jomtien, tel: 0-6378 3880; www.thaibungy.com. Claiming to operate the original and safest bungee jump in Thailand, this company offers a 50-metre (165-ft) launch over a fishing lake behind the beach. A jump costs B1,400 (inclusive of insurance and a "courage" certificate), with additional jumps getting progressively cheaper; the 4th jump is free.

Golf

Thais are great golfing buffs, going so far as to employ some of the golfing world's stellar architects to design international-class courses. The area around Pattaya plays host to at least 18 golf courses. At around B500–2,000, green fees are considerably lower than abroad, and most clubs are happy to allow non-members access. Check www.thaigolfer.com for more details.

Bangphra International: 45 Moo 6, Bangphra, Si Racha, tel: 0-3834 1149. This venerable par 72 course is one of the area's oldest, dating back to 1958, but the first nine holes were completely redesigned in the 1980s.

Laem Chabang International Country Club: 106/8 Moo 4, Si Racha, tel: 0-3837 2273; www.laemchabanggolf.com. Rated one of the region's best, this 27-hole

course (par 72) was designed by Jack Nicklaus.
Phoenix Golf Club: Th. Sukhumvit km 158, Pattaya, tel: 0-3823 9391. With sea views, this 27-hole course (par 72) was designed by Dennis Griffith and is ideal for long hitters. Large clubhouse with excellent facilities.

Go-Karting

K.R. Go-Kart Grand Prix: 62/125 Moo 12, Th. Thepprasit, tel: 0-3830 0347. Burn some rubber at this 1,100-metre (1,200-yd) track. There are different engine sizes (80–110cc) to suit both novice and experienced drivers, and a clubhouse. A 10-minute ride costs from B300–700.

Horse Riding

Horseshoe Point Riding Academy & Club Aviva: tel: 0-3873 5050; www.club-aviva.com. Has two indoor rings, an outdoor sand field, jumping field, polo field and natural trails. Both horses and ponies are stabled here. Short 15-minute rides start at B220, while a longer 2-hour trail ride costs B1,540.

Paintball

Paintball World: Th. Hat Jomtien, tel: 0-3823 2796; www.thailandpaintball.com. Why anyone would want to come to a beach, get dressed in army fatigues and attack people with paint may be baffling to some, but this is one of a few paintball parks in Pattaya.

Sailing

Ocean Marina Yacht Club: 274/1-9 Moo 4, Th. Sukhumvit km 157, Sattahip, tel: 0-3823 7310; www.oceanmarinayachtclub.com. Those with very deep wallets

might want to charter their own yacht or catamaran for a half-day, sunset or overnight cruise.

Skydiving & Parachuting

Pattaya Airpark: 108/1 Moo 9, Hui Yai, Pattaya, tel: 0-6374 1718/9; www.pattayaairpark.com. Located around 15 km (9 miles) south of Pattaya along Thanon Sukhumvit, it offers tandem skydives every weekend (weekday dives can also be arranged). A single jump in the drop zone costs B10,000, or B15,000 with a video of your jump recorded on DVD. Also has hour-long Ultralight flights for B3,500. Advance bookings required.

Submarine

Yellow Submarine: Th. North Pattaya, tel: 0-3841 5234; www.thaisubmarine.com. For those who do not want to get wet, book a trip with the Yellow Submarine. The 2-hour trip involves a boat ride first to Ko Sak southwest of Pattaya where the submarine is moored. Climb aboard and the vessel will slowly sink up to 30 metres (98 ft) for a close-up, albeit limited, view of marine life; the visibility will vary according to the time of year.

Water Theme Park

Pattaya Park: 345 Hat Jomtien, tel: 0-3825 1201/8; www.pattayapark.com. Centred around Pattaya Tower, this water theme park and amusement ride area called "Funny Land" has plenty that will thrill both kids and adults. Ascend the tower for panoramic views, then descend by either the Sky Shuttle cable car, Speed Shuttle, or the adrenalin-pumping Tower Jump. The water park also has slides and a whirlpool.

Wind- & Kite-surfing

Blue Lagoon Water Sports Club: 24/20 Moo 2, Na Jomtiem Soi 14, Sattahip, tel: 0-3825 5115/6. This is one of Thailand's few professional kite-surfing schools. Also rents out kayaks and windsurfers.

SPAS

Cliff Spa: Royal Cliff Beach Resort, 353 Th. Phra Tamnak, tel: 0-3825 0421; www.royalcliff.com. Sits on a hill with wonderful views of the bay. It has 18 luxurious treatment suites plus a complete range of facilities. Spa Café serves healthful cuisine and herbal teas.
Devarana: Dusit Resort, 240/2 Th. Hat Pattaya, tel: 0-3837 1044; www.devarana.com. Devarana, meaning "garden in heaven", is one of Pattaya's most expensive spas, with plush suites for couples.
Hard Rock Spa: Hard Rock Hotel Pattaya, Th. Hat Pattaya, tel: 0-3842 8755; www.hardrockhotelpattaya.com. Housed beside the vast hotel pool, the comfortable treatment rooms are designed in a modern minimalist style while the club has a gym, steam and sauna and plunge pool.

BELOW: therapist at Devarana spa giving a shoulder massage.

KO SAMET

TRANSPORT

GETTING THERE

By Taxi

Taxis in Bangkok can be booked for the 200-km (124-mile) journey to Ban Phe pier in Rayong province. The ride will take approximately 3 hours and will cost about B1,500. Be sure to confirm the rate before boarding. Near the 7-11 store opposite Ban Phe pier, taxis await passengers for rides back to Bangkok, Pattaya (B500–1,000) or on to Trat (B1,500), the jump-off point for Ko Chang.

By Bus

Air-conditioned buses leave every hour (5am–9pm) from **Ekamai Bus Terminal** in Bangkok for Ban Phe pier in Rayong. The journey takes around 3–3½ hours and the fare is B146 one way.

By Minivan

Private tour companies in Bangkok operate tourist minivans departing from Thanon Khao San and designated tour agents and hotels in Bangkok to Ban Phe pier for about B250 per person. Return trips can be arranged with resorts and tour counters on Ko Samet or at travel agents near Ban Phe pier. Typically, operators will try to cram the van full before leaving (11 pax), putting considerable delay on your journey.

By Boat

Fishing boats leave Ban Phe pier across from the bus station every hour or when there are enough passengers. Decide which beach you will be staying at before picking your boat. The journey to the main Na Dan pier on Ko Samet takes around 30 minutes and costs B50 one way. Some boats continue onto Ao Wong Deuan, but there are also direct boats from Ban Phe to Ao Wong Deuan, the 40-minute ride costing B60. If there are a few of you, consider hiring a speedboat as it's much faster. Expect to pay about B800 to Hat Sai Kaew or Ao Phai, and B1,000 to Ao Wong Deuan.

GETTING AROUND

With Ko Samet only 6 km (4 miles) from north to south, walking to most places is relatively easy. The island has little in the way of paved roads and *songthaew* trucks are the only transportation option. These trucks shuttle visitors from Na Dan pier to the beaches for B10–50, depending on distance. Motorcycles are available for hire (B400 per day) but this is quite pointless with little more than one dirt track running down the centre of the island.

RESTAURANTS

Ko Samet doesn't have much in the way of quality stand-alone restaurants. Almost all eateries and bars are contained within the small resorts.

Thai & Western

Naga Bungalows
Ao Hin Khok. Tel: 0-3864 4034. Open: daily B, L & D. $–$$. A longtime favourite with backpackers, this restaurant-bar is run by an Englishwoman and is known for its bakery and late-night revelry. The restaurant sits up the hill and serves decent Western breakfasts as well as sandwiches, pizzas, burgers and Thai dishes. Overlooking the beach, the bar gets busy during the evening happy hour.

Samed Villa
89 Moo 4, Ao Phai. Tel: 0-3864 4094. Open: daily B, L & D. $$. www.samedvilla.com
Under Swiss ownership, this resort is very popular with Bangkok expats. The restaurant is the usual run-of-the-mill island affair, though it raises the bar just enough to distinguish itself from the crowd. Service is prompt and friendly. Large selection of Thai, seafood and Western dishes.

Sea View Restaurant
Ao Prao Resort, Ao Phrao. Tel: 0-3864 4101/5. Open: daily B, L & D. $$$. www.samedresorts.com
If you're hungering for an elegant dining experience away from the slew of beach barbies, then this place is about as good as it gets. The selection of Thai food, steaks and international dishes are well presented but by no means a gastronomic epiphany.

PRICE CATEGORIES

Price per person for a three-course meal without drinks:
$ = under US$10
$$ = US$10–$25
$$$ = US$25–$50

ACCOMMODATION

Expensive

Ao Prao Resort
60 Moo 4, Ao Phrao. Tel: 0-3864 4101/5. www.samedresorts.com

The island's most upscale resort rests on the only beach on the sunset side of Ko Samet. It therefore sees fewer visitors, adding to its exclusivity. The elegant bungalows come with modern conveniences, including cable TV. Also has the most upscale restaurant on the island, though don't expect too much. (48 rooms)

Le Vimarn
Moo 4, Ao Phrao. Tel: 0-3864 4101/7. www.samedresorts.com

Under the same ownership as nearby Ao Prao Resort, this teakwood resort with sea-facing infinity pool is located on the more secluded sunset side of the island. Decked out in an elegant blend of traditional and contemporary, there are three types of cottages and villas to choose from. A spa and a restaurant are centred around a pond. (28 rooms)

Moderate

Sai Kaew Beach Resort
8/1 Moo 4, Hat Sai Kaew. Mobile tel: 0-1874 8087. www.samedresorts.com

Decked out in summery blues and whites, this is one of a new breed of small-scale contemporary resorts on Ko Samet, a part of the growing Ao Prao Resort group. Situated at the northern tip of Hat Sai Kaew, the resort has three types of rooms and a swimming pool. Ask about their long-stay promotions. (40 rooms)

Samed Villa
89 Moo 4, Ao Phai. Tel: 0-3864 4094. www.samedvilla.com

Located at the end of Ao Phai beach on a headland with nice views out to sea, this popular family-run resort is under Scandinavian management. On most weekends it fills up with Bangkok expats, so book ahead. It was recently upgraded and is now one of the island's best places to stay. The bungalows are good value with air-conditioning, hot shower and TV. The restaurant does great Thai and international food. (30 rooms)

Budget

Tubtim Resort
13/15 Moo 4, Ao Tub Tim. Tel: 0-3864 4025. www.tubtimresort.com

This rustic resort is a longtime favourite with Bangkok's hip set, and has a gay-friendly vibe. Family-run, the resort has both cheap wooden huts and concrete air-conditioned bungalows. The beach is one of the prettiest, and the evening barbecue by the bar fills up fast. (75 rooms)

PRICE CATEGORIES

Price categories are for a double room without breakfast and taxes:
Expensive = US$100–200
Moderate = US$50–100
Budget = under US$50

ACTIVITIES

NIGHTLIFE

Naga Bungalows: Hat Hin Kok. tel: 0-3864 4034. Perched on a hillside looking down onto the beach, Naga has one of Ko Samet's busiest beach bars, though its popularity ebbs and flows somewhat depending on what its competitor, Silver Sand (see below), is having at the same time. Daily happy hour and decent upbeat music.

Silver Sand: Ao Phai, mobile tel: 0-1996 5720. With little else on offer late night, the beach bar here is usually crammed to the hilt. Sprawling with beach mats, it occupies a large area, with the decibels cranked high to the ire of those trying to rest at the nearby hotels. Nightly fire juggling entertainment draws the crowds, who don't seem put off by the somewhat moody bar staff.

Talebure Bed & Bar: Ao Wong Deuan, mobile tel: 0-1762 3548. This modern minimalist place – with whitewashed timber and dark wood floors – is a marked difference from your average ramshackle Ko Samet bar hut. Popular with weekending Bangkok trendsters, the bar and resort sits at the southern end of the bay at Ao Wong Deuan.

OUTDOOR ACTIVITIES

Diving

Ploy Scuba Diving: Hat Sai Kaew, mobile tel: 0-6143 9318; www.ployscuba.com. Part of a reputable chain of dive shops. Professionally managed, with courses in several languages.

Samed Resorts PADI Dive Centre: Ao Prao Resort, Ao Phrao, tel: 0-3864 4100; www.aopraoresort.com. This expensive resort-linked dive centre is well run and offers basic, open water and advanced dive courses.

KO CHANG

TRANSPORT

GETTING THERE

By Air

Bangkok Airways operates three daily flights (8.30am, 11am and 4pm) from Bangkok to the new Trat airport. The journey takes less than an hour. From the airport take a 20-minute taxi or *songthaew* ride to Laem Ngop pier. Larger hotels will arrange transportation (by minivan from the airport and boat to Ko Chang) for around B200–250 per person for shared transfers and considerably more for private transfers (B750 and up).

By Taxi

Travelling by road from Bangkok is not the best way of getting to Ko Chang because of the 492-km (190-mile) distance. You can arrange for a taxi in Bangkok to make the 5-hour ride to Laem Ngop pier in Trat Province for a flat rate of B2,500. Make sure you agree on the rate beforehand. For the return journey to Bangkok, private

taxis are available near Laem Ngop pier for around the same price.

By Bus

Air-conditioned buses leave daily from Bangkok's **Ekamai Bus Terminal** for Trat every 90 minutes between 6am and 11.30pm. Tickets cost B223 one way. In addition there are five daily bus departures from **Northeastern (Mo Chit) Bus Terminal** between 6am and 11pm. The ride takes around 6 hours. From Trat bus station take a *songthaew* truck to Laem Ngop pier, about 17 km (11 miles) away.

By Minivan

Private tour companies in Bangkok operate tourist minivans departing from Thanon Khao San and designated tour agents and hotels in Bangkok to Laem Ngop pier in Trat for about B500 per person. Return trips can be arranged with resorts and tour counters on Ko Chang or at travel agents near Laem Ngop pier. Typically operators will try to cram the van full before leaving (11 pax), putting considerable delay on your journey.

By Boat

Passenger and car ferries leave from three different piers in Laem Ngop. The journey on the passenger ferry to Tha Dan Kao pier on Ko Chang (which most people use) takes around 45 minutes and costs B45 one way. During the peak season from Nov to Apr, boats depart hourly from 6am to 5pm; at other times of the year, departures are once every two hours. Larger car ferries depart from other points on Laem Ngop, and they accept non-vehicular passengers as well.

GETTING AROUND

With one paved road that runs almost all round the island, *songthaew*s are the only way of getting around. From Tha Dan Kao pier in Ko Chang, expect to pay B30 to Hat Sai Khao, B50 to Ao Khlong Phrao and Hat Kai Bae, B70 to Hat Tha Nam. Motorcycles (B250–300 per day) and cars (B1,000–2,000 per day) can be rented, but exercise caution as there are steep hills on both sides of the island.

RESTAURANTS

Thai & Western

Blue Lagoon
Ao Khlong Phrao. Mobile tel: 0-1940 0649. Open: daily B, L & D. $. www.kohchangcookery.com
The lagoon certainly isn't very blue, but the Thai food here is considered among the island's finest. Also serves some

decent international fare. Runs a cookery school and some bungalows too.

Hungry Elephant
Opp Sky Bar, btw Hat Sai Khao and Hat Khai Muk. Mobile tel: 0-9985 8433. Open: daily L & D. $$.
This unassuming streetside restaurant

that few tourists venture to is well known among Bangkok expats. Run by a friendly Thai couple (the husband's father was the chef at the French embassy in Bangkok), the menu has Thai staples plus some excellent French dishes.

Kai Bae Marina
Hat Kai Bae. Mobile tel: 0-7044 0385. Open: daily B, L & D. $$.
Under Austrian ownership, this restaurant has no-frills decor, but it fills up every evening. The appeal is the broad menu that includes a Thai seafood section, as well as pizzas, steaks

and dishes with a definite northern European bias. Whatever your choice, it's all good.

Kharma

Hat Kai Bae. Mobile tel: 0-6759 7529. Open: daily L & D. $$.

Run by a Swede and her Thai partner, this simple eatery and bar is located roadside along Kai Bae. It serves a diverse range of good Thai food, some of the island's only Mexican fare, plus Swedish-leaning European dishes. Start with a cocktail and a game of pool before tucking into homemade pasta with Swedish meatballs.

Salak Phet Seafood

43 Moo 2, Salak Phet. Tel: 0-3955 3099. Open: daily B, L & D. $–$$. www.kohchangsalakphet.com

Considered by many to be the best seafood place on the island, this restaurant and resort on

stilts in the southeast of the island is a part of the fishing village of the same name. Great for crabs, squid, shrimp and fish that you can choose yourself from the sunken nets below the pier.

Tonsai Restaurant

Hat Sai Khao. Mobile tel: 0-9895 7229. Open: daily L & D. $–$$.

On the opposite side of the road from the beach, the novel setting of this restaurant – a banyan tree house – is what initially attracts, but it's the delicious selection of Thai and fusion cuisine at bargain prices that keeps diners coming back for more. Very chilled out; lie back on cushions and sample cocktails from the extensive list before munching on salads and curries.

15 Palms

Hat Sai Khao. Tel: 0-3955 1095. Open: daily B, L & D. $–$$.

This British-style eatery and bar is located in the heart of Hat Sai Khao, fronting the Palm Garden Hotel. Serves Thai food, breakfasts, burgers, familiar international fare and a selection of wines and spirits. There's a pool table in the rear, and laid-back dance grooves play in the background. Wireless internet available.

International

Ban Nuna

31/2 Moo 4, Hat Sai Khao. Tel: 0-3955 1230. Open: daily B, L & D. $$.

This German- and Thai-owned restaurant and bar has a leafy terrace garden and two levels of seating, of which the upper has Thai floor cushions. Open for breakfast, the artistically-presented menu

covers a broad range, from Thai to pancakes, pizza, pasta, schnitzel, and barbecued kebabs.

Invito

Hat Sai Khao. Tel: 0-3955 1326. Open: daily L & D. $$$.

This is the island's most upmarket independent restaurant, situated in a none too ideal location beside a string of trashy beer bars. The cosy eatery serves fine Italian cuisine including homemade pasta and a wide selection of pizzas cooked in an open wood-fired oven. Portions are lean for the prices.

PRICE CATEGORIES

Price per person for a three-course meal without drinks:
$ = under US$10
$$ = US$10–$25
$$$ = US$25–$50

ACCOMMODATION

Expensive

Amari Emerald Cove Resort

88/8 Moo 4, Ao Khlong Phrao. Tel: 0-3955 2000. www.amari.com

A part of the successful Amari chain, this is one of the island's biggest and best sleeping options. The rooms are tastefully done up in a stylish contemporary Asian design. The beach-front pool is large and, thankfully, rectangle (which is more suited to

laps than free-form pools). Also on site is the excellent Sivara Spa, plus three restaurants and a lobby bar to relax in. (165 rooms)

Barali Beach Resort

77 Moo 4, Ao Khlong Phrao. Tel: 0-3955 7238. www.baraliresort.com

These contemporary Asian-style villas are representative of the recent upmarket development on Ko Chang. The cosy, private villas come with TV, stereo, hairdryer, and safe; some have beauti-

ful sunken bathtubs. The infinity pool almost touches the ocean. At the time of writing, a new lobby area was under construction. (40 rooms)

Nirvana Resort

12/4-5 Moo 1, Ban Bang Bao. Tel: 0-3955 8061. www.nirvanakohchang.com

With only a wisp of dark sand at the southern tip of the island near the village of Ban Bang Bao, this is not the best of beaches, but the resort more than compensates with fresh and seawater

swimming pools and tasteful, individually-styled rooms. The 1- and 2-bedroom bungalows are backed by jungle, with walks that lead to secluded viewpoints. (11 rooms)

Moderate

Bhumiyama Beach Resort

Hat Tha Nam. Tel: 0-3955 8067. www.bhumiyama.com

The only upmarket resort to be set up on the back-packer retreat of Lonely

Beach, this pleasant resort is built around a lovely tropical beach-front garden with ponds and a central swimming pool. Away from the main building, the better rooms occupy two-storey houses with Thai accents. (46 rooms)

Koh Chang Tropicana Resort & Spa
17/3 Moo 4, Ao Khlong Phrao.
Tel: 0-3955 7122.
www.kohchangtropicana.com
Located right next to the Barali *(see page 143)*, this resort charges much lower rates for similar facilities. In an effort to meld the resort with nature, the rooms have large picture windows which look out onto lush grounds embellished with canals, fountains and wooden bridges. There is a large circular pool by the oceanfront and a reasonably good spa beside the restaurant. (74 rooms)

Koh Chang Kacha Resort & Spa
88-9 Moo 4, Hat Sai Khao.
Tel: 0-3955 1421.
www.kohchangkacha.com
Having recently under-gone expansion on one side (which gives the resort something of a split personality), Kacha Resort is now double the size and one of Hat Sai Khao's best hotels in this price range. The new extension includes a lovely pool and spa with a main hotel building and sea-view villas, while the older section has more verdant gardens and some large split-level family bungalows located right on the beach. (80 rooms)

Mac Resort Hotel
7/3 Moo 4, Hat Sai Khao.
Tel: 0-3955 1124.
www.mac-resorthotel.com
One of Hat Sai Khao's original bungalow back-packer flops, Mac has come a long way and now represents the new face of the island. While somewhat squeezed by neighbouring develop-ments, the small resort centres round a nice pool with bungalows skirting one side and the newer (and more expen-sive) hotel rooms above the restaurant and lobby area. (24 rooms)

Sea View Resort & Spa
10/2 Moo 4, Hat Kai Bae.
Tel: 0-3955 2888.
www.seaviewkohchang.com
This steep hillside resort is located at the south-ern tip of Hat Kai Bae and doesn't have much of a beach of its own, but its views of the small offshore islets are awesome. Self-con-tained and with a variety of room types, the resort has plenty of leisure facilities to keep guests occupied, and the spa is one of the island's best. (126 rooms)

Budget

Saffron on the Sea
13/10 Moo 4, Hat Khai Muk.
Tel: 0-3955 1253.
e-mail: info@saffrononthesea.com
A small, low-key resort with a welcoming atmos-phere and nestled in a garden on the rocks just south of Hat Sai Khao. There are just seven tastefully-styled rooms with air-conditioning or fan. Said to serve the best breakfasts on the island. (7 rooms)

Treehouse Lodge
Two locations: Hat Tha Nam & Hat Yao. Mobile tel: 0-1847 8215. www.treehouse-kohchang.de
Amid the ongoing upmar-ket developments on the island, this long-running backpacker magnet on the southern headland of Hat Tha Nam is a rarity. The Thai- and German-run rustic hideaway, with its hodgepodge collec-tion of grass-roof shacks, is for the hard-ened traveller. The rooms don't have elec-tricity, and all share bath-rooms. Jutting into the sea, the eatery and bar on stilts is where most people choose to hang out. A second, more remote lodge is also found on the island's southernmost tip of Hat Yao. (40 rooms)

KO MAK

Budget

Monkey Island Resort
Mobile tel: 0-1535 9119.
www.monkeyislandkohmak.com
This funky resort with a primate theme was built by the same people who own the popular Monkey Shock restaurants in Bangkok. Located in the middle of Ao Kao bay, the accommodation consists of large 2-bedroom air-conditioned Gorilla Huts, smaller fan-cooled Chimpanzee Huts with outdoor showers, and the over-priced shared bathroom Baboon Huts. The restaurant serves mostly Thai food. In the evenings, head to the beachfront Orangutan Bar for sundowners. (29 rooms)

PRICE CATEGORIES

Price categories are for a double room without breakfast and taxes:
Expensive = US$100–200
Moderate = US$50–100
Budget = under US$50

BELOW: poolside, Amari Emerald Cove Resort.

ACTIVITIES

NIGHTLIFE

Bars

Breezes: Amari Emerald Cove Resort, 88/8 Moo 4, Ao Khlong Phrao, tel: 0-3955 2000. A lively hotel lobby bar found in the island's plushest hotel. Open round the clock, prices aren't exactly cheap but there are regular promotions and theme nights to lure punters in. Attractive and friendly bar staff.

Lek Bar: Kai Bae Beach Resort, Hat Kai Bae, tel: 0-7065 4231. Also known as Nick and Lek's bar, this popular hangout on Hat Kai Bae is run by a Brit and his Thai partner. Has a rustic island look with a garden, nightly live music, a pool table and sports programmes on TV.

Sabay Bar: 7/10 Moo 4, Hat Sai Khao, tel: 0-3955 1098; www.sabaybar.com. Whether you come here for sundowners, or later in the night to catch the live band while lying out on beach mats, Sabay is easily the busiest bar on Hai Sai Khao, possibly the entire island. There is a two-floor air-conditioned bar plus nightly fire juggling shows on the beach to keep customers entertained.

Live Music Venues

Oodies: 7/20 Hat Sai Khao, tel: 0-1835 1271. Situated by the side of the road opposite the beach on Hat Sai Khao, this openfronted music bar gets busy with a more mature set who gather here in the evenings to enjoy the live blues, folk, rock, and Thai music. The Thai and French food served here is good too.

OUTDOOR ACTIVITIES

Diving

Dolphin Divers: 38/7 Moo 4, Ao Khlong Phrao, mobile tel: 0-7028 1627; e-mail: dolphindivers@mail.com. A small and friendly company with multilingual courses. Diving is done around the main island as well as nearby islands like Ko Wai, Ko Rang, Ko Mak and Ko Kut.

Water World Diving: Ko Chang Plaza, 17/3 Moo 4, Hat Chai Chet, mobile tel: 0-6139 1117; www.waterworldkohchang.com. Professional and well-equipped outfit with a comfortable boat to get to the dive sites. Competitive prices and multilingual courses.

Catamaran Sailing

Sea Adventures: Hat Sai Khao, mobile tel: 0-4728 6387. For a unique experience, book a seat on this newly built 13-metre (40-ft) British-owned catamaran. There are day-long tours of Ko Chang and several of the outer islands. For B1,200 per person, you get an English-speaking crew, snorkel and mask, a barbecue lunch on a deserted beach, and hotel pick-up.

Trekking

Mr Anong: mobile tel: 0-6152 5271. A one-man trekking outfit. Led by the knowledgeable Mr Anong, full-day treks cost B1,200 per person.

Trekkers of Ko Chang: tel: 0-3952 5029, mobile tel: 0-1578 7513. Selling itself as an eco-friendly company, it has several full-day treks into Ko Chang's jungled interior, all led by experienced guides.

Elephant Treks

Jungleway: mobile tel: 0-9223 4795, www.jungleway.com). Offers a half-day tour where you get to see the elephants bathing and feeding at Ban Kwan Chang camp, followed by a 90-minute trek on elephant back into the forest (B900 per person). Also organises treks into the island's interior.

SPAS

Bodiwork Spa: Sea View Resort, Hat Kai Bae, tel: 0-3955 7222. Located in a Thai-style pavilion beside the ocean-view swimming pool, it offers a range of pampering and holistic treatments.

Koh Chang Tropicana Resort & Spa: 17/3 Moo 4, Ao Khlong Phrao, tel: 0-3955 1184; www.kohchangtropicana.com. The spa at this tastefully designed resort offers several traditional Thai therapies as well as facials, scrubs and aromatherapy massages.

Sivara Spa: Amari Emerald Cove Resort, Ao Khlong Phrao, tel: 0-3955 2000; www.amari.com. This is probably the island's most expensive spa, but entering its soothing confines will transport you to seventh heaven. Excellent service.

COOKING CLASSES

Ko Chang Thai Cooking School: Blue Lagoon, Ao Khlong Phrao, mobile tel: 0-1940 0649; www.kohchangcookery.com. The cookery school at this resort overlooks a lagoon and operates under the guidance of local chef Khun Ya. Full- and half-day classes available.

GULF OF THAILAND COAST

This narrow strip of land, blessed with sandy beaches, good weather, rich forests and interesting historic towns, also contains two of Thailand's famous national parks. Popular destinations in this area include historically-rich Petchaburi, beach getaways Cha-am and Hua Hin, and the celebrity-friendly Pranburi

Map on page 148

Wedged between the Gulf of Thailand and the Andaman Sea, southern Thailand geographically resembles an elephant's trunk snaking down narrowly from below the Central Plains to the tip of the Malay Peninsula. The Isthmus of Kra is the name for this land bridge connecting mainland Asia with the Malay Peninsula, which at its narrowest point in Chumphon is only 44 km (27 miles) from coast to coast.

The 600 km (373 miles) or so from Bangkok to Surat Thani province is blessed with miles and miles of sandy beaches and equable weather *(see margin tip page 152)*, plus lushly-forested interiors and historic towns that harbour plenty of attractions worth exploring. The southern rail line and Highway 4, also known at Petchkasem Highway, are the two principal links to the south, although there are also airports in Surat Thani and Hua Hin.

The upper section of the Gulf coast is home to two of the country's best-known national parks: Kaeng Krachan, also the country's largest, and Khao Sam Roi Yot. The town of Petchaburi with its ancient temples is a worthy stop before travellers continue to the beachside enclaves of Cha-am and Hua Hin, popular with Bangkokians as weekend getaways. Further south, Pranburi is growing in reputation as a high-end boutique resort hideaway. Prachuap Khiri Khan and Chumphon see few foreign tourists, except those departing from Chumphon's port for the boat ride to Ko Tao *(see page 179)*; the latter is more easily accessed from Ko Samui.

PETCHABURI

Historically rich **Petchaburi ❶** is one of Thailand's oldest towns and has been an important trade and cultural centre since the 11th century.

LEFT: Petchaburi's Wat Kamphaeng Laeng.
BELOW: making the trek up to Khao Wang.

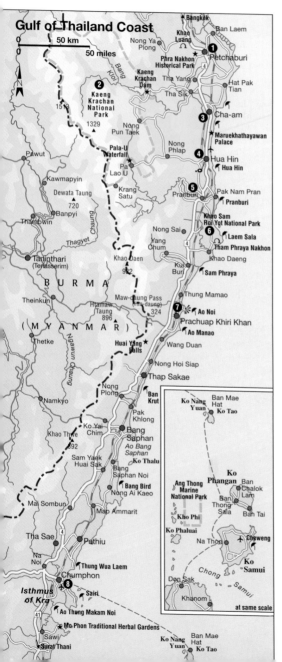

Gulf of Thailand Coast

Lying on the Petchaburi River some 120 km (75 miles) south of Bangkok, the town has come under the influence of the Mon, Khmers and Thais at various times, and has over 30 temples that reflect the differing cultures and architectural styles of its past invaders.

A pleasant place to while away a day or two, Petchaburi is easily navigable on foot. It has a laid-back provincial atmosphere with little in the way of modern conveniences.

Khao Wang

Just west of town and providing a useful geographical reference is the 92-metre (302-ft) hill called **Khao Wang** (Mount Palace). Commissioned in 1860 as the summer residence of King Mongkut (Rama IV), the entire complex is now known as **Phra Nakhon Historical Park** (daily 9am–5pm; admission charge; tel: 0-3240 1006). It is a curious melange of Thai, Chinese and Western architectural styles taking the form of shrines, temples, pagodas and other structures. Many of these offer fabulous panoramas of the vicinity, especially at sunset.

The hilltop buildings include three throne halls (two of which have been turned into a museum housing an assortment of furniture and collectables belonging to King Mongkut), a neo-classical observatory (the king was an avid astronomer), a large white *chedi* and the **Wat Maha Samanaram**. The steep cobblestone trail to the peak winds through forest and well-kept gardens populated by inquisitive monkeys. The easier option is to take the rickety cable car (daily 8am–5pm) on the Petchkasem side of the hill; its entrance is marked by a line of souvenir shops.

Other key temples

Some of Petchaburi's more important religious sites include the five laterite Khmer *prang* of the originally Hindu

Wat Kamphaeng Laeng (daily 8am–6pm; free), which possibly marks the southernmost point of the Khmer kingdom. Located on Thanon Phra Song, the temple dates from the 12th century. Although the towers have undergone some restoration work they are still dishevelled enough to look authentic.

Just around the corner on Thanon Phongsuriya is the 17th-century **Wat Yai Suwannaram** (daily 8am–6pm; free). The temple is best known for its fading murals of Hindu gods that date back to the 18th century. Its large grounds hold a lovely teak pavilion, as well as a catfish-filled pond. Jutting out into the pond is a small stilted *ho trai*, or scripture library.

Back across the river and along Thanon Damneon Kasem are the five white stucco-covered *prang* of the town's most dominant temple, **Wat Mahathat** (daily 8am–6pm; free). As with any Mahathat (Great Relic) temple, the 14th-century site has relics of the Buddha enshrined, but is probably better known for the intricate depictions of angels and other mythical creatures in the low-relief stucco on the gables of the main temple buildings.

Monkeys at Khao Wang. Avoid feeding them even if they seem tame.

Khao Luang cave

An interesting excursion only 5 km (3 miles) from town is **Khao Luang** cave (daily 8am–6pm; admission charge). Shafts of sunlight filter down from naturally-hewn holes in the cave roof, creating a splendid visual. Rays illuminate some of the hundred or more Buddha images that rest in the three main chambers of the cave, contributing to the site's spiritual aura.

Beside the entrance to the cave is **Wat Bunthawi**, a temple with wonderfully-carved wooden door panels. The hilly approach to the cave is occupied by a large group of monkeys seeking handouts from visitors. Unofficial guides wait near the approach to the cave, offering to turn on the cave lights for a fee.

Ban Puen Palace

As the railway line south brought greater access to this part of Thailand, a number of palaces were

BELOW: Buddhist ceremony at Khao Luang cave.

Suspension bridge spanning the river at Kaeng Krachan National Park.

BELOW: orchid blooms at Kaeng Krachan National Park.

erected for the royal family in times past. Situated beside the Petchaburi River, along Thanon Ratchadamneon, is the **Ban Puen Palace** (daily 8am–4pm; tel: 0-3242 5555; admission charge). The structure looks more at home in Germany's Black Forest than here in the coastal flats of Petchaburi. Built in 1910 for King Rama V (the same year he died), this stately Germanic home was modelled after the summer palace of Keiser Wilhelm, and designed by a German architect. The grandiose two-storey palace was intended as a rainy season hideaway for the king. Although little in the way of furniture remains to convey its original splendour, the porcelain-tiled dining room and inner courtyard with its pond and fountain are interesting enough to explore, as are the expansive gardens by the river bank.

KAENG KRACHAN N P

Located some 60 km (37 miles) southwest of Petchaburi town is the vast 3,000-sq km (1,158-sq mile) **Kaeng Krachan National Park ❷** (daily 6am–6pm; admission charge)

The park – the largest in Thailand – is the source of the Petchaburi and Pranburi rivers and covers almost half of Petchaburi Province. It is a haven for numerous species of large mammals, including tigers, elephants, leopards, bears, deer, gibbons and monkeys. With around 300 species of resident and migratory birds, the park is also a prime bird-watching spot. The topography varies between rainforest and savannah grasslands, and harbours both a freshwater lake and rugged mountain ranges. It is possible to ascend the park's tallest peak, the 1,207-metre (3,960-ft) **Phanoen Tung**, for superb views of the lush countryside, or trek to the 18-tier **Tho Thip Waterfall**. Swimming and boating in the vast reservoir created by the **Kaeng Krachan Dam** are other popular activities.

Considering Kaeng Krachan's close proximity to Bangkok, surprisingly few tourists venture here. Trekking is the park's main activity; guides can be hired at the park's headquarters at the end of the road beyond the dam. On the southern

edge of Kaeng Krachan, towards the mountain range that divides Thailand from Burma, is the area's spectacular **Pala-U Waterfall**. Best seen during the rainy season, the falls have 11-tiers and are surrounded by dense forest. Accommodation consists of basic park lodgings, but the easiest way to visit the park is on a tour organised by hotels in Hua Hin.

Tours to Kaeng Krachan National Park often include a stop at the **Wildlife Rescue Centre** in Kao Look Chang, where you can visit animals that have been abused in captivity and hear about the centre's uphill battle to save local wildlife (by appointment only; tel: 0-3245 8135; www.wfft.org). Around 24 km (15 miles) from Petchaburi, the centre cares and rehabilitates over 30 rescued gibbons, as well as bears, macaques and langurs.

CHA-AM

Popular as a weekend getaway with Bangkokians is the long stretch of sand at **Cha-am ❸**. Around 40 km (25 miles) south of Petchaburi (or some 178 km/111 miles from Bangkok), the beach has a different vibe compared to Hua Hin further down the coast, and is fairly quiet during the weekdays with plenty of seafood stalls and cheap restaurants along the beachfront Thanon Ruamchit to choose from. At weekends, however, the mood becomes more raucous as families and college students arrive in droves, picnicking (and boozing) under the casuarina trees and beach brollies, floating on rubber inner tubes and riding on inflatable banana boats. Small hotels are starting to spring up on either side of the main stretch, mainly frequented by foreign tourists who tend to stick to their resort turf. The sand underfoot is a bit rough and the waters are less than pristine but Cha-am does offer good value for money when it comes to hotels and food.

Maruekhathayawan Palace

Some 10 km (6 miles) south of Cha-am heading towards Hua Hin, is the seaside **Maruekhathayawan Palace** (daily 8am–4pm; tel: 0-1941 2185; admission charge). Built in 1923 from golden teakwood, the airy stilted structures were designed by an Italian architect and are European in style – supposedly based on sketches made by King Vajiravudh (Rama VI). Beautifully renovated in summery pastel shades, the three palace wings are interconnected by long raised covered walkways.

The palace served as a retreat for King Vajiravudh during the last two years before his death in 1925. After the king's death, the palace lay abandoned for decades before being restored and opened to the public. The magnificent audience chamber is the centrepiece of the palace structure, with many of the smaller fretwork-topped rooms decked out in period furnishings. Despite its proximity to Hua Hin, the lovely palace grounds sees few foreign visitors and only gets busy at weekends with local visitors.

Maruekhathayawan Palace was used as a retreat by King Vajiravudh between 1923–25.

BELOW: fun on the sand at Cha-am beach.

HUA HIN

TIP

The Gulf of Thailand coast covered in this chapter has weather similar to that of the rest of Thailand *(see page 287)* but although the rains here continue well into Nov, the effects of the monsoon are milder. The best months of the year are from Dec to Mar while Apr and May are the hottest months. The rainy months stretch from July to Nov.

BELOW:
aspects of the Hua Hin Railway Station.

Prachuap Khiri Khan is Thailand's narrowest province and its coast is fringed with mountains and lovely quiet beaches, the most popular of which is the 5-km (3-mile) long sandy beach at **Hua Hin ④**. Located 203 km (126 miles) from Bangkok and less than four hours away by road or rail, Hua Hin has long had an air of exclusivity, thanks to the private residences maintained by Thai royalty and Bangkok's wealthy elite. Partly because of this, it retains more of a Thai family ambience than other beach destinations in Thailand.

The royal connection can be seen at the seafront teak wood summer residency called **Klai Kangwon Palace**, which means "Far from Worries". Built in 1926 for King Rama VII, the Spanish-style villa is still regularly used by the royal family and is not open to the public.

One of the country's first rail lines linked Bangkok to Hua Hin at the start of the 20th century, transporting the capital's wealthy to the southern shores. Hua Hin thus had the aura of a European spa town, with the royals coming here for the clean air. Today, the coastal town is beginning to reclaim that mantle as several exclusive spa retreats – like the award-winning Chiva Som – cater to the needs of moneyed travellers. A string of large brand-name resorts, like Hilton, Hyatt and Marriott, have also opened in recent years, along with local (and equally expensive) concerns like the Dusit and Anantara.

Hua Hin sights

Today, some visitors still choose to take the train to Hua Hin, arriving at the charming **Hua Hin Railway Station**. Built in the early 1920s, the station evokes the romance of a bygone era, with the cream-and-red coloured royal waiting room, once used by King Rama VI and his entourage, still intact.

Thanon Damneon Kasem leads from the railway station directly to the beach and another historic landmark, the colonial-style **former Railway Hotel**. Constructed in 1922, the Victorian-inspired building was the country's first resort hotel before being restored to its

original wood-panelled glory as the **Sofitel Central Hua Hin Resort**. Even if you don't stay here, have afternoon tea or dine at one of its eateries and then stroll through its large manicured gardens filled with topiary creatures, including a huge elephant that you can walk through.

Beside the hotel, Thanon Damnern Kasem ends at an alley that is the main access point to Hua Hin beach. The walkway is lined with stalls proffering tourist tat, and on the beach are boys with ponies for hire for trots along the beach.

Today, the wide and sweeping run of Hua Hin beach is backed by the summer homes of Bangkok's elite, along with a slew of faceless condo developments. Some of the beach-front homes, which fuse elements of Thai and Western architecture, date back almost a century, and are owned by influential families. A few of these historic abodes have been restored and converted into unique boutique resorts, like **Baan Bayan** and **Baan Talay Dao**, while **Baan Itsara** has become one of Hua Hin's better restaurants. Hua Hin is also

fast gaining a reputation as a place to retire, and more and more condos and beach houses are being built to accommodate the upsurge.

The beach, punctuated by occasional boulders that give it a scenic beauty, lacks the character of Thailand's palm-fringed island bays, but is great for long undisturbed strolls. The beaches further south of town, **Suan Son** and **Khao Tao**, are nicer and more secluded, but again, not extraordinary. While the sea is generally calm during the low season period of May to September (with jellyfish an occasional problem), the winds can whip up the water towards the end and start of the year. This is when windsurfers and kite-surfers take to the water.

Outside Hua Hin

For a bird's eye view of Hua Hin, head up steep **Khao Hin Lek Fai** hill for some of the best panoramas of the beach. Around 3 km (2 miles) west of town, turn down Soi 70 and follow the signposts for the viewpoints (six different spots are marked around a recreational park) from which the

Map on page 148

Try to make a three or four line caption for margin picture.

BELOW: Hilton Hua Hin is one of several luxury hotels on the beach.

Giant Buddha image at Khao Takiab.

scenery can be enjoyed. Dawn and sunset are the best times to stop here.

Visible a few kilometres south of town is **Khao Takiab** (Chopstick Hill), a rocky outcrop which marks the end of Hua Hin beach. It is a steep climb to the top but the views of the surrounding coast are worth the sweat. The hill is split into two windswept peaks, the nearest is festooned with several small shrines and has a steep staircase that leads down to a towering 20-metre (66-ft) tall Buddha image. Dramatically standing just above the crashing surf, the image looks back toward Hua Hin beach with its hands outstretched.

On the other brow is **Wat Khao Lad** with its lofty pagoda atop a tall flight of stairs. A little further round the headland is a garish Chinese shrine with a large statue of the Goddess of Mercy, Kwan Im. A road splitting the two peaks leads to one of Hua Hin's most popular seafood restaurants **La Mer** *(see page 160)*.

Activities

These days, as tourism with all its associated trappings increases its grip, the image of the resort as a low-key family getaway may become a thing of the past. The town's nightlife has picked up in the last few years as more "beer bars" (but no go-go bars as yet) open with more professional girls recruited to draw in customers. It's a familiar pattern in Bangkok and Thailand's other resorts; once single male tourists descend en masse, working girls also begin their migration. However, Hua Hin still has a long way to go before it resembles the likes of Pattaya.

Along with this upsurge in nightlife, a number of new restaurants have appeared too. While Hua Hin was always known as a place for wonderfully fresh seafood, the diversity of culinary options has expanded beyond just Thai. These days, Japanese, Korean, Scandinavian, German, French and Italian eateries reflect the nationalities of the major tourist arrivals. The restaurants and bars are all clustered into a small area around Thanon Naresdamri and behind on the parallel Thanon Phunsuk. Soi Bintabaht has the highest concentration of girly bars, and the pier area along Naresdamri serves some of the best grilled seafood in town.

Hua Hin sees a lot of activities and events usually organised at weekends to cater to the Bangkok crowds. These include the annual **Hua Hin Jazz Festival** and the popular **King's Cup Elephant Polo Tournament**, usually held in September. The entertaining competition raises money for elephant preservation. Around 15 teams from around the world compete according to rules set by the World Elephant Polo Association – yes such an association exists! With three elephants per team playing on a pitch, a game comprises of two 10-minute *chukkas*, with a 15-minute interval.

Another annual event in tune with the historical legacy of the coastal

BELOW: Hua Hin Vintage Car Parade takes place in Dec.

resort is the **Hua Hin Vintage Car Parade**, which saw its third anniversary in 2005. The December rally sees over 50 classic motorcars driving up from Bangkok to the Sofitel Central resort in Hua Hin before taking a lap down the town's streets, providing for great photo opportunities. For the latest information and listings, pick up a copy of the monthly English-language magazine *Hua Hin Observer* or the *Hua Hin Today* newspaper.

Hua Hin may not boast as many golf courses as Pattaya, but what Hua Hin lacks in numbers, it makes up for in heritage. In the 1920s, the king and members of the country's aristocracy played their first game at the **Royal Hua Hin Golf Course**, Thailand's first ever golf course. Presently, there are seven courses within striking distance of the town, with more under construction.

PRANBURI

The beaches south of Hua Hin towards **Pranburi ❺** have started to see some development. Around 20 minutes drive from Hua Hin, Pak Nam Pran, the mouth of the Pranburi River, marks the beginning of a clean but fairly unremarkable beach that runs down towards Sam Roi Yot National Park. Here are found some of Thailand's most exclusive beachfront hideaways, including the magnificent **Evason** and its newer sister property, the **Evason Hideaway**, along with plush celebrity-friendly **Aleenta**. Most people who stay at these places tend to remain within the luxurious confines of their hotel, although some resorts organise tours to the mangrove-lined Pranburi River estuary and to Sam Roi Yot.

Located 63 km (39 miles) south of Hua Hin is **Khao Sam Roi Yot National Park ❻**, which translates as "Three Hundred Mountain Peaks" and refers to the dramatic landscape of limestone pinnacles jutting up from the park's mangrove swamps to heights above 600 metres (1,968 ft). Carved from the rugged coastline, the 98-sq km (38-sq ft) park (daily 6am–6pm, admission charge) features beaches, marshes and brackish lagoons, forests, caves and offshore islands. Wildlife includes a multitude of migratory birdlife that congregate on the marsh and mud flats, unusual crab-eating macaques and the rare serow – a mountain goat-antelope. At certain times of the year, pods of dolphins also swim along the park's shores.

Reached by boat or by foot along a steep half-hour trail from Hat Laem Sala, **Tham Phraya Nakhon** is the park's most famous attraction; the huge cave has a large sinkhole that allows shafts of light to enter and illuminate the grand Thai-style pavilion or *sala* called **Phra Thinang Khuha Kharuhat**. It was built in the 1890s for a visit by King Chulalongkorn (Rama V). Other noteworthy caves are **Tham Sai** and **Tham Kaeo** (Jewel Cave), the latter with glistening stalactite and rock formations. The park's best viewpoint is at the

Map on page 148

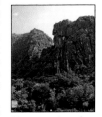
Limestone pinnacles at Khao Sam Roi Yot National Park.

BELOW: the plush Aleenta resort in Pranburi.

Map on page 148

In 1868, King Mongkut, an astute astronomer, visited Khao Sam Roi Yot National Park to view a total eclipse of the sun, which he had foretold. The king's prediction, to the astonishment of local astrologers, was only four minutes off the mark. Sadly, Mongkut contracted malaria from this trip and died a week after his return to Bangkok.

300-metre (984-ft) **Khao Daeng** outcrop at the southern end of the park.

Most Hua Hin and Pranburi hotels organise day trips to the park, but independent travellers can catch a train or bus to Pranburi, and from there take a *songthaew* to the fishing village of Bang Pu, inside the park. From here, catch a short boat ride or walk across the headland from the village to the park checkpoint on **Hat Laem Sala** beach. There is accommodation run by the Forestry Department here, but a better option is to stay at a hotel, like the **Dolphin Bay Resort** *(see page 162)*, located at **Hat Phu Noi** beach a few kilometres north of the park.

SOUTH OF PRANBURI

The coastline south of Khao Sam Roi Yot is still lined with miles and miles of sandy beaches, yet most foreign tourists make the jump directly to Chumphon *(see page 179)* for ferry connections to Ko Tao *(see page 179)*, or to Surat Thani and then by boat to either Ko Samui *(see page 166)* or Ko Phangan *(see page 172)*. While this stretch of the Gulf of Thailand coast may not be

geared towards pampering foreign visitors, you will be rewarded by a less commercial face of Thai tourism.

Prachuap Khiri Khan ❼, about 85km (53 miles) from Hua Hin, is an interesting town to explore as are the beaches of **Ao Manao**, 4 km (3 miles) south of Prachuap town, and **Ban Krut**, 70 km (43 miles) south. Both beaches have limited facilities in the way of accommodation and restaurants. Offshore from the town of **Bang Saphan Yai** further south is **Ko Thalu**, one of the first islands south of Bangkok that is good enough for snorkelling and diving.

Located 184 km (114 miles) from Prachuap Khiri Khan and considered the start of southern Thailand is **Chumphon** ❽. It has several good beaches including **Thung Wua Laem**, 12 km (7 miles) north of Chumphon town, and **Ao Thung Makam Noi**, about 25 km (16 miles) south. Some 20 km (12 miles) offshore are the reef-fringed islands of **Ko Ngam Yai** and **Ko Ngam Noi**, popular with divers, while 80 km (50 miles) away is **Ko Tao** *(see page 179)*, another diving hotspot. ❑

BELOW: the famous *sala*, or pavilion, at Tham Phraya Nakhon.

GULF OF THAILAND COAST

PETCHABURI

TRANSPORT

GETTING THERE

By Taxi

A taxi in Bangkok can be booked for the 120-km (75-mile) ride to Petchaburi. The ride will take 1½ hours and cost B1,000–1,500. Be sure to agree on the rate before boarding.

By Bus

Buses leave from Bangkok's **Southern Bus Terminal** every 30 minutes between 5am and 9pm, stopping at Petchaburi and Cha-am before heading to Hua Hin. The journey to Petchaburi takes around 1½ hours (B112).

By Train

There are 12 departures on the Southern Line from Bangkok's **Hualamphong Station** between 7.45am and 10.50pm daily. Trains take around 2 hours (depending on the service) to get to Petchaburi. Ticket prices vary, depending on the train and class of travel.

GETTING AROUND

Samlor (three-wheel motorcycles) and *songthaew* trucks are Petchaburi's principal mode of public transport. Rates for trips around town average B10–20. Motorcycle taxis are common with fares ranging from B20–30 for a short journey. If you prefer to get around on your own, motorcycles (B250 per day) and bicycles (B120) can be rented at the Rabieng Rim Nam Guesthouse (tel: 0-3242 5707).

RESTAURANTS

The eating out scene in Petchaburi is uninspiring. Most of the better restaurants are confined to the area's small hotels and there are few independent eateries.

Thai

Rabieng Rim Nam Guesthouse
1 Th. Chisa-In. Tel: 0-3242 5707. Open: daily B, L & D. $.
There are few eateries with English-language menus in Petchaburi town, so this rustic wooden restaurant that juts out over the Petchaburi River is a real find. Part of a guesthouse popular with backpackers, this simple eatery attracts a mix of foreigners as well as locals. There is a broad menu of Thai cuisine and art displays line the walls of the restaurant.

Thai & Western

Fisherman's Village
170 Moo 1, Hat Chao Samran. Tel: 0-3244 1370. Open: daily B, L & D. $$.
www.thefishermansvillage.net
A rare find for this part of Thailand, this beachfront restaurant (on nearby Hat Chao Samran) is part of a boutique resort, with dining on the breezy wooden deck or within the warmly-lit interior. As well as all the major Thai favourites, the menu also has a selection of pastas, steaks and several Western dishes. Good-value wine list.

PRICE CATEGORIES

Price per person for a three-course meal without drinks:
$ = under US$10
$$ = US$10–$25

ACCOMMODATION

Expensive

Fisherman's Village
170 Moo 1, Hat Chao Samran.
Tel: 0-3244 1370.
www.thefishermansvillage.net
Probably Petchburi's only upmarket boutique resort, this getaway on the nearby beach at Hat Chao Samran promotes the merits of its undeveloped location as an alternative to Hua Hin. Built in classic Asian style, there is also a swimming pool, spa and a good restaurant. (34 villas)

Moderate

Rabiang Rua & Village Wing Resort
80/1-5 Moo 1, Th. Anamai, Hat Chao Samran. Tel: 0-2967 1911/2. www.rabiangrua.com
Located on the beach at Hat Chao Samran, this is a popular weekend getaway for Thais. Both Boat House and Village Wing rooms available. Note: little English is spoken by the staff.

Budget

Rabieng Rim Nam Guesthouse
1 Th. Chisa-In. Tel: 0-3242 5707.
This popular backpacker haunt is centrally located beside a busy bridge over the river. Cheap but don't expect much with small box-like rooms and shared bathrooms. A good place to glean local info. Also has one of the best restaurants in town. (9 rooms)

PRICE CATEGORIES

Price categories are for a double room without breakfast and taxes:
Expensive = US$100–200
Moderate = US$50–100
Budget = under US$50

CHA-AM

TRANSPORT

GETTING THERE

By Taxi

A taxi in Bangkok can be booked for the ride to Cha-am, 178km (111 miles) away. The cost is about B1,500–2,000, and it will take about 2½ hours to get there. Resorts in Cha-am can also arrange for car or minivan transfers. Limousines can be arranged at Bangkok International Airport to Cha-am. Depending on the car used, it will cost between B2,800 and B5,000.

By Bus

Buses leave from Bangkok's **Southern Bus Terminal** every 30 minutes daily between 5am and 9pm, stopping at Petchaburi and then at Cha-am. Travel time is about 2½ hours to Cha-am; the one-way ticket price is B142.

By Train

There are 12 departures on the Southern Line from Bangkok's **Hualamphong Station** between 7.45am and 10.50pm daily. Trains take around 3 hours (depending on the service) to get to Cha-am. Ticket prices vary, depending on the train and class of travel.

GETTING AROUND

Cha-am is best suited for those with their own transport. Motorcycles, bicycles and cars can be rented from numerous resorts. Along the beach road you can take a two-seater *samlor* for around B20 while vendors also rent three-person bikes for B60 an hour. Motorcycle taxis are common with fares ranging from B20–30 for a short ride.

RESTAURANTS

The eating out scene in Cha-am is uninspiring. Most of the better restaurants are confined to the hotel and there are few independent eateries.

International

Crawford's
252/6 Th. Chad Laird.
Tel: 0-3247 1774. Open: daily B, L & D. $$.
Eclectic looking bar and restaurant tucked back on a parallel road to the Cha-am beachfront. The bar is part of the patio garden while upstairs is a dining room with a piano. The food has a Brit-Gaelic leaning, but there are also Thai dishes on the menu. Popular with expats.

Rabiang Lay
Veranda Resort & Spa,
737/12 Th. Mung Talay.
Tel: 0-3270 9000.
Open: daily L & D. $$$.
www.verandaresortandspa.com
Cha-am's most stylish beachfront eatery is a crisp white minimalist affair with design-oriented furniture and both terrace and indoor seating. It specialises in fusion seafood and has a popular bar mixing up tropical cocktails and innovative smoothies. Also has a good wine list. The restaurant is part of the Veranda resort and therefore mainly frequented by hotel guests. Best to book a table if you're not staying here.

Thai

Poom
274/1 Th. Ruamchit.
Tel: 0-3247 1036. Open: daily B, L & D. $$.
With a sea-view patio, this simple outdoor restaurant has been serving some of Cha-am's best Thai-style seafood for over a decade. It's so popular with locals that advance bookings are essential, especially on weekends.

PRICE CATEGORIES

Price per person for a three-course meal without drinks:
$$ = US$10–$25
$$$ = US$25–$50

ACCOMMODATION

Expensive

Dusit Resort & Polo Club
1349 Th. Petchkasem.
Tel: 0-3252 0009.
www.huahin.dusit.com
Located along Cha-am's main beachfront and around a 10-minute drive to Hua Hin, this is a large beachfront hotel with expansive gardens and plenty of water elements. The décor is a blend of colonial-style and traditional Thai. (300 rooms)

Veranda
737/12 Th. Mung Talay.
Tel: 0-3270 9000.
www.verandaresortandspa.com
New on the scene and making waves for its contemporary elegance and style. The large pool and pond elements are the central features of this boutique-style resort and its trendy beachfront brasserie is unique in the area. The regular rooms are slightly cramped, but the sea-view villas are very spacious. (97 rooms)

Casuarina
284 Moo 3, Hat Puk-Tien.
Tel: 0-3244 3080.
www.casuarinathailand.com
Named after the casuarinas that line much of the beach here, this is a new boutique resort with garden and beachfront villas decked out in modern minimalist design. Its avant garde style may not appeal to some but it's popular among Bangkok's style mavens. Located on Puk Tien beach to the north of Cha-am. (32 rooms)

Moderate

Casa Papaya
810/4 Th. Petchakasem.
Tel: 0-3247 0678.
www.casapapayathailand.com
A cute family-run boutique resort just south of the main Cha-am beach. Done in peachy pastel shades, it's more evocative of the Mediterranean. Rooms are either beachfront and garden-view or sea-view bungalows, all with hammocks out front. (12 rooms)

PRICE CATEGORIES

Price categories are for a double room without breakfast and taxes:
Expensive = US$100–200
Moderate = US$50–100

HUA HIN AND PRANBURI

TRANSPORT

GETTING THERE

By Air

An air shuttle service operated by **Siam GA** has four daily flights (8am, 11.30am, 3pm, 6.30pm) from Bangkok International Airport to Hua Hin Airport. The small Cessna 11-seater planes take 40-minutes and cost B5,200 return. Bookings (Bangkok: tel: 0-2535 7050, Hua Hin: tel: 0-3252 2300; www.sga.aero) must be made at least two days in advance. Most hotels will pick up guests from the airport.

By Taxi

A taxi from Bangkok to Hua Hin, 203 km (126 miles) away, will take about 3 hours. Expect to pay about B1,500–2,500 and make sure you agree on the rate beforehand. Limousines can be arranged at Bangkok International

Airport to Hua Hin for B2,800 to B5,000, depending on type of car and location of drop off. Pranburi, for instance, is 23 km (14 miles) south of Hua Hin and transfers will cost more. Resorts in Hua Hin and Pranburi can also arrange for transfers by car or minivan. Make enquiries at the time of booking.

By Bus

Buses leave from Bangkok's **Southern Bus Terminal** every 30 minutes between 5am and 9pm, making stops at Petchaburi and Cha-am first before arriving at Hua Hin. Journey time is roughly 3 hours to Hua Hin. One-way tickets cost B160.

By Train

There are 12 daily departures on the Southern Line from Bangkok's main **Hualamphong Station** between 7.45am and 10.50pm. Trains take around 3½ hours (depending on the service) to get to Hua Hin, which has a quaint colonial-style station. Ticket prices vary, depending on the train and class of travel.

GETTING AROUND

Samlor (three-wheel motorcycles) and *songthaew* trucks are Hua Hin's principal mode of public transportation. Rates for short rides around town average about B10–20 while a ride to resorts in Pranburi costs around B40–50. Motorcycle taxis are common, with fares ranging from B20–30 for a short journey.

Motorcycles and cars are available for hire from stands and shops all over town.

RESTAURANTS

International

Brasserie de Paris
3 Th. Naresdamri. Tel: 0-3253 0637. Open: daily L & D. $$$.
This European-flavoured bistro has excellent steaks and meats at reasonable prices. Spread over two floors, the upstairs looks out to sea. The staff are attentive and the Belgian owner Thierry is very personable. The set meals are a great-value option.

Great American Rib Company
8/4 Sailom Pavilion, Th. Damneon Kasem. Tel: 0-3252 1255. Open: daily L & D. $$–$$$.
www.greatrib.com
Branch of the hugely popular Bangkok original, this Hua Hin outlet in a shopping plaza has indoor and terrace seating. The specialty is the wood-smoked ribs in barbeque sauce, but equally good are the combo platters, steaks and burgers. Save room for the huge desserts.

Mamma Mia
19 Th. Damneon Kasem. Tel: 0-3253 3636. Open: daily L & D. $$$.
Run by Milan native Claudio, this authentic Italian eatery has a colourful modern look and sits beside one of Hua Hin's busiest roads. Spilt over two floors, upstairs is a pizzeria, while downstairs there are plenty of authentic Italian dishes, including handmade pastas and mouthwatering desserts, to choose from.

Japanese

Hagi
Sofitel Central Hua Hin Resort, 1 Th. Damneon Kasem. Tel: 0-3251 2021. Open: daily D only. $$$–$$$$.
If all the Thai-style seafood gets a bit much, then treat yourself at Hua Hin's swankiest Japanese restaurant. The decor is a blend of traditional and contemporary Asian design, and the cooking and sushi preparation is done right in front of diners at the teppanyaki area or the sushi counter.

Thai

Baan Itsara
7 Th. Naeb Kehardt. Tel: 0-3253 0574. Open: daily L & D. $$–$$$.
Set in one of Hua Hin's former beachside residences, this restaurant occupies a large old Thai house with indoor and al fresco dining. The menu is Thai with an obvious seafood leaning. Try the homemade ice cream or sorbet for dessert.

Chao Lay
15 Th. Naresdamri. Tel: 0-3251 3436. Open: daily L & D. $$–$$$.
This is the mother of all Hua Hin's seafood eateries and is hugely popular with local diners. Set on a jetty over the sea, the Thai-style ocean cuisine is very fresh at this no-frills restaurant.

La Mer
111/2 Khao Takiab. Tel: 0-3253 6205. Open: daily L & D. $$–$$$.
On the side of Khao Takiab hill at the southern end of the beach, this is Hua Hin's best positioned restaurant for dramatic evening views. A huge restaurant spread over several platforms, it's seafood all the way on its large menu. Not particularly glam but it's the food and view that packs them in.

Let's Sea
83/155 Soi Talay 12, Th. Takiab. Tel: 0-3253 6022. Open: daily L & D. $$–$$$.
www.letussea.com
One of the few independent dining options

along the beach, this is probably Hua Hin's most stylish restaurant and bar. Contemporary Asian in design, it's the look and mood of this place rather than the somewhat average Thai food that keeps the people coming back.

Sasi

83/159 Th. Takiab. Tel: 0-3251 2488. Open: daily D. $$.

www.sasi-restaurant.com

This garden-theatre has a wooden stage over a large pond where every evening a 2-hour show of costumed traditional dance and martial arts takes place from 7pm. The price includes a set menu of popular Thai dishes. This is a good place to sample both local culture and food.

Supatra-by-the-sea

122/63 Th. Takiab. Tel: 0-3253 6561. Open: daily L & D. $$–$$$.

www.supatrabythesea.com

Right at the end of Hua Hin beach, this lovely restaurant overlooks Khao Takiab hill. A sister of Bangkok's hugely popular Supatra River House restaurant, expect well-executed Thai dishes served on the torch-lit garden terrace or up in the main pavilion. There are two small pavilions reserved for private parties.

You Yen

29 Th. Naeb Kehardt. Tel: 0-3253 1191. Open: daily L & D. $$–$$$. www.youyen.com

Run by a local family, this beautiful old wooden Thai house on the seafront has seating in the garden next to the beach or in the house itself. The extensive menu is Thai with an obvious accent on seafood.

ACCOMMODATION

HUA HIN

Luxury

Anantara

43/1 Th. Phetchkasem. Tel: 0-3252 0250. www.anantara.com

Luxurious hideaway tucked among verdant gardens and fronting the beach. Rooms are spacious and have strong Thai accents with the more expensive ones facing the beach and lagoon. Highly-rated spa plus Italian and Thai restaurants. (187 rooms)

Chiva-Som

73/4 Th. Petchkasem. Tel: 0-3253 6536. www.chivasom.com

Chiva-Som resort harnesses the best of traditional Thai hospitality with a relaxing location beside Hua Hin beach. This multi-award winning spa resort has a superb range of spa facilities, including a unique floatation tank, Pilates room, gym, water therapy suites, indoor and outdoor pools and a tai-chi pavilion. Extensive spa treatments plus surprisingly tasty spa cuisine at its in-house restaurants. (57 rooms)

Expensive

Sofitel Central Hua Hin

1 Th. Damneon Kasem. Tel: 0-3251 2021. www.sofitel.com

Historic colonial-style hotel nestled in a tropical garden. Although in the heart of Hua Hin beach, it feels very private. As well as six swimming pools, there's a spa and fitness centre, plus several international dining options. (207 rooms)

Baan Bayan

119 Th. Petchakasem. Tel: 0-3253 3540. www.baanbayan.com

Set in a century-old beachfront residence, this place is a real gem, evoking a bygone era yet replete with all the mod cons of a boutique resort. The lovely wooden house is surrounded by a large garden. Both sea- and garden-view rooms, plus a pool and bar. Popular for weddings and private parties. (21 rooms)

Hua Hin Marriott Resort & Spa

107/1 Th. Phetchkasem. Tel: 0-3251 1881. www.marriott.com

This chain hotel has more style and ambience than its American counterparts and prides itself on impeccable service. A 5-minute drive into town, right on the beach and with four dining options, guests have little reason to leave the resort. Rooms are spacious and equipped with all modern amenities. (216 rooms)

Moderate

Baan Talay Dao

2/10 Soi Takiab. Tel: 0-3253 6024. www.baantalaydao.com

Centred round a 90-year old teakwood beach house, this resort lies on a nice stretch of Hua Hin beach towards Khao Takiab. Mainly studio rooms but there are also several nice villas and suites that are arranged around the pool and jacuzzi area. (32 rooms)

Veranda Lodge

113 Soi 67. Tel: 0-3253 3678. www.verandalodge.com

A short distance from the main drag, this elegantly furnished mid-range hotel has a small pool and restaurant that fronts the beach. The one- and two-bedroom suites come with kitchenettes, and the roof terrace Veranda Grill is a popular restaurant. (18 rooms)

Budget

City Beach Resort
16 Th. Damneon Kasem. Tel: 0-3251 2870. www.citybeach.co.th
This centrally located high-rise looks and feels dated, but is still good value for money. There's a pool and most rooms have sea views. One of Hua Hin's late night party spots, Star Planet, is located here. (162 rooms)

PRANBURI

Expensive

Aleenta
Pak Nam Pran. Tel: 0-2519 2044. www.aleenta.com
This is one of the best resorts along this stretch of coast and occasionally plays host to A-list celebrities. Private and intimate, the

Aleenta resort is all about simple and clean lines yet luxurious at the same time. Pool, restaurant, bar and spa. Romantic dinners can also be set up on the beach with advance notice. (10 suites, 3 villas plus 5 suites in the new Frangipani Wing with its own infinity pool)

Evason Hua Hin Resort & Evason Hideaway
Pak Nam Pran. Tel: 0-3263 2111. www.sixsenses.com
Evason is a contemporary retreat with 185 tastefully designed Asian-accented rooms, a large pool and two beachfront restaurants. Its Six Sense spa is set among lily ponds with an outdoor pavilion for treatments. Next door is the recently opened luxury **Evason Hideaway**, with 55 private villas (over US$400 a night), each with pool and butler service.

Purimuntra Resort
Pak Nam Pran. Tel: 0-3263 0550. www.purimuntra.com
Another new boutique resort along Pranburi's strip of increasingly stylish and expensive beach hotels. Designed with a contemporary Asian feel, choose between rooms in the main building, or beach and poolside villas. (19 rooms)

Moderate

Huaplee Lazy Beach
Pak Nam Pran. Tel: 0-3263 0555. www.huapleelazybeach.com
This small boutique-style resort has six funky maritime-accented rooms and one two-bedroom villa. It recently opened another resort (called **Brassiere Beach** – no kidding) with six villas near Sam Roi Yot National Park (6 rooms and one villa)

SAM ROI YOT N P

Budget

Dolphin Bay Resort
227 Moo 4, Hat Phu Noi, Sam Roi Yot. Tel: 0-3255 9333. www.dolphinbayresort.com
Located north of Sam Roi Yot National Park, this well-managed resort lies on a beach whose waters are a breeding ground for dolphins. The family-oriented resort has two swimming pools, and regular rooms and bungalows as well as 1–3 bedroom apartments (72 rooms)

PRICE CATEGORIES

Price categories are for a double room without breakfast and taxes:
Luxury = over US$200
Expensive = US$100–200
Moderate = US$50–100
Budget = under US$50

ACTIVITIES

NIGHTLIFE

Dance Bars & Clubs

Hua Hin Brewing Company: Hilton Hua Hin Resort & Spa, 33 Th. Naresdamri, tel: 0-3253 8999. This microbrewery at the front of the Hilton hotel is crammed with tourists and cruising bar girls every night. The house band provides the main entertainment.
Star Planet: City Beach Resort, 16 Th. Damneon Kasem, tel: 0-3251 2870. This place is more of

a Thai-oriented late nightspot. Live music by the resident band, plus the typical posse of working girls.
Stepz: Grand Hotel, 222/2 Th. Petchkasem, tel: 0-3251 1499. Another Thai-style nightspot aimed more at the Thai market. Music centres on the band that plays Thai and Western covers.

Bars & Pubs

Jungle Juice Bar & Restaurant: 19/1 Th. Selakam, tel: 0-6167 7120. Claiming to be voted the "Best Expat Bar" in Hua Hin, this friendly low-key place with a menu

of Brit-style pub grub is a regular haunt for long-term residents.
Monsoon: 62 Th. Naresdamri, tel: 0-325 1062. This charming old two-floor wooden bar sits just behind the seafront. Upstairs is a restaurant, while on the ground floor, tapas and cocktails are served in the evening.
Sasi's Bar: 83/159 Th. Takiab, tel: 0-3251 2488; www.sasi-restaurant.com. The bar sits on the ground floor of an old converted wooden house. Inside is a long bar with sofa seating, while out front there is al fresco seating around a pond.

Satchmo Club: Sofitel Central Hua Hin Resort, 1 Th. Damneon Kasem, tel: 0-3251 2021. The resident band takes centrestage at Sofitel's plush lounge bar, playing jazz and easy listening sounds throughout the night.

Kathoey Cabaret

Blue Angel: Soi Bintabaht (behind Fresh Inn Hotel), tel: 0-6892 2856. Not at all sleazy, there are two shows at 8pm and 9.45pm at this transsexual cabaret theatre. Campy and entertaining.

SHOPPING

Rashnee Thai Silk Village: 18/1 Th. Naeb Kehardt, tel: 0-3253 1155; www.thaisilkvillagehuahin.com. Set up as a workshop and village, a guided tour will show how silk is extracted from cocoons and then transformed into cloth.

Hua Hin Night Bazaar: Th. Petchkasem (corner of Soi 72). Open from early evening until around midnight, this large market is packed with souvenir stalls, tailor shops and eateries.

Satukarn Square: Th. Damnoen Kasem (corner of Soi 76). Open-air eateries and tourist-oriented stalls selling clothes and handicrafts.

OUTDOOR ACTIVITIES

Adventure Tours

Hua Hin Adventure Tour: 69/8 Th. Petchkasem, tel: 0-3235 0314; www.huahinadventuretour.com. Offers a variety of adventure tours into Kaeng Krachan and Sam Roi Yot national parks. Trips range from 1-day excursions to 3-day camping, trekking, kayaking and rock-climbing tours.

Boat Cruises & Fishing

Mermaid Cruises: 77/5 Moo 1, Pak Nam Pran, Pranburi, tel: 0-4800 7400; www.huahincruises.com. Board its teakwood pleasure boat the *Peacock* and embark on one of several trips – evening squid fishing, all-day fishing, or cruises to Monkey Island and Sam Roi Yot National Park.

Thai Boxing

Grand Sport Stadium: Th. Petchkasem (next to Grand Hotel), tel: 0-9754 7801. Usually has matches two nights a week at 9pm. The norm is five to six bouts per night, with Thai and international boxers (including women).

Go-Karting

JWS Motorsport: Soi 2 Th. Petchkasem, tel: 0-3254 7199. Karts include 13hp senior race karts, 6hp junior karts, and two-seater karts; B400 for 12-minutes of race time. Open all day. Call for hotel pick up.

Golf

Majestic Creek Country Club: 164 Moo 4 Tambon Tabtai, tel: 0-3252 0162. Opened in the early 1990s, this 18-hole par 72 course is one of the country's longest and was designed by Thailand's leading golf architect.

Royal Hua Hin Golf Club: tel: 0-3251 2475. Opened in 1924, this is Thailand's oldest golf course and is located close to town. The course follows the undulating topography and is fringed by large mature trees.

Kite-Boarding

Hua Hin Kite Centre: Soi 75/1, tel: 0-1591 4593; www.kiteboardingasia.com. Offers 1- to 3-day training in the vogue sport of kite-boarding. Hua Hin beach has a long windy season (Nov– Apr) making it perfect for both wind-surfing and kite-boarding.

SPAS

Chiva-Som: 73/4 Th. Petchkasem, tel: 0-3253 6536; www.chivasom.com. Comprehensive range of facilities and a qualified team of holistic experts, homeopaths and personal trainers who can recommend tailor-made programmes.

Mandara Spa: Anantara Resort & Spa, 43/1 Th. Phetchkasem, tel: 0-3252 0250; www.anantara.com. Housed within the tropical luxury resort, the Mandara Spa is a chain of spas in Asia with a well-deserved reputation.

The Spa: Hilton Hua Hin Resort, 33 Th. Naresdamri, tel: 0-3253 8999; www.huahin.hilton.com. Based on the four elements – fire, earth, air, water – the spa offers a wide range of specialised treatments and packages.

Six-Senses Spa: Evason Hua Hin Resort & Spa, Pak Nam Pran, tel: 0-3263 2111; www.six-senses.com. A well regarded spa with a full range of facilities and therapies.

COOKERY SCHOOL

Baan Khrai Wang: 11 Th. Naeb Kehardt, tel: 0-3253 1260/1; www.thaiculinaryschool.com. This cookery school is located in an old summer villa beside the seafront. Morning and evening classes with up to four dishes taught.

Ko Samui, Ko Phangan and Ko Tao

Ko Samui conjures images of an idyllic island paradise, but Ko Phangan is equally paradisiacal except that it's often overshadowed by wild, anything-goes, all-night Full Moon Parties. If you prefer to dive or snorkel, head to the pristine dive haven of Ko Tao

Map on page 166

Located some 80 km (50 miles) from the mainland town of Surat Thani in the southern Gulf of Thailand, palm-fringed **Ko Samui** is the biggest of 80 islands that make up the Samui Archipelago, an island chain that also includes the party island of **Ko Phangan**, the dive mecca of **Ko Tao** as well as pristine **Ang Thong Marine National Park**. With only a handful of the islands hosting any significant settlement, much of the area remains unspoiled, with perfect white sand beaches ringed by colourful coral reefs, and rugged forested interiors.

The coconut islands

For over a century, the immigrant Chinese from Hainan and Muslim fishermen on these islands derived their incomes from coconut plantations and fishing. While tourism dominates today, many of Ko Samui's poorer islanders still make their living off the coconut plantations.

Ko Samui is an hour's flight from Bangkok, 644 km (400 miles) away. The Samui Archipelago's three largest islands are firmly entrenched on the tourist map. While Ko Samui increasingly tailors itself to the higher end of the market, Ko Phangan and Ko Tao still gear themselves to backpackers, the first of whom stumbled upon these shores in the 1970s. Convenient ferry connections between the three islands make it easy to sample the unique pleasures of each while on a single holiday.

The Samui Archipelago saw a significant jump in tourists in 2005, as holiday makers scrambled to find alternative destinations away from the tsunami-hit resorts along the Andaman coast. Now that tourism has picked up along the Andaman coast, it will be interesting to see if the Samui area continues to draw the same numbers as it did post-tsunami.

LEFT: the rocks of Hat Lamai on Ko Samui.
BELOW: buses at Ko Samui airport.

Ko Samui is sometimes called the "Coconut Island", thanks to its vast coconut plantations.

KO SAMUI

When foreign backpackers first began travelling to Ko Samui in the 1970s, travellers' tales of this island paradise soon began to surface – it was only a matter of time before Samui's secret was out. The simple A-frame huts that once sheltered budget travellers can still be spotted on the island's peripheral beaches, but nowadays the most scenic bays have been taken over by minimalist-style, luxury boutique resorts that blend with the palm-lined beachfronts.

At 247 sq km (95 sq miles), Ko Samui's raw beauty is still largely intact, and its laidback vibe the reason the island attracts so many repeat visitors. Many have secured their own piece of tropical paradise by buying holiday houses or condos on the island – which are more affordable (and offer better value for money) compared to those in Phuket.

Ko Samui is also fast becoming Thailand's hottest spa destination, with a wide variety of extravagant hotel-based pampering spas as well as independent day spas and retreat centres that claim to restore both physical and spiritual health. For those who tire quickly of the soft

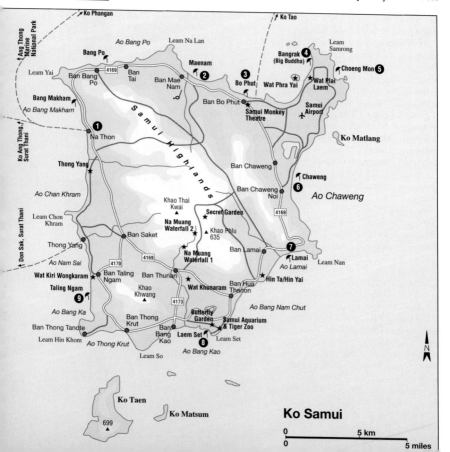

Ko Samui

0   5 km

0   5 miles

sandy beaches, the jungle treks and waterfalls of Samui's interior offer a different kind of escape.

Ko Samui still has some way to go before matching the yachting marinas and theme parks of Phuket, but having recently added an 18-hole golf course and two large supermarket chains to its list of amenities, it looks destined to follow in the same footsteps. The island's rapid rise, however, has not been without consequence. Severe water shortages are becoming a regular occurrence during the driest months, while the rainy season sometimes brings flood waters rushing down from deforested hills to many of the island's roads and beachfront properties.

For better or worse, Ko Samui is becoming increasingly cosmopolitan. Dining choices are becoming varied and upscale, with more design-conscious eateries independent of hotels opening by the month. While the nightlife scene is always busy, the island is short on atmospheric bars and clubs, with most socialising taking place in dingy "beer bars", Brit-style pubs and meat market clubs.

Some long-term repeat visitors to Samui complain that the island's idyllic charms are fraying at the edges. Aside from the obvious upsurge in construction, the behaviour and attitude of the locals have come under rap. While most of Samui's population still exude the famous southern hospitality, there are increasingly disturbing reports of opportunistic rip offs and a seemingly uncaring attitude that borders on rudeness. Road rage and assault have also been reported, along with unsympathetic and at times compliant responses by the local police. The brutal murder of a young female British backpacker at the start of 2006 has done nothing to improve the island's reputation.

Getting to Ko Samui

It is possible to fly direct to Ko Samui's airport (located in the northeastern tip of the island) from Bangkok, Phuket and Krabi. The tropical escape begins the minute you touch down at the island's international airport. With its quaint open-plan buildings and manicured

Map on page 166

TIP

The southwest monsoon brings intermittent rains to the Samui archipelago from June to Oct. From Nov to Jan, the northeast monsoon takes over, with Nov being the wettest month. Given the rather unpredictable wet weather pattern, the best time to visit the islands is from Feb to May – although there are plenty of fine days through to Sep.

BELOW: Ko Samui's palm-fringed coast.

BELOW:
Hat Maenam is in the north of Ko Samui.

gardens, this is one of Thailand's most picturesque arrival points. Many people also travel by boat from mainland Surat Thani (Ban Don pier) to the busy port town of **Na Thon ❶** on Ko Samui's northwest coast.

Na Thon, which is also the island's administrative centre, has little of interest to visitors, save for a few Chinese-influenced old wooden shophouses, souvenir shops for last minute purchases, banks, restaurants, travel agents, a few faceless hotels, and an immigration office for visa extensions.

Ko Samui's roads are generally well paved and the ring road, Route 4169, that loops the island is eminently driveable. Yet, accidents are frequent (mainly caused by intoxicated drivers) and great care should still be taken if driving your own car or riding a motorbike.

Hat Maenam

The first beach of note on the north coast is **Hat Maenam ❷**, about 13 km (8 miles) from Na Thon and 6 km (4 miles) from the airport. The 4-km (2½-mile) long stretch of beach is fairly isolated and quiet. The golden yellow sand underfoot is a little coarse and the beach is pleasant but quite narrow. Numerous budget hotels have sprung up here in addition to the deluxe-class **Santiburi**. Nights can be quiet in Maenam due to the near absence of bars and clubs; for that you have to head south to Chaweng.

Hat Bo Phut

East of Maenam is **Hat Bo Phut ❸**. While the beach is nice enough and of similar standard to Maenam, the 2-km (1-mile) long Bo Phut is better known for the quaint seafront lane of old wooden shophouses known as **Ban Bo Phut** or **Fisherman's Village**. The old timber shacks have been tastefully converted into restaurants, bars and shops, making this one of the nicest places on the island to wander around in.

Of all the islands in the gulf, Ko Samui has the most off-beach attractions, many of which can be enjoyed by the whole family. Largely set up for tourists, but also a mark of the island's coconut plantation heritage,

Map on page 166

the trained "monkey work coconut" shows at **Samui Monkey Theatre** in Bo Phut (daily 10.30am, 2pm, 4pm; admission charge; tel: 0-7724 5140) reveal how southern Thais use simian labour to assist them in harvesting coconuts from towering palms. The expert pig-tailed macaques can gather up to 500 coconuts each a day.

Hat Bangrak

Northeast of Bo Phut and part of a headland is **Hat Bangrak ❹**, better known locally as **Big Buddha Beach**, which takes its name from **Wat Phra Yai**, or Big Buddha Temple (open daily 8am–5pm; free). Standing tall across the bay on a small islet linked by a causeway at the end of the beach is the 12-metre (39-ft) high golden seated Buddha image.

At low tide, the water can retreat quite far out, exposing a swathe of mud. There is some budget accommodation set behind the beach but most of it isn't particularly nice. As the Big Buddha statue is a popular photo stop for island tours of Ko Samui, swarms of vendors hawking souvenirs frequently crowd the path leading to the entrance of the temple.

A short hike and a left turn from the temple entrance is **Wat Plai Laem**, an interesting little temple whose base takes the form of a giant lotus flower in the middle of a large fish-filled pond. Atop the pond is a giant pink statue of the multi-armed Chinese Goddess of Mercy Kwan Im.

Hat Choeng Mon

On the other side of the headland is **Hat Choeng Mon ❺**, a small but serene white sand bay backed by casuarinas trees. It has a relatively undeveloped ambience, save for a couple of upmarket resorts. There is hardly any nightlife here but then busy Chaweng beach is only a short drive away. Several of the island's premier beach resorts, like the **Imperial Boathouse**, **Tongsai Bay**,

and the all-villa **Sala Samui Resort & Spa** occupy prime positions along this scenic stretch of beach.

Hat Chaweng

The island's busiest beach by far, and arguably still the prettiest, is the 6-km (4-mile) long **Hat Chaweng ❻** on the east coast. The beach is roughly divided into three sections: North Chaweng, Central Chaweng and Chaweng Noi (south). The stunning powdery white sand beach facing clear turquoise waters follows the shore from the headland in the north near the small island of **Ko Matlang**, all the way down to the curving bay and rocky end point of Chaweng Noi.

North Chaweng beach is sheltered by a coral reef, which means that while the sea is sheltered from strong winds during the monsoon season, the waters can also be still as a mill pond at other times of the year. It is also less crowded than **Central Chaweng**, which has the highest concentration of development. Behind the rather cramped line of beach resorts, Chaweng Beach Road is a largely faceless

Temple structure at Wat Phra Yai in Ko Samui.

BELOW: giant Buddha statue at Wat Phra Yai, Hat Bangrak

Its obvious how these boulders – Grand-father Rock and Grandmother Rock – in Hat Lamai got their quirky names

sprawl of somewhat tourist-oriented shops, restaurants and bars. However, recent upmarket shopping arcades like **Iyara Plaza**, **Central Plaza** and **Living Square**, are a sign of things to come.

Past a tiny spit of land is the relatively quiet beach enclave of **Chaweng Noi**, which is thinner on accommodation and restaurants.

Hat Lamai

South of Chaweng over a rocky ridge that has stunning viewpoints back towards the Chaweng shoreline is Samui's second most populous beach, **Hat Lamai** ❼. The beach is lovely and far less hectic compared to Chaweng, with better accommodation choices for budget travellers, although there are also several boutique resorts. Lamai is also the home of the island's original wellness centres, namely **The Spa Samui** and **Tamarind Springs**.

A little beyond the beach's southern tip are two naturally hewn suggestive rock formations known as **Hin Ta** (Grandfather Rock) and **Hin Yai** (Grandmother Rock). As they resemble male and female genitalia, the rocks are the subject of much phototaking (and sniggering).

Dining at Lamai doesn't have a patch on Chaweng's breadth and quality, and unfortunately, Lamai gets a bad rap for its slightly lascivious nightlife scene, with its slew of raunchy girly bars and the sex workers who prop them up.

Inland attractions near Lamai

Taking Route 4169 inland from Hat Lamai leads to one of the temples featured on most around-the-island tours, **Wat Khunaram** (open daily 8am–5pm; free). The temple is famous as the home of mummified monk Luang Phor Daeng. His body is still seated in the same meditating position he held when he died over 20 years ago.

Continuing past the village of Ban Thurian is **Na Muang Waterfall 1**, where in the wet season, a cascade of water plunges some 20 metres (66 ft) into a large pool. Getting to **Na Muang Waterfall 2** involves a fairly strenuous 1½-km (1-mile) trek; a more novel way would

be an elephant ride offered near the entrance to Na Muang Waterfall 1.

Another of Lamai's attractions is the **Samui Aquarium & Tiger Zoo**, located within the Samui Orchid Resort in south Lamai (daily 9am–6pm; daily show at 1pm, admission charge; tel: 0-7742 4017; www.samui orchid.com). The aquarium exhibits are nothing to write home about; more entertaining is the daily bird and Bengal tiger show. Visitors also have the opportunity to become a sea lion trainer for a day with the help of professional trainers.

South and west coasts

The south and west coast beaches aren't as pretty although a few beautiful resorts have nestled along these shores. Some visitors intent on a more secluded holiday much prefer the beach at **Hat Laem Set ❽** (also sometimes referred to as **Hat Na Thian**) along the south. The charming **Laem Set Inn** with its elegant rooms is the accommodation of choice here. The road leading to Laem Set Inn will also take you to the **Butterfly Garden** (daily 8.30am–5.30pm; admission charge; tel: 0-7742 4020) where the rainbow-coloured wings of a variety of butterflies can be viewed within its net-covered compound.

Rounding the southern coast and heading to the west is **Hat Taling Ngam ❾**, the site of the spectacular **Le Royal Meridien Baan Taling Ngam**. Occupying a vantage position on a steep hill, the views of the coast here make up for the rather ordinary beach resting at the bottom of the hill.

Activities

Ko Samui's waters offer the typical gamut of watersports – jet skiing, kayaking, windsurfing, waterskiing, parasailing, deep-sea fishing and sailing. The **Ko Samui International Regatta** (www.samui regatta.com), which celebrated its fourth year in

2005, has helped establish the island as a yachting base and a few companies now charter luxury boats.

Although Ko Samui has numerous dive shops, the waters around the island are not particularly good for diving and snorkelling. Most dive trips head out to **Ang Thong Marine National Park**, **Hin Bai** and **Ko Tao** *(see below and pages 178 and 179)*.

For land-based action, hire a four-wheel drive jeep and embark on an island safari exploring the winding dirt trails that lead up into the mountainous hills. The more adventurous can rent a mountain bike and explore the interior of the island.

ANG THONG N P

Although Ko Phi Phi's Maya Bay *(see page 251)* was the chosen location setting for the film *The Beach*, it was the dramatic scenery of **Ang Thong Marine National Park** near Ko Samui that was Alex Garland's original inspiration for the best-selling novel. Lying some 31 km (19 miles) west of Ko Samui, the 42 islands that make up the Ang Thong archipelago stretch over a 100-sq km

Map on page 166

Famous mummified monk Luang Phor Daeng at Ko Samui's Wat Khunaram.

BELOW: Ko Samui's jungle-filled interior invites exploration.

Getting to Talay Nai lake on the island of Ko Mae Ko involves a 20-minute trek, but the vistas of the blue-green waters encircled by towering limestone cliffs is well worth the effort.

BELOW:
sea-canoeing among the limestone formations of Ang Thong Marine National Park.

(39-sq mile) expanse of land and sea. Virtually uninhabited by humans, the islands are home to a diversity of flora and fauna, including macaques, langurs and monitor lizards. Pods of dolphins are known to shelter in the waters late in the year.

Meaning "Golden Bowl", Ang Thong Marine National Park takes its name from the **Talay Nai** (inland sea), an emerald-green saltwater lagoon encircled by sheer limestone walls that are covered with vegetation. A principal stop on any day trip to the island chain, the picturesque lake can be reached by a trail from the beach on the island of **Ko Mae Ko**.

Several tour companies on Ko Samui operate day trips, including kayaking expeditions to the archipelago, which usually include a stop on the largest island of **Ko Wua Talab**, or Sleeping Cow Island. Aside from a beach and the park's headquarters, there is a steep climb 400 metres (1,312 ft) up to a lookout point with unrivalled views of the surroundings, with Ko Samui and Ko Phangan in the distance. Also involving an arduous climb is Ko Wua Talab's other

highlight, **Tham Bua Bok**, or Waving Lotus Cave. It is named after lotus-shaped rock formations.

Diving and snorkelling at Ang Thong Marine National Park is usually best experienced at the northern tip of the island chain around the islet of Ko Yippon. Although visibility isn't crystal clear, the shallow depths make it easy to view the colourful coral beds, inhabited by sea snakes, fusiliers and stingrays. There are also shallow caves and archways to swim through.

KO PHANGAN

The second largest island in the Samui archipelago, **Ko Phangan** is blessed with numerous seductive white sand beaches and rich forest topography, yet the island's current international reputation stems almost exclusively from the infamous Full Moon Party *(see page 176)*, which takes place at Hat Rin on the island's southern tip. With an infamy rivalling that of Ibiza and Goa, the lunar gathering has steadily grown since its first party back in the late 1980s. Nowadays, the monthly

beach party is a point of hedonistic pilgrimage for some 10,000 revellers from all over the world.

Lying around 20 km (12 miles) north of Ko Samui, or a 40-minute boat journey, Ko Phangan became a an outpost on the shoestring traveller's map in the 1980s, around the same time as Ko Samui. But while the latter rapidly developed into a hub for package holiday-makers and flashy beach homes for the wealthy, Ko Phangan has largely remained an enclave of backpackers, drug-craving revellers and new age nirvana seekers. However, pockets of the 193-sq km (75-sq mile) island are becoming built up, particularly Hat Rin and its vicinity, which now looks and feels like a separate resort when compared to the rest of the island.

While most revellers confine themselves to the southern cape beaches of Hat Rin Nok (Sunrise Beach) Hat Rin Nai (Sunset Beach), and nearby Leela Beach, there are plenty of other more isolated bays that skirt the mountainous interior, attracting travellers who are still searching for the mythical oasis that Alex Garland wrote about in *The Beach*. Increasingly better roads have made the furthest reaches of the island more accessible, but even so, a couple of coves such as Hat Kuat (Bottle Beach), can be reached ony by boat.

Located around halfway up the west coast, the island's administrative centre and main arrival point is the small town of **Thong Sala ❶**. Apart from fishing boats unloading their daily haul, the port is usually busy with ferries, catamarans and speed boats travelling to and from Ko Samui, Ko Tao and Surat Thani. Accommodation touts pounce on new arrivals as soon as they set foot on the pier, which can be helpful if no reservations have been made and it is close to the full moon. The town has all the usual tourist-friendly services – internet cafés, banks, shops, and a few restaurants and bars. Aimed more at locals, there is also a morning and night market and two Thai boxing stadiums.

Ban Khai and Ban Tai

East of Thong Sala, the south coast is endowed with a continuous stretch of beach running all the way up to the Hat Rin cape, though the shallow reefs make the water often impossible to swim in. The most popular beaches here are between the villages of **Ban Tai ❷** and **Ban Khai ❸**; the former is a small fishing village with boats clogging up part of the seafront. Both basic and more comfortable family-run bungalow accommodation are found along the length to Thong Sala, with Ban Khai, the closest to Hat Rin, the only spot with any night activity.

Hat Rin

East of Ban Khai is where all the beach action is. Certainly not Ko Phangan's most serene beaches anymore, the original appeal of **Hat Rin** was that it had two beaches within

There are no official tourism offices in Ko Phangan. Your best source for information is the website managed by the Phangan Batik shop in Thong Sala: www.kohphangan.com. The site has a wealth of information and useful tips on what to do on the island. Phangan Batik also operates a tour agency and an internet cafe on its premises.

BELOW: verdant Ko Phangan from the air.

easy walking distance – across a flat headland – where both sunrise and sunset views could be enjoyed.

Hat Rin Nok , or Sunrise Beach, is the wider, more popular bay, and is where the main nightlife cranks up, climaxed by the monthly Full Moon party. Hat Rin attracts a global melting pot of young clubbers and alternative lifestyle devotees, who find this tiny pocket of Thailand the perfect place to express their inner selves (fuelled, of course, by booze and drugs). This is the lure for many, though more jaded travellers will regard the scene as one big cliché.

The less attractive of the two beaches is **Hat Rin Nai** ❺, or Sunset Beach, a thinner stretch of sand lined with beach huts that offer respite from the late-night cacophony over at Hat Rin Nok. There is a pier towards the southern end of this beach for boats shuttling to Ko Samui. The walk between the two beaches is jam-packed with accom-

modations, shops, restaurants, internet cafés, travel agents and the like.

Further towards the island's southern tip is pretty **Leela** beach. It is around a 15-minute walk to Hat Rin Nai, and has a more peaceful atmosphere, removed from the main Hat Rin mayhem.

East coast beaches

There are several small but fine bays that run north up the east coast from Hat Rin, but a lack of roads make boat transportation (from Hat Rin) the only way to venture there. Development is therefore patchy along this coast. **Hat Yuan** ❻ and **Hat Yao** (not to be confused with the longer Hat Yao on the west coast), and particularly **Hat Thian** ❼, are popular with travellers who seek isolated and undisturbed beaches.

At the top of the east coast are the increasingly popular twin bays of **Ao Thong Nai Pan Noi** ❽ and **Ao Thong Nai Pan Yai** ❾, described

Lots of vendors offer cheap massages by the beach at Hat Rin Nok and Hat Rin Nai.

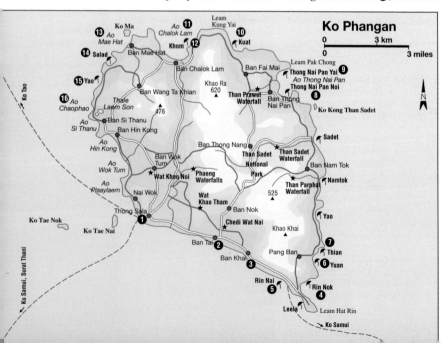

by many as the island's most beautiful coves. There is a good choice of cheap accommodation at both bays, separated by a headland that can be traversed in about 20 minutes. Getting to these beaches is a nightmare though as the 12-km (8-mile) road, actually a dirt track, from Ban Tai in the south is riddled with potholes.

North coast beaches

The north coast has two bays that are worth seeking out. The first is **Hat Kuat** ⑩, or Bottle Beach. There is a decent road from Thong Sala up to Ao Chalok Lam *(see below)*, from where you can take a boat to Bottle Beach. It is one of Ko Phangan's best bays and with its own insular scene that attracts lots of repeat visitors. The splendid white sand beach is backed by steep hills and, like elsewhere in Ko Phangan, most accommodation is at the budget end.

The second bay to the west, **Ao Chalok Lam** ⑪, holds a large fishing village. Ban Chalok Lam is the island's second port, with a pier in the centre of the large curving bay that is usually busy with fishermen

who supply the seafood restaurants here with the freshest catch. The small white sand cove of **Hat Khom** ⑫ along this stretch and closer to the headland east is the best bit of beach here, ringed by a coral reef offshore. The 10-km (6-mile) road from Thong Sala in the south to Ao Chalok Lam is decent, in fact one of the island's best roads, so getting there is not a problem.

West coast beaches

The west coast beaches stretching from Ao Mae Hat all the way to Thong Sala in the south are considered more attractive than those along the southeast shores, but somehow they see fewer visitors compared to the Hat Rin area.

Starting from the northwest corner is **Ao Mae Hat** ⑬, which has a sand bank at low tide that connects to the reef-fringed tiny island of **Ko Ma** (Horse Island). The reef that runs up the coast from Ao Chaophao *(see page 177)* all the way to Ko Ma is considered by some to be the island's best snorkelling and diving site.

Further down the coast is scenic

Map on page 174

TIP

The advantage of staying on any of the west coast beaches are fewer crowds and beautiful sunset views with the islands of the Ang Thong Marine National Park framed against the horizon.

BELOW: longtail boat at Ao Thong Nai Pan Noi.

Full Moon Fallout

An essential stop on any backpacker's tour of Southeast Asia, the Full Moon Party is dubbed the "world's biggest beach party", and despite the Thai government's intermittent calls for the event to be scrapped, this Ko Phangan cash cow is too vital to pull the plugs on. The party takes place on Hat Rin Nok, or Sunrise Beach, with the focal point of the all-night rave at the southern end of the beach in front of Paradise Resort.

The event itself builds in momentum from sunset to sunrise, with Paradise Resort regarded as the main hub of this no-holds barred party. This is where the party circuit's most popular DJs spin their tunes, although there are DJs vying for attention at the main bars all the way along the beach. As each bar leans towards a different groove, the dance hotspots shift periodically, depending on who is spinning what, where and when.

The Full Moon Party (or F-M as people in the know refer to it) draws thousands of global partiers throughout the year, though the peak season of December and January sees the wildest bounce fests. Guesthouses fill up as the full moon approaches, with some only taking bookings for a minimum of

four or five nights. Those craving beauty sleep should choose accommodation well away from Hat Rin Nok as the party scene can be loud on most nights, cranking up to ear drum-bursting on full moon.

For those who desire distance from the monthly mayhem, transport from other beaches to the party is plentiful. And if you prefer to nurse a post-party hangover within the confines of a luxury hotel in Ko Samui, numerous boats do make the night time crossing between the two islands.

Generally, people spend the night getting wasted on cheap booze concoctions, being painted up in fluorescent ink, then alternate between dancing and passing out on the beach. Aside from all the music, dance, booze and fleeting romances (mostly of the one-night stand variety), a lot of party-goers are there to sample what first gave F-M its notoriety – partaking of illicit substances. However, today's F-M is no longer an open display of magic mushroom omelettes and teas, Speed and Ecstasy punches, and ganja cookies. Drug taking is still prevalent, but with plain-clothed and uniformed police on patrol, any purveying or indulging is done with discretion. Penalties for possession of or being under the influence of illegal drugs are extremely harsh in Thailand.

The party is a bane for international embassies in Bangkok as every month, at least one excessive party-goer loses the plot after ingesting some psychotropic cocktail, with officials left to unravel the person's fractured mind before shipping him or her back home. Party-goers should be extremely vigilant as to what they are ingesting or smoking; the local methamphetamine *yaa baa* (crazy drug) is one of the most common yet most addictive drugs around.

Sunrise is met with triumphant cheers, and the chance to raise the tempo once more for anyone who might be thinking about collapsing into bed. The beach party winds up late morning but for those who still have their brain cells and eardrums intact, the traditional after party kicks off at Backyard Bar up the hill. For more info and current F-M dates, check out www.fullmoon-party.com. ❑

LEFT: Hat Rin with Full Moon party animals.

Hat Salad , with good snorkelling just off the northern edge of the beach. Next is an attractive 1-km (½-mile) long sandy stretch called **Hat Yao**, or Long Beach. It has become very popular in recent years and is giving Hat Rin a run for its money with its range of accommodation, bars, restaurants and other facilities. Further south is a nice small bay called **Ao Chaophao**, which has a decent range of facilities. The inland **Laem Son Lake** demarcates Ao Chaophao from the next beach, **Ao Si Thanu**. Further down the coast are three more beaches of note: **Ao Hin Kong** and **Ao Wok Tum**, both of which are divided by a small stream that empties into the sea, followed by **Ao Plaaylaem**.

Inland attractions

The beach at Ao Thong Nai Pan Yai was a favourite stop-off for King Chulalongkorn who made numerous visits to Ko Phangan between 1888 and 1909, when just a few hundred Thai and Chinese islanders eked a living from coconuts, fishing and mining tin. Another of the king's

haunts was **Than Sadet Waterfall**, which flows out to **Hat Sadet** beach in the next cove down the east coast from Ao Thong Nai Pan Yai, or some 12 km (7 miles) up from Hat Rin. The island's largest falls, Than Sadet, meaning Royal Stream, has boulders carved with inscriptions by King Chulalongkorn, King Rama VII and the present monarch Rama IX.

The island's other cascades are **Than Praphat Waterfall** on the way to the east coast beach of Hat Nam-tok, **Than Prawet Waterfall** located near Ao Thong Nai Pan Noi, and **Phaeng Waterfall** halfway across the island on route from Thong Sala to Ban Chalok Lam village. All these falls come under the umbrella of **Than Sadet National Park**, a 65-sq km (25-sq mile) reserve that aims to protect the biodiversity of Ko Phangan's forested interior as well as the small outlying islands that are within the park's boundaries.

If the soul also needs centring, then the cave monastery at **Wat Khao Tham**, at the top of a hill near the village of Ban Tai, holds 10-day meditation retreats taught by an

Map on page 174

Wat Khao Tham is popular as a meditation retreat.

BELOW: Ao Mae Hat on the northwest tip of Ko Phangan is connected to the tiny isle of Ko Ma.

Australian-American couple. The retreat is silent and places emphasis on the key principle of compassionate understanding. Early registration is advised as places for the retreat fill quickly. The cost is B4,000; for more information and registration check **www.watkowtahm.org**.

Diving and snorkelling

As with Ko Samui, the majority of Ko Phangan's diving is conducted at a handful of dive sites some distance from the island at **Ang Thong Marine National Park** *(see page 171)*, **Hin Bai** (Sail Rock) and around **Ko Tao** *(see page 179)*. Snorkelling and diving closest to Ko Phangan is best experienced along the reefs on the northwest tip of the island, around **Ko Ma**, **Ao Mae Ha**t and **Hat Yao**. Ko Ma is Ko Phangan's best dive site with fairly shallow depths of up to 20 metres (66 ft) and various types of coral, including a multi-coloured anemone garden. The area is frequented by blue-spotted stingrays, giant grouper and reef sharks.

Located about halfway between Ko Phangan and Ko Tao, **Hin Bai** is regarded as one of the best dive sites in the Samui archipelago and is suitable for all levels of divers. The rugged rock emerges like an iceberg from the water; most of its bulk is hidden below the surface reaching depths of up to 30-plus metres (98-ft). The granite pinnacle is circled by large schools of pelagic fish, but the highlight is a dramatic vertical chimney that can be entered at 19 metres (62 ft) below, with an exit at 6 metres (20 ft) from the surface.

Nightlife and entertainment

Apart from the notorious full moon parties, Ko Phangan has plenty of other regular weekly and monthly party nights to keep extreme party animals bouncing until that ultimate night arrives again. Those who like canned commercial dance music will have to make do with a mix of trance, techno and drum 'n' bass – the music of choice at the island's main nightspots. The so-called **Half Moon** parties shape up twice a month, a week before and after full moon, held at a hypnotically-lit outdoor venue in Ban Tai. The lovely

Hin Bai, or Sail Rock, is a popular diving spot in the Gulf of Thailand and easily accessed from Ko Tao or Ko Phangan.

BELOW: diving among the coral reefs off Hin Bai (Sail Rock).

waterfall setting for the pre-full moon **Paradise Party** attracts a large party contingent to the waterfalls that are found off the road to Ban Chalok Lam.

Famous for its post-full moon all-day recovery session, the funky two-floor **Backyard Bar** up the hill behind Hat Rin Nok on the way to Leela beach also holds regular party nights, with differing musical slants. Hat Rin's bars tend to be ephemeral but mainstays include **Pirate's Bar**, along with **Cactus Club** and **Drop-In Club**. For more information on the island's entertainment scene, pick up a copy of *Phangan Info* (www.phangan.info) or see page 191 for nightlife listings.

KO TAO

Located around 40 km (25 miles) northwest of Ko Phangan and 60 km (37 miles) from Ko Samui, **Ko Tao**, or Turtle Island, is the northernmost inhabited island in the Samui archipelago. The remote and tiny 21-sq km (8-sq mile) island is said to draw its name from its rather loose geographical shape of a diving turtle; others have attributed its name to the once-prevalent number of turtles that swam in these waters. Today, the laid-back island might just as well be called "aqua lung" island for the density of affordable dive schools that operate diving expeditions to its coral-abundant waters, making this one of the world's best places to learn how to dive.

A few years ago, Ko Tao had little appeal for non-divers, and if you had no intention of submerging into its briny depths, listening to the endless evenings of divers' tales in the bars and restaurants could quickly become tiring. Less than a decade ago, the island consisted solely of rustic back-packer bungalows. More recent development however has seen better accommodation options and entertainment venues, with plenty more activities to occupy landlubbers. And the bonus of having a large percentage of visitors studying in dive schools or out on dive trips is that the island's beaches are relatively peaceful and relaxing during the day.

Due to its remoteness, Ko Tao was seldom visited and there are few historical elements for visitors to peruse, save for the initials of King Rama V (Chulalongkorn) carved into a large boulder at the southern end of Hat Sai Ree beach. The king visited the island in 1899, and the spot has become a place where locals pay their respects. In the 1930s and 40s, the island was used as a political prison, but since the 1980s, Ko Tao has been welcoming increasing numbers of overseas visitors.

West coast beaches

Ko Tao is accessed by ferries and speed boats from the mainland port of Chumphon *(see page 156)*, some 80 km (50 miles) to the east; or from Ko Samui, Ko Phangan or Surat Thani to the south.

Ko Tao is a rugged rock, topped with tropical forest and fringed with

Map on page 180

TIP

Koh Tao is too tiny and undeveloped to have a tourism office. Your best bet for information and tips on the island are the following websites:
www.kohtao.com
www.on-koh-tao.com.

BELOW: a flame-thrower performing at Ko Phangan's Full Moon Party.

some picturesque secluded bays. The island's main arrival point is the small but lively village of **Ban Mae Hat ❶** on the west coast. It is little more than a one-street village lined with a post office, banks, shops, cafés, bars and other tourist-related infrastructure.

North of the village is the small, shallow bay of **Ao Hat Mae**. There is some accommodation here but it may be too close for comfort to the village for some. Much nicer is the 2-km (1-mile) long **Hat Sai Ree ❷**, the island's longest and most popular curve of white sand. Sai Ree is lined with hotels to suit most budgets, getting gradually quieter further north with the ever-growing **Ban Hat Sai Ree** village backing the beach just over the halfway mark. Beyond Sai Ree, the road makes an incline up towards the northern tip of the island, with several more out-of-the-way cliff-top resorts, including attractive **Thipwimarn**, whose restaurant offers stunning sunset views.

South coast beaches

Ko Tao's southern shores have quite a few small but pretty beaches that are found in either direction from the island's second busiest beach of **Ao Chalok Ban Kao ❸**, a well protected bay that is literally jammed with resorts, dive shops, eateries and bars. The large headland at the east end of Ao Chalok Ban Kao has a fantastic viewpoint atop the **John Suwan Rock**, with vistas in either direction. To the east of the promontory is the long yet quiet **Ao Thian Ok ❹**, and further still is **Hat Sai Daeng**.

Within walking distance to the west of Ao Chalok Ban Kao are several small and scenic bays located around **Ao Jun Jeua**, **Hat Sai Nuan** and **Ao Jansom**. Unfortunately, the monsoon season from June to October bring high winds and heavy seas, causing disruptions to ferry schedules and a lot of flotsam to be washed up on these beaches.

Dive shops are aplenty on Ko Tao but as most offer more or less the same services, it's best to shop around and ask people for recommendations.

BELOW: taking the plunge at Ko Tao.

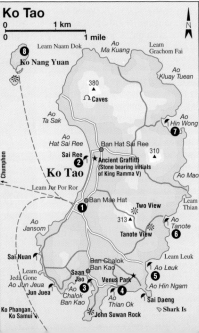

East coast beaches

The east coast of the island has several isolated inlets with scant sleeping options, and although none have outstanding beaches, there is plenty of good snorkelling and diving to be experienced. The dirt trails to the eastern shores can be treacherous (the only other way is by boat) and once you are there, it can be awkward and expensive to venture back west. Most resorts along this coast offer basic facilities, with some generating electricity only between sunset and sunrise. Heading north from Hat Sai Daeng, the bays include lovely **Ao Leuk** ❺, the scenic horseshoe-shaped **Ao Tanote** ❻, the tiny cape of **Laem Thian**, and eventually remote **Ao Hin Wong** ❼.

North coast

A short boat ride off the island's northern tip is the picture-perfect **Ko Nang Yuan** ❽, a gathering of three small islets joined together by mere wisps of sand that can be walked across at low tide. The setting is incredible, both above and below sea level, so much so that dive trips and boat tours from around the island, as well as Ko Samui and Ko Phangan, all converge here, somewhat spoiling the idyll. With simple bungalows spread across the three outcrops, only the **Nangyuan Island Dive Resort** (tel: 0-7754 6088; www.nangyuan. com) has the rights to operate here, with outside visitors charged B100 just to step foot on the island.

Diving and snorkelling

As a premier dive destination, Ko Tao's reputation has diminished slightly in the last decade, mainly due to the hefty increase in the number of divers; at the more popular sites the undersea human traffic can be annoying. Even so, visibility in the warm water is usually very clear – sometimes over 30 metres (98 ft) – and there are a variety of dive sites to choose from. While sightings of giant groupers and turtles are not uncommon, and territorial disputes with triggerfish best avoided, an encounter with an underwater giant such as a whale shark or a manta ray is still a special event.

Unlike the lengthy journey times

Map
on page
180

BELOW:
Stunning Ko Nang
Yuan is a must-see.

Map on page 180

A man and his canoe at Ko Nang Yuan.

BELOW: taking a break at Ko Tao.

to dive sites from Ko Samui and Ko Phangan, Ko Tao is fortunate to have more than 25 chartered dive sites close by that can be reached in less than 30 minutes. The close proximity and favourable conditions (outside the Nov-Dec monsoon), make the island's waters an ideal place to learn how to dive.

Some of the best dive sites are found off Ko Nang Yuan, including the granite boulder and swim-throughs of **Nang Yuan Pinnacle**, the pair of coral-coated rock formations known as the **Twins**, and **Green Rock** with its tunnels and swim-throughs. About 5 km (3 miles) northwest of Ko Tao, the **Chumphon Pinnacle** is a very popular site with depths of up to 38 metres (125 ft) and regular sightings of large groupers and other sizeable fish. In the opposite direction, the **Southwest Pinnacle**, some 7 km (4 miles) from Ko Tao, is rated as one of the best soft-coral reefs in the Gulf of Thailand with currents that attract large schools of pelagic fish. Other frequently visited sites are **White Rock**, **Hin Wong Pinnacle** and **Shark Island**.

With nearly 50 dive schools and competitive dive packages that include accommodation, a few resorts refuse to take in non-divers during the peak season. Advance reservations are advised. The majority of schools offer PADI open-water certification with rates averaging from B6,000 to B9,000. Qualified divers can expect to pay B800 for fun dives, which are discounted if you bring your own equipment.

Activities

Ko Tao's compact size makes the island an ideal place for walking, with the reward of panoramic hill top views or a hidden pristine cove at the end of your journey. If hiking the rugged coast is too strenuous, day-long boat trips around the island can be chartered independently with longtail boat operators at beaches and piers, or through your guesthouse. A round-island tour will cost around B1,000 for the boat, but operators may ask for more depending on how many people are aboard.

Watersports like kayaking, wakeboarding and waterskiing can be done on Ao Tanote or Hat Sai Ree.

Entertainment

Some of the healthy diving camaraderie on Ko Tao spills over into its lively nightlife scene. The island is also an escape for Ko Phangan visitors who seek a reprieve from that island's party town atmosphere. There are regular party nights with guest DJs (fliers and posters notify fresh-faced arrivals of the latest place to shake their booty). As the island develops, the nightlife on offer is moving from basic beach bars blaring loud trance and techno to the dreaded fire-jugglers and cheap Thai whiskey scene of Ko Phangan. Fortunately, cooler lounge bars like **Papa's Tapas** (*see page 192*) serving absinthe and fat Cuban cigars offer a welcome diversion. ❑

K O SAMUI, KO PHANGAN AND KO TAO

K O   S A M U I

TRANSPORT

GETTING THERE

By Air

Bangkok Airways is the only airline that flies to Ko Samui. Thanks to its virtual monopoly, prices are grossly inflated. From Bangkok, there are 15 daily flights (flight time: 80 minutes) to Ko Samui. Bangkok Airways also connects Ko Samui with Phuket and U-Tapao (Pattaya), and there are impending plans to fly to Trat (Ko Chang).

Bangkok Airways also flies from Ko Samui direct to Singapore and Hong Kong. For these international flights, a B300 airport departure tax applies.

If you haven't made arrangements with your hotel for an airport pick-up, you can take a taxi. The driver will quote B400 for a ride to Chaweng but B200 is more realistic. Private minivans also take passengers to the different beaches, though they usually wait until the van is full before leaving. Typical minivan fares are B70 to Bo Phut, B100 to Chaweng and Maenam, and B120 to Nathon and Lamai.

By Bus

Private tour companies along Bangkok's Thanon Khao San run bus services from there to Surat Thani (the jump-off point for Ko Samui). The ride takes about 10 to 11 hours and costs B450 to B650, depending on type of bus and whether the ferry ticket to Ko Samui is included. Air-conditioned buses leave daily from Bangkok's **Southern Bus Terminal** as well from 9.30am to 11pm. The cost and duration are about the same as that of private companies.

Much quicker is the **Lomprayah** (tel: 0-2629 2569) VIP bus (www.lomprayah.com) from Bangkok (departs 6am or 9pm) or Hua Hin (departs 9.30am or 12.30am) to Chumphon, which connects with the Lomprayah catamaran (departs 1.20pm or 7am) to Ko Samui (via Ko Tao and Ko Phangan). The trip takes about 10½ hours during the day or just over 15 hours overnight. A one-way ticket costs B1,000 to B1,400.

By Train

There are nearly a dozen daily train departures to Surat Thani from Bangkok's **Hualamphong Station** from 7.45am to 10.50pm. The journey takes around 9 to 12 hours (depending on the train service). The station is in Phunpin, 13 km (8 miles) from Surat Thani Town.

By Boat

If you don't fly direct to Ko Samui, all land transport will deposit you at Surat Thani. Here, several companies operate passenger and car ferries to Ko Samui from Don Sak, Ban Don and Pak Nam Tapi piers. Boats leave approximately every 1 to 2 hours from 5am to 7pm and take around 1½ to 2½ hours (depending on the boat). There is also a slow 6½-hour night ferry from Ban Don pier. Depending on the operator, tickets cost B80 to B200. Most ferries arrive at Ko Samui's main pier at Na Thon, which is around 40 minutes by songthaew to Chaweng beach. Some ferries carry on to Ko Phangan from Na Thon pier.

GETTING AROUND

Songthaew trucks are the island's principal mode of public transport. Drivers always try to overcharge so make sure you hand over the correct fare. A journey down the length of Chaweng beach is B20, from Na Thon to Chaweng B50, with no journey costing more than B50. Late at night they operate more like taxis and the fare should be agreed on beforehand.

Metered taxis are becoming prevalent on the island but drivers rarely turn on the meter, preferring to quote extortionate rates for relatively short distances.

Motorcycle taxis are cheaper, with fares ranging from B20 to B30 for a short journey, and B150

to B200 for a longer ride from, say, Chaweng to Na Thon.

A variety of motorcycles, from mopeds to choppers (B200–500), as well as jeeps (B800–2,000), can be hired at all the main beaches. Motorcycle accidents are frequent so wear a helmet.

RESTAURANTS

HAT CHAWENG

Thai & Western

Budsaba
Muang Kulaypan Hotel, 100 Moo 2, Hat Chaweng. Tel: 0-7723 0849/51. Open: daily B, L & D. $$. www.kulaypan.com
This lovely Thai restaurant sits on the beach at the front of the stylish Muang Kulaypan hotel. Nestle under intimate, rustic grass-roof pavilions with floor cushions and order classic Thai dishes while being entertained by live classical Thai music and dance performances.

Chez Andy
Central Chaweng. Tel: 0-7742 2593. Open: daily D. $$–$$$. www.chez-andy.com
It won't win any awards for decor and ambience, but with staff eager to please and some of the best steaks on Samui, this Swiss-owned steakhouse and grill is a magnet for meat-lovers. The menu has European and Thai favourites, and imported Angus and Kobe beef. A cheaper alternative is the all-you-can-eat

international buffet. Kids under 10 eat free.

Montien House
Hat Chaweng. Tel: 0-7742 2169. Open: daily B, L & D. $$. www.montienhouse.com
This is one of the better beach set-ups along the central stretch of Chaweng in the evening. The Thai food at this hotel restaurant is familiar and good, though the Western dishes are quite forgettable. The moon-lit beach atmosphere is the main attraction.

Poppies
South Chaweng. Tel: 0-7742 2419. Open: daily 6.30am–midnight. $$$. www.poppiessamui.com
A decade old, this enduring beachfront restaurant has long been an island favourite. Sit under the stars beside the boutique resort's pool or in the authentic Ayutthaya-style teak pavilion as you dine on well-presented and refined Thai and international dishes.

Rice
91/1 Moo 2, Hat Chaweng. Tel: 0-7723 1934. Open: daily L & D. $$$. www.ricesamui.com
Smack in the heart of Chaweng's evening

entertainment scene, this new fine-dining place is hoping to raise the bar on the island's cuisine credentials. With a contemporary Asian look, the split-level Mediterranean, international and Thai restaurant has a large lily pond in front and a glass elevator to carry diners up to the third level where a more exclusive gourmet experience awaits at the rooftop Rice & Stars.

International

Betelnut
43/04 Moo 3, Soi Colibri, Hat Chaweng. Tel: 0-7741 3370. Open: daily D only. $$$–$$$$. www.betelnutsamui.com
The tiny street may look unassuming, but it has several of the island's best dining options, including the excellent Betelnut. Owned by American Jeffrey Lord, the restaurant's design is simple but tasteful, leaving the focus on the small but innovative selection of Californian-meets-Thai fusion fare.

Coco Blues Company
161/9 Moo 2, Hat Chaweng. Tel: 0-7741 4354. Open: daily

B, L & D. $$–$$$.
www.cocobluescompany.com
This is one of Chaweng's liveliest entertainment and dining spots and sees a steady flow of patrons. In the evenings, the island's best live bands entertain here, but just as appealing is the New Orleans-style menu of Cajun and Creole dishes.

The Cliff
Between Hat Chaweng and Hat Lamai. Tel: 0-7741 4266. Open: daily L & D. $$$. www.thecliffsamui.com
An airy and modern clifftop restaurant set between the island's two busiest beaches. The view from this vantage point is its main appeal, but the Mediterranean fare is also very good. The menu includes dishes cooked in zesty *piri piri* sauce, pastas, steaks and burgers.

PRICE CATEGORIES

Price per person for a three-course meal without drinks:
$ = under US$10
$$ = US$10–$25
$$$ = US$25–$50
$$$$ = over US$50

The Islander

Central Chaweng. Tel: 0-7723 0836. Open: daily B, L & D. $$.
Always busy, this two-storey restaurant and bar is on the central stretch of Chaweng Beach Road. Several TVs screen sports, while the menu has an extensive range of international favourites. Look out for the daily specials on the board.

Prego

North Chaweng. Tel: 0-7742 2015. Open: daily L & D. $$–$$$.
Situated on the quieter north end of Chaweng, opposite the Amari hotel, this stylish Italian restaurant is open and airy, with soothing water elements that add to the mood. The menu, which includes wood-fired oven pizza and fresh seafood, is reasonably priced given the quality of the food and ambience.

Red Snapper Bar & Grill

Chaweng Regent Hotel. Tel: 0-7742 2389. Open: daily D. $$$. www.chawengregent.com
Located within the Chaweng Regent Hotel, this tastefully designed eatery combines a comfy lounge bar with live Latin music nightly. The food has a Mediterranean leaning, with juicy steaks and grilled seafood providing the backbone. All main dishes give you access to the large salad buffet.

ELSEWHERE

Thai & Western

Napasai

Napasai Resort, Hat Maenam. Tel: 0-7742 9200. Open: daily L & D. $$$–$$$$. www.pansea.com
This resort restaurant is nestled on the breezy hillside above Maenam beach and features both authentic French and royal Thai cuisine. Sit at one of the wooden outdoor *sala*, or opt for air-conditioned comfort inside – with glass walls that allow a view of the tropics outside. Imaginative seafood and imported meat dishes plus indulgent desserts.

The Patio

Pavilion Samui Boutique Resort, Hat Lamai. Tel: 0-7742 4420. Open: daily L & D. $$–$$$. www.pavilionsamui.com
Part of the plush Pavilion boutique hotel, this lovely open-air beachfront eatery on Lamai is surrounded by ponds and fountains. The extensive menu has Italian and Thai dishes, plus some enticing desserts and potent cocktails.

The Shack

Fisherman's Village, Hat Bo Phut. Tel: 0-7724 6041. Open: daily D only. $$$.
It may look like little more than a shack, but this American-owned place is a firm favourite with the island's expats. Photos of blues legends hang on the wall, and blues is the music of choice here. The chalkboard menu has a selection of local seafood and imported Australian meats, but save room for the homemade ice-cream and New York cheesecake.

Zazen

177 Moo 1, Zazen Boutique Resort & Spa, Hat Bo Phut. Tel: 0-7742 5085. Open: daily L & D. $$$–$$$$. www.samuizazen.com
Stylish and romantic, this restaurant looks out to the sea with Ko Phangan as a backdrop. Sit in an open-sided area with its Balinese-style roof or on the candlelit terrace. The European chef serves up a blend of Asian and European cuisine using healthy organic ingredients. You can order dishes à la carte or choose from one of the four set menus available.

ACCOMMODATION

HAT CHAWENG

Luxury

Poppies

South Chaweng. Tel: 0-7742 2419. www.poppiessamui.com
Oozing tropical Thai ambience, this popular resort is one of south Chaweng's cosiest hideaways. Set in a lush garden with streams and a free-form pool, the private cottages are decorated in traditional Thai style. The hotel restaurant is considered an island must-try. (24 cottages)

Expensive

Buri Rasa Village

Hat Chaweng. Tel: 0-7723 0222. www.burirasa.com
A new entrant to the scene, this lovely boutique resort just south of Chaweng's busiest stretch is already making waves. Tastefully designed with a Thai village ambience, the rooms and suites feature DVD players and Wi-Fi internet access but retain an old-world charm with four-poster beds. Features a stylish, pool perfect for lazing at, plus a restaurant and beach bar. (32 rooms)

Muang Kulaypan

Hat Chaweng. Tel: 0-7723 0849. www.kulaypan.com
One of the island's stand-outs, this boutique hotel designed in Zen-inspired minimalist style has one of the largest beach frontages on Chaweng. Has a stylish black-tiled swimming pool and Thai restaurant with traditional dance and music in the evenings. (41 rooms)

Moderate

Chaweng Villa
Hat Chaweng. Tel: 0-7723
1123. www.chawengvilla.com
Set a little close to the
main nightlife activity,
this beachfront resort
with its tropical garden
setting and vine-covered
roofs is good value.
Aside from the small
pool, there are three
beachfront eateries and
a busy bar. (48 rooms)

Budget

Charlie's Huts
Hat Chaweng. Tel: 0-7742 2343.
There's supposedly no
advance reservations at
this long-standing
Chaweng cheapie, but
with few other bargain
options around, this rus-
tic wooden hut establish-
ment is always full. Set
within a beachfront tropical garden. The staff
could be more amicable.

HAT LAMAI

Expensive

Pavilion Samui
Hat Lamai. Tel: 0-7742 4030.
www.pavilionsamui.com
The Pavilion has been on

PRICE CATEGORIES

Price categories are for a
double room without
breakfast and taxes:
Luxury = over US$200
Expensive = US$100–200
Moderate = US$50–100
Budget = under US$50

Lamai for years but was
recently upgraded into
an upmarket resort, with
prices and facilities to
match. Lovely pool, spa
and an attractive beach-
front. More expensive
rooms have bathtubs on
the balcony. (58 rooms)

Tamarind Villas
Hat Lamai. Tel: 0-7723 0571.
www.tamarindvillas.com
Known primarily as a spa
and wellness centre, this
hillside retreat features
nine villas aimed at
families or couples who
want a healthy holiday. In
a large tree-shaded
setting, the residences
vary from a cave-cum-
tree house to the magnif-
icent hilltop house with
panoramic view. (9 villas)

Moderate

Jungle Park
Hat Lamai. Tel: 0-7741 8034.
www.jungle-park.com
Situated at the northern
tip of Lamai beach, this
French-run outfit has a
pool and garden, and
beachfront bungalows
with air-conditioning, TV
and minibar. Also a bar,
massage area and a
busy seafront restaurant
serving Thai-French cui-
sine on site. (24 rooms)

Long Island Resort
Hat Lamai. Tel: 0-7742 4202.
www.longislandresort.com
Located on the northern
stretch of Lamai, this
mid-range resort became
much more hip and
upmarket recently, but
thankfully retains its laid-
back vibe. Offers a range
of rooms (priced from

budget to moderate) and
there's a nice pool, bar
area and spa. (40 rooms)

Budget

The Spa Resort
Hat Lamai, Ko Samui. Tel: 0-
7723 0855. www.spasamui.com
This retreat is one of the
island's first and best
health spa resorts, plus
it's eminently affordable.
Surrounding a pool, the
rooms vary in standard
and rate, and generally
have to be booked
weeks in advance.
Guests mainly come for
the detox programmes.
(32 rooms)

HAT CHOENG MON

Luxury

Sala Samui Resort & Spa
Hat Choeng Mon. Tel: 0-7724
5888. www.salasamui.com
This recent addition to
the island's luxe resorts
has raised the bar with
its lavish Thai-style
villas, most of which
have their own private
pool. The main pool is
fringed by a lily pond and
has pavilions for outdoor
massage. (69 rooms)

HAT BO PHUT

Expensive

Bandara Resort & Spa
Hat Bo Phut. Tel: 0-7724 5795.
www.bandararesort.com
Stylish resort right on

Bo Phut beach with
contemporary and Thai-
style design elements.
Both rooms and villas
available, plus a good
in-house spa and a
beachfront restaurant.
(151 rooms)

Moderate

Peace Resort
Hat Bo Phut. Tel: 0-7742 5357.
www.peaceresort.com
This long-standing resort
on Bo Phut beach has a
relaxed family vibe and,
despite being fairly large,
still retains an intimate
atmosphere. There's a
nice pool and all the bungalows have their own
balconies. (102 rooms)

Budget

The Lodge
Hat Bo Phut. Tel: 0-7742 5337.
www.apartmentsamui.com
Right in the heart of
Fisherman's Village, this
place has cosy rooms
with hardwood floors and
balconies with sea
views. The two upper-
floor Pent Hut rooms
are more expensive.
The beachfront bar
does great breakfasts
and evening cocktails.
(10 rooms)

HAT MAENAM

Luxury

Santiburi Resort
Hat Maenam. Tel: 0-7742 5031.
www.santiburi.com
The Santiburi touts itself

as the island's first golf resort, but even if the rolling greens don't entice you, the luxury resort has plenty else to offer. Located on quiet Maenam beach, it has a huge oval-shaped pool with suites in the main building and lovely villas set in the large gardens (the more expensive ones face the beach). (71 rooms and villas)

Expensive

Paradise Beach Resort
Hat Maenam. Tel: 0-7724 7227. www.samuiparadisebeach.com This has spacious bungalows, deluxe rooms and Thai-style suites, all set around a lush garden and two pools on Maenam beach. A bit worn in places, the resort is quiet and more suited to older couples and fam-ilies. Slightly overpriced for what you get. (95 rooms)

HAT TALING NGAM

Luxury

Le Royal Meridien Baan Taling Ngam
Hat Taling Ngam. Tel: 0-7742 9100. www.meridien.kosamui.com Located on a steep hill-side on the quiet south-west side of the island, this grand resort has five swimming pools and several restaurants which make up for its rather inadequate beach and isolated location. The stunning villas are capacious and embell-ished with traditional Thai antiques and furnishings. (70 rooms)

ACTIVITIES

NIGHTLIFE

Dance Bars & Clubs

Gecko Village: Bo Phut, tel: 0-7724 5554; www.geckosamui.com. This happening beach bar on Bo Phut beach features some of Ko Samui's best DJ-spun dance beats, with big international names making guest appearances.
Green Mango: Soi Green Mango, Chaweng, tel: 0-7742 2148. Ko Samui's best-known club, this huge barn of a venue is crammed on most nights. The music is main-stream Euro-dance and the crowd largely drunken holidaymakers.
Mint: Soi Green Mango, Chaweng, tel: 0-7089 8726; www.mintbar.com. A loud pumping bar aimed at a dance crowd with a more discern-ing music sense. Occasionally hosts internationally known DJs.
Reggae Pub: Chaweng Lagoon, tel: 0-7742 2331. A Samui main-stay, it's become more tired than trendy, but still stays busy with cruising single men and the work-ing girls they hope to meet. Main-stream dance sounds with a touch of Bob Marley.

Bars & Pubs

Ark Bar: Chaweng, tel: 0-7742 2047; www.ark-bar.com. On the central stretch of Chaweng beach, this is a bar and restaurant with a mainly Brit clientele. The dance music picks up from early evening onwards.
Coco Blues Bar: Chaweng, tel: 0-7741 4354; www.cocobluescompany. com. America's Deep South comes to Samui. Cajun and Creole food alongside live blues bands at this two-floor restaurant and bar.
Sweet Soul Café: Soi Green Mango, Chaweng, tel: 0-7741 3358. The warm-up spot for those moving onto Green Mango just opposite, but with better music and a more intimate vibe.
Tropical Murphys: Chaweng, tel: 0-7741 3614; www.tropicalmurphys. com. The island's premier Gaelic haunt is a two-level pub and restaurant with appetising dishes, local and imported beers on tap and live band music.
Unique: Chaweng, tel: 0-7741 3388. A stylish entrant to the bar scene, this split-level minimalist bar is more discerning in its choice of music and attracts a similarly discerning crowd.

Kathoey Cabaret

Christy's Cabaret: Chaweng, tel: 0-7741 3244. Packing them in every night for the 11pm free show, Christy's is Samui's most popular (but not the only) *kathoey*, or transsexual, cabaret act.

SHOPPING

As Samui's development contin-ues unabated, shops geared to both tourists and residents are beginning to spring up all over the island. By far the greatest concen-tration is in and around Chaweng, with at least two major supermar-ket chains (Tesco Lotus and Tops) having set up shop, as well as small boutique arcades like Iyara Plaza, Living Square and Central Plaza. In addition, market stalls and shops along Chaweng's main drag peddle the same counterfeit clothing, bags, sports shoes, CDs and DVDs you find in Bangkok.

Also commonly found in Chaweng are painters' studios that produce replicas of your favourite masterpieces, as well as handi-craft and home furnishings stores.

OUTDOOR ACTIVITIES

Diving

Coral Grand Divers: Bo Phut, tel: 0-7743 0531/2; www.coralgrand divers.com. This PADI dive centre has branches at Bo Phut, Lamai and Chaweng on Ko Samui, as well as on Ko Tao, the Similan Islands on the Andaman Coast, and on Phuket. The emphasis is on small, personalised groups.

Discovery Dive Centre: Amari Palm Reef Resort, Chaweng, tel: 0-7741 3196; www.discoverydivers.com. A small but well-equipped dive centre with its own speed boat. As well as offering courses and fun dives, it also rents out underwater video and photography equipment, in addition to kayaks, windsurfing boards and catamarans.

Dive Indeep: 162/8 Chaweng, tel: 0-7723 0155/6; www.diveindeep. com. This PADI dive centre has been on Ko Samui for over 15 years. Apart from the usual courses, it also organises snorkelling trips to Ko Tao and has free introductory dives for first-timers and introductory dive courses for kids.

Go-Karting

Samui Go-Kart: 101/2 Moo 1, Bo Phut, tel: 0-7742 7194. Open from 9am till late, this jungle-fringed track has three types of karts, the slowest of which are suitable for kids.

Cable Ride

Canopy Adventures: Best Beach Bungalow, Chaweng, tel: 0-7741 4150/1. Suspend from the trees above and glide through the forest canopy in Ko Samui's lush interior. The 2- to 3-hour trip includes six treetop rides, a swim in a waterfall and a drink at their jungle bar.

Golf

Santiburi Samui Country Club: 12/15 Moo 4 Maenam, tel: 0-7742 1700; www.santiburi.com. Opened in 2004, this lush 18-hole (par 72) course, the island's only one, lies on the hills behind quiet Maenam beach on Samui's northern coast.

Kayaking

Blue Stars: Chaweng, tel: 0-7741 3231; www.bluestars.info. This outfit runs 1-and 2-day kayak trips around Ang Thong Marine National Park. The 2-night trips feature a barbeque dinner and overnight camping on a desolate beach. The departure point on Ko Samui is Na Thon pier.

Sailing

Siam Commercial Boat Charters: 83/51 Moo 2, Bo Phut, tel: 0-7743 0434. Has a small fleet of luxury sporting yachts that are professionally crewed and have full waiter service on board.

SIGHTSEEING TOURS

Living Thailand Tours: 20 Moo 1 Namuang, tel: 0-7741 8680/1; www.livingthailandtours.com. Pick from a wide range of tours that cover everything from jungle walks and buffalo-cart riding to an elephant safari and even Thai cooking.

Mr Ung's Magical Safari: Moo 3, Chaweng, tel: 0-7723 0114; www.ungsafari.com. Mr Ung runs three tours – a full- and half-day "safari", as well as a day of deep sea fishing. The full-day safari includes an optional elephant ride, plus four-wheel-drive jeep tours into the lush jungled interior and a waterfall swim.

SPAS

Four Seasons Tropical Spa: Chaweng, tel: 0-7741 4141; www.spafourseasons.com. This elegant day spa (no relation to the Four Seasons hotel chain) offers a wide range of pampering services. Try the soothing hot-stone massage for something different.

The Spa Resort: Lamai, tel: 0-7723 0855; www.spasamui.com. One of Thailand's longest-running spas, this no-frills resort is well-known for its fasting and cleansing programmes. Often booked up in advance. Also has yoga, Reiki and traditional Thai massage classes.

Tamarind Retreat: 205/7 Moo 4, Samui Ring Rd, tel: 0-7742 4436; www.tamarindretreat.com. A truly inspired setting, this well-regarded spa has rustic timber pavilions under which you can enjoy its range of therapeutic massages. Also offers classes in yoga, tai chi and *qigong*.

COOKERY SCHOOL

Samui Institute of Thai Culinary Arts (SITCA): Chaweng, tel: 0-7741 3172; www.sitca.net. A professionally run school that has been featured widely in the media. It conducts hands-on morning (B1,200) and late afternoon/dinner (B1,600) courses. Budding chefs learn to cook three to four dishes, and end up eating them. The school also runs 3-day fruit and vegetable carving courses.

KO PHANGAN

TRANSPORT

GETTING THERE

By Air

It is possible to fly from Bangkok to Ko Samui on **Bangkok Airways** and then take a ferry to Ko Phangan. A slightly cheaper option is to fly **Thai Airways** to the mainland airport at Surat Thani, then take a connecting bus to the pier and then connect by ferry to Ko Phangan.

By Bus and Train

Surat Thani is the jump-off point for Ko Phangan, so the bus and train transportation is the same as Ko Samui's *(see page 183).*

By Boat

From **Surat Thani**, there are six daily ferries departing from either Don Sak, Ban Don or Pak Nam Tapi piers to Thong Sala pier on Ko Phangan. The boats take around 1½–2½ hours and tickets cost B200–320 (depending on the service). A slow night ferry from Surat Thani's Ban Don pier makes the same journey in about 7 hours (B200).

From **Ko Samui**, there are four daily ferries from Na Thon pier to Thong Sala pier on Ko Phangan. The ride takes 30 to 45 minutes and tickets cost about B120. Additionally there are several daily ferries and speedboats from Mae-Nam and Bangrak (Big Buddha) beaches in Ko Samui bound for Hat Rin on Ko Phangan.

GETTING AROUND

Songthaew trucks traverse the main roads, with the average fare around B50 from Thong Sala town to anywhere on the island, except Ban Khai (B30) or further-flung places like Ao Thong Nai Pan (B80). Motorcycle taxi fares range from B20 to B30 for a short journey, to B150 to B200 from Thong Sala to Hat Rin. Note: *songthaews* don't move until they are full, so if you wish to charter one, expect to pay about B250 or more for a trip.

Motorcycles (B150–500) and jeeps (B800–1,500) can be hired at the island's main centres. The roads are tricky and accidents common, so exercise caution.

RESTAURANTS

Outside of Hat Rin and Thong Sala, there are few independant restaurants. Most eateries are contained within guesthouses, and while the food is passable, don't have too high expectations. Most menus have the familliar Thai and Western staples.

Thai & Western

Outback Bar
Hat Rin. Tel: 0-7737 5126. Open: daily L & D. $$.
This expat-run watering hole with a friendly vibe sits towards the pier and attracts a regular crowd who come for the pool tables, sports on the big screen TV, and pub grub. Serves pies, steaks, burgers, as well as Indian and Thai food.

The Village Green Restaurant & Bar
Ao Chaophao. Tel: 0-7734 9217. Open: daily B, L & D. $$.
www.villagegreen.phangan.info
This two-level restaurant is one of the west coast's best eateries, serving a hearty menu of international and Thai dishes. Full English-style breakfasts, as well as pastas, pizzas, steaks and seafood for lunch and dinner. Located on Ao Chaophao, about 15 minutes' drive from Thong Sala.

International

A's Coffee Shop
Thong Sala. Tel: 0-7737 7226. Open: daily B, L & D. $–$$.
Located within the Buakao Inn Guest House, this is a longtime favourite with visitors. It has a great variety of dishes, from traditional Thai to Pacific Rim cuisine, with specialities like pizza baguettes, German, English and American breakfasts, and excellent pastas, all washed down by espresso, cappuccino and large margaritas. It occasionally holds live gigs on weekends.

Bamboozle Bar and Restaurant
Hat Rin. Mobile tel: 0-9587 0142. Open: daily L & D. $–$$.
The island's best (and only) Mexican restaurant and bar is located just off the main drag between the Hat Rin Nok and Hat Rin Nai beaches and set in a garden. The half-price margaritas on Mondays are a real bargain.

PRICE CATEGORIES

Price per person for a three-course meal without drinks:
$ = under US$10
$$ = US$10–$25

Emotion of Sushi
Seagarden Plazaa, Hat Rin.
Mobile tel: 0-1079 1073. Open:
daily B only. $$.
Located just off Hat Rin
Nok (Sunrise Beach),
this sushi and sashimi
eatery has sofas and
a bar on the ground
floor and a modern
air-conditioned seating
area upstairs.

Om Ganesh
Hat Rin Nai. Tel: 0-7737 5123.
Open: daily B, L & D. $–$$.
Om Ganesh is a relaxing
two-storey restaurant
located near the Hat Rin
pier. Prepared by a cook
with over two decades of
experience in New Delhi,
the restaurant serves
excellent curries and
Indian breads.

The Shell
Hat Rin. Tel: 0-7737 5149.
Open: daily B, L & D. $$.
Unbelievably great
Italian cuisine is found
around the rustic
surrounds of Hat Rin
Lake (or swamp, rather).
The Shell makes its own
pastas, pizzas and
gelato, and the fresh
coffee is excellent.

Vantana
Thong Sala. Tel: 0-7723 8813.
Open: daily B, L & D. $–$$.
Brit-owned Vantana
serves traditional English grub with plenty of
other cuisines thrown in.
Favourites include
bangers and mash,
steaks, fish fingers and
Sunday roasts with York-
shire pudding.

ACCOMMODATION

Expensive

Cocohut Village
Ban Tai (Leela Beach). Tel: 0-
7737 5368. www.cocohut.com
Located on quieter Leela
beach, yet still within
walking distance of Hat
Rin's main action, this
popular resort sprawls
over 100 metres (328 ft)
of prime beachfront
land. It has six different
types of rooms, ranging
from the simple guest-
house with shared bath-
rooms to the more
expensive pool-facing
executive suites. There's
also an internet café and
a restaurant with huge
video screen. (67 rooms)

Panviman Resort
Ao Thong Nai Pan Noi. Tel: 0-
7744 5101. www.panviman.com
This is one of Ko
Phangan's few upscale
sleeping options. It is
perched atop the head-
land that divides the
pretty northeastern bays
of Thong Nai Pan Yai and
Thong Nai Pan Noi. Clus-
tered around the pool,
the stylish cottages and
hotel rooms have mod-
ern amenities including
air-conditioning, minibar,
satellite TV, hot water,
and DVD players (in the
more expensive villas).
(75 rooms)

Santhiya Resort & Spa
Ao Thong Nai Pan Noi. Tel: 0-
7723 8333. www.santhiya.com
This brand-new resort
has just opened on
idyllic Thong Nai Pan Noi
bay. Decked out in a
blend of traditional and
modern Thai style with
teakwood finishing, the
rooms have ceiling-to-
floor windows as well as
verandahs with great
views of the pool and
gardens or the sea. One-
and two-bedroom villas
are even more luxurious.
(59 rooms)

Moderate

Green Papaya Resort
Hat Salad. Tel: 0-7737 4230.
www.greenpapayaresort.com
Under Thai and French
management, this resort
has deliberately limited
itself to just 18 rooms
so as to ensure privacy
and a personalised
touch. Set around a
pool, the wooden bunga-
lows come in five price
ranges, with the execu-
tive suites featuring
private terraces and out-
door jacuzzis. The
unique restaurant is built
like a boat. (18 rooms)

Sarikantang
Ban Tai (Leela Beach). Tel: 0-
7737 5055. www.sarikantang.com
Situated on the tip of Hat
Rin at pleasant Leela
beach, this small, mod-
ern boutique resort has
a modern Asian minimal-
ist feel to it. Like most of
the island's newer and
more upscale resorts, it
offers several types of
rooms to suit different
budgets. Pick from the
basic but comfy wooden
bungalows, or if you feel
like splurging, plump for
the ocean-view suite with
separate living room,
DVD player and outdoor
bathtub. (37 rooms)

Vimarn Samut Resort
Hat Rin. Tel: 0-7737 5027.
www.vimarnsamut.com
A small mid-range hotel
with rooms over two
floors, balconies that
look out to the sunset
side of Hat Rin, and a
restaurant right on the
beach. Rooms are
modern and clean but
somewhat short on
ambience. (18 rooms)

Budget/Moderate

Haad Son Resort
Hat Son. Tel: 0-7734 9103.
www.haadson.info
Occupying the rocky
headland at the end of
an uninhabited pristine
white sand beach, this is
one of the best resorts
on the west coast. A
variety of rooms, from
thatch-roof huts to
air-con poolside villas.
The sunset views are to
die for, and the executive
penthouse suites
come with private pools.
(47 rooms)

PRICE CATEGORIES

Price categories are for a
double room without
breakfast and taxes:
Expensive = US$100–200
Moderate = US$50–100
Budget = under US$50

ACTIVITIES

NIGHTLIFE

Bars & Dance Clubs

Backyard Bar: Hat Rin Nok, tel: 0-7737 5244. A long-established Ko Phangan favourite and the home of the Full Moon Party after-bash, this bar is located up the hill behind Hat Rin Nok. Generally quiet outside its regular parties.

Cactus Club: Hat Rin Nok. Popular mainstay on this beach. It also organises fun day trips to interior waterfalls and nearby beaches.

Drop-In Club: Hat Rin Nok, tel: 0-7737 5444. Located between Cactus Club and Paradise, this long-established bar has the usual beach mat and cushion set-up on the sand, and plays more listener-friendly commercial music.

Pirate's Bar: Ao Chaophao. This imaginatively designed bar takes the form of a boat built into the rock face at the end of the beach. To cash in on the Full Moon Party phenomenon, it hosts the monthly Moon-Set Party a few days before the real McCoy starts.

Sheesha Bar: Ao Chalok Lam, tel: 0-7737 4161; www.sheesha-bar.com. Positioned near the fishing pier in the sleepy village of Chalok Lam, Sheesha's modern Asian design sets the scene for a relaxing night out with beachfront daybeds and hookah pipes to puff away on.

OUTDOOR ACTIVITIES

Diving

Chaloklum Diving: Ao Chalok Lam, tel: 0-7737 4025; www.chaloklum-diving.com. Located on the north coast, this outfit has been operating for a decade now. It has its own boat and a policy of running courses for small groups, ensuring maximum attention. Courses taught in English and German.

Hat Yao Divers: Sandy Bay Bungalows, Hat Yao, mobile tel: 0-6279 3085; www.haadyaodivers.com. Located on the island's west coast, this reputable European-run outfit has its main office at Hat Yao beach, another branch on Ao Chaophao and a retail centre in Thong Sala. It offers all the main PADI and speciality courses.

Phangan Divers: Hat Rin, Hat Yao, Ko Ma and Ao Thong Nai Pan, tel: 0-7737 5117; www.phangandivers.com. With four branches on Ko Phangan alone, this is one of the island's first and most comprehensive dive schools. As well as PADI courses, fun dives and snorkelling equipment rental, it also operates an Instructor Development Centre for professional certification.

Health & Fitness Centres

Jungle Gym & Health Café: Thong Sala and Hat Rin, tel: 0-7737 5115; www.junglegym.co.th. Two branches on Ko Phangan. Apart from the usual weight training equipment, it specialises in training wannabe *muay thai* (Thai boxing) fighters. Also teaches yoga, Brazilian jiujitsu, yoga and belly dancing.

Yoga Retreat: opposite Hat Salad, tel: 0-7737 4310; www.yogaretreat-kohphangan.com. Qualified expat instructors offer courses on Hatha yoga and Pilates. The centre is set in a tranquil garden just a short walk from Hat Salad beach. Also has a herbal steam room and plunge pool.

SIGHTSEEING TOURS

Phangan Adventure: Lotus Dive Centre, Ao Chalok Lam, tel: 0-7737 4142; www.phanganadventure.com. This is the island's first adventure activities centre, organising a variety of water- and land-based activities. On offer is wakeboarding, waterskiing, sailing, deep-sea fishing, kayaking and diving trips, while on land, there is mountain biking, trekking, hiking and round-island tours of Ko Phangan.

Snoop Dogg Boat Trip: Hat Rin, tel: 0-7737 5364. Snoop Dogg's well-known and reputable boat trip goes round the island daily, starting in Hat Rin and visiting some of the island's best natural attractions, including Than Sadet Waterfall, Ao Thong Nai Pan and Hat Kuat, before heading to Ko Ma for a spot of snorkelling. Travel agents on Hat Rin and Thong Sala all sell tickets; otherwise book with Snoop Dogg directly.

SPAS

When the neurons are shot after a heavy dose of partying, Ko Phangan has a couple of establishments to detoxify the body and purify the mind. For a holistic retreat experience, consider **The Sanctuary** (mobile tel: 0-1899 2269; www.thesanctuarythailand.com) on Hat Thian, a centre offering fasting, colonic cleansing and yoga. Or else try the **Monte Vista** (mobile tel: 0-1747 7329; www.montevistathailand.com) near Thong Sala, which has similar services as well as palm reading, meditative painting and more.

KO TAO

TRANSPORT

GETTING THERE

By Bus, Train & Air

Surat Thani is the jump-off point for Ko Tao, so the plane, bus and train transportation is the same as Ko Phangan's (see page 189).

Alternatively, you can use Chumphon as a base to get to Ko Tao. Buses travel regularly from Bangkok's **Southern Bus Terminal** to Chumphon (7 hours), from where you can take a ferry to Ko Tao. There are also regular train departures to Chumphon from Bangkok's **Hualamphong Station**.

By Boat

From **Chumphon**, the boat ride to Ko Tao takes about 1½–3 hours.

There are at least six daily boat departures from the pier at Pak Nam port in Chumphon to Ban Mae pier on Ko Tao. Depending on the operator, tickets cost around B200 to B400 one way.

From **Surat Thani**, the boat to Ban Mae pier on Ko Tao takes about 6½ hours (once daily). From **Ko Phangan**, it takes about 1½ to 2½ hours (2–3 times daily); and from **Ko Samui** the ride takes 1½ to 3 hours (2–3 times daily). These varying travel times reflect the type of boats used, ranging from catamarans and speedboats to ferries.

GETTING AROUND

Songthaew trucks run along the island's main road from Hat Sai Ree to Ao Chalok Ban Kao in the south. The average fare from the main village of Mae Hat to either Hat Sai Ree or Ao Chalok Ban Kao is B30; travel to farther beaches like Ao Leuk will cost B80. Motorcycle taxis run the same routes for around the same price and they can also access some of the dirt tracks. Rates rise considerably later at night. Motorcycles (B150–500 per day) and jeeps (B800–1,500 per day) can be hired, but most of the island's tracks are still not sealed so caution is advised. Depending on sea conditions, longtail boats carry passengers to the island's less accessible beaches, with fares from Mae Hat to Ao Chalok Ban Kao costing B150, to Ko Nang Yuan B100, and to Ao Tanote B300. Some boats will only leave with a minimum number of people; otherwise charter the boat.

RESTAURANTS

Thai & Western

New Heaven Restaurant & Bakery

New Heaven Bungalows, Ao Thian Ok. Tel: 0-7745 6462. Open: daily D only. $–$$. www.newheavenresort.com
This family-run restaurant, bakery and bungalows is famous for its hilltop location that looks out across a beautiful bay. Large menu of simple international and Thai fare, with an emphasis on seafood. The kitchen closes early but the cocktail bar stays open till late.

Suthep

Hat Sai Ree. Open: daily B, L & D. $–$$.
This welcoming eatery and bar with garden terrace and cushioned seating is a popular haunt for the island's expats. Run by a Brit and his Thai wife, it serves a broad selection of Western and Thai favourites.

International

Café del Sol

Mae Hat. Tel: 0-7745 6578. Open: daily B, L & D. $–$$.
This pleasant little eatery serves a broad selection of authentic French, Italian and other international fare, cooked up by a Gallic chef. Tuck into big breakfasts, homemade pastas, bruschettas, tender steaks and smoked salmon. Good wines and coffee too.

Papa's Tapas

Hat Sai Ree. Tel: 0-7745 6298. Open: daily D only. $$. www.papastapas.info
There's sophisticated indulgence at this recently-opened tapas and cocktail lounge. Run by a Swedish chef and his mixologist counterpart, this elegant venue serves up inventive tapas and cocktails. There is also a hookah room to enjoy flavoured tobacco and Cuban cigars. The restaurant menu features innovative dishes like teriyaki spare ribs, panfried chorizo sausages and a wide selection of vegetarian dishes.

PRICE CATEGORIES

Price per person for a three-course meal without drinks:
$ = under US$10
$$ = US$10–$25

ACCOMMODATION

Expensive

Jamahkiri Resort & Spa

Ao Thian Ok. Tel: 0-7745 6400. www.jamahkiri.com

This top-end resort is perched over huge boulders and houses the island's most pampering spa. Decorated in dark woods and silks, there are four room sizes, all with flat-screen TVs, DVD players and bathtubs. Terrace restaurant, plus a pool and fitness centre

PRICE CATEGORIES

Price categories are for a double room without breakfast and taxes:
Expensive = US$100–200
Moderate = US$50–100

that opened in mid-2006. (12 rooms)

Moderate

Charm Churee Villa

Ao Jansom. Tel: 0-7745 6393. www.charmchureevilla.com

Perched on pretty Ao Jansom, this eclectic mix of bungalows is one of the island's better mid-range options. There are a variety of hillside cottages and villas, all with air-conditioning. The seafood restaurant has great views. (30 rooms)

Koh Tao Cabana

Hat Sai Ree. Tel: 0-7745 6505. www.kohtaocabana.com

Tucked away at the northern tip of Sai Ree,

this resort is built around boulders in a picturesque hillside setting. Rooms range from concrete bungalows to rustic wooden huts. Pricey considering the absence of a swimming pool. No TV in the rooms either. (33 rooms)

Koh Tao Grand Coral Resort

Hat Sai Ree. Tel: 0-7745 6431. www.kohtaocoral.com

These salmon-pink coloured cottages are clustered around a free form swimming pool and located on the far end of Sai Ree beach. All have nice wooden interiors and private terraces. Small restaurant on site. (45 rooms)

Ko Tao Resort

Ao Chalok Ban Kao. Tel: 0-7745 6133. www.kohtaoresort.com

Located on a lovely crescent-shape beach in the south, Ko Tao Resort is an efficient Thai-run dive-oriented hotel with a swimming pool, restaurant and a variety of rooms. (51 rooms)

Thipwimarn Resort

Hat Sai Ree. Tel: 0-7745 6409. www.thipwimarnresort.com

This tastefully-designed clifftop resort is a cosy private retreat with 11 rooms and private access to a small beach below. The bonus is the spectacular sunset views from its circular restaurant. (11 rooms)

ACTIVITIES

NIGHTLIFE

AC Bar: Hat Sai Ree, tel: 0-7745 6197. One of the island's original nighttime hangouts, this is a loud pumped up dance bar.

Dragon Bar: Mae Hat Centre, tel: 0-7745 6423. One of the island's hippest hangouts. Inventive cocktails, a pool table and DJs who spin great music.

Dry Bar: Hat Sai Ree. A chilled-out bar with customers lying on beach mats from sunset till late.

Pure: Hat Sai Ree, tel: 0-7891 2796; www.pure-lounge.com. Fringed by the large rocks at the southern end of Hat Sai Ree, this lounge bar with glowing red lighting is built over a wooden deck.

Whitening: Mae Hat, tel: 0-7745

6199. Stylish beach bar offers innovative cocktails, cool dance beats and Friday night parties.

OUTDOOR ACTIVITIES

Diving

Big Blue Diving: Hat Sai Ree and Mae Hat, tel: 0-7745 6050/2; www.bigbluediving.com. One of Thailand's best dive companies, with a well-deserved reputation.

Easy Divers: Mae Hat, tel: 0-7745 6010; www.thaidive.com. With a branch on Mae Hat and Ko Nang Yuan, it runs regular, speciality courses and live-aboard trips.

Planet Scuba: Mae Hat, tel: 0-7745 6110; www.planet-scuba.net. One of Thailand's most reputable

dive outfits with over two decades of experience.

Scuba Junction: Hat Sai Ree, tel: 0-7745 6164; www.scuba-junction.com. Located halfway up Hat Sai Ree beach, this outfit has its own boat and runs a wide range of courses.

Watersports

Black Tip Diving & Watersports: Ao Tanote, tel: 0-7745 6488/9; www.blacktipdiving.com. In addition to dive trips, it has wakeboarding and waterskiing lessons on Ao Tanote, plus operates banana boats and hires out kayaks.

Switch Watersports: Ban's Diving Resort, Hat Sai Ree, tel: 0-7745 6061; www.switchkohtao.com. Full range of watersports on Hat Sai Ree, including wakeboarding, waterskiing and banana boat rides.

NORTHERN ANDAMAN COAST

This region is well known for its pristine diving and snorkelling hotspots – the famed Similan and Surin islands – as well as the awesome limestone formations at Phang Nga Bay. Also worth exploring are land-based attractions like waterfalls, hot springs and jungle trails

Bangkok

T he Andaman Coast along western Thailand stretches from Ranong on the Isthmus of Kra all the way south to Satun near the Malaysian border. This chapter only covers the land and sea attractions as far south as Phang Nga. This region provides easy access to the renowned scuba and snorkelling hotspots of Similan and Surin islands, as well as to the dramatic limestone karsts towering out of the waters around Phang Nga Bay.

RANONG

Located 600 km (370 miles) from Bangkok and 300 km (185 miles) from Phuket, it's difficult to understand why people would want to visit **Ranong**. As the province with the highest annual rainfall in Thailand, it's certainly not for its sunny skies. And despite its coastal location, Ranong is not blessed with beautiful beaches but instead hosts a large port, its atmosphere pungent with the aroma emanating from boats filled with dead fish.

What Ranong does offer, however, is easy access to a number of inland attractions, as well as to the undeveloped islands of Ko Chang and Ko Phayam, both reached in about 2 to 3 hours. Its proximity to **Myanmar** (25 minutes by boat) also makes it easy for foreigners in South Thailand who

have to leave the country to renew their visas. The harbour is filled with companies offering to make the border run and sort out the paperwork.

Ranong Town

The run-down **Ranong Town** ❶ offers a limited choice of accommodation and even the most expensive hotels need a good lick of paint. Good places to eat are few and far between and nightlife is limited, but it is a good base from which to explore the inland attractions.

Map on page 196

LEFT: the Similan Islands in the Andaman Sea is a diver's haven.
BELOW: Punyabun \Waterfall in Ranong.

Outside Ranong Town

The **Punyaban Waterfall**, about 15 km (9 miles) north of Ranong Town and off Highway 4, is frequently over shadowed by the larger Ngao Water fall *(see below)*, but is no less beau tiful. Punyaban's cascading waters can be witnessed from a few levels. Access to its base is possible by scal ing a few boulders, while a 300-metre (985-ft) nature trail leads to an elevated lookout – from here the water below hits the rocks spectacu larly and disperses into a fine mist.

About 2 km (1½ miles) southeast of town is **Raksawarin Park ②**, where Ranong's most famous attraction, the natural **Hot Springs** (open daily 8am–5pm; free), is found. Heated to around 65 degrees C (150 degrees F), the water is too hot to bathe in. There are concrete pools circled by stone seats where people can stop, sit and inhale the reviving steam.

The dirt road through Raksawarin

Park past the Hot Springs leads to a junction that forks one way to the village at **Hat Som Paen**. This one-time tin mining village has a creek running though the temple of **Wat Hat Som Paen** (open daily 8am–5pm; free), where giant carp swim freely and can be fed with locally sold fish food. Superstitious locals believe the carp to be angels who should be treated with respect.

Ranong's only beach, **Hat Chan Damri ③**, which overlooks the British-named **Victoria Point** in Myanmar, is approximately 9 km (6 miles) from town. It is a small but pleasant beach when the sun is shin ing, but the monsoon rains frequently litter its sands with broken palm leaves, twigs and fallen coconuts.

The large **Ngao Waterfall**, 13 km (8 miles) south of Ranong is situated within **Khlong Phrao National Park** (daily 8am–4.30pm; admission charge). Originating deep within the dense forest, water pours down the

Hot springs pool at the Jansom Hot Spa Ranong Hotel (see page 204).

BELOW: Wat Hat Som Paen at dusk.

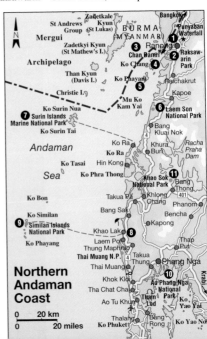

cliff and can be seen from a distance.

Directly across Highway 4 from Ngao Waterfall are the so-called **Ghost Mountains**, so named because of their complete lack of trees. This series of grass-covered hills changes its colour to golden brown during the hot summer months.

Ko Chang

The quiet and undeveloped island of **Ko Chang ❹** in Ranong Province could not be further removed from the other Ko Chang found along the Eastern Seaboard *(see page 129)*. This island is part of the **Mu Ko Phayam National Park**, and home to islanders who moved from Surat Thani and Ko Phangan decades ago and who now live in small fishing communities around the island.

Accessible from both Ranong (2½ hours) and Laem Son National park (1 hour), the boat ride to Ko Chang is particularly scenic even in bad weather. During the monsoon season from May till October, boats stop running altogether as the seas are too dangerous to cross, and accommodation on the islands shut down.

Most of Ko Chang's golden sand beaches are stretched along the west coast, the longest being **Ao Yai**. Spanning 4 km (3 miles), it is where most of the accommodation is found. The absence of electricity on the island has deterred large resorts, and basic beach bungalows are presently all the island has to offer. Calm waters and shallow coral reefs make for safe swimming and snorkelling, and as there is no pier, beach access is only possible by longtail boat and then a wade through the water on nearing the shoreline of Ao Yai.

There are no cars on the island and two concrete tracks lead to Ko Chang's only village. It is easily reached in 30 minutes on foot; paths are flat and there is plenty of shade, but all you will found is a minimart and small restaurant.

Reaching the smaller beach of **Ao Lek** on the east coast requires a 5 km (3 mile) trudge from the village. It's not worth the trip as there is no accommodation or facilities along this beach. This seclusion and privacy, however, may appeal to some.

Map on page 196

TIP

From May to Oct, the southwest monsoon brings heavy rain to the entire Andaman Coast. While this means that some of the islands further away cannot be accessed because of rough seas, it's not unusual to get days of intermittent sunshine even during the peak rainy season months.

BELOW: hot springs and playful young monks at Ranong.

Ko Phayam

Smaller than Ko Chang but with a more developed edge is the nearby island of **Ko Phayam ⑤**, 15 minutes by boat from Ko Chang. A backdrop of forested hills shadow white sandy beaches, and monkeys, boars and sea birds inhabit the island. Ko Phayam has a population of around 500, who mainly eke a living by growing cashew nuts and coconuts. Awaiting incoming boats at the pier are hoards of motorcycle taxis and touts trying to entice guests to their bungalows.

The two main beaches are on opposite sides of the island, so the pier is fairly quiet with just a handful of convenience stores and an internet café. Like Ko Chang, the roads are small, many moving from concrete to dirt trails as they progress inland, and also like Ko Chang, there are no cars. As the walk to the other side of the island can take a good hour, motorcycle taxis on the island do a brisk trade. There are no restaurants on either of the beaches, so meals are confined to the hotel you stay at.

The waters around Laem Son National Park are prime game fishing grounds.

BELOW:
signage at the Laem Son National Park.

The longest and most popular beach, and the site with the most accommodation is **Ao Yai** on the southwest coast. Most bungalows are set slightly back from the white sand beachfront behind a border of palm and pine trees, which allow for uninterrupted views from anywhere along the sand.

Ao Khao Khwai on the northwest coast is the second base for visitors, but being smaller and having fewer bungalows makes it a less popular choice. Nonetheless, it has clear water, a fine stretch of sand and lots of corals near the shore, making it good for snorkelling. Its nickname, Buffalo Bay, comes from the curvature of its two sides, resembling a pair of buffalo horns.

Laem Son National Park

Reaching into both Ranong and Phang Nga provinces, **Laem Son National Park ⑥** covers an area of 315 sq km (120 sq miles), of which roughly 85 percent is sea. Offshore from its 60 km (37 miles) of coastline are a number of small islands where the waters teem with fish and are

considered prime locations for game fishing. Bird watchers often visit in the hope of spotting a few of the park's 130 bird species, while nature lovers can observe animals like common tree shrews, Malayan flying lemurs, slow loris, macaques, civets and mouse deer. With the exception of the abundant wildlife, the park is generally quiet year round.

Fringed by casuarinas, the beach at **Hat Bang Ben** is home to the park's headquarters and the main entry point for visitors. From massive stretches of beach to vast open sea and towering trees, everything here is supersized; only the waves are small, making Bang Ben safe for swimming throughout the year. A scattering of islands offshore make for a picturesque view from virtually anywhere along the shore, and its flat compacted sand is easy to walk on.

A number of the islands in Laem Son National Park are easily reached by excursions organised at local guesthouses or by chartering a longtail boat. A 40-minute trip leads to the dramatic boulder formations at **Ko Khang Khao**, where the smooth white sand and colourful pebbles are as popular with sunbathers as the coral and marine life offshore with snorkellers and scuba divers. It is **Ko Kam Yai**, however, which is just over an hour by boat, that is considered the most beautiful island in the national park area. Its pristine reefs hover very close to shore, making for excellent snorkelling and scuba diving.

SURIN ISLANDS

The five islands that make up the **Surin Islands Marine National Park** ❼ (open Nov–May; admission charge) lie some 55 km (34 miles) from the coast and are renowned for their superlative diving and snorkelling spots. Not surprisingly, they are mainly visited by divers on liveaboard boats. The scenery above water is equally spectacular, with numerous sandy bays and coves backed by verdant jungle. The Surin Islands were uninhabited until World War II, and today, has only a few hundred permanent residents. The ecology of the islands has suffered badly over the years due to fishermen using dynamite to blast fish up to the water's surface. Mooring posts to prevent anchor damage have helped coral re-growth in recent years, while dynamite fishing has been banned.

The two main islands of **Ko Surin Nua** and **Ko Surin Tai** are separated by a 200-metre (655-ft) narrow channel of small beaches and pockets of mangroves that can be waded across at low tide. These islands are virtually uninhabited, although Ko Surin Tai is home to a small community of *chao lay* or sea gypsies, and Ko Surin Nua houses the park's headquarters and the island's only accommodation – rustic bungalows and a campsite. The other three islands, **Ko Ri, Ko Khai** and **Ko Klang** are just small, rocky islets covered with sparse vegetation and are not worth exploring.

Map on page 196

TIP

The boat trip from Ranong to the islands off its coast is unbearably slow. Occasionally, there is a speedboat service, which takes less than half the time for only a little extra *(see also page 203).*

BELOW: a Surin islander taking a break.

Muslim men outside the mosque at Khao Lak. Muslims form a significant percentage of the local population in these parts.

BELOW: Khao Lak's beaches were wiped clean after the tsunami.

Diving in the Surin Islands

The Surin Islands' most popular dive site, **Richelieu Rock**, is only just exposed at low tide. It is one of the world's top locations for sightings of whale sharks, with February to April being the best time. On average, 10 percent of all dives in a year at Richelieu result in an encounter with this 20-metre (65-ft) behemoth.

Around 60 km (37 miles) northwest of the Surin Islands are the renowned **Burma Banks**, where the three submerged peaks of **Silvertip**, **Roe** and **Rainbow** rise to within 15 metres (50 ft) of the sea's surface before plunging back into the surrounding 300-metre (980-ft) deep waters. Encounters with silvertip, nurse and, occasionally, grey reef sharks, are a near certainty. The only way to dive these sites is on board a live-aboard dive charter arranged out of Khao Lak, Phuket or Ranong.

KHAO LAK

Frequented primarily by diving enthusiasts, the sleepy beach resort of **Khao Lak** ❽ is the closest access point to the marine-life saturated

Similan Islands that lie some 60 km (37 miles) offshore. Khao Lak was steadily emerging as an upmarket alternative destination to neighbouring Phuket until the colossal tsunami struck on 26 December 2004. Khao Lak was one of the two areas in Thailand – the other being Ko Phi Phi – where the gigantic earthquake-generated waves caused the most substantial damage and loss of life.

Geographically, Khao Lak's flat floodplain landscape gave the waves nowhere to go but straight inland, where in parts they reached distances of almost 3 km (2 miles). A naval boat washed over 2 km (1 miles) inland by the churning sea stands today as testament to the astonishing power of nature. While other areas of Thailand recovered swiftly, Khao Lak did not and still suffers from the after effects of the world's most talked about natural disaster. By mid-2006, significant reconstruction was in progress, and there is a sense, too, that things are moving on. Hotels are re-opening, shops and restaurants are being rebuilt and many would argue that the beach is more beautiful than

ever before with resorts relocating further from the seafront. Considering the extent of damage, Khao Lak has come a long way and is certain to regain its former charms over time.

Khao Lak's beaches

The view over Khao Lak when arriving from Phuket, located 80 km (50 miles) to the south, is quite stunning. As the narrow mountain road winds down to the beaches below, turquoise waters lapping against the sand give an impression of an unspoilt haven. Khao Lak is in fact made up of a string of beaches, each separated by rocky outcrops, keeping them quiet and secluded while also appearing to merge into one and other.

From north to south, the beaches are **Bang Sak**, **Pakarang Cape**, **Khuk Khak**, **Bang Niang**, **Nang Thong** and finally, **Khao Lak**. The last is a relatively small beach stretching 800 metres (2,625 ft). Most of the development is centred on Bang Niang, Nang Thong and Khao Lak beaches. Swimming conditions in the high season are excellent on all beaches, but during the monsoon season, it is better to keep to the north towards the rocky headland where the currents are not so strong.

SIMILAN ISLANDS

Promoted in nearly every dive shop and diving website and mentioned in countless brochures throughout Thailand is the beautiful **Similan Islands National Park** ❾ (open Nov–May; admission charge), situated 100 km (62 miles) northwest of Phuket but most easily accessible from Khao Lak, the nearest mainland point 60 km (37 miles) away.

Similan, derived from the Malay word *sembilan*, means nine, in reference to nine small islands that make up this 128-sq km (50-sq mile) marine national park. For easy reference, the islands are numbered from north to south in descending order,

starting with **Ko Bon** (No. 9), **Ko Ba Ngu** (No. 8), **Ko Similan** (No. 7), **Ko Payoo** (No. 6), **Ko Miang** (collective name for islands No. 4 and 5), **Ko Pahyan** (No. 3), **Ko Phayang** (No. 2) and **Ko Hu Yong** (No. 1).

With the exception of Ko Ba Ngu and Ko Miang, the islands are uninhabited and for years, prior to their rise in popularity among the dive fraternity, were visited only by sea gypsies. Today, the islands are mainly visited by daytrippers from Phuket and Khao Lak and divers on multi-day live-aboard boats.

Like most places in Thailand, the reefs suffered greatly in the past, thanks to dynamite fishing and indiscriminate anchoring of boats and trawlers. Since 1987, fishing has been banned and boundaries set for moorings, allowing the reefs to return to their former pristine state.

Diving the Similans

There are more than 20 dive sites around the Similan Islands. Trips from Phuket and Khao Lak take in any number of these depending on the dive operator and length of expe-

TIP

Because the famous Burma Banks dive site is located within the territorial waters of Burma (Myanmar), the only way to visit it is by travelling onboard a live-aboard dive cruise boat that would have the required papers to be granted access.

BELOW: snorkelling in the clear waters of the Similan Islands.

Snorkelling is a worthwhile activity in the Similan Islands even if most visitors tend to be divers.

BELOW: powder-like beaches and clear aquamarine waters are the hallmarks of the Similan Islands.

dition. The eastern side of the islands feature hard coral gardens where the most popular activity is drift diving along slopes that lean dramatically from the surface down to depths of 30–40 metres (100–130 ft). Popular sites include the so-called **Christmas Point** and **Breakfast Bend**, both at Ko Ba Ngu, where soft coral growth and colourful sea fans are among the largest found in Thailand. The napoleon wrasse, a rare sight in Thailand, is occasionally seen at Breakfast Bend along with leopard sharks resting on the sands beneath.

The western side of the Similan Islands offer faster paced and more exhilarating diving, with currents swirling around huge granite boulder formations, and dramatic holes and overhangs. Colourful soft corals grow so thick on many of these boulders that the rock is no longer visible. Most dive sites on the west coast are best seen with a guide, since navigation can be tricky. Popular sites include **Fantasy Reef** and **Elephant Head** at Ko Similan where clown fish, lionfish and the occasional turtle visit.

AO PHANG NGA

Under an hour by road from Phuket airport, 65 km (40 miles) away, is the mainland town of **Phang Nga**. The town has little attraction for tourists, and there are a few caves and waterfalls nearby but with the exception of the most famous, **Tham Phung Chang** (Elephant Belly Cave), none are overly impressive. Located about 3 km (2 miles) from the town, the hill that the 1,200-metre (3,937-ft) tunnel burrows into resembles a crouching elephant of sorts. Phang Nga tour operators organise trips that take people through the cave by means of wading, rafting and canoeing through water before finally emerging on the other side of the hill.

The main attraction of this area is really **Ao Phang Nga**, the site of Thailand's most striking jungle-clad limestone rock formations, monoliths and cliffs. Spread over a coastal area of 400 sq km (155 sq miles) between Phuket and Krabi, the islands are part of the **Ao Phang Nga National Park** ➓. While impressive by day and evocative of a Chinese brush painting, the spectacular vistas of towering karsts are most captivating at night when the moon casts haunting shadows off the eerie rock structures into the watery depths around them. Sheltered from both northeast and southwest monsoon seasons, the blue-green waters around the bay are calm year-round.

Trips to the bay are mostly arranged from either Phuket or Krabi, but they can also be booked in Phang Nga Town itself. A more interesting way of exploring Phang Nga is by sea canoe. These low-lying craft allow access under the jagged edges of the limestone karsts which shelter hidden lagoons within.

Ko Ping Kan and Ko Panyi

Thailand has long been sought after as an exotic film locale, and in 1974, one of the rocky pinnacles of Phang

Nga was featured in the film *The Man with the Golden Gun*. **Ko Ping Kan** is better known today as **James Bond Island**. The small beach here is perpetually crowded with daytrippers who pose for pictures with the geological oddity called **Ko Tapu** behind them. Rising from a precariously thin base 200 metres (650 ft) out of the water, the rocky outcrop seems destined to tip into the water at some point. Bond fans are unlikely to care though and there is something undeniably cool about standing at the same location where 007 once did.

All tours of Ao Phang Nga also make a stop at nearby **Ko Panyi**, a Muslim village built entirely over the water and nestled against towering cliffs. Come lunchtime each day, it transforms from a quiet fishing community into a bustling hive of restaurants and souvenir shops with the arrival of 3,000 or so tourists on their way to or back from James Bond Island. Overnight tours of Ao Phang Nga stop here for the night, but the accommodation is very basic.

Apart from stopping off at James Bond and Ko Panyi islands, most tours will pass by a number of rocks and uninhabited islands whose names take after the strange shapes they resemble. Another popular stop is **Khao Khien** (Painting Rock) to see ancient cave art painted onto its inner walls. An array of animals, including monkeys, elephants as well as fish and crabs are depicted alongside human stick figures.

KHAO SOK NATIONAL PARK

Easily accessible from Phuket on the east and Surat Thani on the west, **Khao Sok National Park ⑪** (open daily; admission charge) is often dismissed as simply another national park. However, alongside the usual flora, fauna, rivers and forests, are some features that make Khao Sok unique. It is home to the world's oldest evergreen rainforest, 160 million years to be exact, and its location at the mountain ridge between the east and west coasts makes it the wettest area in Thailand (rains from both the Gulf of Thailand and the Andaman Sea coasts deposit as much as 3,500 mm (138 inches) of rainfall annually) Within the park's dense rainforest lies

Map on page 196

If in the Phang Nga area, a worthwhile detour is the Tham Suwankhuha cave temple, located 10 km (6 miles) south of Phang Nga Town.

BELOW: exploring Ao Phang Nga's James Bond Island (Ko Tapu is on the left).

Map on page 196

Waterfall at Cheow Lan Lake, Khao Sok National Park.

BELOW: bungalows by Cheow Lan Lake, Khao Sok National Park.

the world's second largest flower, the *Rafflesia Kerrii*, measuring 80 cm (31 inches) in diameter when in bloom.

Geographically, much of the 740-sq km (285-sq mile) park comprises limestone mountains, most in the 400–600 metre (1,300–2,000 ft) range, with the highest at 960 metres (3,150 ft). Lowland rainforest dominates, but there are also many towering trees, some reaching heights of around 65 metres (215 ft). Mammals including elephants and leopards roam free (though are rarely spotted) while cobras, tarantulas and scorpions make frequent appearances.

Jungle trails

Of the nine trails in the park, eight follow the same route for the first 5 km (3 miles) along the **Sok River**, after which they split. One continues a further 2 km (1 mile) to the **Ton Gloy Waterfall** where swimming is possible, while another to the **Bang Leap Nam Waterfall** which is not as large but easier to reach. **Tan Sawan Waterfall** is the most difficult to reach, and involves a clamber over the river across slippery and sometimes steep rocks. The ninth trail leads in a different direction altogether, following the **Bang Laen River** all the way to **Sip-et Chan Waterfall**.

You can tackle these jungle trails yourself, but half-day tours booked from Phuket or Krabi will have experienced guides who will point out rare flora and signs of animal life that the untrained eye could easily miss.

Another popular day trip is to **Cheow Lan Lake**, some 60 km (37 miles) from the main accommodation area. It is home to over 100 small islands and was formed in the 1980s when the **Ratchprabha Dam** was built to provide water for a hydroelectric power plant. Mountains and cliffs surrounding the river can be explored, but only on a guided trek. Activities on the lake include boat trips, fishing and canoeing, as well as walks around it to locations such as **Nam Talu Cave**. The lake is at its most beautiful in the early morning when the hooting of gibbons can be heard from deep within the mists hanging over the lakes and mountains. ❏

NORTHERN ANDAMAN COAST

RANONG & SURROUNDINGS

TRANSPORT

GETTING THERE

By Air

Ranong Airport is situated 24 km (15 miles) north of Ranong Town. **Phuket Air** previously operated daily flights from Bangkok, but ceased flying in early 2006. No official statement has been released to confirm whether this is a temporary or permanent situation, so do check with the airline before travelling.

Alternatively travellers can fly into Phuket or Krabi *(see pages 230 and 260)* and then take a bus *(see below)* from either of these places to get to Ranong.

By Road

All the air-conditioned buses that travel daily from Bangkok's **Southern Bus Terminal** to Phuket and Krabi pass the Ranong bus station just off Highway 4. The 600-km (373-mile) journey takes around 9–10 hours. It is also possible to get to Ranong from either Phuket or Krabi, some 300 km (185 miles) away by bus (the ride takes about 4–5 hours).

GETTING AROUND

Ranong

Songthaew trucks and motorcyle taxis are the primary mode of transportation on Ranong. These run frequently from Thanon Ruangrat in the town centre to locations near the town and to Laem Son National Park, 60 km (37 miles) south of Ranong.

Ko Chang & Ko Phayam

The islands of Ko Chang and Ko Phayam can be reached by boats departing from the Ranong port area. Timetables frequently change and getting a straight answer is difficult, but at the time of print, these boats departed at 9.30am and took just under 3 hours (despite claims of 1–2 hours). A quicker speedboat service occasionally operates; use this if available as it is much faster and tickets only cost about B100. The kiosk is at the same pier. Note: boats only make the trip if there is enough demand.

The only form of transport on Ko Chang and Ko Phayam are motorcycle taxis, which travel across dangerously bumpy dirt tracks. The only other way to get around is on foot, but tracks are uneven and poorly signposted.

Surin Islands

The closest mainland base to the Surin Islands is Khura Buri pier, about 110 km (68 miles) south of Ranong Town. Boats depart daily at 9am and take between 4 and 5 hours to reach the islands. It is also possible to take a boat from Amphoe Kapoe pier in Ranong Town. Trips leave daily during the November to April high season and take around 7 hours to get there. Note: most people who travel to the Surin Islands are divers on live-aboard boats.

BELOW: beachside *tuk-tuk* drivers.

RESTAURANTS

RANONG TOWN

There are a few good eateries in Ranong, but outside of this town, in places like Ko Chang and Ko Phayam, the only places worth eating at are the restaurants attached to the small hotels *(see page 207)*. Don't expect any gourmet stuff though – the food will be decent at best.

Thai & Western

Coffee House
173 Th. Ruangrat. Tel: 0-7782 2447. Open: daily B, L & D. $.
This unassuming little roadside restaurant looks basic from both the inside and out, but the food is fantastic and good value for money. Large selection of freshly made breads with a wide choice of fillings; the chicken and cheese baguettes are delicious.

Gardener's
Th. Ruangrat. Tel: 0-7783 0111. Open: daily B, L & D. $.
Appropriately named open garden-style restaurant serving Thai and Western dishes but best known for its coffee and ice-cream selection. Popular lunchtime meeting point for Ranong's expats.

Namtal Restaurant
Jansom Thara Hotel, 2/10 Th. Petchkasem. Tel: 0-7781 1511. Open: daily 6pm–2am. $$.
International restaurant with an emphasis on Asian dishes (the Chinese options being the best). Live music nightly from 7pm to 1am.

Princess Café
Royal Princess Ranong. 41/144 Th. Tamuang. Tel: 0-7783 5240. Open: daily B, L & D. $$.
Probably the most refined place to eat in Ranong, where proper sit-down meals can be enjoyed in a comfortable and relaxed environment. A house band and singer perform nightly from 8pm, and although the international menu is not fantastic, the Thai food is very good.

Sophon's Hideaway Bar and Restaurant
Th. Ruangrat. Tel: 0-7783 2730. Open: daily L & D. $–$$.
Very popular Australian-owned restaurant serving everything from Thai to Italian. Look out for the Aussie-inspired daily specials, which often include ostrich steaks. Service is slow, but can be forgiven as it's done with a smile.

Taxi Pizzeria
Th. Ruangrat. Open: daily L & D. $.
Italian restaurant where, ironically, the Italian is a hit or miss. The small Thai selection is much, much better. The restaurant is raised slightly above street level, so it's a good spot for people-watching while you eat.

Thai

Woodhouse Guest House
Near Royal Princess Ranong, Th. Tamuang. Mobile tel: 0-9866 3672. Open: daily B, L & D. $.
Basic Thai restaurant below the Woodhouse Guest House, which advertises food, yet only seems to serve it in the high season. The Thai dishes, when available, are fantastic though. The bubbly and exuberant owner is a fountain of information on what to do in Ranong.

PRICE CATEGORIES

Price per person for a three-course meal without drinks:
$ = under US$10
$$ = US$10–$25

ACCOMMODATION

RANONG

Moderate

Jansom Beach Resort
Hat Chan Damri. Tel: 0-7782 1611.
As the only hotel on Chan Damri beach, the Jansom is peaceful and quiet with lovely views of Myanmar (Burma) from your room. The down-side is the long walk up a lot of rocky steps to reach your room, but the sea breezes at the top make it bearable. (42 rooms)

Jansom Hot Spa Ranong
2/10 Th. Petchkasem. Tel: 0-7781 1510.
www.jansomhotsparanong.com
Despite being the most well known, this hotel is by no means the best. From the paintwork to the lifts, this 1960s throwback appears old and rundown and the staff is less than welcoming. The hotel justifies its prices due to the hot spring water baths on site. (220 rooms)

Royal Princess Ranong
41/144 Th Tamuang. Tel: 0-7783 5240.
www.royalprincess.com
Easily the best hotel in Ranong Town. Rooms are clean and decently appointed and the staff is friendly. Hot spring water is provided in all guest rooms as well as in the swimming pool and jacuzzi areas. (138 rooms)

Budget

Woodhouse Guest House
Near Royal Princess Hotel, Th. Tamuang. Tel: 0-9866 3672.
This guesthouse may be one of Ranong's cheaper options, but its

atmosphere is far more welcoming than some of the more expensive options. There are two rooms per floor, with each pair sharing a bathroom, but everything is clean and the guesthouse never feels crowded. (16 rooms)

LAEM SON N P

Budget

Andaman Peace Resort
Hat Bang Ben. Mobile tel: 0-1211 0895.
Rooms have direct sea views, making it far more scenic than its main competitor, Wasana Resort, but the food at the attached restaurant is not great and staff have trouble speaking English. (12 rooms)

Wasana Resort
Hat Bang Ben. Tel: 0-7782 4311.
This seems to be the best-equipped resort, offering tours and renting canoes. Staff are friendly, speak good English and are more than

happy to give advice. The food served at the restaurant is as good as it gets within the park. There is no sea view, but the beach is within walking distance. (8 rooms)

KO CHANG

Budget

Cashew Resort
Ao Yai. Tel: 0-7782 0116.
Ko Chang's first and largest resort has a variety of bungalows made from wood and bamboo to solid stone. There are more facilities here than at many other resorts, including a dive school and a beach bar with pool table. Open only from mid-October to May. (25 rooms)

Ko Chang Resort
Ao Yai. Tel: 0-7782 0176.
These very basic but clean beach bungalows are set directly on the rocks with lovely views of the sea, meaning a short clamber is necessary. The resort has its

own daily boat to and from Ranong. Open only from November to May. (13 rooms)

Sunset Resort
Ao Yai. Tel: 0-7782 0171.
Shaded beach bungalows with a pleasant attached restaurant. Beach volleyball is played daily at sunset in front of the resort and the staff are happy to advise on fishing and other nearby activities. Open mid-October to May only. (15 rooms)

KO PHAYAM

Budget

Aow Yai Bungalows
Ko Phayam. Tel: 0-7782 1753.
These popular bungalows are set in a large pine and coconut plantation right in the centre of Ao Yai bay. There are three styles of bungalows, all decent on the inside, but the lowest priced do not have their own toilets or showers. (16 rooms)

Baan Suan Kayoo
Ko Phayam. Tel: 0-7782 0133.
www.gopayam.com
Thatched roof cottages built on a gentle slope where winding paths lead through a cashew nut garden toward the beach. Cottages range from simple to superior; the latter have larger beds and Western-style toilets. Ask about the packages which include transfers and tours. (17 rooms)

Bamboo Bungalows
Ko Phayam. Tel: 0-7782 0012.
www.bamboo-bungalows.com
This popular cluster of bungalows open year round is one of the livelier places in the evenings, when guests from nearby hotels come to enjoy the music on the beach. Nestled about 100 metres (330 ft) back from the beachfront. (25 rooms)

PRICE CATEGORIES

Price categories are for a double room without breakfast and taxes:
Moderate = US$50–100
Budget = under US$50

ACTIVITIES

NIGHTLIFE

The limited nightlife options in Ranong have much more of a Thai following than a foreign one, and even in the high season, bars here are often quiet. The nightlife scene is probably more happening on the offshore islands of Ko

Chang and Ko Phayam – although not by much more. Ko Chang, with its lack of electricity and therefore inability to put on loud music or lights, all but shuts down in the evenings. Although Ko Phayam is a little busier than Ko Chang at night, there are still no bars as such, but rather just extensions to the guesthouses that play music and serve cold beer.

SHOPPING

There is a large market, open both during the day and at night, found on Thanon Ruangrat in Ranong Town. The stalls here sell a varied selection of items, including Thai food, handicrafts and household decorations such as silk flowers.

With the exception of this market though, the retail options found in Ranong are rather limited.

OUTDOOR ACTIVITIES

Diving

Ranong's two leading dive operators offer day trips and live-aboards to the Surin Islands, as well as to nearby Ko Phayam.
Aladdin Dive Safari: Ranong Pier, tel: 0-7782 0472; www.aladdindive safari.com. Takes only small groups of no more than four persons and conducts regular 10-day expeditions to the outlying islands. PADI dive courses can be completed at nearby Ko Chang, or as part of the longer dive safaris.
A-One Diving: 256 Th. Ruengrad, tel: 0-7783 2984; www.a-one-diving.com. This multilingual dive com-

pany has operated since 1999. Catering to both scuba divers and snorkellers, it specialises in live-aboards, but will also arrange PADI courses with most of the theoretical and practical training conducted at Ko Phayam.

SPAS

Spas around Ranong focus on one thing and one thing only – the natural mineral waters of the nearby Raksawarin Hot Springs. The selling point for any Ranong spa is the therapeutic natural baths in which to soak away stress and tension.
Jansom Hot Spa Ranong: tel: 0-7782 2516; www.jansomhotspa ranong.com. Mineral water is pumped directly into the men's and women's communal baths. This is the best known of the

town's spas, but overcrowding at certain times of day can be a source of annoyance. It is generally quieter later in the evening.
Royal Princess Spa: 41/144 Th. Tamuang, tel: 0-7783 5240; www.ranong.royalprincess.com. This hotel spa welcomes non-guests as well as those staying at the hotel to use its swimming pool, gym, massage and spa facilities as well as the hot spring water jacuzzi that is replenished daily. Facilities are cleaner and less crowded than other hotels in the area.
Siam Hot Spa: 73/3 Moo 2, Th. Petchkasem, tel: 0-7781 3551; www.siamhotspa-ranong.com. Open: daily 10am–10pm. Probably the nicest of Ranong's spas, although surprisingly, also reasonably priced. Separate men's and women's jacuzzi pool, sauna and steamroom. Cafe/bakery on site. Located directly opposite the Raksawarin Hot Springs.

KHAO LAK & SIMILAN ISLANDS

TRANSPORT

GETTING THERE

By Air & Road

Khao Lak is situated just off Highway 4, some 780 km (485 miles) south of Bangkok and 80 km (50 miles) north of Phuket. The easiest way to get there is to fly to Phuket *(see page 230)* and take one of the airport minibuses (B2,200) or taxis (B1,300) from there. The journey time from Phuket airport to Khao Lak is just over an hour. Few people ride the bus from Bangkok as the journey is a back-breaking 12 hours long.

GETTING AROUND

Khao Lak

Motorcycle taxis and *songthaew* trucks are the primary mode of transportation along Khao Lak's several beaches. *Song-thaews* can be hailed from the road, and fares range from B20 to B30 for anywhere within Khao Lak. They can be also chartered like taxis but agree on the price before you get in. Alternatively, motorcycles and cars can be hired. Inquire at your hotel reception desk.

Similan Islands

The easiest departure point for the Similan Islands is from Khao Lak, but Phuket is also a jump-off point for a large number of Similan-bound diving and snorkelling excursions. Boats only operate from Nov–Apr, after which time the waters are deemed too rough and dangerous to cross.

Thap Lamu pier, located about 8 km (5 miles) south of Khao Lak, is where boats depart on the 3-hour journey to the Similan Islands. Most tours from Phuket travel by road to Thap Lamu pier and then make the connection to the islands by boat.

RESTAURANTS

KHAO LAK

International

Khao Lak Seafood
19/1 Moo 7, Khuk Khak.
Tel: 0-7642 0318. Open: daily
L & D. $–$$.
Favoured by residents
and widely known to
serve the best fresh
seafood in Khao Lak,
this unassuming little
restaurant is busy
throughout the year and
well worth a visit.

Mex's Biker Bar
5/14 Moo 7, Khao Lak.
Tel: 0-7642 0603. Open: daily
9am–late. $–$$.
With an incredibly Ameri-
can vibe despite being
German-owned, the dark
wood interior of this

place is adorned with
Harley Davidson para-
phernalia. On the menu
is typical pub grub like
chicken and ribs, accom-
panied by massive por-
tions of french fries.

**Pizzeria Spaghetteria
Italica**
5/3 Moo 7, Khuk Khak.
Tel: 0-7642 0271. Open: daily
L & D. $–$$.
Homely Italian-managed
restaurant that makes
fresh pasta on the
premises, and sauces
that use quality imported
herbs and meats. Basic
decor, but with a wide
selection of pizza and
pasta, as well decent
home-made *gnocchi*. The
four-cheese *penne* is
particularly good. End
the meal with real Italian
coffee or liqueur.

Thai

Baan Thai
Le Meridien Beach Resort and
Spa, 9/9 Moo 1, Khuk Khak.
Tel: 0-7642 7500. Open: daily
D only. $$$.
This simple yet elegant
restaurant overlooks a
natural lagoon and
offers a healthier range
of Thai dishes than the
usual deep-fried options
and dishes doused in
coconut milk.

Beau Seafood Restaurant
12/9 Moo 2, Khuk Khak.
Open: daily L & D. $.
Housed in a bamboo
building set back from
the road and surrounded
by jungle. Run by the ever
smiling Khun Pen, who
serves Thai food using
fresh fish and shellfish
bought daily from local

fishermen. The snapper
with "three flavour"
sauce is a must-try.

Jai Restaurant
5/1 Moo 7, Khao Lak.
Tel: 0-7642 0390. Open: daily
B, L & D. $.
Attached to the popular
bungalows at the start of
the beach road, this
inexpensive Thai restau-
rant serves the usual
suspects. The *som tam*
(northeastern spicy
papaya salad), washed
down with a lemon shake
makes for a light lunch.

PRICE CATEGORIES

Price per person for a
three-course meal
without drinks:
$ = under US$10
$$ = US$10–$25
$$$ = US$25–$50

ACCOMMODATION

KHAO LAK

Luxury

The Sarojin
60 Moo 2, Khuk Khak. Tel: 0-
7642 7900. www.thesarojin.com
Arguably Khao Lak's
most luxurious resort,
The Sarojin is the ulti-
mate embodiment of
indulgence, with direct
access to a secluded
11-km (7-mile) stretch of
private beach. Rooms
are situated in low-rise
buildings and each is
appointed luxuriously

with strong Thai accents.
Ground-floor rooms have
access to private
gardens while the ones
upstairs have capacious
terraces. Two restau-
rants, a bar, a pamper-
ing spa and an exquisite
infinity pool complete
the picture of elegance.
(56 rooms)

Expensive

Khao Lak Merlin Resort
7/7 Th. Petchkasem.
Tel: 0-7642 8300.
www.merlinphuket.com/khaolak
With three swimming
pools, a fitness room,

spa and tennis courts,
this resort caters to
more than just the
sedentary sun-worship-
per. For children there is
a kids' club and play-
ground, and for adults, a
pool bar, beach bar and
lounge. Rooms are large
yet homely in appear-
ance, many with high
ceilings that add to the
sense of spaciousness.
(209 rooms)

La Flora
59/1 Moo 5, Khuk Khak.
Tel: 0-7642 8000.
www.khaolak-hotels.com/laflora
A series of small low-rise
buildings set among

tropical gardens house
the villas and guest-
rooms in this lovely
resort. Marble floors and
contemporary artwork
on the walls accentuate
the modern Asian ambi-
ence, and a beautiful
mosaic-tiled sea-facing
pool adds a touch of
luxury. (70 rooms)

**Le Meridien Khao Lak
Beach and Spa Resort**
9/9 Moo 1, Khuk Khak.
Tel: 0-7642 7500.
www.lemeridien.com
Set within 20 ha (50
acres) of sandy beach
and tropical gardens.
Rooms are luxurious and

large, with lounge areas and 29-inch flat-screen TVs. Bathrooms have separate baths and rain showers with glass panelling that allows an unobstructed view of the living and balcony areas. Three restaurants, two bars and one excellent spa. (243 rooms).

Moderate

Best Western Palm Galleria Resort
43/1 Moo 2, Khuk Khak.
Tel: 0-7623 6378.
www.khaolak-hotels.com/palmgalleria

This four-star resort is in an ideal location, with easy access to both the town and the beach. Guestrooms are clean and spacious, and have private balconies and separate shower stalls and bathtubs. A reasonably good deal considering that most of Khao Lak's resorts are rather upmarket. (74 rooms)

Khaolak Bhandari Resort
26/25 Moo 7, Nang Thong.
Tel: 0-7642 0751.
www.khaolak-hotels.com/bhandari
Set slightly back from the beach amid tropical

gardens, the romantic Thai-style pavilions that form this resort twist around palm trees and a large, curved swimming pool. Has a good restaurant serving Thai and Western options, and an open-air bar. (58 rooms)

Budget

Jai Restaurant and Bungalows
5/1 Moo 7, Khao Lak.
Tel: 0-7642 0390.
One of the few budget places to stay at in Khao Lak. Rooms are clean

and service is friendly, considering the low prices. Bungalows with small private terraces are set behind Jai Restaurant, just off the main road and a few minutes' walk from the beach. (15 rooms)

PRICE CATEGORIES

Price categories are for a double room without breakfast and taxes:
Luxury = over US$200
Expensive = US$100–200
Moderate = US$50–100
Budget = under US$50

ACTIVITIES

NIGHTLIFE

Simply put, Khao Lak is the last place those in search of nightlife should visit. Dance bars and clubs are non-existent, and Khao Lak's few pubs and bars are quiet and generally shut early.
Happy Snapper Bar: 5/2 Moo 7, Khuk Khak, tel: 0-7642 3540. This multi-level bar is the liveliest of Khao Lak's night spots with a live band or resident DJ nightly.
Mex's Biker Bar: 5/14 Moo 7, Khuk Khak, tel: 0-7642 0603. Laid-back ambience with pool tables and darts. Popular after-work hangout for locals and a magnet for tourists with its friendly vibe. Also serves good pub food.
Tarzan Bar: 21/1 Moo 7, Khuk Khak, mobile tel: 0-1089 1412. Laid-back and relaxed bar that is popular with both locals and expats. Small and intimate with a pub-type atmosphere and music that plays late into the night.

OUTDOOR ACTIVITIES

Golf

Thai Muang Beach Golf and Marina: 157/12 Moo 9 Limdul Rd, tel: 0-7657 1533. This 18-hole course is just a 30-minute drive from Khao Lak or Phuket. Has an interesting placement of bunkers and water hazards, but it is most popular for its scenic beachside location.

Diving

Several dive sites are easily reached from Khao Lak, making it a major haven for scuba enthusiasts. In addition to being the main gateway to the Similan Islands, the wreck diving site of *Boonsong* where an old tin mining boat sank in 1984 is easily accessible from there. So too is the tin mining boat called *Premchai*, which in August 2001

sank to its watery grave at a depth of 21 metres (69 ft).
Divers Land: 4/56 Moo 7, Khuk Kak, tel: 0-7642 3710; www.divers land.com. Khao Lak's first integrated diving resort, with accommodation, restaurant, fitness and training centres as well as dive equipment sales and service centres all on one site. Organises both diving and snorkelling trips.
Scuba Diving Adventures: 9/1 Moo 7, Khuk Khak, tel: 0-7642 0795. Founded by an Austrian couple in 1995, this dive shop offers 3- to 10-day excursions to the Similan Islands on either a speedboat or catamaran.
Sub Aqua Diver Centre: 5/21 Moo 7, Khao Lak, tel: 0-7642 0165; www.subaqua-divecenter.com. Professional and well-established multilingual dive outfit offering daily excursions to the Similan Islands onboard one of three modern speedboats. Offers a range of PADI courses, as well as introduction to scuba and fun courses tailored for children.

AO PHANG NGA & KHAO SOK NATIONAL PARK

TRANSPORT

GETTING THERE

By Air and Road

Phang Nga is 790 km (490 miles) south of Bangkok and 90 km (55 miles) north of Phuket. The easiest way to get to Phang Nga is to fly to Phuket (see page 230) or Krabi

(see page 260) and take an airport minibus (B1,800) or taxi (B900). Phang Nga is midway between Phuket and Krabi on Highway 4.

GETTING AROUND

Motorcycle taxis and songthaew trucks are the primary mode of

transportation in Phang Nga. But the town is also small enough to get around on foot.

Tours of Phang Nga Bay and Khao Sok National Park are best handled by travel agencies in Phang Nga. Generally, however, more people tend to visit these places from their base in Khao Lak, Phuket or Krabi. Enquire with travel agents at these places.

ACCOMMODATION

PHANG NGA TOWN

Budget

Phang Nga Guest House
99/1 Th. Phetkasem.
Tel: 0-7641 1358.
Basic but comfortable rooms with choice of fan or air-conditioning. This is one of the better budget options in town, conveniently situated and with friendly staff. (12 rooms)

AO PHANG NGA

Note: both options in the expensive category are on the island of Ko Yao Noi, which is ideally located to enjoy the panoramas of Phang Nga Bay.

Expensive

Ko Yao Island Resort
Ko Yao Noi. Tel: 0-2673 0966.

www.koyao.com
Eco-friendly property with a small number of one- and two-bedroom villas along a short stretch of beach. Villas are either ocean-facing or tucked away in a tropical garden. Restaurant serves Mediterranean and Thai dishes. Has a bar but no pool. Prices drop by half during the off season. The resort can arrange transfers from either Phuket or Krabi. (15 rooms)

The Paradise Koh Yao
Ko Yao Noi. Tel: 0-2233 1399.
www.theparadise.biz
This beautiful resort is nestled in a secluded spot adjacent to a stretch of private beach. Rooms have semi-outdoor bathrooms, open living areas, air-conditioning and postcard-perfect views of lovely Phang Nga Bay. The resort can arrange transfers from either Phuket or Krabi. (70 rooms)

Budget

Phang Nga Bay Resort
Ko Panyi. Tel: 0-7641 2067.
www.thaihotel.com/phangnga/
phangngabay
Accomodation in the Phang Nga Bay area is scarce; this one is found on Ko Panyi island. Rooms are a bit dated, but are clean and spacious, and facilities include karaoke rooms, pool table, tennis courts and a restaurant overlooking the bay. (88 rooms)

KHAO SOK N P

Budget

Bamboo House
Khao Sok. Tel: 0-1787 7484.
www.krabidir.com/bamboohouse
Basic but clean and comfortable stilted wood bungalows with separate bathroom and hot showers. Its restau-

rant serves Thai and Western food. Staff are very friendly and in high season there is a monthly full-moon barbeque by the Sok River. It also organises trekking tours of Khao Sok and other activities. (17 rooms)

**Khao Sok
Rainforest Resort**
Khao Sok. Tel: 0-7739 5135.
www.krabidir.com/khaosokrain
forest
Fantastic location right by the river and just 100 metres (330 ft) from the main bridge. Incredibly tall stilted bungalows sit among the treetops and even the restaurant has a jungle feel to it, with vines creeping over its open walls. It's a bit of a walk up there, but definitely worth it for the spectacular mountain views. Various jungle activities and trekking tours can be booked at the resort. (12 rooms)

PHUKET

Thailand's largest resort island is a base for dive trips to several world-famous dive sites. If brash Patong proves overwhelming, you can escape to any one of 16 natural coves, carpeted with blinding white sand and strung along the island's western coastline, or head to Phuket Town to see its temples and market

As Thailand's smallest province but largest island at 587 sq km (225 sq miles), **Phuket** has witnessed a tourism boom rivalled only by Pattaya. With tourism came development, driving its dramatic growth from the sleepy little seaside town it was in the 1970s to a busy and bustling, sometimes even sophisticated, island destination it has evolved into today. With so many visitors flocking to the island, savvy businessmen have jumped on the construction bandwagon. There are hotels to suit different budgets, but recent development has seen the construction of expensive boutique hotels and upmarket villa-style houses along with shops, schools and hospitals of international standards. Not surprisingly, all this has encouraged many foreigners to take up permanent residence in Phuket.

The stunning white sand beaches along the 48-km (30-mile) long west coast are separated by picturesque headlands. Some are small and pristine with intimate hidden coves, while others teem with noisy jet-skis, crowds of sun worshippers, and vendors trawling the sands selling colourful sarongs and souvenirs.

Phuket is a base for dive trips to several renowned dive sites in the surrounding seas, and the number of operators offering courses, organ-

ised excursions and live-aboards is astounding. Phuket is also an excellent base for the exploration of islands, national parks and mainland beaches like Khao Lak and Krabi.

People and economy

Of the approximate 300,000 people living in Phuket, the majority are Buddhist, with Muslims comprising around 35 percent of the population. Many locals make their living from the island's rubber and pineapple plantations, but since the 1980s,

Map on page 214

LEFT: Laem Promthep at sunset.
BELOW: plantation worker extracting latex from a rubber tree.

Phuket

0   5 km

0   5 miles

N

tourism has overtaken agriculture as the main source of income. When the tsunami hit Phuket and the surrounding areas on 26 Dec 2004 – the peak of the high season – Phuket suffered very badly. Some beaches (like Bang Thao and Nai Narn) escaped relatively unscathed, while others (like Patong and Kamala) were hit hard. The loss of life, injuries and damage to property were considerable. Not surprisingly, the scale of damage at Patong was the greatest because it is so heavily built up.

In the months following the tsunami, it was not uncommon to see shops and restaurants shutting their doors in defeat during what was supposed to be the high season. Even massive discounting of hotel room rates could not entice the tourists back. Thankfully, due to rapid rebuilding and focused tourism campaigns overseas, this quiet spell did not last long, and today, Phuket is back on its feet again. Indeed with beaches swept clean of debris and buildings renovated and given a fresh lick of paint, Phuket is literally sparkling once more.

PHUKET TOWN

Not surprisingly, many people head straight for the beaches and give **Phuket Town** a miss. But the town is worth at least a day trip as there are some sights which are rich in culture and tradition. Only 20 minutes drive from Patong, the town can seem busy and unattractive, and with an impossible to follow one-way traffic system. By foot and with the aid of a good maps it's not difficult to navigate, but by car it's easy to get lost.

Phuket Orchid Garden and Thai Village

Not quite in Phuket Town but in its outskirts about 2½ km (1½ miles) away at Thanon Thepkrassatri is a popular stop on most standard tours of Phuket island, the **Phuket Orchid Garden and Thai Village ❶** (daily 8am–9pm; admission charge; tel: 0-7623 7400). Apart from its collection of rare orchids, the Thai Village is also a cultural centre that hosts traditional dances and elephant shows, a handicraft centre and Thai restaurants. The staged wedding ceremony – while a little kitschy – rivals a Las

Map on page 214

Orchid blooms aplenty at the Phuket Orchid Garden and Thai Village.

BELOW: Phuket Town's market area.

BELOW: a butterfly at the Butterfly Garden and Insect World.

Vegas show for glitz and glamour, with a ceremony steeped in Thai culture and tradition, and even a grand entry on elephant back.

Phuket Butterfly Garden and Insect World

At the start of Thanon Yaowaraj heading towards Phuket Town centre is the **Phuket Butterfly Garden and Insect World** ❷ (daily 9am–5.30pm; admission charge; tel: 0-7621 5616). Inside are over 40 species of butterfly in a natural rainforest environment and an enclosure full of rare and native birds of Thailand. An ideal outing for children, information boards point out the differences between butterflies and moths, and there are educational exhibits of live eggs, larvae and pupa.

A large pond brimming with koi fish is a reminder that until 2004 there was also an aquarium here. This has since been replaced with Insect World, where stick insects, tarantulas, scorpions and other creepy crawlies go about their daily business, unaware of watchful eyes marvelling at them.

Khao Rang

Just south of the Butterfly Garden is **Khao Rang**; a spiralling road leads to a summit revealing (according to most brochures) panoramic views over Phuket town. In reality, the view is far from spectacular, as roads and traffic are all that can be seen from here. However, the leafy surrounds and the quiet makes it a peaceful place to have a picnic. The park is popular with locals, and is a favourite escape for young courting couples. **Tung-Ka Café** (tel: 0-7621 1500) at the peak of the hill serves delicious and cheap Thai food daily for lunch and dinner.

Chinatown

In the heart of Phuket Town, between Thanon Thalang and Thanon Deebuk, is the **Chinatown** area, where old colonial houses and Sino-Portuguese style mansions dominate. Originally built by Europeans, they were designed for Chinese sensibilities. Oddly, the combination of Eastern and Western influence has produced some fine architecture. As many are now privately owned, they can be viewed only from the outside. These residences are easily recognised by their tiled roofs, artistically-chiselled exteriors and tall, spiralling pillars at their fronts.

Chinese temples

Due to the strong Chinese presence in Phuket, a number of temples in Phuket are Taoist in character. A few in particular stand out. **Sanjao Sam San** (daily 8am–6pm; free) at Thanon Krabi, erected in 1853 in dedication to Tien Sang Sung Moo, the Patron Saint of Sailors and Goddess of the Sea, is recognisable by the gold statues which stand proudly outside and intricate carvings that adorn the inner walls.

Also worth a visit is the **Put Jaw Temple** (daily 8am–6pm; free) on Thanon Ranong, dedicated to

Kwan Im, the Chinese Goddess of Mercy. At a little over 200 years, this is the oldest Chinese Taoist temple in Phuket. It not overly impressive from the outside, and is better known for what happens within. In the middle hall, resting before an image of Kuan Im, are a number of odd-looking fortune telling devices, including a pair of wooden divining blocks, which when dropped to the floor by devotees imply a "yes" or "no" answer to a question – depending on which side they fall on. Your fortune can also be told by the aid of divining sticks *(see margin tip on page 216)*.

Jui Tui Temple (daily 8am–6pm; free), just next to Put Jaw is much more ornate. On the altar inside is the red-faced statue of Kiu Ong Ya, one of the Nine Emperor Gods to whom the temple is dedicated. This temple is the main location for the annual November Vegetarian Festival *(see page 43)* when the streets come alive with thousands who flock here to witness devotees perform grotesque acts of self-mutilation.

Across from Jui Tui Temple on the corner of Thanon Ranong is the

Central Market where you can watch Thai housewives as they banter with the merchants among piles of vegetables, fruit and fish. The uninitiated however may find the pungent scents overpowering.

Crocodile World

To witness a true feast though, visit the **Crocodile World and Sea Aquarium** ❸ (daily 9am–6pm; admission charge), 10 minutes away on Thanon Charoen. Here you can see the fearsome saltwater predators eagerly chomp down on whole raw chickens. Thailand is home to two species of crocodile, the Siamese and the saltwater. In the 1960s, the two species were cross-bred, resulting in a hybrid that tolerated captivity better and produced leather of a higher quality.

PHUKET'S INTERIOR

Most visitors confine themselves to Phuket's beaches and see little else of the island. This is a real pity as the lush interior is filled with verdant jungle-covered hills interspersed with rubber and pineapple planta-

Map on page 214

Koi fish at Phuket's Crocodile World and Sea Aquarium.

BELOW: the entrance to Jui Tui Temple in Phuket Town.

The southwest monsoon brings heavy rain from May to Oct to the Andaman Coast, including Phuket. Nov is the start of the dry season but Dec to Feb is best. Apr and May are the hottest months and Sep the wettest. Hotel rates in Phuket are the lowest from May to Oct and many people take advantage of this as there can be intermittent days of sunshine in between rainy spells.

BELOW: Wat Phra Thong and its half-buried Buddha statue.

tions. Phuket's compact size and relatively good roads will allow you to access trails that lead through primary rainforest to take a dip at hidden waterfalls and still be back at your beachside hotel come nightfall.

Thalang area

About 12 km (7 miles) north of Phuket Town is a large roundabout that dominates Thanon Thepkrasattri (Route 402). It is known both for its ability to annoyingly halt free flowing traffic and for the striking statues of two women encircled by flags. Called the **Heroine's Monument**, these female figures stand proud with drawn swords and honour Lady Chan and Lady Muk, the widow of the governor of Phuket and her sister, who led the successful defence of the island against the invading Burmese in 1785.

The statues mark the entry into the **Thalang** district. Thalang Town itself is rather run down, but it is a district steeped in history, having moved from several different locations before taking up its current position in the geographical centre of Phuket

in 1894. A short distance northeast of the monument is the **Thalang Museum** (daily 9am–4pm; admission charge; tel: 0-7631 1426). The museum contains a few interesting artefacts and displays on Phuket's past. Everything from Phuket's prehistoric cave dwellers and its ethnic diversity as a maritime crossroads to the island's invasion by the Burmese and the great tin mining boom of the 19th century are recounted here.

Return to Route 402 and continue to **Thalang Town** to see one of Phuket's most famous temples, **Wat Phra Thong ④** (daily 8am–6pm; free), a little way north beyond the main crossroads. Inside the main hall is the statue of a golden Buddha that is half buried in the ground. From the chest up it measures about 2 metres (7 ft). Over the years, thanks to stories circulating that the Buddha image was cast in gold, many people, including an invading Burmese army, have tried to dig it out of the ground. To date, none have succeeded in unearthing it, and most have met with grisly deaths, or so the story goes, as a result of a curse asso-

ciated with the image. The statue is in fact made of brick and plaster, with a thin layer of gold covering it.

Khao Phra Taew National Park

East of Thalang Town is **Khao Phra Taew National Park ❺** (daily 6am–6pm; admission charge), a pretty but hardly spectacular protected reserve. This is Phuket's largest tract of virgin rainforest, covering an area of 22 sq km (8½ sq miles). A leisurely 20-minute walk from the park's entrance, over some occasionally steep rocks, leads to **Bang Bae Waterfall**. It's a nice spot for lunch and a swim, but is not overly remarkable as it's neither high nor carries much water, and at certain times of year is totally dry. A further 3 km (2 mile) along the same route is **Ton Sai Waterfall**, which although more impressive, is also at risk of drying up during the summer months.

The rainforest is particularly lush during the May to October monsoon season when flowers bloom and the greenery is more vibrant. Guides are available at the information centre at the park entrance and should be used for treks; unless you are an expert, the rare fan-shaped *lang khao* palms and telltale signs of wildlife are easy to miss. Tigers and bears once roamed the park, but today it is far more common to see monkeys, civets and other small animals.

Gibbon Rehabilitation Centre

A 15–20 minute walk from Bang Pae Waterfall leads to the **Gibbon Rehabilitation Centre ❻** (daily 10am–4pm; free; tel: 0-7626 0491; www.warthai.org). This is a non-profit organisation that aims to stop the poaching of Thailand's gibbons for tourist attractions and the pet trade. The gibbons are kept in large enclosures but as the whole purpose is to reintroduce them to the wild, it's not possible to see them up

close. Although located within the national park, the Gibbon Rehabilitation Centre receives none of the money from park fees and relies solely on donations from visitors.

WEST COAST

Phuket's western coastline is its main claim to fame. Over centuries, the coast has been sculpted by pounding waves into 16 coves stretching from north to south and carpeted in powdery white sand.

Sirinat National Park

A large chunk of the northwest cape is given over to **Sirinat National Park ❼**. Formerly called Nai Yang National Park, it was renamed in 1992 in commemoration of Her Majesty Queen Sirikit's 60th birthday. The 90-sq km (35-sq mile) park, of which 75 percent comprises the surrounding seas, encompasses the beaches at **Hat Nai Yang** and **Hat Nai Thon** as well as the northern mangrove area at **Hat Mai Khao**.

Casuarinas are the most common tree found in the park, and many species of bird, mammal and insect

Map on page 214

Gibbons kept as pets are re-introduced to the wild at Phuket's Gibbon Rehabilitation Centre.

BELOW: water buffalo at Khao Phra Taew National Park.

live within its mangrove forests. The park's marine environment is diverse and its coral reefs are among the most pristine found around Phuket. Located in water between 4–7 metres (12–23 ft) deep are extensive plate and tree corals as well as sea fans and sea anemones. The 600-metre (1,970-ft) long **Thachatchai Nature Trail** at the northern end of the park follows signs along a wooden walkway highlighting various species of flora and fauna common to this region.

Endangered turtle species lay their eggs at Hat Mai Khao between Nov and Feb each year.

Hat Mai Khao

Despite being the longest of Phuket's beaches at over 17 km (11 miles) long, the secluded location of **Hat Mai Khao** ❽ at the top north of the island also makes it one of the quietest. The sands are more golden than white and a little coarse underfoot, but the waters are very clean. There is little to do at Hat Mai Khao other than soak up the sun. As the beach is part of the protected Sirinat National Park, development is virtually non-existent, which is perhaps why hundreds of olive ridley sea turtles, as well as the odd giant

BELOW: JW Marriott Resort & Spa on Hat Mai Khao.

leatherback turtle, come ashore to lay their eggs here between November and February each year.

The only hotel on this beach is the luxury **JW Marriott Resort & Spa**. Initially criticised for encroaching on national park land, the hotel has managed to change the tide of opinion against it by initiating the **Marine Turtle Foundation**. All guests who stay at this hotel are encourged to donate US$1 a day to support local conservation efforts that help ensure the turtles' yearly return.

Hat Nai Yang

Despite housing the headquarters of Sirinat National Park and being a protected area, **Hat Nai Yang** ❾ hosts a few hotels. Still, it is very laid back and quiet compared to the beaches further down the coast. In the low season it is virtually deserted, but high season sees a strip of thatched wooden beach huts serving cold beer and seafood. The beach itself is a beautiful curving bay lined with evergreen trees that provide both visual relief and shade. A large coral reef around 1 km (½ mile) offshore is home to many different species of fish, and Mai Khao's nesting turtles sometimes stray onto the shores of Nai Yang as well.

Hat Nai Thon

The smallest of Sirinat National Park's three beaches, and one of the most isolated on the island is **Hat Nai Thon** ❿, which due to its position at the foot of a series of high hills is harder to reach and requires a journey along a long and winding road passing jungle and rubber plantations. The beach is not totally deserted, however, and a few sun beds are available for hire. Nai Ton is sheltered from the wind and waves and offers good swimming and snorkelling along its rocky headlands that attract rich marine life year round. Offshore are the

remains of a wrecked tin dredger; found at a depth of 16 metres (52 ft), it is a favourite spot with divers.

Ao Bang Thao

The 8 km (5 mile) stretch of beach at gently curving **Ao Bang Thao** ⓫ is dominated by the Laguna Resort, an integrated development of five luxury hotels, the most exclusive being the **Banyan Tree Phuket** with its 18-hole golf course and multi-award-winning spa. The developers chose this location for a reason; the sand on Bang Tao beach is among the whitest on the island, and the water is crystal clear. Beware of the strong undertow, however, during the monsoon season. All accommodation is at the northern end of the beach, so a walk south will often lead to a virtually deserted patch of sand.

Ao Pansea and Hat Surin

Phuket's most exclusive resort, the luxury **Amanpuri** occupies prime position at **Ao Pansea** ⓬. This ultra exclusive hotel is the ultimate in luxury, with Thai-style pavilions interspersed in a coconut plantation

on a sea-facing headland. The beach runs for only 300 metres (984 ft) and although the law in Thailand states that all beaches are public, Pansea seems to be an exception as it's closed off by headlands on either side of the bay. The other end of Ao Pansea is anchored by the **Chedi** resort, much more afffordable, but still beyond the reach of many.

Beyond the Chedi resort, the beach becomes **Hat Surin** ⓭. It is not as pristine as Phuket's other beaches and the sand is more of a golden hue than white, but it's nonetheless popular and surprisingly busy in the high season considering the limited facities available. Again, beware of the undertow during the monsoon season. Vendors frequently set up makeshift stalls at the beach car park and sell freshly grilled prawns and barbecued mackerel.

Hat Kamala

Patong received the most coverage when the tsunami hit Phuket in December 2004, but it was the quieter **Hat Kamala** ⓮ that took the brunt of the killer waves. Damage to

Map
on page
214

TIP

Even if you can't afford to stay at the famed Amanpuri resort (by far Phuket's most expensive) go there for lunch (or a drink) if only to soak in the ambience, architecture and the views from its lofty perch at the top of a cliff. There are lots of Aman wannabe resorts in Phuket these days, but none can equal the Amanpuri.

BELOW: Hat Surin, pretty but be careful of the undertow during the monsoon season.

Having been through the catastrophic tsunami in Dec 2004, Phuket now has an early warning system and clearly marked evacuation routes if ever a tsunami should hit its shores again.

BELOW:
Hat Patong is by far Phuket's busiest beach.

this area of mostly Muslim villages was severe and the area took longer to recover than any other in Phuket. As of 2006 though, the beach looks back to normal and the damaged hotels have been rebuilt. There is still some evidence though, of what occurred, in the mounds of concrete and rubble at various locations inland. Kamala is only a few minutes away from the hustle and bustle of Patong yet could not be more different in character; the beach is calm, relaxed and peaceful with few vendors touting for business.

In the heart of Kamala is the **Phuket Fantasea** ⓯ (daily except Thurs 5.30–11.30pm, show time 9pm; tel: 0-7638 5333, www.phuket-fantasea.com). The 57-hectare (140-acre) complex, which cost a massive US$60 million to construct, touts itself as a night-time cultural theme park. Visitors can pose for photos while riding elephants and cuddling tiger cubs, although the latter are quickly taken from you after the flash goes off and passed on to the next paying customer. The show itself combines acrobatics, pyrotechnics and illusions, and a whole menagerie of performing animals, including at one point over 40 elephants on stage – all at the same time.

Hat Patong

Love it or hate it, Phuket would not be the successful tourist magnet it is today without **Hat Patong** ⓰. Patong, with its multitude of shops, restaurants, street stalls, neon lights, flashy bars and glitzy discos, sums up what many visitors like to see. But individual tastes differ and for every person who is drawn here, there is another who despises it and can't escape quickly enough. The beach is crowded and the constant barrage of hawkers gets annoying, but the location is naturally beautiful. Touts from restaurants and tailors go overboard enticing you into their shops, but at least there is plenty to buy and the variety is good. Restaurants are overpriced, but the range of cuisines on offer is immense and caters for every palette. And while the nightlife in certain areas is seedy and the prostitution blatant, you can have a fun

and entertaining night if you don't take it all too seriously.

The 3 km (2 mile) stretch of Hat Patong was one of the areas worst hit by the tsunami. The beach in the days that followed, totally bereft of deckchairs, umbrellas and people, was a sad but strangely beautiful sight: for the first time in over a decade, it was possible to catch a glimpse of what attracted developers there in the first place.

Unfortunately, after months of reconstruction, Hat Patong is now back to its unsightly pre-tsunami congested state. Sunburnt bodies shelter under rows of beach umbrellas and even in the low season it is virtually impossible to find a quiet spot on the sand. On the plus side, the sea is crystal clear outside of the monsoon season, and is good for swimming or snorkelling, but care should be taken not to get too close to the jet skis and banana boats whizzing by close to the shore.

Note: not many people are aware that only one hotel, the **Phuket Cabana**, is right on the beach. All other properties are tucked behind the beachside Thanon Thaveewong.

Patong nightlife

In the heart of Patong is **Soi Bangla**, the epicentre of the seedy sex trade with bar after bar of young Thai prostitutes, *kathoey*, or "lady-boy" transsexuals, and the explicit "ping-pong" sex shows. Despite the blatant commercial trade, the atmosphere is relaxed and feels surprisingly safe. While single men may get hassled to buy drinks for the bar girls, women, couples and even families can amble down the street, stop in a bar or two and be treated no differently than they would elsewhere on the island.

Showing how easily Thai men can morph into the opposite sex is **Simon Cabaret** (show time nightly at 7.30pm and 9.30pm; admission charge; tel: 0-7634 201; www.phuket-simoncabaret.com), a popular show located on Thanon Sirirat heading south out of Patong. Some people find the show rather dull, with the performing "lady-boys" or *kathoey* miming the lyrics and acting and dancing in an exaggerated manner, but the sight of so many men dressed up as alluring women draws in curious gawkers every night.

Phuket has a fairly large gay district that mainly centres around the network of lanes that make up the **Paradise Complex** near the Royal Paradise Hotel on Thanon Raja Uthit.

Hat Karon Noi and Hat Karon

Past Hat Patong is **Hat Karon Noi**, sometimes referred to as Relax Bay. Although it is a public beach, this crescent of sand is dominated by a single hotel, **Le Meridien Phuket**, making access to it a little difficult.

The 4-km (3-mile) long beach at **Hat Karon** ⑰ is Phuket's second most popular beach after Hat Patong. The sand is golden in colour and the beach is rarely packed; its beauty only hampered slightly by the ugly sand dunes and grassy

Map on page 214

TIP

To see the "lady-boys" at Simon Cabaret without suffering through the show, head to the car park around 11pm when they all come out and line up for photos. This is a better opportunity to see them up close and personal.

BELOW: Patong's Soi Bangla comes alive at night.

Waitresses in costume at Karon's Dino Park and Mini Golf Course.

BELOW:
it is easy to see why Hat Kata Yai is one of Phuket's best beaches.

embankment leading up to the road backing it. It was this elevated position that spared Karon from the same degree of tsunami damage that Patong suffered. During the rainy season, large waves make Hat Karon excellent for surfing although unsafe for swimming. There is a good range of hotels, most of which, like in Patong, are tucked behind the beachside Thanon Karon road.

One of Karon's most prominent attractions is the kitschy **Dino Park and Mini Golf** (daily 10am–10pm; admission charge; tel: 0-7633 0625; www.dinopark.com). It is impossible to miss this sight with its huge dinosaur statue towering outside and staff dressed in Flintstone costumes. At night, an elephant stands at the entrance, waiting to be fed bananas. The tables are carved out of stone and set among pretty waterfalls and jungle vines, but the food is overpriced and bland. More impressive is the mini golf course, which trails over rocks and across rivers, passing screeching dinosaurs with smoking nostrils and clusters of half-hatched eggs.

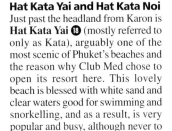

Hat Kata Yai and Hat Kata Noi

Just past the headland from Karon is **Hat Kata Yai** ⓱ (mostly referred to only as Kata), arguably one of the most scenic of Phuket's beaches and the reason why Club Med chose to open its resort here. This lovely beach is blessed with white sand and clear waters good for swimming and snorkelling, and as a result, is very popular and busy, although never to the point of discomfort. The southern end of the beach is home to the **The Boathouse** hotel, which has a well-known fine-dining restaurant. At night, the beach is quiet and romantic, and there are a number of seafood restaurants lit by fairy lights overlooking the waves lapping the shore.

Separated by a rocky headland is **Hat Kata Noi** ⓲, which shares the same white sand and clear blue-green waters as the preceding beach but is even prettier and more peaceful. The sprawling but unattractive **Kata Thani Resort** has almost complete run of this beach. At the southern end of the beach are some decent corals for snorkelling.

Kata Hill Viewpoint

A sharp, steep mountain road leads out of Kata, one that cars sometimes struggle with and motorbikes splutter trying to crest. On a sunny day, the view from this road is breathtaking. A number of small, reggae-type bars have opened up along the road in recent years, building simple wooden platforms out over the hillside towards the sea; any of them would be good for watching the setting sun. At the peak is the **Kata Hill Viewpoint** ⓴ from which the three stunning bays of Kata, Karon and Patong can be seen at one fell swoop. This famous scene appears on postcards island wide; photography conditions are better in the morning, as even on a seemingly perfect day the clouds can roll in by mid-afternoon and block the view.

Hat Nai Harn

South of Kata and lying between two ridges is stunning white sand **Hat Nai Harn** ㉑, the epitome of a chilled and laid back Thai beach. For this it can thank the **Samnak Song Nai Harn Monastery**, which occupies a large portion of the beachfront land, and therefore thwarted development. Popular with expats who are frequently seen exercising their dogs along the beach on Sunday mornings, Nai Harn is a quieter alternative to the island's other beaches. It offers some conveniences in the form of a few small bars, restaurants and shops. An open lagoon, the cause of much controversy when the trees bordering it were ripped out in early 2005, backs the beach. Officially, the trees were cleared to make way for a public pathway, but right now it looks like a blight on the landscape.

SOUTH COAST

The south coast beaches from Laem Promthep onwards are largely mediocre at best and mainly used as a staging point for explorations of the islands off the southern coast.

Laem Promthep

Leading up the mountain from Nai Harn is another viewpoint that features on many a postcard of Phuket, **Laem Promthep** ㉒ (Promthep Cape). This busy point overlooking a splendid headland stretching into the blue Andaman Sea is packed every evening throughout the year when hoards of tourists flock to see the mango-hued sun sink slowly over the horizon. When the conditions are right, the sunset vistas here are breathtaking. **Promthep Cape Restaurant** *(see margin tip)*, overlooking the cape and serving cheap Thai food, is surprisingly quiet considering the number of visitors who make it up here.

Hat Rawai

A base for the vast majority of Phuket's foreign residents, **Hat Rawai** ㉓ offers all the attractions of island life but without the intrusive tourist facilities of Kata, Karon and Patong. Rawai is often picturesque with its rows of small fishing and longtail boats waiting to journey to the nearby islands, but at low tide, the exposed rocks make it

Map on page 214

TIP

The views at Promthep Cape Restaurant (tel: 0-7628 8851; open daily lunch and dinner) are much better than the mostly mediocre food. The fresh oysters, reared in the owner's farm, are far more impressive. Service is slow, but the staff are friendly and the prices reasonable.

BELOW: aerial view of Kata, Karon and Patong beaches from the Kata Hill Viewpoint.

unsuitable for swimming and snorkelling. Rawai is famous for its street vendors who barbeque freshly caught seafood along the beach road throughout the day and the fresh seafood restaurants which open in the evenings. To the south of the beach is a small *chao lay* (sea gypsy) village that can be visited.

The most exclusive hotel in the area, the **Evason Resort and Spa**, has its own private beach in addition to having access to an offshore island, **Ko Bon**, for its guests to use.

Nearby on Thanon Viset is the **Phuket Seashell Museum** (daily 8am–6pm; admission charge), with an interesting display of over 2,000 different species of shells and fossils; some of the latter are reputedly over 380 million years old.

Ao Chalong

North of Rawai is **Ao Chalong**, which is known mainly for a temple and its pier, from which many scuba expeditions and boat trips to nearby islands depart from.

Wat Chalong ㉔ (daily 8am–6pm; free), located inland of Rawai

on Route 4021 is Phuket's most important Buddhist temple and the largest of the island's 29 Buddhist monasteries. Architecturally, it's not much different from other Thai temples, but it is one of Phuket's most ornate and among the most visited by both Thais and foreigners. The temple is associated with the revered monks Luang Pro Chaem and Luang Pho Chuang, famous herbal doctors and bone setters who tended to the people of Phuket during the tin miners' rebellion of 1876. Far from being just physical healers, they also mediated in the conflict, bringing both parties together to resolve disputes. Today, many Thais visit the temple to pay homage to the two statues that honour the monks.

SOUTHERN ISLANDS

The waters around Phuket's southernmost tip are dotted with a number of islands. All can be reached by the longtail boats lining Hat Rawai beach or the pier at Ao Chalong. If staying overnight at islands like Ko Racha, the resort there will arrange the boat transfer for you.

Ko Bon

Nearest to shore is the small but pretty **Ko Bon ㉕**. Jointly owned by the five-star Evason Resort and Spa on Hat Rawai and by local businessmen, the island can be reached in just 10 minutes. Unfortunately, it has no fresh water or electricity and no accommodation. One side of the island is owned by the Evason Resort and is intended for the private use of its guests (free boat transfers are provided from Hat Rawai). It is possible to walk from one side to the other, and although the Evason's beach is beautiful, the food and drink prices at its clubhouse match those of the resort on the mainland.

Most daytrippers head for the other side where **Sit Lo Chia**, a small Thai and seafood restaurant, is all that rests on the sandy beachfront. Some of the coral close to shore was damaged by the tsunami, and larger fragments are still strewn on the beach, too heavy to be moved (but ironically look quite pretty). Coral in the deeper waters remains undamaged and while the Evason's beach is better for swimming, the water in front of Sit Lo Chia is particularly good for snorkelling.

Ko Hae

Abou 20 minutes from mainland Phuket, and often combined on a day trip with Ko Bon is **Ko Hae ㉖** (Coral Island). Amenities are better than at Ko Bon, with a number of restaurants, a few small shops and a choice of watersports. Overnight stays are possible at the **Coral Island Resort** (tel: 0-7628 1060), the island's only accommodation; nights are generally very quiet when all the daytrippers have returned to Phuket. The crystal clear turquoise waters around the island make it particularly good for both swimming and snorkelling, and there is a shallow coral reef within easy swimming distance of the beach.

Ko Kaeo

Known to locals as Buddha Island, **Ko Kaeo ㉗** is by far the least visited by daytrippers due to its lack of facilities, giving visitors the chance to have their own private beach for the day. Only a 10-minute boat ride from mainland Phuket, the pretty island is home to a number of Buddha statues and shrines, hence its name.

Ko Racha

Around 20 km (12 miles) off the coast of Rawai are **Ko Racha Noi**, a small uninhabited island with more rocks than beaches, and the larger **Ko Racha Yai ㉘**. Of the many islands within close proximity of Phuket, Ko Racha Yai is undoubtedly the most exclusive, as it's the site of a luxury resort known simply as **The Racha** on the northeast coast along **Ao Batok**. In 2004, it was voted one of the top 100 hottest new resorts in the world by *Condé Nast Traveller* magazine. High season sees Ko Racha Yai transform into a bustling hotspot, with daytrippers arriving on longtail boats and filling out the beaches. The shoreline of the beach in front of The

Map on page 214

Ko Kaeo island has numerous Buddha statues and shrines, hence its name, Buddha Island.

BELOW: pristine Ao Batok on Ko Racha Yai.

Spectacular undersea life awaits divers in the waters around Ko Racha Yai and Noi.

Racha is picturesque, the sand almost talcum powder-like and the waters crystal clear turquoise. Watch out for the small corals and rocks, however when you wade into the waters.

Ko Racha offers some of the best diving in the Phuket area and is often compared to the waters around the Similan Islands. The **Bungalow Bay** reef offshore of Ao Batok has clear waters and soft coral gardens, with good visibility and currents that allow gentle drift diving along sloping reefs. Elsewhere on the island are more white sand beaches and snorkelling spots. Resting at the bottom of a grassy slope on the eastern coast is **Ao Kon Kare**, a small sandy beach with **Lucy's Reef** within swimming distance, a nickname given to the staghorn coral found here. Further up the east coast, a submerged wreck is found off **Ao Ter** at depths of 25–35 metres (80–115 ft); it is popular with more advanced divers. On the northern coast is **Ao Siam**, where shallow waters not only make for good snorkelling but also prevent boats from docking, keeping this beach less busy than those on other parts of the island. Siam Bay still shows some evidence of tsunami damage in the form of ruined bungalows and beach bars close to shore, but there is talk of rebuilding in the near future.

The smaller **Ko Racha Noi** also has a few good dive sites for experienced divers; depths here are generally greater and currents stronger. On the southwest side of the island, lots of interesting reef fish are drawn to a 27-metre (88-ft) shipwreck, while a large pinnacle at the northern tip attracts stingrays and reef sharks.

Phuket's other dive sites are scattered around the Andaman Coast *(see pages 200, 201, 254 and 259).*

EAST COAST

The east coast of Phuket was once the bank of a flooded river. Unlike the west, this side of the coastline comprises mainly limestone shoals and virtually no sandy beaches.

Laem Panwa

The only real beach spot on the eastern coast of Phuket is **Laem Panwa**, 10 km (6 miles) southeast from

Phuket Town. This quiet cape is frequently filled with yachts sailing around **Ao Yon** , where a totally unspoilt stretch of sand sheltered by headlands on both sides makes it good for swimming year round. Only a handful of hotels and restaurants stand in the Laem Panwa area, and as *tuk-tuks* and motorcycle taxis rarely journey over the winding mountain road to get here, the beach is often deserted.

Khao Khad Viewpoint (reached by following signs along Thanon Sakdidej which lead through Muang Tong village) is one of the island's best kept secrets and a beautiful spot from which to gaze out to the sea. From this elevated point, Phuket Town lies to one side, Chalong Bay to the other, and the shadowy outline of Ko Phi Phi *(see page 251)* island can be seen in the distance.

On the southernmost tip of Laem Panwa on Route 4129 is the **Phuket Aquarium & Marine Biological Research Centre** (daily 8.30am–4pm; admission charge; tel: 0-7639 1128). It re-opened in April 2005 after over two years' renovation. The impressive display of sharks, tropical fish, reefs and a touch pool with star fish and sea cucumbers is an excellent primer before taking that first diving or snorkelling trip.

Ko Sirey

To the east of Phuket Town and separated from the mainland by a small bridge is the tiny island of **Ko Sirey** , home to a small *chao lay* (sea gypsy) fishing community and the **Phuket International Dog School** (tel: 0-7621 6336) but not a lot else. This dog training complex has regular dog shows featuring movie stars of the four-legged variety – one "actor" had his cameo appearance in the 2004 film *Bridget Jones: The Edge of Reason*. The *chao lay* village is one of the largest in Phuket, but it is poverty stricken

and not very pleasant to walk around; many people who have visited before feel uncomfortable about intruding. More pleasant to visit is the smaller but more welcoming community on **Hat Rawai** *(see page 226)*.

Naga Pearl Farm

The jetty at Ao Po, north of Phuket Town, is the departure point for the 30-minute boat ride to the island of **Ko Nakha Noi** . This is where you find the **Naga Pearl Farm** (daily 9am–3.30pm; admission charge; tel: 0-7742 3272), where full-sized South Sea pearls worth thousands of dollars are cultivated. It also displays a replica of the world's largest pearl, the original of which is currently housed at the Mikimoto Pearl Museum in Japan. Visitors can wander round and see pearls at various stages of cultivation, from the nurturing of the baby oysters to the extraction of pearls from their shells years later. Longtail boat operators at Ao Po can arrange a boat ride to the island (about B300 per person for a return trip) or else book a guided tour directly with the farm. ❑

Map on page 214

TIP

If you must visit Ko Sirey, or any sea gypsy village, have consideration for its inhabitants. The village, after all, is their home and not a living museum for visitors to wander at will. Be sensitive when exploring the village, tempering it with consideration for the villagers' mood.

BELOW: sea gypsy children collecting mussels on a Phuket beach.

P HUKET

TRANSPORT

GETTING THERE

By Air

Phuket International Airport (tel: 0-7632 7230/5) is located in the north of the island. Though most visitors to Phuket stop off in Bangkok first for a few days, many also fly directly to Phuket from Cambodia (Siem Reap Airways), Hong Kong (Dragonair), Kuala Lumpur (Malaysia Airlines, Air Asia, Thai Airways), Sydney (Thai Airways) and Singapore (SilkAir, Jetstar Asia, Tiger Airways, Thai Airways). Internally, Thai Airways offers daily flights from Bangkok, while Bangkok Airways flies daily from Bangkok and Ko Samui. Several budget airlines fly to Phuket from Bangkok, including One-Two-Go (Orient Thai Airlines), AirAsia and Nok Air *(see pages 103–4 for details of domestic airlines)*.

By Road

Air-conditioned buses from the **Southern Bus Terminal** in Bangkok make the 14-hour overnight trip to Phuket. But with so many cheap flights there, it makes little sense

taking this uncomfortable option. From the bus terminal in Phuket Town (Th. Phang Nga, tel: 0-7621 1977) there are air-conditioned buses departing daily for nearby Krabi, Phang Nga, Ranong, Surat Thani, Satun, Hat Yai and Trang.

By Boat

Boats from Krabi and Ko Phi Phi to Phuket normally drop passengers off at Rassada pier in Phuket Town. It takes roughly 2½ hours from Ko Phi Phi and 3 hours from Krabi. Boats from Ko Lanta travel via Krabi or Ko Phi Phi. Between May and October, boats may stop operating due to wet weather.

The islands south of Phuket, like Ko Bon, Ko Hae, Ko Kaeo (Buddha Island) and Ko Racha, can be visited by chartering a longtail boat from Rawai beach, and, except for Ko Racha, can be reached in 10 to 20 minutes. Visitors to further flung Ko Racha usually join a day trip on a larger, quicker boat from Chalong pier. Depending on sea conditions, transfer time is 45–60 minutes to Ko Racha. The Racha resort on the island can also arrange both the land transfer from the airport and the boat trip for hotel guests – albeit at inflated rates.

GETTING AROUND

From the Airport

Travelling to Phuket Town from the airport takes about 45 minutes, while Patong beach can be reached in around half an hour. Even during the high season, traffic flows freely. If you plan to drive, Hertz and Avis *(see page 231)* both have car rental counters at the airport.
Taxi: In the Arrival Hall, airport taxis and limousines cab be hired at set rates displayed on a board. After paying the fare, a coupon is issued which is then given to the driver. Prices start at B200 to B400 for the nearby northern beaches, rising to B550 to B750 for different locations in Patong. Trips to hotels on Kata and Karon have a flat fare of B650.
Minibus: If you are part of a large group, book an 8-seater minibus. The fares are around B900 to Phuket Town, B1,200 to B1,500 to Patong and B1,300 to Kata and Karon. Tickets are sold next to the limousine booths.
Airport Bus: Tickets for the airport bus can be bought on boarding or from designated booths in the

arrival hall. Passengers to Phuket Town are usually dropped off first, so if you are staying at one of the beaches it can take a while to get there. At around B300 to Phuket Town, it is a cheaper option than taxis. A larger airport bus, route 8411, also runs daily between the airport and town.

Taxis & Tuk-tuks

Public transport in Phuket is notoriously poor. There are few metered taxis and those that have meters will never use them. Taxi fares have to be negotiated except for taxis boarded from taxi stands at major shopping centres and some beaches, where prices are fixed.

*Tuk-tuk*s are plentiful, but prices are among the highest in Thailand, costing nearly as much as taxis. Agree on a price before getting in a *tuk-tuk*, and be aware that prices will rise at night and during rainy spells. Unlike those in Bangkok, Phuket's *tuk-tuk*s have four wheels instead of three and are painted bright red. These converted open-air vans have two benches in the back, and are not very comfortable on long journeys. Expect to pay about B200 to B250 for a trip between Phuket Town and Patong, and about B150 to B200 between Patong and Kata or Karon, although it comes down to what you can negotiate in the end.

Motorcycle taxis are a cheaper but more risky way to travel, with at least one death per week from road collisions during the high season.

Buses

Small, blue public buses called *songthaew* shuttle from the market on Th. Ranong in Phuket Town to the main beaches. They leave every half hour between 8am and 6pm. Those to Rawai and Nai Harn depart from Th. Bangkok. There are no *songthaew* connections between beaches, so this would require unnecessary travelling to and from the town departure point. *Songthaews* also move very slowly and stop frequently to cram in as many locals as possible.

Rented cars

Driving in Phuket can be challenging. Motorists frequently resist giving way, and exceed the speed limit. It is not uncommon to see trucks overtaking on blind corners. As a result, road accidents are shockingly common, most involving motorcyclists. An alarming number of people drink and drive, in part because of limited public transportation.

The roads outside of town are less busy, making driving almost pleasurable. Note, however, that scenic roads during the day become pitch black and hazardous at night.

Car rental ranges from B1,200 to B2,000 a day. Use a reputable company because many of the independent beachfront businesses do not provide insurance. **Avis**, Phuket Airport, tel: 0-7635 1243; www.avisworld.com. **Budget**, 36/1 Moo 6, Thalang, tel: 0-7620 5398; www.budget.co.th **Hertz**, Phuket Airport, tel: 0-7632 8545; www.hertz.com.

RESTAURANTS

PHUKET TOWN

International

Salvatores
15-17 Th. Rasada. Tel: 0-7622 5958. Open: daily except Mon L & D. $$–$$$.
www.salvatoresrestaurant.com
Watching owner/chef Salvatore at work in the kitchen, it is easy to see why *Tatler Thailand* voted this the country's (not just the island's) best Italian restaurant. Begin with the gnocchi with lamb sauce, followed with homemade ice-cream and round off with fresh ground Italian coffee. The tables in its rustic interior are fully booked most nights so reservations are strongly recommended.

Watermark Bar and Restaurant
22/1 Moo 2, Th. Thepkasattri. Tel: 0-7623 9730. Open: daily L & D. $$$.
www.watermarkphuket.com
Overlooking the yachts at the Boat Lagoon Marina, the atmosphere in this dockside retreat is chic, and although the clientele is a bit pretentious, the food is not. Everything on the menu is delicious; the fresh mint and green pea risotto with baby prawns is particularly good.

Thai

Natural Restaurant
Soi Phutorn. Tel: 0-7622 4287. Open: daily 10.30am–11.30pm. $.
Unique restaurant with jungle decor and chunky wooden tables hidden by branches and vines. Serves all the classic Thai dishes, including *mussaman gai* (chicken curry with potato) and *hu mook* (steamed fish with chilli and coconut). Food is no better or worse than at other Thai restaurants but the setting and reasonable prices make it a must.

Tung-Ka Café
Rang Hill, Th. Korsimbi. Tel: 0-7621 1500. Open: daily 11am–11pm. $.
Perched on the peak of

Rang Hill is this popular restaurant now in operation for more than 30 years. *Plaa nueng menao* (steamed lemon fish) is particularly good, and although the wine list is limited there is no corkage fee if you bring a bottle. Most impressive at night when Phuket Town becomes a mass of twinkling lights.

AO BANG TAO

International

The Red Room
293/25-6 Th. Srisoonthorn.
Tel: 0-7627 1136. Open: daily
L & D. $$–$$$.
Despite the enticing red glow on the outside giving it an alarming brothel-like appearance, the red candles and red walls within create a rather seductive ambience. Try the fillet of salmon drizzled with champagne lemon dill sauce, or the tuna with capsicum and garlic sauce. Features live jazz on Friday evenings.

The Supper Club
Unit 20/382 Th. Srisoonthorn.
Tel: 0-7627 0936. Open: daily
6pm–1am. $$$–$$$$.
Chic ambience with food to match. Serves mouthwatering meat dishes including grilled tenderloin of beef and rack of lamb as well as tasty vegetarian options. The goat cheese with pesto balsamic dressing is simply divine.

Tatonka
382/19 Moo 1, Th. Srisoonthorn. Tel: 0-7632 4349. Open: daily except Wed, D only. $$$.
Spanish-style al fresco eatery with vine-covered trellises and wall murals. The innovative fusion cuisine, prepared in an open kitchen, presents seemingly bizarre combinations, including Peking duck pizza and sashimi spring rolls – a must-try for adventurous diners.

HAT KAMALA

International

Rockfish
33/6 Hat Kamala. Tel: 0-7627 9732. Open: daily 8am–late.
$$$–$$$$.
Trendy food at reasonable prices considering Tatler's *Thailand's Best Restaurants 2005* guide voted this three-storey open-sided house Phuket's top eatery. Despite some flashy dishes such as kingfish wrapped in spinach leaves with red curry sauce, the atmosphere is casual and the sunset beach views are lovely.

HAT PATONG

International

Baan Yin Dee
7/5 Th. Muean Ngen.
Tel: 0-7629 4104. Open: daily
7am–midnight. $$$.
www.baanyindee.com

Grand piano music accompanies an elevated view of the bay to create an intimate atmosphere inside this elegant restaurant. Serves innovative fusion cuisine such as yellow curry prawns with cointreau and apples, and good Thai food toned down slightly for delicate palates.

Da Maurizio
223/2 Th. Prabaramee.
Tel: 0-7634 4079. Open: daily
noon–midnight. $$$$.
www.damaurizio.com
One of the finest of Phuket's restaurants with waves breaking on rocks close to tables and flickering candlelight bouncing off the interior cave-like walls. Food is exquisite – start with the bacon-wrapped goat cheese and savour it with a glass of chilled crisp white wine – it simply doesn't get any better. Advance bookings are essential.

Indian

Baluchi
Horizon Beach Resort, Soi Kep Sap. Tel: 0-7629 2526. Open: daily L & D. $$.
Phuket's only award winning Indian restaurant serves authentic North Indian dishes. Set menus available for lunch and dinner as well as extensive a la carte selection. Mutton *rogangosh* is the house speciality although the *tandoori nisa* (barbecued tiger prawns) is also very impressive.

Thai

Baan Rim Pa
223 Th. Prabaramee.
Tel: 0-7634 0789. Open: daily
noon–midnight. $$$–$$$$.
www.baanrimpa.com
Famous clif-hugging restaurant in the style of an old teak house. Known for its ambience and quality food. Serves outstanding Royal Thai cuisine, retaining all the flavour but without the chilli kick. Arrive early and have a drink on the terrace while enjoying the sea views. Reservations are essential.

Savoey Seafood
136 Th. Thaweewong.
Tel: 0-7634 1174. Open: daily
L & D. $$.
Impossible to miss with its prime beachfront location and elaborate outdoor displays of fresh fish and ridiculously huge "Phuket lobsters". Selected seafood is whisked away and returned cooked to your liking, whether deep fried, grilled or steamed with Thai herbs.

HAT KARON

International

Las Margaritas
Soi Islandia Park Resort.
Tel: 0-7628 6400. Open: daily
L & D. $$.
Fusion cuisine from as far across the globe as Mexico, India, Hawaii, the Mediterranean and of course Thailand. Of

the extensive selection of dishes, the Mexican offerings are the best. The sizzling chicken fajitas go down well with a bottle of Corona.

Wildfire
509 Th. Patak. Tel: 0-7639 6139. Open: daily B, L & D. $$.
Split-level restaurant combining four dining options in one place: haute cusine, bar and delicatessen, a Brazilian-style grill, and a pizzeria with a wood-fired oven serving freshly-baked pizzas by the beach.

Thai & Western

On The Rock
Marina Phuket Resort.
Tel: 0-7633 0625. Open: daily B, L & D. $$.
Cosy little restaurant within the Marina Phuket Resort, aptly named after the sea-facing rocks on which its elevated deck rests. Menu is predominantly Thai with a few Western dishes. Reservations recommended.

Red Onion
486 Th. Patak. Tel: 0-7639 6827. Open: daily B, L & D. $.
Although similar in appearance to its competitors on either side of the road, the food is better and the staff friendlier at this open-air eatery. The Western options are mediocre, but Thai classics like *gaeng keow waan gai* (green chicken curry), washed down with Thailand's favourite Chang beer, are all brilliant.

HAT KATA

International

Capannina
30/9 Moo 2, Th. Kata.
Tel: 0-7628 4318. Open: daily noon–11pm. $$.
Italian-managed terracotta and mustard coloured eatery serving the usual Italian fare: antipasti, fresh breads, homemade pasta and risotto. The real draws though are the huge stone-fired oven pizzas. The large measures a whopping 60 cm (24 inches) in diameter!

The Coffee Pot
110/3 Th. Taina. Tel: 0-7633 3203. Open: daily 8am–10.30pm. $$.
This great little restaurant could be easily missed were it not for the wafting aroma of steaks and chops being grilled by the Aussie chef on the huge open barbecue at the front. The Sunday roast with all the trimmings and freshly-baked bread is a real feast.

Mom Tri's Boathouse Wine and Grill
182 Th. Kata. Tel: 0-7633 0015.
Open: daily D only. $$$–$$$$.
www.boathousephuket.com
This is an internationally-acclaimed restaurant with a panoramic view of Kata Bay. Has a fine, if pricey, wine list, although its zesty vodka sorbet is just as impressive. Serves a selection of well-prepared Thai, European and seafood

dishes – try the exquisite Rock Lobster Trilogy.

Thai

Kata Mama
South end of Hat Kata Yai.
Tel: 0-7628 4301. Open: daily 8am–midnight. $.
This popular family-run operation serving home-style Thai dishes and seafood has been around for over 35 years. Serves favourites such as fried fish with garlic and pepper, and barbecued prawns with chilli sauce.

HAT NAI HARN

International

L'Orfeo
95/13 Soi Saiyuan.
Tel: 0-7628 8935. Open: daily except Wed, D only. $$.
A wonderfully romantic spot if you can get a table. Sirloin tips are a house speciality, served on wooden chopping boards with a choice of sauce. Desserts change regularly, but keep an eye out for the zesty lemon mascarpone mousse.

Regatta Bar and Grill
Le Royal Meridien Phuket Yacht Club. Tel: 0-7638 1156. Open: daily B, L & D. $$$.
Classy dining with live music accompaniment. The cuisine is mainly contemporary Italian, but seafood specialities also feature strongly. Arrive early for sunset cocktails at the bar, which overlooks Nai Harn beach.

AO CHALONG

International

The Green Man Pub and Restaurant
82/15 Moo 4, Th. Patak.
Tel: 0-7628 0757. Open: daily 11–2am. $$.
www.the-green-man.net
Owner Howard Digby-Johns' eccentricities, raucous laugh and zest for life keep patrons coming back for more at this English-style pub with a menu so huge it comes in a ring binder. Traditional Sunday roast and Friday curry nights. The giant onion *bhajis* are a meal in themselves.

Thai

Kang Eang 2
9/3 Th. Chaofa. Tel: 0-7638 1323.
Open: daily 10am–10pm. $.
Seafood restaurant directly overlooking the sea where a small fireworks display erupts at 8pm nightly, making it the perfect place for a birthday or anniversary celebration. Mostly seafood either barbecued or steamed and accompanied with a variety of sauces.

PRICE CATEGORIES

Price per person for a three-course meal without drinks:
$ = under US$10
$$ = US$10–$25
$$$ = US$25–$50
$$$$ = over US$50

ACCOMMODATION

PHUKET TOWN

Moderate

Metropole Hotel
1 Soi Surin, Th. Montri.
Tel: 0-7621 5050.
www.metropolephuket.com
Large and ugly from the
outside, but nicer inside
and in a great location
close to the town's main
shops and attractions.
Staff are friendly, and
service is of a high
standard. (228 rooms)

Royal Phuket City Hotel
154 Th. Phang Nga. Tel: 0-7623
3333. www.royalphuketcity.com
This centrally-located
hotel is large yet welcoming and easily the best in
town. Facilities include a
sandwich corner, café
and the trendy bar/night-
club Zanzibar in the
adjoining annexe, plus
fitness centre and swim-
ming pool. (251 rooms)

HAT MAI KHAO

Expensive

**JW Marriott Phuket
Resort & Spa**
Moo 3, Mai Khao. Tel: 0-7633
8000. www.marriott.com
Located a few minutes
from the airport, this
self-contained sanctuary
has extensive facilities
including seven restau-
rants, fitness centre,
spa and watersports
facilities. Set in sprawl-

ing landscaped grounds,
this is the only property
of note on Mai Khao
beach and sits just adja-
cent to a national park
and a turtle-nesting
sanctuary. Some people
like the isolation while
others feel it's too far
away from the town and
the main beaches. (246
rooms and 13 suites)

HAT NAI YANG

Expensive

Indigo Pearl
Nai Yang. Tel: 0-7632 7006.
www.indigo-pearl.com
Located within Sirinat
National Park and by the
beach, the former Pearl
Village is slated to re-
open at the end of 2006
after undergoing major
renovations and a name
change. The design
mixes contemporary with
Thai accents, if the web-
site pictures are anything
to go by. (292 rooms)

AO BANG TAO

Luxury

Banyan Tree Phuket
33 Moo 4, Th. Srisoonthorn.
Tel: 0-7632 4374.
www.banyantree.com
Most exclusive of the
five hotels within the
Laguna Phuket complex
and has won numerous
awards and accolades

over the years. Luxurious
Thai-style villas with
landscaped gardens and
private outdoor pools.
Excellent spa on site.
Perfect getaway for hon-
eymooners. (108 rooms)

Expensive

Dusit Laguna
390 Th. Srisoonthorn. Tel:
0-7632 4324. www.dusit.com
Low-rise, modern Thai
style buildings contain
bright and airy rooms
with wooden floors. Part
of the Thai-owned luxury
Dusit group, it's located
right on Bang Thao
beach. All rooms have
balconies, and there are
six restaurants to chose
from. (226 rooms)

**Sheraton Grande
Laguna Phuket**
10 Moo 4, Th. Srisoonthorn.
Tel: 0-7632 4101.
www.sheraton.phuket.com
It's water water every-
where at this large and
luxurious Sheraton. Sits
on its own small island
in the centre of a lagoon,
with Bang Tao beach at
the front and forests at
the back. Lagoon-style
pools wind through the
entire property. (252
rooms and 83 villas)

AO PANSEA

Luxury

Amanpuri
118/1 Moo 3, Pansea. Tel: 0-
7632 4333. www.amanpuri.com

Without a doubt
Phuket's most exclusive
retreat, situated on a
headland with its own
private beach and a fleet
of luxury boats. The
Amanpuri is all about
understated elegance. It
naturally attracts A-list
celebrities and the very
rich who seek privacy.
The beach is located at
the bottom of a long
flight of steps. (40
rooms and 31 villas)

Expensive

The Chedi
118 Moo 3, Pansea. Tel: 0-7632
4017. www.ghmhotels.com
Overshadowed by the
nearby Amanpuri, rooms
here are simple
thatched cottages, each
with private verandah
and teakwood floors. As
the cottages hug a cliff,
expect to climb a lot
stairs which sometimes
take a circuitous route.
It has one of Phuket's
most inviting swimming
pools and a gorgeous
beachfront. (108 rooms)

HAT SURIN

Luxury

Twin Palms Phuket
106/46 Moo 3, Surin.
Tel: 0-7631 6500.
www.twinpalms-phuket.com
Modern and stylish
resort only a 5-minute
walk from Surin beach.
Contemporary decor

with white walls and bed-linen contrasting with dark wooden floors and furniture. All the usual amenities expected from a luxury resort plus the hip Oriental Spoon restaurant serving innovative Western and Thai dishes. (76 rooms)

Expensive

Treetops Arasia
125 Moo 3, Th. Srisoonthorn. Tel: 0-7627 1271.
www.treetops-arasia.com
Aptly named due to its elevated positioning high on the tree-covered Surin hill, this boutique resort has a perfect, uninterrupted view of the bay and is within walking distance of the beach. This is a great place to be during the monsoon season when massive storms over the open sea light up the sky. (48 rooms)

HAT PATONG

Luxury

Ban Yin Dee
7/5 Th. Muean Ngen. Tel: 0-7629 4104. www.baanyindee.com
A boutique-style resort with the ambience of a private villa. Distinct Thai-style design with triangular arching roofs and extensive use of teak, marble and rattan throughout. Three swimming pools and a 12-person jacuzzi with a bird's eye view of Patong beach. (21 rooms)

Expensive

Burasari Resort
31/1 Soi Ruamjai. Tel: 0-7629 2929. www.burasari.com
Burasari is a maze of exotic plants, flowers and waterfalls set around a swimming pool. The decor is a blend of contemporary and Thai, and the resort itself is perfectly located: just a minute's walk down a quiet street off the main beach road – keeping it secluded yet in the midst of the action. (90 rooms)

Holiday Inn Resort
52 Th. Thaweewong. Tel: 0-7634 0608.
www.phuket.holiday-inn.com
Improved and upgraded as part of a massive refurbishment following the tsunami, the Holiday Inn is only a 5-minute walk from the beach. Has four swimming pools with fountains, sandstone sculptures and jacuzzis. Very popular during the high season. (405 rooms)

Moderate

Novotel Coralia Phuket
282 Th. Prabaramee. Tel: 0-7634 2777.
www.accorhotels-asia.com
Set slightly up a hill on the far end of Patong, the Novotel is popular because of its friendly service and international reputation. It could do with some renovations, but it is comfortable and clean, with spacious rooms and rates that are lower than other hotels in the same category. (215 rooms)

Budget

Expat Hotel
163/17 Th. Ratutit. Tel: 0-7634 2143.
www.phuket.com/patong/expat.htm
Situated on the back road near the central street of Soi Bangla and a 5-minute walk from the beach, the Expat Hotel is a favourite with return guests. Its old-style decor keeps prices lower than many other Patong hotels in the same price range. Clean rooms, friendly service and large swimming pool make it great value for money. (46 rooms)

HAT KARON

Expensive

Hilton Phuket Arcadia Resort & Spa
333 Th. Patak. Tel: 0-7639 6433. www.hilton.com
Phuket's largest hotel is housed in this rather odd looking circular structure set in a prime location at the centre of Karon. The beach itself is located a short walk across the road. The inside is far more appealing and there are excellent facilities including pool and spa, tennis and squash courts, jogging and walking tracks and a putting green. (679 rooms)

Le Meridien Phuket Beach Resort
Karon Noi. Tel: 0-7634 0480.
www.lemeridien.com
Located in a sheltered bay with a private beach on its doorstep. Facilities are top rate: two massive adjoining swimming pools, spa, numerous restaurants, bars and shops, golf driving range and one of the island's largest and most modern gyms. Rooms are spacious and tastefully furnished. (407 rooms)

Moderate

Central Karon Village
8/21 Moo 1 Karon. Tel: 0-7628 6300. www.centralhotelsresorts.com
Perched on a hill with sweeping views of the beach, the trade-off is no direct beach access. As the hotel is located at the northern end of Karon, it has in fact easy access to Patong beach. Rooms are contemporary in look with pure white linens contrasting against bold, bright-coloured walls and cushions. (72 rooms)

HAT KATA

Expensive

Mom Tri's Boathouse
Kata Yai. Tel: 0-7633 0015.
www.boathousephuket.com
Prime beachfront location along the broad Kata

PRICE CATEGORIES

Price categories are for a double room without breakfast and taxes:
Luxury = over US$200
Expensive = US$100–200
Moderate = US$50–100
Budget = under US$50

Yai beach. All rooms (albeit on the smallish side) have sunset-facing sea views. Award-winning Boathouse Wine & Grill on site. (33 rooms and 3 suites). Note: south of the Boathouse and located on the cliff just above the headland is the **Villa Royale**. Under the same management as the Boathouse, many of its Thai-style villas have stunning sea views and are only a short walk to the smaller and more intimate Kata Noi beach. Prices here are in the luxury category (27 villas).

Club Med

Kata Yai. Tel: 0-7633 0455.

www.clubmed.com

Set directly in front of Kata Yai beach, Club Med is spread out rather than built up, so it blends into the landscape and keeps the beach view clear. Price is inclusive of all accommodation, food and drink, and use of all resort facilities except motorised water sports. (297 rooms)

Katathani Hotel and Beach Resort

Kata Noi. Tel: 0-7633 0010/4.

www.katathani.com

Located on quiet Kata Noi where guests have pretty much the run of the stunning beach. The resort is large and spread out so it never seems overcrowded. Rooms (the standard ones feel cramped) have been given a makeover in teak-wood and sandstone but the star attraction here is the beach. (479 rooms)

HAT NAI HARN

Luxury

Le Royal Meridien Phuket Yacht Club

23/3 Moo 1, Th. Vises. Tel: 0-7638 0200. www.lemeridien.com

As the only hotel with direct access to Nai Harn beach, Le Royal Meridien, with the sparkling sea to its front and a lagoon at its back, is in high demand year-round. Rooms, all with private terraces are massive and tastefully furnished. All have sea views, most overlooking the bay and nearby Promthep Cape. Popular with those seeking a quiet beach away from the hustle and bustle further up the island. (110 rooms)

HAT RAWAI

Expensive

Evason Resort and Spa

100 Th. Viset. Tel: 0-7638 1010.

www.six-senses.com

Popular with couples and honeymooners, the romantic and stylish Evason is secluded and set back from the main road. It has two beach-front restaurants, its own pier and exclusive access to the island of Ko Bon for its guests, partly to make up for its smallish but nonetheless pleasant beach-front. (260 rooms)

Expensive

The Mangosteen Resort & Spa

99/4 Moo 7, Soi Mangosteen. Tel: 0-7628 9399.

www.mangosteen-phuket.com

Intimate resort with a sea view to one side and mountains to the other. Rooms are octagonal in shape and many have private jacuzzi baths. The salt-water swimming pool bends and twists its way around the resort's buildings and restaurant. No direct beach access unfortunately; a shuttle bus is offered to Nai Harn beach and takes only 5 minutes. (40 rooms)

LAEM PANWA

Expensive

The Panwaburi

84 Moo 8, Th. Sakdidet. Tel: 0-76200800. www.panwaburi.com/en/HOME/index.html

Boutique resort set over 10 acres of tropical landscape with a curved swimming pool overlooking a private 80-metre (260-ft) long beach. All guests receive personalised Thai pyjamas with their name in Thai script sewed on. (79 rooms)

Moderate

Cape Panwa Hotel

27 Moo 8, Th. Sakdidet. Tel: 0-7639 1123. www.capepanwa.com

Located among palm trees and set slightly to the back of a quiet

beach. Rooms are sea facing and are large and comfortable. Holds weekly Thai cooking classes. (246 rooms)

KO RACHA YAI

Luxury

The Racha

Ko Racha Yai. Tel: 0-7635 5455.

www.theracha.com

This is without a doubt the island's most exclusive resort. The Racha has a chic, modern style with its minimalist white-on-white toned villas and luxurious open-air garden bathrooms with rain showers. If the budget allows, plump for the villas with private pools, or at the very least, the large deluxe villas. A dramatic rooftop glass-edged infinity swimming pool overlooks the turquoise bay. (70 villas)

KO HAE

Moderate

Coral Island Resort

Ko Hae (Coral Island). Tel: 0-7628 1060.

www.coralislandresort.com

The only choice for an overnight stay on this island. All cottages are air-conditioned with terraces overlooking the sea. Has the island's only swimming pool. Offers diving and snorkelling trips. (64 rooms)

THE ARTS

Dinner, Dance & Drama

There are not very many venues that offer traditional dance or theatre but the few that do have shows that are so extravagant they virtually have a monopoly on this form of entertainment. Apart from the Phuket Fantasea listed below, the **Phuket Orchid Garden and Thai Village** (see page 215) is another place where can you watch traditional Thai dance.

Phuket Fantasea: 99 Moo 3, Hat Kamala, tel: 0-7638 5000; www.phuket-fantasea.com. Winner of the Thailand Tourism Best Attraction award for three consecutive years, this huge theme park hosts a show featuring acrobatics, dance, drama and even animals and pyrotechincs. It's more of a Las Vegas-style spectacle than a traditional form of entertainment, but many people find it enjoyable. Daily except Thurs, 5.30–11.30pm; showtime is 9pm.

Art Galleries

For quality reproduction paintings head to Patong's Thanon Phrachanukhro, which has rows of shops all bearing canvases. All hold similar stock, but the **Manu Art Gallery** (53-57 Th. Phrachanukhro) is one of the few to display prices and staff are not as pushy.

Elsewhere on the island, original pieces can be found at significantly higher prices.

Phuket Art Gallery: 74 Th. Talang, Phuket Town, tel: 0-7625 8388; www.phuketartgallery.com. Located inside a historic two-storey Sino-Portuguese house. Displays and

sells many photographs, water-colours and oil paintings featuring both abstract and contemporary work by Thai and Asian artists.

Sea-Nam Watercolour Gallery and Coffee Corner: 29/1 Th. Thepkrasattri, tel: 0-1892 0566. Owned by artist and teacher "Mr Zone" who specialises in watercolours. Original pieces depict flowers, land and sea scapes.

World of Paintings: Phuket Grande Tropicana Hotel, 48 Th. Ruamjai, Patong, tel: 0-7634 0397; www.worldofpaintings.net. Boutique art gallery displaying only original work. Regular exhibitions by local and international artists.

NIGHTLIFE

Phuket, although falling under the same Social Order laws as Bangkok (see page 113), shows no similar restraint. Bars at some of the quieter beaches may close early, but Patong in particular always has more than its fair share of all-night offerings. The scene in Phuket Town, Karon and Kata beaches is more subdued; elsewhere on the island, it's almost non-existent.

Hat Patong

The choice of entertainment in Patong is diverse, with heaving clubs and sex shows on one street contrasting with chic and trendy cocktail bars on the next. Most of the scene in Patong takes place along **Th. Bangla** and the tiny streets that radiate off it (like Soi Eric, Soi Easy etc) all the way past the **Th. Rat-U-Thit** junction and also **Soi Sunset**. Most common are the raucous "beer bars", simple open-

air bars with wooden tables and stools, and hordes of young women in skimpy dress beckoning to customers. Listed here are less sleazy spots that couples would be more comfortable in.

ACTIVITIES

Dance Bars & Clubs

Banana Disco: Th. Thawiwong, tel: 0-7634 0301. Basement disco on the beach road, just before Soi Bangla. This busy venue is air-conditioned and so is never uncomfortable despite the heaving crowds. Plays Top 40 hits and has a large dance floor.

Safari Pub and Disco: 28 Th. Siriat, Patong Hill, tel: 0-7634 1079. Outdoor safari-themed disco surrounded by trees, waterfalls and jungle vines. Several dance floors and intensely loud music. Doesn't shut until daylight.

Tai Pan Disco: Th. Rat-U-Thit, www.taipan.st. Located on the back road running parallel with Patong beach. Has both DJ-spun music and live bands. Full of young Thai bar girls and may get a bit sleazy but generally a fun night out.

Bars & Pubs

Joe's Downstairs: 223/3 Th. Prabaramee, tel: 0-7634 4254. Opened in 2006, Joe's is Phuket's newest "be-seen" place. Contemporary in design and mostly white, from the long white cocktail bar to the white walls, tables, chairs and silk cushions.

Molly Malone's: 68 Th. Thaweewong, tel: 0-7629 2774. Popular Irish pub at the centre of Patong with both an indoor bar and outside drinking and dining area. Features live music.

Scruffy Murphy's: 5 Th. Bangla, tel: 0-7629 2590. Another popular Irish pub with a nice party atmosphere and Celtic Rock bands playing nightly. Serves standard but tasty range of pub grub.

Kathoey Cabaret

Simon Cabaret: 8 Th. Sirirat, Patong, tel: 0-7634 2114; www.phuket.simoncabaret.com. Popular show that draws in crowds both for its exaggerated theatrical performances and for the chance to have photos taken with Phuket's most convincing *kathoey* or transsexual "lady-boys".

Phuket Town

Jammin Music Club: 78/28 Th. Bangkok, tel: 0-7622 0189. This Caribbean-style club features reggae as well as Thai and English chart hits. Like its name suggests, it is jam-packed on weekends. Runs a free bus to and from the beaches.
Timber Hut: 118/1 Th. Yaowarat, tel: 0-7621 1839. Relatively quiet until around 11pm, after which the place goes wild with live rock and roll and dancing until the early hours.
Watermark Bar: Boat Lagoon Marina, 22/1 Moo 2, Th. Thep-kasattri, tel: 0-7623 9730. People love or hate the Watermark, seeing it as either pompous and pretentious or modern and trendy. Either way, this harbourside bar is undeniably sophisticated.

Hat Karon

Angus O'Toole: 516/20 Th. Patak, Karon. Popular Irish bar located at the end of a plaza, slightly off the main road. Shows live sports matches, serves cold draught Guinness and an excellent Irish-style breakfast.
Dino Bar: Karon, tel: 0-7633 0625. Roadside bar with a Stone-Age theme, attached to the Dino

Park mini-golf course. Perfect for watching the world go by.
Hangover Corner: 94/4 Th. Taina, Karon, tel: 0-7633 3020. Aptly named bar serving a variety of cocktails, shooters and beers. There are many similar looking bars along this stretch of road, but this one seems to attract a livelier crowd.

Hat Kata

Bamboo Pub and Restaurant: Kata Centre, tel: 0-7628 4244. One of many similar looking bars along this stretch.
The Boathouse: Kata Yai, tel: 0-7633 0015. This elegant beach-front bar is the perfect location to sip a few cocktails and watch the sunset. Live music every evening and jazz on Sat from 8pm.
Ratri Jazztaurant: Kata Hill, tel: 0-7633 3538; www.ratrijazztaurant.com. Relatively new addition to the Phuket jazz scene, having opened in Dec 2005. Features an oyster bar with sunset views. Live jazz performed nightly.

Ao Chalong

The Green Man Pub and Restaurant: 85/15 Moo 4, Th. Patak, tel: 0-7628 1445; www.the-green-man.net. English-stye pub with beer on tap and a large, open beer garden. Holds regular Thurs night pub quizzes, curry and Bollywood nights on Fri, and reduced-price drinks at weekends. It serves ridiculously cheap (and large) Bloody Marys on Sunday mornings from 11am onwards.

Hat Nai Harn

The Red Lion: 14/83 Th. Nai Harn, mobile tel: 0-1956 1036. Inte-grated lounge bar with a Thai-style dining area offering fusion cuisine,

and a warmly-lit lounge area with masses of floor cushions and bamboo furniture on the upper level. The downstairs bar features regular drinks promotions and is popular with both expats and tourists.

Gay Venues

Phuket's gay scene isn't as hot and happening as in Bangkok or Pattaya, with most of it taking place around the **Paradise Complex** along Th. Rat-U-Thit. Here, bars, clubs and saunas cater to a colourful gay clientele. Phuket also has its very own gay festival (see www.gaypatong.com) that takes place in Feb each year.
Boat Bar: Soi 5, Paradise Complex, Patong, tel: 0-7634 1237; www.boatbar.com. Located near the main entrance of the Royal Paradise Hotel. Popular and trendy gay dance club, and considered the place to be seen at.
Galaxy: Soi Sunset, Patong. Plays good music and exudes a happy-go-lucky atmosphere. Mixed venue, but with a large gay clientele, many of whom are foreign residents of the island.

SHOPPING

While Bangkok offers a greater variety of shops, the emergence of large shopping malls such as Central Festival on the outskirts of Phuket Town has increased the opportunities to go on a spending spree in Phuket. These malls often have small stalls displaying local goods such as jewellery and beach wear while the larger shops within sell international brand names like Levi's and Nike.

All the beaches are lined with stalls selling designer knock-off T-shirts and handbags as well as bootleg CDs and DVDs. DVD prices are usually fixed at B100, but be sure to ask to see the quality first.

Generally, prices can double or even triple during the high season so always bargain and never accept the first price you hear. A huge open-air clothing and souvenir market facing Karon beach is one of the few places that indicate prices on their goods. While you may end up paying a little bit extra, many are glad to avoid the hassle of bargaining for better deals.

Shopping Malls

Central Festival: 74–75 Moo 5, Th. Vichit, tel: 0-7621 1111. Phuket's biggest and best shopping venue opened in late 2004 on the outskirts of Phuket Town. The three-storey mall contains numerous shops, the Central Festival Department Store, restaurants and a cinema. It will soon have a bowling alley when its fourth floor is opened.

Ocean Shopping Mall: 38/1-15 Th. Tilok-U-Thit, Phuket Town, tel: 0-7622 3057. This mall has a supermarket, cheap clothes, cosmetics and many craft stalls. It has two branches in Patong.

Robinsons: 36 Th. Tilok-U-Thit, Phuket Town, tel: 0-7625 6500. Occasionally offers items not found elsewhere. Ground floor supermarket, plus clothes and household goods in the main department store.

Antiques

Chan's Antiques: 99/42 Moo 5, Th. Chalermprakit, tel: 0-7626 1416. Home to Phuket's largest collection of antiques from Thailand and neighbouring countries. Even if not shopping, with so many displays, it is fascinating to walk around this old Thai-style building

on the outskirts of Phuket Town.
Soul of Asia: 37–39 Th. Ratsada, Phuket Town, tel: 0-7621 1122. Elegant gallery converted from two old Chinese shophouses. Contains over 700 sq metres (7,535 sq ft) of paintings and antiques.

Fashion & Clothing

The best and widest range of clothes are found in the **Central Festival Department Store**, in the Central Festival mall. Local brands are excellent value for money should you be small enough to squeeze into them, and international labels such as Nike and Levi's are considerably cheaper here than in Europe and the US. Cheaper clothes, however, can be found at streetside stalls and markets.

Tailors

The majority of Phuket's tailors are situated around Patong and Kata beaches. Many have overbearing touts who try and cajole you into going inside, which unfortunately often acts as a deterrent to doing just that. Prices are competitive, so it is best to look at the quality and design of the garments in shop windows. The following shops are recommended.
King's Fashion: 146 Th. Thaweewong, Patong, tel: 0-7634 0192.
Mr Singh's Fashion Gallery: 26/2 Th. Rat-U-Thit, Patong, tel: 0-7634 5038.

Handicrafts/Home Decor

Art and Gift Gallery: Canal Village, Laguna Shopping Unit 16, 390/1 Moo 1, Th. Srisoonthorn, Bang Thao, tel: 0-7627 0616; www.artandgiftgallery.com. Reputable shop that sells an interesting array of handicrafts and home

decor items. Goods can be personalised with name or company logo. Lots of gift ideas here.
Jim Thompson: Central Festival Phuket, tel: 0-7624 9615. This brand, which is synonymous with quality Thai silk, has three stores in Phuket alone, the largest of which is found at the Central Festival mall. Wide range of fabrics, clothing, accessories and home decor items.
Thai Terrific: 382/91-92, Laguna Phuket, Th. Srisoonthorn, Bang Thao, tel: 0-7627 1126. Unique decor items including leather vases, handblown glass, handmade candles and spa products. Collection updated regularly.

OUTDOOR ACTIVITIES

Bungee Jumping

Jungle Bungee: Th. Vichitsongkram, tel: 0-7632 1351; www.phuketbungy.com. Fully licensed, insured and (supposedly) accident-free since its opening in June 1992. Jumps overlook a beautiful wooded area surrounding a lagoon. A breathtaking site – if you can keep your eyes open long enough to enjoy it!

Deep-Sea Fishing

Aloha Tours: 44/1 Th. Visit, Chalong, tel: 0-7638 1215; www.thai-boat.com. Experienced crew take boats out daily in search of the massive tuna, marlin and king mackerel that all thrive in Phuket's surrounding waters.
Wahoo: 48/20 Moo 9, Chalong , tel: 0-7628 1510; www.wahoo.com.ws. Phuket's most famous fishing company, with a fleet of boats all fully equipped with first-class fishing gear.

Diving & Snorkelling

Phuket's only notable snorkelling spots are around the headlands at Kata Yai and Kata Noi beaches. Shacks along the sand rent snorkelling gear by the day or hour. Better snorkelling can be found on trips to nearby islands and most dive operators offer a cheaper snorkelling-only option. Phuket is a popular base for many day trips and live-aboard excursions. Conditions are best during the December– April dry season when seas are calm and the water at its clearest. Most dive shops offer everything from introductory dives to advanced dive master certification. Prices vary, but so too are the condition of boats and equipment. The following are recommended:

Dive Asia: 24 Th. Karon, Kata, tel: 0-7633 0598; www.diveasia.com. Offers numerous training pro-

BELOW: Phuket is a good base to pick up diving in Thailand.

grammes in different languages as well as dive day trips and all inclusive live-aboards.

Fantasea Divers: 43/20 Moo 5, Th. Viset, tel: 0-7628 1387; www.ocean-rover.com. One of the best live-aboard options available. Spacious boat holds a maximum of 16 passengers and 12 crew. All indoor areas are air-conditioned.

Scuba Cat Diving: 94 Th. Thaweewong, Patong, tel: 0-7629 3120; www.scubacat.com. Phuket's first National Geographic dive centre is Canadian-owned and English-managed. The most prominent on Patong due to its central location and outdoor training pool.

Golf

Blue Canyon Country Club: 165 Moo 1, Th. Thepkasattri, tel: 0-7632 8088; www.bluecanyonclub.com. Beautifully landscaped on a 720-acre (290-hectare) green with two award-winning 18-hole courses. First golf course to ever hold the Johnny Walker Classic twice and has played host to such greats as Nick Faldo and Tiger Woods.

Laguna Phuket Golf Club: 34 Moo 4, Th. Srisoonthorn, Bang Thao, tel: 0-7627 0991; www.laguna phuket.com/golfclub. An 18-hole course that trails around scenic lagoons, coconut groves and rolling fairways. Water features loom over 13 holes, making this one of Phuket's more challenging golf courses.

Go-Karting

Patong Go Kart Speedway: 118/5 Th. Vichitsongkram, tel: 0-7632 1949. Formed in 1990, this 750-metre (2,460-ft) racetrack has go-karts capable of speeds of up to 110 km (70 miles) per hour. Open daily and floodlit to enable night rides. Situated at the foot of

Patong Hill in the Kathu district, next to Jungle Bungee.

Horse Riding

Phuket Laguna Riding Club: 394 Moo 1, Bang Tao, tel: 0-7632 4199; www.phuket-bangtao-horseriding. com. All levels are welcomed to ride along the beach and over the hills. Experienced guides lead the way. Three tours offered and transportation to and from the riding club is included.

Sailing

SY Stressbreaker: mobile tel: 0-1894 3966; www.thailand-sail.com. Offers adventure sailing in the Mergui Archipelago aboard a 19-metre (63-ft) ketch that comfortably sleeps eight. Experienced British skipper along with his qualified scuba instructor and sailor wife arrange everything from diving and kayaking to the food and drinks. In constant demand and highly recommended.

Meroja: 86 Th. Patak, Kata, tel: 0-76330087; www.meroja.com. Offers the *Meroja*, a 26-metre (85-ft) ketch for charter into the waters of the Andaman Sea. The well-equipped boat sleeps 11 people and is manned by a competent European skipper, a Thai chef and two deck hands.

Shooting

Phuket Shooting Range: 82/2 Th. Patak, tel: 0-7638 1667. Deafening shooting range with choice of gun. Price per pellet depends on the total number purchased. Open: daily 9am–6pm.

Sea Canoeing

Phuket is the best base to book tours to see the magnificent limestone karsts of Ao Phang Nga (see page 202). Cruises are the usual way of visiting Phang Nga Bay. The **June Bahtra**, an old Chinese junk, offers day and evening sunset cruises with dining options and can be booked through any tour company in Phuket. Or check its website at www.asian-oasis.com.

The more novel way to explore Ao Phang Nga, however, is by sea canoe. These low-lying craft enable you to enter the area's limestone karsts when the tide is low enough to explore hidden islands. The following companies are the best in the business:

Phuket Panwa Canoe: 63/259 Th. Virach Hongyok 3, tel: 0-7635 5918; www.phuketdir.com/pktpanwa canoe. Tours by inflatable canoe start in the early morning, visiting a number of caves and lagoons as well as Naka and James Bond islands. Lunch is included, and although groups are fairly large, the reasonable price reflects this.

Sea Canoe (Thailand): 367/4 Th. Yaowarat, Phuket Town, tel: 0-7621 2252; www.seacanoe.net. Its reputation is the best in the business and is not without reason. Staff are well trained and the specially designed kayaks are more sturdy than the inflatable ones used by other operators. Evening trips to marvel at the sun melting into the ocean against the backdrop of limestone cliffs are among the most popular excursions.

Thai Boxing

Muay Thai Stadium: Saphan Hin, Phuket Town, tel: 0-7639 6591. Thai boxing matches every Fri night. Tickets can be bought at the door or from any travel agency.

Patong Boxing Stadium: Soi Kebsap 2, Th. Sai Nam Yen, tel: 0-7634 5578. Fights can be seen at 8pm every Mon, Thurs

and Sat between sinewy Thai fighters and foreigners who have been training in preparation.

SPAS

The spa industry is big business in Phuket. All across Thailand there are small, streetside shophouses offering cheap Thai massages, but Phuket has taken this one step further. The majority of hotels have spas which are part of the hotel. But while these spas are undeniably luxurious, the prices can be equally sky high. More recently, a clutch of day spas have emerged on the scene, which on the whole offer the same range of treatments but at more reasonable prices. Many will arrange transportation to and from your hotel.

Aspasia Spa: 1/3 Th. Laem Sai, Kata, tel: 0-7633 3033; www.aspasiaphuket.com. Emphasis on organic products such as oatmeal and fruit juice for moisturising and rice grains for exfoliation. Therapists are well trained in dispensing various massage, body scrubs and facial treatments.

Atsumi Healing Centre: 34/18 Soi Pattana, Rawai, tel: 0-1272 0571; www.atsumihealing.com. Natural therapy centre specialising in 7-day detox programmes. Complimenting it are morning yoga sessions followed by daily colonic irrigation. Don't expect it to be easy, but weight loss is guaranteed and minor conditions such as colds and infections often miraculously disappear during the detoxification process.

Banyan Tree Spa: Banyan Tree Resort and Spa, 33 Moo 4 Th. Srisoonthorn, tel: 0-7632 4374; www.banyantreespa.com/phuket. The spa has won numerous accolades (including World's Best Spa

Resort by readers of Condé Nast Traveller). Surroundings are indulgent with open-air spa pavilions containing Thai artefacts and even fish ponds. Highly skilled therapists are trained in rare and unique treatments. Expect to pay highly for such indulgences.

Body and Mind Day Spa: 558/7-12 Th. Patak, Karon, tel: 0-7639 8274. Hugely popular due to its quality service and luxury surroundings at incredibly reasonable prices. Offers all the usual massage options plus a variety of body wraps, scrubs and facials.

Hideaway Day Spa: 382/33 Th. Srisoontorn, Bang Tao, tel: 0-7627 1549; and 157 Th. Nanai, Patong, tel:0-7634 0591; www.phuket-hideaway.com. Concentrating solely on massage, this independent spa was established in 1987 and has since become famous for administering the best Thai massages on the island. Therapists are highly skilled and treatments are given under open-air Thai pavilions.

SIGHTSEEING TOURS

Most generic sightseeing tours are operated by independent travel or tour agents, located in Phuket Town and at the beaches. They will advise and book tours and transportation at very short notice. Inquire at your hotel reception. For specialist nature tours of Phuket and surroundings, contact:

Siam Safari: 45 Th. Chaofa, Chalong, tel: 0-7628 0116; www.siamsafari.com. This is one of the longest-running tour companies in Phuket, offering a range of land-based tours incorporating jeep safaris, elephant trekking, canoeing and visits to Thai villages and national parks.

KRABI, KO PHI PHI AND KO LANTA

This region is dominated by a geographical wonder that attracts rock-climbing enthusiasts: sheer limestone peaks that rise dramatically out of the water. And if the pristine beaches of Krabi do not impress you, head to the legendary Ko Phi Phi and other nearby islands

Bangkok

The lush and sprawling 4,708-sq km (1,818-sq mile) **Krabi Province** lies just east of Phuket. Parts of mainland Krabi were once submerged under water millions of years ago. As a direct result of changing sea levels, these areas evolved to become land while previously flat plains were sculpted into towering limestone peaks. Scattered in the waters of the Andaman Sea, including at Ao Phang Nga *(see page 202)*, are hundreds of these sheer-sided limestone outcrops known as karsts. Krabi is a popular destination for sports enthusiasts who scale these challenging rock faces.

Many of the islands around Krabi Province are tiny or uninhabited, the best known being **Ko Phi Phi** and **Ko Lanta**, where the beaches are legendary. The former was badly hit by the tsunami in December 2004 and parts of it are still recovering; Ko Lanta, fortunately, suffered minimal damage.

Krabi mainland is blessed with a string of white sand beaches that attract thousands during the dry season from November to April *(see margin tip page 245)*. Many of these too were spared the full onslaught of the tsunami, and tourism is picking up again. Inland on Krabi mainland are lush rainforests that harbour rare species of birds and wildlife. Cam-

era crews often travel miles to take advantage of Krabi's idyllic surroundings for commercials, television shows and even movies, including the 2004 blockbuster *Around the World in 80 Days*.

Map on page 244

KRABI PROVINCE

Krabi Town

Located some 180 km (112 miles) from Phuket, **Krabi Town ❶** is the main jump-off point for travellers en route to the beaches and islands of

LEFT:
sea canoeing along the Krabi coast.
BELOW:
Krabi Town children.

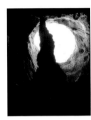

The limestone pinnacles of Khao Khanab Nam.

BELOW: Buddha statue at Wat Tham Seua

Krabi Province. Thanon Maharat, which is the central point in the busy and compact town, is where the main market and most of the restaurants and shops are found. A concentration of guesthouses and hotels are located on Thanon Chao Fa, a few minutes from **Chao Fa Pier**. The pavements around Chao Fa Pier become a bustling hub of activity in the evenings when grills are fired up and saucepans and woks clatter in unison to whip up a feast of freshly caught grilled seafood and various stir fries.

At the bottom of Krabi Town is **Thara Park**, an attractively landscaped and shaded spot overlooking the **Krabi River**. On the river's opposite bank are dense mangroves and a small but thriving fishing community who live in wooden huts raised on stilts. Longtail boats can be hired at Chao Fa pier to explore these mangrove forests, which shelter many types of fish, crabs, shrimps and shellfish, and are important nesting grounds for hundreds of bird species.

Most tours of the mangroves will include a stop at the limestone pinnacles of **Khao Khanab Nam ②**. The two 100-metre (328-ft) pinnacles that rise dramatically from the side of Krabi River have come to represent the town. Legend has it that two ceremonial *krabi* (swords) were discovered here in ancient times. Inside one of the peaks are a series of caves with impressive formations of stalactites and stalagmites. In one of the caves, skeletons – thought to belong to people who took refuge here before being cut off by a massive flood – have been found.

KRABI'S INTERIOR

Wat Tham Seua

More commonly referred to as "Tiger Cave Temple", **Wat Tham Seua ③** (daily 8am–6pm; admission charge) was founded by Jamnien Silasettho, a monk and teacher of

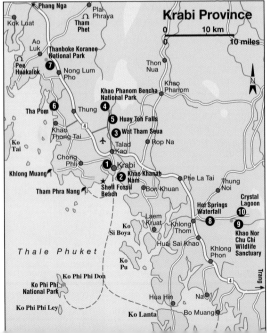

Krabi Province

meditation. The temple is set amid forests and cliffs 9 km (6 miles) from Krabi Town and is easily reached by car or motorbike. At the rear of the temple is a concrete staircase; clambering up the 1,272 steps to the 600-metre (1,970-ft) peak brings you to a small shrine and a footprint of the Buddha immortalised in a flat rock. The hour-long ascent is exhausting, but the fantastic view of the surrounding area at the top makes up for it. A second staircase, next to a large statue of Kwan Im, the Chinese Goddess of Mercy, takes you on a different route up 1,237 steps.

Scattered around this forest are towering limestone rock faces and a large cave with a Buddha image. Flanking one side of this statue is a human skeleton encased in glass while on the other side are several ticking clocks. Both are intended to serve as a poignant reminder of the fragility of time and life.

Khao Phanom Bencha N P

Covering an area of 50 sq km (19 sq miles) is **Khao Phanom Bencha National Park ❹** (daily 8am–6pm; admission charge) about 20 km (12 miles) to the north of Krabi Town. The park is the site of a dramatic 1,397-metre (4,583-ft) tall limestone karst called **Khao Phanon Bencha**, or "Five-Point Prostration Mountain". The reserve officially lists 218 species of birds and 32 mammals including leopards, Asiatic black bears and even tigers, although sightings of the last are extremely rare. The cascading waterfalls flowing down the mountain slopes are another of the park's attractions, the main one being the 11-tiered **Huay Toh Falls ❺**. Situated 350 metres (1,150 ft) from the park headquarters, the tiers are at varying heights; the highest at 80 metres (262 ft).

Tha Pom

Some 34 km (21 miles) north from Krabi Town is an unusual canal that most locals refer to as **Tha Pom ❻** (daily 8am–6pm; admission charge). On signages leading to this attraction, however, the name appears as **Tha Pom Khlong Song Nam**, which translates as "Canal of Two Waters". A 700-metre (2,300-

Map on page 244

TIP

The southwest monsoon brings heavy rain from May to Oct to the Andaman Coast, including Krabi, Ko Phi Phi and Ko Lanta islands. Room rates can drop as much as half during the wet months so some people take advantage of this and hope for the best. There can be intermittent days of sunshine in between rainy spells.

BELOW: monks at Wat Tham Seua.

ft) boardwalk takes you on a trail past mangrove and forest, eventually leading to the main attraction, a stream of clear water with two distinct colours. The water will appear colourless in poor weather, but on a good day, when the sun's rays penetrate the water, it creates a seemingly invisible line between its turquoise blue and emerald green layers. This phenomena apparently happens during high tide when tidal seawater meets fresh spring water running off the mountainside.

The amazing coloured waters of the Crystal Lagoon.

Thanboke Koranee N P

About 45 km (28 miles) northwest of Krabi Town is **Thanboke Koranee National Park** (daily 8am–6pm; admission charge), with its many caves and waterfalls. One of the park's highlights is the cave called **Pee Huakalok**, where an oversized human skull was found over half a century ago. Superstitious locals believe that the ghost of this head dwells within the cave and have immortalised their fear forever with its name. *Pee* is Thai for ghost, *hua* means head and *kalok* is skull. The

walls of the cave are embellished with hundreds of colourful cave paintings and prehistoric drawings, estimated by archaeologists to be between 2,000 and 3,000 years old. Accessible by boat from **Bor Tor Pier**, 7 km (4 miles) south of nearby Ao Luk, the cave burrows deep into a hill surrounded by water and mangroves.

Hot Springs Waterfall

Some 55 km (34 miles) southeast of Krabi Town, past the town of Khlong Thom on Highway 4, is another unusual phenomenon, the **Hot Springs Waterfall** (daily 8am–5pm; admission charge). This is where an underground hot spring leaks water through the earth's surface and cascades down smooth boulders. It is quite an experience to let the soothing warm water wash over you before you take a dip in the cool waters of the stream, a sort of natural hydrotherapy in the middle of the jungle. This picturesque waterfall is a popular place to relax in but is relatively small and can get crowded around lunchtime when large tour groups arrive. If travelling on your own, early morning is the best time to get here.

Khao Nor Chu Chi Wildlife Sanctuary

A 10-minute drive east of the Hot Springs Waterfall is the **Khao Nor Chu Chi Wildlife Sanctuary** (daily 8am–5pm; admission charge), also known as Khao Pra Bang Khram Wildlife Sanctuary. This is said to be the last patch of lowland rainforest in Thailand and one of the few locations in the world where the endangered bird species known as *Gurneys Pitta* can be found.

A 3-km (2-mile) trail from the park leads through a shaded path to the **Crystal Lagoon** . Bacteria and algae living in this emerald-coloured pond cause a variation of colours ranging from pale green where the

BELOW: Hot Springs Waterfall at Thanboke Koranee National Park.

temperature is cooler to a greenish blue where the temperature peaks at around 50°C (122°F). It's safe to swim in but the calcium carbonates in the water make it unsuitable for drinking, and a sign at the entrance asks you to refrain from using shampoo or soap. Be cautious of slippery moss at the water's edge – the best way in is to sit first and slowly inch your way into the pond to avoid a painful and ungraceful splash.

KRABI'S BEACHES

Hat Khlong Muang and Hat Noppharat Thara

Only a handful of small hotels are fortunate enough to share the secluded white sands at **Hat Khlong Muang ❶**. Backed by lush vegetation, this lovely beach is extremely quiet and has a nice ambience to it. Set away from Krabi Town (but only a 30-minute drive away), it has clean waters that are pleasant to swim in

year round. Most of the accommodation at Hat Khlong Muang is simple save for the five-star **Sheraton Krabi** and the stylish boutique-style **Nakamanda** resort.

An extended finger of land called Hang Nak Cape separates Khlong Muang from the next beach, **Hat Noppharat Thara ❷**, which has beautiful, uninterrupted views out towards a cluster of limestone islands. Shady casuarinas back this 2-km (1-mile) long beach and seafood vendors congregate around the car park. The western end of the beach is quiet and because it is separated by a canal, can only be accessed by longtail boat. The middle section is similarly quiet, with a visitor's centre and the park headquarters while the eastern section is the busiest.

Ao Nang

A few minutes drive from Hat Noppharat Thara, and sharing the same view of the limestone cliffs in the

 Map below

A free back massage at Krabi's Hot Springs Waterfall

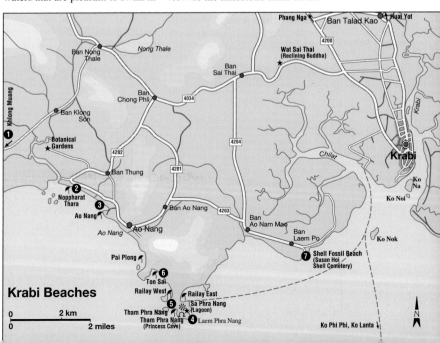

Krabi Beaches

0 — 2 km
0 — 2 miles

distance, albeit obstructed by a line of longtail boats, is **Ao Nang ❸**, the most commercial and developed beach on mainland Krabi.

Located 22 km (14 miles) east of Krabi Town, Ao Nang gets somewhat crowded in the high season but is not yet so built up as to be completely ruined. With the rapid construction currently going on though, this will likely change in the future.

Ao Nang beach is rather ho hum, and would be nicer were it not for the longtail boats congesting its shore; at high tide there is very little space to relax. The quiet is also shattered by the loud and piercing drone from the engines of these longtail boats. The splendid backdrop of the limestone cliff-studded Andaman Sea however makes up for it. At the north of the beach is a cluster of open-air seafood restaurants, usually owned by the small hotels behind them. With displays of snapper, barracuda and shellfish, these restaurants fill up rapidly in the evenings. Other restaurants serving mostly Thai and Italian food are found along the main beach road.

The Krabi coastline is strewn with islands which make for fun exploration. Most tour agencies sell the well-known "Krabi Four Islands" tour, covering Ko Poda, Ko Tup, Ko Kai and Phra Nang Cave.

BELOW: view of Hat Railay East and Hat Railay West beaches.

Laem Phra Nang (Railay Bay)

Surrounded by sheer limestone cliffs on three sides and only accessible by boat, the peninsula of **Laem Phra Nang ❹**, better known as **Railay Bay**, feels more like an island paradise than the mainland beach that it actually is. This stunning peninsula has four beaches, each with crystal clear turquoise waters, powder white sands and sheer-sided limestone cliffs that seemingly melt into the waters below, making it one of the world's leading rock climbing destinations.

Hat Railay West and Hat Railay East

Most arriving boats head straight to the western side of the peninsula, to **Hat Railay West**. The absence of a pier demands a short wade to the shore, but this has fortunately also prevented ferry loads of daytrippers landing on its pristine white sands. Although still developing, Railay West is a world away from nearby Ao Nang. Its tastefully designed resorts (no ramshackle guesthouses here) along with nice landscaping

has prevented it from turning into a busy backpacker haunt. Accommodation is more expensive than on the other Krabi beaches, but that is the premium to be paid for direct access to such a lovely beach.

On the opposite side of the peninsula is **Hat Railay East**. Backed by dense mangroves, this is a less scenic beach and is unsuitable for swimming due to the incredibly low tides and the jagged rocks along the foreshore. Still, the lower-priced bungalows here get their fair share of trade. Access between the two Railay beaches is easy – a 5-minute walk along a flat paved pathway takes you from one beach to the other. The same people appreciating the mango-streaked sunsets on Railay West are often seen a few hours later enjoying fire shows and all-night parties at Railay East.

Hat Tham Phra Nang

The undeniably prettiest beach on Railay Bay, if not the whole of Thailand, is **Hat Tham Phra Nang** ❺ where the extravagant and ultra-expensive **Rayavadee Resort** occu-

pies prime position (there is no other accommodation here). Set amid 11 hectares (26 acres) of coconut groves and surrounded by towering limestone cliffs, Tham Phra Nang is endowed with the softest of white sands, limpid turquoise blue waters and beautiful coral reefs offshore. Although staying at the Rayavadee gives you the most direct access to this beach, many daytrippers from Railay West and Railay East flock to Tham Phra Nang to sunbathe, swim and snorkel.

Hat Tham Phra Nang is named after a princess (*phra nang*) whom locals believe resides in the area. Near the Rayavadee Resort, at the beach's eastern end, is **Tham Phra Nang** (Princess Cave) where a collection of wooden phallic-shaped objects sit as an offering to her, its supplicants hoping she will bestow the surrounding mountains and sea with fertility. The cave is not as spectacular as it's made out to be and is little more than a series of small overhangs, but a map at its base highlights the way towards a **viewpoint** *(see margin tip)* and **Sa Phra Nang** (Princess Lagoon), which are both far more impressive.

Map on page 247

TIP

Check the tide before scaling the cliff towards the viewpoint high above Hat Tham Phra Nang. When the tide is at Hat Railay East, it makes for much more stunning views from the top.

BELOW: the gorgeous Hat Tham Phra Nang.

The Shell Fossil Beach at Krabi, also known as the Susan Hoi Shell Cemetery.

BELOW: longtail boats moored at Hat Ton Sai.

The route to each sight is straightforward but neither is suitable for the young, elderly or unfit, and good shoes are a must. The most challenging part of the walk is at the beginning, which involves clinging to ropes to clamber up a fairly steep incline; after this, the pathway becomes easier to follow. Veering to the left as the pathway splits leads to a viewpoint with spectacular vistas of the east and west bays of Railay. Continuing straight leads to a sharp rock face with yet more ropes, this time used to almost abseil down into the Princess Lagoon. The lagoon is suitable for swimming, but is not crystal clear and does have some rocks.

Hat Ton Sai

From Hat Railay West, it is possible at low tide to walk to the nearby **Hat Ton Sai ❻**. Longtail boats can also be hired to make the 5-minute journey, or if feeling energetic, you may simply swim to the beach. Budget travellers are attracted to Ton Sai by its cheaper accommodation and more convivial atmosphere. Of all the beaches on the Laem Phra Nang

headland, Ton Sai has the most vibrant nightlife, with beach bars open until the early hours and hosting monthly full moon parties. The view out to sea is as beautiful as that of Railay's, with limestone monoliths in the foreground and to the sides, but the sand is not as white, and at low tide the beach becomes muddy and makes swimming difficult.

Rock climbing

Sheer limestone cliffs facing mile upon mile of tranquil sea make Railay Bay a favoured spot for rock climbers. Most of the roughly 650 routes that have developed since Krabi's cliffs were first scaled in the late 1980's are located in this peninsula. Among the most popular climbs is the challenging yet phenomenal **Thaiwand Wall** on the southern end. There are a range of other climbs suited for beginners right through to professionals, involving limestone crags, steep pocketed walls, overhangs and hanging stalactites. Any of the climbing operations around Railay will advise on the best climbs, some of which are accessed by a combination of boat and a hike through the jungle.

Shell Fossil Beach

Some 17 km (11 miles) from Krabi Town with its entrance marked by a small Chinese temple is the **Shell Fossil Beach ❼** (also known as Susan Hoi Shell Cemetery). Extending right to the edge of the sea are the remnants of a 75-million-year accumulation of shell deposits – which look like large concrete slabs from afar. This phenomenon can only be seen at two other locations worldwide, one in Japan and the other in the US – the one in Krabi is the only coastal site. Visitors either love or hate this sight but some people appreciate the enormity of witnessing evidence of life that existed millions of years before man.

KO PHI PHI

Lying in the Andaman Sea between Phuket and Krabi (about two hours by boat from either location) are the twin islands that make **Ko Phi Phi**. The two island jewels – the larger **Ko Phi Phi Don** and the smaller **Ko Phi Phi Ley** – are part of the protected **Mu Ko Phi Phi National Park**, but somehow, development, especially on Ko Phi Phi Don, seems to have run amok over the years, ruining its natural beauty. From afar though, the islands are still stunning with their mountains and lovely arcs of soft white sand washed by gin-clear waters. Ko Phi Phi Don is where all the accomodation and facilities are while Ko Phi Phi Ley is uninhabited and mainly visited on daytrips.

The islands' rise to fame is characterised by both fortune and tragedy. As recently as in 1998, Ko Phi Phi was still considered a quiet, idyllic retreat. Turquoise waters bordering limestone cliffs and palm tree-filled interiors made it a postcard perfect location, and visitors would leave feeling they had seen a truly tropical island. Then came the major blockbuster film, *The Beach*, which was shot mainly at **Ao Maya** (Maya Bay) in 1998 on Ko Phi Phi Ley. Within one year, thousands were flocking to Ao Maya in the hope of seeing this utopian image of the perfect unspoilt beach up close and personal. While Ko Phi Phi Ley was spared development, it suffered from overcrowding and this took a toll on its ecology. The larger Ko Phi Phi Don also saw a rash of construction – resorts, restaurants and bars built quickly to cater to the onslaught of tourists.

The December 2004 tsunami hit Ko Phi Phi as its busiest time. Its popularity coupled with the peak tourist season meant that hotels on Ko Phi Phi Don were fully booked and every tourist facility was at its maximum capacity. When the tsunami waves hit the narrow centre of Ko Phi Phi Don, the damage it caused was immense; numerous shops, restaurants and hotels were reduced to rubble and thousands of lives lost. The most evident damage is opposite the main **Ton Sai village** at **Ao Lo Dalam**

Map on page 252

Close-up view of rock climbing winches and hooks.

BELOW: rock climbing at Railay Bay.

where entire resorts were washed away. By mid-2006, much rubble was still evident; some hotels have re-opened but others are in the process of rebuilding. Given the scale of the disaster, Ko Phi Phi's recovery has been a lot swifter than predicted but it will take at least another year before it gets back on its feet again.

There are no roads on the island, so walking from one place to another is generally the only way to get around. Most dive sites around Ko Phi Phi were unaffected by the tsunami, and it remains one of Thailand's most popular diving locations.

Ko Phi Phi Don

Ko Phi Phi Don is made up of two elongated islands joined together by a narrow isthmus to create, what looks like from the air, a giant high-backed chair. Most development is concentrated on the bays found on either side of the isthmus – Ao Ton Sai and Ao Lo Dalam.

Boats to the island dock at the main pier at **Ao Ton Sai ❶**, a bay that would be far prettier were it not for the ferries and longtail boats lining it from one end to the other. There are a few information booths at the end of the pier beyond which is **Ton Sai village**, a compact area of restaurants, bars, dive shops, internet cafes and stalls selling everything from sarongs and beaded jewellery to sandwiches and banana pancakes.

Opposite Ao Ton Sai and only a few minutes walk away is **Ao Lo Dalam ❷**, a quieter and prettier bay with a lovely curve of white sand skimming clear blue waters. Following the tsunami, it is now bereft of the numerous hotels that once lined its shores.

Much of the island's accommodation is today located on **Hat Hin Khom ❸**, at the western end of Ao Ton Sai, and on **Hat Yao ❹** (Long Beach) at the southwestern tip of the island. Although these beaches too

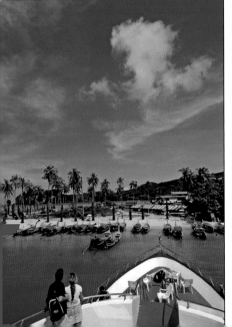

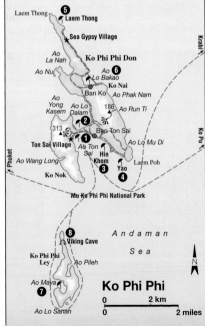

were severely hit by the tsunami, they were able to rebuild more quickly. Prices are typically higher than elsewhere in Thailand and although rooms are generally of above average standard, the elevated prices do not usually reflect the actual quality.

The best snorkelling and the most exclusive resorts are found to the north of the island on **Hat Laem Thong ❺**, where the majority of visitors are either honeymooners or those seeking a more isolated beach. The beach is beautiful and quiet but as boat transportation is scarce in these parts, it is difficult to get to the other parts of the island from here. Hat Laem Thong is also the home of a small community of *chao lay* or sea gypsies. These folk mainly make their living by fishing or ferrying tourists around the islands.

South of Hat Laem Thong along the same northeastern coastline is **Ao Lo Bakao ❻**, which has mainly upmarket accommodation on its quiet beach. Both Hat Laem Thong and Ao Lo Bakao were spared the worst of the huge waves as they are located on the "right" (east) side of the island.

Inland attractions are limited but many people take the 30-minute hike over to the **viewpoint** located high on a bluff at the southern end of Ao Lo Dalam. To get there, follow the path eastwards towards Hat Hin Khom and turn left when it forks inland. Understandably, the scenic point is at its busiest around sunrise and sunset; from here the vista of the twin bays of Ao Ton Sai and Ao Lo Dalam, separated by a thin band of land with the mountain behind, is breathtaking.

Ko Phi Phi Ley

The uninhabited **Ko Phi Phi Ley** is a mere speck at 6½ sq km (2½ sq miles). It lies about 4 km (2 miles) south of Ko Phi Phi Don. Formed entirely from limestone, the island is surrounded by steep karsts rising out of the sea that circle it almost completely. Of the picturesque bays around the island, the most visited are **Ao Pileh** to the east and the aforementioned **Ao Maya ❼** on the west coast. Ao Maya would be a more beautiful spot if not for the daytrippers who descend here in droves and

Map on page 252

Longtail fishing boats, commonly found at the beaches and islands of South Thailand, are a cheap means of transport but the incessant droning noise the engines make is annoying.

BELOW: viewpoint on Ko Phi Phi Don, with the bays of Ao Ton Sai and Ao Lo Dalam on either side.

Harvesting prized birds' nests at the Viking Cave.

frequently leave their litter behind.

Also at Ko Phi Phi Ley is the **Viking Cave** at the northeastern end of the island. Inscribed on the cave walls are coloured chalk drawings of various boats, believed to have been sketched hundreds of years ago by pirates who used the cave as a shelter. Today, the pirates have been replaced by hundreds of swifts who build their nests in crevices high up on the steep cave walls. These nests are collected by local villagers who climb the tall rickety ladders, risking life and limb, to collect the birds' nests so highly prized by Chinese gourmets for their health-giving properties. Swarms of swifts descend on the caves of Ko Phi Phi Ley every year between January and April and built their nests using their saliva as a bonding material.

Diving and snorkelling

Many of the dive sites around Ko Phi Phi are the same ones that can be done out of Phuket, Krabi and Ko Lanta. Around Ko Phi Phi itself, the best diving and snorkelling sites are **Hin Bida** (Phi Phi Shark Point), **Ko Pai** (Bamboo Island), **Ko Yung** (Mosquito Island) and **Ao Maya** on the western side of Ko Phi Phi Ley. The **King Cruiser** wreck between the waters of Phuket and Ko Phi Phi is another favourite dive site.

KO LANTA YAI

Stretching 27 km (17 miles) in length and 12 km (7 miles) in width, **Ko Lanta Yai** is one of only three inhabited islands in an archipelago of over 50. Originally named Pulao Satak, meaning "Island with Long Beaches" by the *chao lay* (sea gypsies) who first settled on the island, the term Ko Lanta generally refers to the largest of these islands, Ko Lanta Yai.

Most visitors to Ko Lanta travel direct from Krabi where ferries leave twice daily on a journey that takes about 2 hours and terminates at **Ban Sala Dan** village on Ko Lanta's northernmost tip. Due to strong winds and rough seas, boats do not operate between May and October. Running from north to south, the island's one main road passes along the western beaches while a few

BELOW: magnificent Maya Bay.

smaller roads lead inland towards the southeastern coast, where there are small settlements of sea gypsies. Development has been mainly confined to the west coast where spectacular sunsets viewed from along a number of striking white sand beaches are a near daily certainty. The east coast is fringed by long stretches of mangroves and swimming is not possible. Ko Lanta will inevitably develop over time but so far it has managed to retain its sleepy island feel. Phone reception is patchy, internet connections are slow and beach bungalows dominate over high-rise developments. The red earth dirt tracks are slowly being replaced with tarred roads, making for easier access but invariably attracting more developers.

When the tsunami struck in December 2004, Ko Lanta was miraculously spared the destruction witnessed in nearby Ko Phi Phi. Some hotels and structures directly on the beachfront along Ko Lanta's west coast suffered slight damage. Reconstruction work has been completed, and hotels and facilities on Ko Lanta are up and running again.

Ban Sala Dan

Whether arriving by passenger or car ferry, the first stop for most visitors is the compact main village of **Ban Sala Dan ❶**. Guests at the more exclusive resorts on Ko Lanta have the luxury of being delivered right to the doorstep, or rather shorestep, of their hotel by private boat transfers.

Concrete posts and overhead hanging cables make Ban Sala Dan village a rather unsightly place, but for a relatively small island it is well equipped with a police post, clinic, tour agents and internet facilities. There are also a few small but well stocked local convenience stores. Along the pier are a number of seafood restaurants where fresh daily catches are displayed on beds of ice.

Hat Khlong Dao

A few kilometres south of Ban Sala Dan is the first of the island's westerly beaches, **Hat Khlong Dao ❷**. Shallow waters and safe swimming conditions make this 3-km (2-mile) stretch of beach a preferred choice with families. Its close proximity to the pier at Ban Sala Dan also appeals to scuba divers seeking an easy access to the nearby dive sites. Despite its attractions – white sand, picturesque hilly backdrop and some of the most dramatic sunsets along the western coast – Khlong Dao rarely seems crowded. The beach is wide enough that even in the peak season it's always possible to find a relatively secluded spot.

Ao Phra Ae

Almost if not equally as popular as Khlong Dao is the neighbouring **Ao Phra Ae ❸** (Long Beach) which is slightly longer at 4 km (3 miles) and shaded by vast stretches of coconut and pine trees. Phra Ae is popular with swimmers and sunbathers, but parts of the seabed are steep and the water not as calm so families with

If you plan to rent a jeep or a motorbike and explore Ko Lanta yourself, be sure to fill up with enough petrol before leaving the main village of Ban Sala Dan. The few petrol stations on Ko Lanta are expensive, difficult to find and shut annoyingly early.

BELOW: Muslim islanders on Ko Lanta.

small children should consider other options. There are lots of acommodation choices though and an ample variety of restaurants.

Hat Khlong Khong

Just south of Ao Phra Ae is laid back **Hat Khlong Khong ❹**, which although not great for swimming is one of the island's best beaches for snorkelling; at low tide the rocky underlay reveals an assortment of fish and other marine life. Accommodation is generally cheaper than on the more northerly beaches with an emphasis on clean but basic beachfront bungalows. Most have attached restaurants and beach bars which spring to life in the evenings, enticing customers with tables on the sand and colourful performances by flame throwers and fire eaters.

Inland diversions

There are limited attractions on Ko Lanta apart from its stunning beaches.

Some 4 km (2½ miles) south of Hat Khlong Khong, the road splits into two. The left fork leads all the way to the east coast of the island, where few tourists venture to. A turn-off at the 3-km (2-miles) mark to the right leads to the **Tham Mai Kaeo ❺** caves. It is best to get your hotel to organise this trip as finding the caves on your own is a bit of a challenge – you need to clamber up a steep hill, often with the help of tree branches. The combination of slippery paths, rickety bamboo ladders and confined spaces make this an inadvisable activity for the physically challenged. The expedition leads through a labyrinth of winding tunnels and caverns, past dramatic rock formations. At the end, after negotiating a steep slope with the aid of a rope, is a deep pool, where you can cool off.

If the thought of being up before dawn is not one that results in dread, a sunrise trip to the central peak referred to simply as **Viewpoint**

BELOW:
Ko Lanta fisherman.

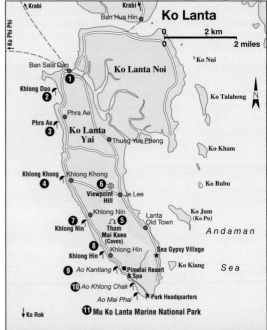

Map
on page
256

Hill ❻ is worth the effort. To get there, continue on the road that heads east (signs along the way will guide you towards this attraction).

As the early morning sky changes from pitch black to soft blue, the haunting, gravestone-like profiles of limestone cliffs will appear almost magically, one by one, until the sea is filled with them. The near 360-degree panoramic vistas amid the crisp morning air is truly breathtaking. The experience can be enjoyed over a "sunrise breakfast" high on the hill at the **Khao Yai Restaurant**. The food is mediocre, but gazing out towards the sea, you will barely realise that.

Hat Khlong Nin and Hat Khlong Hin

Turning right about 4 km (2 miles) from Hat Khlong Khong leads past a few convenience stores and wooden restaurants before emerging at **Hat Khlong Nin** ❼. This lovely beach has a relaxed feel and is imbued with the atmosphere of a small, intimate village. The powdery white sands of Hat Khlong Nin stretch about 2 km (1 mile) in length and calm waters out-

side of the monsoon make it excellent for swimming. Accommodation consists primarily of stylish resorts like **Sri Lanta** and the **Rawiwarin**, most with in-house restaurants and beach bars. At the start of Hat Khlong Nin is the popular reggae-style **Rasta Baby Bar**. A stroll along the beach-front reveals more of the same; at night time the next bamboo beach bar is never more than a short walk away.

At its southern end, Hat Khlong Nin merges with the similar sounding but much smaller and secluded **Hat Khlong Hin** ❽. Separated from the former by a cluster of trees, the waves here are rough during the monsoon season. It is quite empty at the moment and awaits development.

Ao Kantiang

About 6 km (4 miles) from Hat Khlong Hin is the lovely and picturesque bay of **Ao Kantiang** ❾. This bay has a secluded and private feel to it as it's framed on both sides and to the back by jungle-covered hills. To the north and high up on the hill are a handful of small stilted bungalows; there are lovely views

Typical beach bar set-up along Hat Khlong Nin.

BELOW: picturesque Ao Kan Tiang is anchored by Pimalai Resort & Spa at one end.

from the top but it also means climbing up a considerable number of steps to get to it. The southern end of this bay is anchored by the luxury **Pimalai Resort and Spa**. This five-star resort is set in 40 hectares (100 acres) of natural tropical surroundings and has direct access to the 1-km (½-mile) long stretch of pure white sand beach.

Ao Khlong Chak and Ao Mai Phai

Beyond Ao Kantiang, the further south one ventures, the more remote and consequently harder to reach the beaches become. Shortly after the Pimalai Resort and Spa, the road comes to an abrupt halt before morphing into a rugged dirt track; navigating it without the assistance of a four-wheel drive vehicle is a near impossibility. The reward is a cluster of the most scenic and underdeveloped beaches on the island, including **Ao Khlong Chak** ⑩, one of the smallest beaches on the island at just 400 metres (1,310 ft) long. Only a small handful of resorts are found here. Ao Khlong Chak is most

famous for its waterfall, found 1½ km (1 mile) inland, that flows year round.

Beyond this is a short but even bumpier drive leading to the cove of **Ao Mai Phai** (Bamboo Bay). This is the last beach before reaching the headquarters of the Mu Ko Lanta Marine National Park on the southernmost tip. Its difficulty of access and geography – Ao Mai Phai is backed by mountains on three sides – gives this bay a real sense of isolation. The beach is only 500 metres (1,640 ft) in length, but is ideal for swimming; a shallow boulder-strewn stretch at the northern edge is more suited to snorkelling.

Mu Ko Lanta N P

Declared Thailand's 62nd official National Park in 1990, **Mu Ko Lanta Marine National Park** ⑪ comprises the southern tip of Ko Lanta Yai and 15 small surrounding islands. The southernmost tip of Ko Lanta comprises two beaches: **Laem Tanode** and the rocky **Hat Hin Ngam**; the latter is where the park headquarters is situated. A 2½-km (1½-mile) hiking trail leading along a cliff begins here and offers the chance of spotting fauna like fruit bats, deer, wild pigs and reptiles, including monitor lizards, cobras and green snakes. Also here is a small white lighthouse, from which there are scenic views out to the sea and mountains.

Snorkelling and diving

Some of Thailand's finest spots for snorkelling and scuba diving are found in the waters off Ko Lanta. The most visited site for snorkelling, and considered by many to be one of Thailand's best, is **Ko Rok**, about 47 km (29 miles) south of Ko Lanta. There are actually two islands, **Ko Rok Nai** and **Ko Rok Nok**, graced with powdery white sand beaches and an extensive patch of coloured coral in between. Visibility is very

BELOW: snorkelling near Ko Rok.

good, and many interesting types of reef fish can be found in these waters.

Approximately 20 km (12 miles) from Ko Rok are the twin peaks of **Hin Daeng** and **Hin Muang**, frequently rated one of the world's top 10 dive sites. An incredible variety of marine life thrive at this site. As the only outcrops in this area of deep open sea, they also attract many pelagics, as well as large tuna and barracuda. Schools of grey reef sharks often approach divers and the area has one of the highest incidences of whale shark sightings in the world.

OTHER ISLANDS

Ko Bubu

Those seeking an even quieter retreat than Ko Lanta may wish to visit the smaller islands nearby. At 7 km (4 miles) off the east coast of Ko Lanta, the tiny island of **Ko Bubu** takes just 30 minutes to circumnavigate by foot. This uninhabited island only has a basic restaurant and a few simple bungalows on the western coast, where the small but stunning gently-sloping beach is fringed by turquoise waters ideal for swimming. Boat transfers can be arranged for guests of **Bubu Bungalows** (tel: 0-7561 2536), the only resort on the island; there is no other regular service. Longtail boats at Krabi and Ko Lanta can, however, be chartered for the journey.

Ko Jum (Ko Pu)

Larger than Ko Bubu, but still small and pleasantly underdeveloped is the island of **Ko Jum** (Ko Pu), to the northwest of Ko Lanta. The flat southern part is covered in palms and casuarinas, and the mountainous northern tip reaches a height of 395 metres (1,296 ft). The island is gifted with powdery white sand beaches and clear waters with plenty of healthy coral reefs. The best part is that it has yet to sustain any impact from tourism. Some 3,000 permanent residents reside on Ko Jum, earning a living mainly from fishing and its rubber plantations. Accommodation is limited to basic and mid-range bungalows but due to the lack of facilities most people visit only for the day. ❑

Maps on pages 256 & 244

Sea gypsy (chao lay) fisherman on Ko Jum mending his net.

BELOW:
Ko Bubu at dusk.

KRABI, KO PHI PHI AND KO LANTA

KRABI TOWN AND BEACHES

TRANSPORT

GETTING THERE

By Air

Krabi International Airport (tel: 0-7563 6541/2) is located about 18 km (11 miles) east of Krabi Town. Although the majority of visitors to Krabi and its surrounding islands stop off in Bangkok first for a few days, it is also possible to fly directly to Krabi from Singapore on budget airline **Tiger Airways** (www.tigerairways.com), which has several flights a week serving this route. Domestically, **Thai Airways** offers multiple daily non-stop flights to Krabi from Bangkok, as well as from Phuket and Chiang Mai.

If you haven't made arrangements with your hotel for pick-up at the airport, use one of the airport taxis. Fares are about B350 to Krabi Town and approximately B600 to B700 to Krabi's beaches. Travel time from Krabi Airport to the town centre takes around 30 minutes, with Ao Nang beach taking slightly less time. Pay the posted fare at the counter in the Arrival Hall and avoid the touts that hover outside the terminal.

By Bus & Taxi

Air-conditioned buses depart from Bangkok's **Southern Bus Terminal** daily for Krabi on the 12-hour overnight journey. Tickets range in price, as do levels of comfort. There are also direct buses from Phuket (3½ hours), Hat Yai (6 hours) and Ko Samui (2½ hours via Surat Thani on the mainland). Travel agents in any of these areas will advise on buying tickets. Note: in Krabi Town, the public buses terminate at Talat Kao, about 5 km (3 miles) north of town, while private tour buses end up at Andaman Wave Master station in the town centre. Local buses and taxis run from both stations to the beaches and the pier.

Taking a taxi from Phuket, Hat Yai or Ko Samui is quicker. From Phuket Airport, for instance, a taxi to Krabi will cost B2,200 and make the trip in 2½ hours. If you can get a cheap air ticket to Phuket (see page 230), you could fly to Phuket and then take a taxi to Krabi.

By Boat

During the high season, it's possible to take a boat from Phuket via Ko Phi Phi to Krabi. The journey from Ko Phi Phi is approximately 2 hours; from Phuket it's just under 3 hours. Boats from Phuket and Ko Phi Phi arrive at the new **Krabi Passenger Pier** on Th. Tharua (and not Chao Fa Pier as they did previously). Inquire with travel agents at either of these destinations as there are boats of varying quality and speeds.

GETTING AROUND

Non-metered taxis, motorcycle taxis and *tuk-tuk*s can be hired from Krabi Town and the beaches. The drivers in town often speak limited English, although those who operate around the beaches are more than adept at negotiating prices. Expect to pay between B200 and B400 for a short half-hour ride on a taxi or *tuk-tuk* (both charge about the same rates). Local bus services are provided by *songthaews* – converted pick-up trucks with two wooden benches in the back. These are difficult to use if you don't speak the language.

Krabi Town and the beach road are full of rental companies, many offering cheap deals but often without the security of full insurance. Using an internationally recognised firm is advisable. Contact **National Car Rental** at Krabi Airport (tel: 0-7569 1939). Motorcycles are available for hire along Ao Nang beach road but be sure to use a safety helmet.

Longtail boats make the 15-minute trip to both Railay West and Railay East beaches throughout the day. They line up from dusk to dawn along Ao Nang beach and charge a fixed rate of B60 per person each way. Prices rise to B100 after 7pm. They can also be hired for the day, in which case rates are negotiable. There is no pier at both Railay beaches, and the shore is reached by a short wade from the boat.

RESTAURANTS

KRABI TOWN

International

Café Europa
Th. Maharat. Tel: 0-7562 0407. Open: Mon–Sat B, L & D. $–$$. This cosy café is somewhat of an institution in Krabi Town. The limited menu is based around a few signature dishes, including pepper steak, meatballs and goulash, all with side salad and bread. Stacks of Thai and international newspapers and magazines make it a pleasant place to relax over a cuppa.

Thai

Night Market
Soi 10, Th. Maharat. Open: daily D only. $. The best food in Krabi Town, not to mention the one least likely to burn a hole in your pocket. Absorb the atmosphere and sample local delicacies at this local night market. Choices differ nightly, but the *kaab moo* (pork leg), a delicious meaty dish simmered for hours in soy sauce and accompanied with green vegetables and rice, is a good bet.

Ruen Mai
Th. Maharat. Open: daily 11am–9pm. $–$$. Vegetarians love this place as staff can prepare, on request, meat-free versions of any dish on the menu. With a wide selection of unusual local vegetables, the adventurous can try stir-fried *sataw* ("stinky beans") in red curry paste, or wing bean spicy salad. Strong flavours and lashings of chilli are not sacrificed to protect sensitive palates; this is way the locals eat.

AO NANG

Only Ao Nang beach has enough independant restaurants to warrant coverage here. Eating out at Krabi's other beaches is mainly confined to the hotel restaurants along each stretch.

Thai & Western

Azura Nova
142 Ao Nang. Tel: 0-7563 7848. Open: daily L & D. $$. Italian restaurants dominate Ao Nang's beach road, with this being the best. Lovely Mediterranean ambience with tiled floors, marble tables and vines creeping up the walls. Owned by Italians, the food is as authentic as it can get. The pizzas, pastas and risottos are all delicious.

Chanaya's Thai-Dutch Restaurant
Ao Nang (opp Krabi Seaview Resort). Mobile tel: 0-9993 3716. Open: daily B, L & D. $. Quirky rainforest setting with an interior overflowing with plants, a pebbled floor and colourful birds swinging in wooden cages from the ceiling. Choices include salmon, steak and even ostrich. Delicious baguette sandwiches at lunchtime.

Moon Terrace
154 Moo 2, Ao Nang. Tel: 0-7563 7180. Open: daily D only. Open-air seafood eatery on a wooden platform just a few feet from the water's edge. Arrive early to catch the setting sun. The seafood and fish served here are freshly caught every day. The white snapper is delicious and although not on the menu, ask for it steamed with garlic and chilli.

The Roof
Krabi Seaview Resort, Ao Nang. Tel: 0-7563 7242. Open: daily B, L & D. $$–$$$. www.krabi-seaview.com From its elevated rooftop position, The Roof, with its low lighting and flower-filled dining room, is an intimate location for dinner. Serves some Thai dishes but the specialities on the menu are mainly Swiss-German fare and organically bred beef.

Thai

Aning
Ao Nang. Open: daily B, L & D. $. One of the few Thai restaurants that has managed to secure its place along the beach road dominated by Italian eateries. Its orange interior is flamboyant and and the food tasty but toned down. Try the fluffy catfish salad and any of its delicious curries.

PRICE CATEGORIES

Price per person for a three-course meal without drinks:
$ = under US$10
$$ = US$10–25
$$$ = US$25–$50

ACCOMMODATION

KRABI TOWN

Budget

Krabi City Seaview Hotel
77/1 Th. Kongha.
Tel: 0-7562 2885.
www.krabidir.com/krabicityseaview
Located on the waterfront with good views of Krabi River and just 2 minutes' walk from the pier to the nearby islands. Quite basic but all rooms have cable TV, air-conditioning and fridge. (29 rooms)

Moderate

Maritime Park & Spa
1 Th. Tungfah. Tel: 0-7562 0028.
www.maritimeparkandspa.com
About 10 minutes' drive from Krabi Town, this is one of the better resorts outside of the beaches. Within its tropical-style setting are a large free-form swimming pool and a jogging track. (221 rooms)

AO NANG

Expensive

Pavilion Queen's Bay
56/3 Moo 3, Ao Nang.
Tel: 0-7563 7612.
www.pavilionhotels.com
This four-star hotel is perched atop a hill and is only 350 metres (1,150 ft) from the beach. Views of both mountain and sea are stunning, and the swimming pool area has elegant white umbrellas and tall, white Grecian columns. (106 rooms)

Moderate

Ao Nang Villa Resort
113 Ao Nang. Tel: 0-7563 7270.
www.aonangvilla.com
Great location only a minute's walk from the beachfront, with two large free-form swimming pools resting at the foot of Krabi's limestone mountains. The Villa Spa, opened in 2005, is located in a Thai-style house within the resort and is one of Ao Nang's best. (79 rooms)

Cliff Ao Nang Resort
85/2 Moo 2, Ao Nang.
Tel: 0-7563 8117.
www.krabi-hotels.com/thecliff
Voted one of Thailand's top 50 resorts by the Tourism Authority of Thailand. Small, elegant and located in the hills a 10-minute walk from the sea. The mountain views from this elevated position are stunning; if one is content to relax around the pool, this is one of Ao Nang's most peaceful retreats. (22 rooms)

Krabi Resort
232 Moo 2, Ao Nang. Tel: 0-7563 7030. www.krabiresort.net
Situated a 5-minute walk from the beach, this resort spreads over 7 ha (18 acres) and offers a choice of bungalows or cheaper rooms in the main hotel block. One of the few hotels in Ao Nang to have tennis courts. Massive swimming pool. (95 rooms)

HAT KHLONG MUANG

Luxury

Nakamanda Resort & Spa
126 Moo 3, Hat Khlong Muang.
Tel: 0-7564 4388.
www.nakamanda.com
Classy and elegant is a good way to describe this boutique resort. The large and elegant 56-sq m (603-sq ft) villas have Thai-style pointed roofs and are linked by shaded wooden walkways. Sandstone sculptures are scattered on the grounds and the artistically-designed pool is simply stunning. By far the most romantic hotel in the area and worth staying at if the budget allows. (36 rooms)

Expensive

Sheraton Krabi Beach Resort
155 Moo 2, Khlong Muang.
Tel: 0-7562 8000.
www.sheraton.com/krabi
Set directly on Khlong Muang beach, this large resort is spread across a number of blocks but fits in so well with the natural surroundings that it appears smaller. Beautiful sea-facing pool and all the facilities expected from a Sheraton hotel, including the exclusive Mandara Spa. High-speed internet access in rooms. Coffee house, bar, Mediterranean and Thai restaurants. (246 rooms)

HAT THAM PHRA NANG

Luxury

Rayavadee
Hat Tham Phra Nang. Tel: 0-7562 0740. www.rayavadee.com
The most exclusive – and expensive – resort in the entire Krabi Province and hailed by many magazine surveys (including *Condé Nast Traveller*) as being one of the world's best. Tucked away in a headland alongside spectacular Tham Phra Nang beach on one side and the more prosaic Railay East beach on the other. The well-designed villas all but melt into the surroundings. Includes several restaurants and a spa. Very expensive, but a truly magical location. (103 rooms)

PRICE CATEGORIES

Price categories are for a double room without breakfast and taxes:
Luxury = over US$200
Expensive = US$100–200
Moderate = US$50–100
Budget = under US$50

HAT RAILAY WEST

Moderate

Railay Bay Resort & Spa
Hat Railay West. Tel: 0-7562
2570. www.krabi-railaybay.com
The only resort on Railay
Bay to spread from
Railay West beach and
inland all the way to
Railay East. Different
styles of cottages are
available, all with cable
TV and air-conditioning.
Restaurant and swim-
ming pool on site, plus
the Sunset Bar on Railay
West where you can have
a drink while watching
the sun set. (126 rooms)

Sand Sea Resort
Hat Railay West. Tel: 0-7562
2574. www.krabisandsea.com
Pleasant hotel with a
variety of room styles
(and prices). Restaurant,
beachfront swimming
pool, minimart and
internet facilities on site.
(42 rooms)

Budget

Railay Village Resort
Railay West. Tel: 0-7562 2578.
www.krabidir.com/railayvillageresort
Perfectly situated for
sunsets on scenic Railay
West beach. Offers a
choice of bungalows, all
set close to the beach
and among coconut
groves. (48 rooms)

HAT RAILAY EAST

Moderate

Sunrise Tropical Resort
Hat Railay East. Tel: 0-7562
2599. www.sunrisetropical.com
Located on Railay East,
this place is blessed with
dramatic morning sun-
rises. Prettier Railay West
beach is only a 5-minute
walk away. Rooms are
spacious and homely with
wooden floors, and the
resort pool is surrounded
by palms and faces
towering limestone
karsts. Restaurant, internet and massage facili-
ties on site. (28 rooms)

AO TON SAI

Budget

**Krabi Mountain
View Resort**
Ao Ton Sai. Tel: 0-7562 2610.
www.krabimountainview.com
Pleasant bungalow-style
huts situated between
the cliffs and waters of
Ton Sai beach, with
Railay West just a
10-minute walk at low
tide. Rooms are clean
and modern, and offer
good value for money. By
far the best choice of
accommodation on this
beach. Rates include
breakfast. (46 rooms)

ACTIVITIES

NIGHTLIFE

Ao Nang

Irish Rover Bar and Grill: 247/8
Moo 2, Ao Nang, tel: 0-7563
7607. Irish-style pub just off a
side street from the main beach
road. Convivial atmosphere with
Guinness flowing all evening and
sports on overhead TVs.
Luna Beach Bar: Ao Nang. Beach
bar with pool tables, DJs and a lively
atmosphere; doesn't get going till
after midnight. Nightly fire shows
on the beach.

Railay West & East

Bobo's: Bobo Plaza, Hat Railay
West. This quiet beach bar with
its candle-lit tables is the only
purpose-built bar on Railay West
to watch the setting sun. All other
places are basically restaurants
that happen to serve drinks.
Gecko Bar: Hat Railay East. Hip
and happening beach bar set on
the rocks of Railay East. Often has
parties lasting late into the night;
a favourite spot to gather after all
the other beach bars wind down.

SHOPPING

In Krabi Town, the **Vogue Department Store** (285–6 Th. Montri,
tel: 0-7524 3589) has cosmetics
and a supermarket on the first
level, and clothing and sports
gear on the upper levels.

Two night markets located in
the Krabi Town centre spring to
life in the evening. The first, alongside **Chao Fa Pier** at the Krabi
River is mainly a food market

frequented by locals but is well
worth a look for the variety of low-
priced dishes on offer. The second, outside the **City Hotel** on Th.
Srisawat, is more tourist-oriented
and sells clothes and souvenirs.

OUTDOOR ACTIVITIES

Golf

Pakasai Country Club: Ban Lik
Nai, Nua Klong, tel: 0-7561 1984.
This 9-hole course with lake views
is currently Krabi's only golf
course. Games can be arranged
with your hotel or online at
www.krabigolftours.com.
Krabi Driving Range: Th.
Klongkanan, Nua Klong. Just a
few minutes' drive from Ao Nang,
this driving range has a practice
green and two chipping greens,

one with a bunker. Bookings via www.krabigolftours.com or through tour agents.

Deep Sea Fishing

Ao Nang Fishing and Snorkelling: 31/4 Moo 2, Ao Nang , tel: 0-7569 5408. Offers fishing day trips off the coast of Krabi aboard longtail boats. Enjoyable day out and good value for money.

Sea Canoeing

Krabi's limestone cliffs and beautiful bays make it a favoured location for sea canoeing enthusiasts. Tours from mainland Krabi usually depart from Ao Thalane or Ao Luk, where monkeys, otters and tropical birds are a common sight. Away from the main Krabi beaches, one of the prime canoeing areas is around the Railay peninsula (Ko Hong and Ko Bileh are favoured spots). The popularity of this site is not without good reason – aside from the cluster of rocky peaks and hidden caves, the peninsula is accessible only by longtail boat, meaning there are no large boats or noisy jet skis sharing the water with you.

Art Canoeing: 32/12 Moo 2, Ao Nang, tel: 0-7563 7492. Organises sea kayak trips to the islands off Krabi. Also combines the trips with snorkelling.

Sea Kayak Krabi: 40 Th. Maharat, Krabi Town, tel: 0-7563 0270; www.seakayak-krabi.com. Offers both half- and full-day guided canoeing trips to Ao Thalane, Ao Luk and Ko Hong. Lunch is provided on the full day tours.

Sea Canoe Thailand: 367/4 Th. Yaowarat, Phuket Town, tel: 0-7621 2252; www.seacanoe.net. This reputable Phuket-based operator also runs trips to Krabi. Make enquiries with local travel agents in Krabi.

Rock Climbing

Krabi is famous for its limestone cliffs. There are over 150 pegged routes both inland and offshore in the Phra Nang Bay area. Operators in Ao Nang and Railay can advise on the best courses to suit people of different ages and levels of skill and fitness. Most routes are challenging but there are also several beginner climbs. Equipment rentals, instruction and guides are all available. The following companies are recommended.

Hot Rock Climbing School: Bobo Plaza, Hat Railay West, tel: 0-7562 1771; www.railayadventure.com.

King Climbers: Hat Railay East, tel: 0-7563 7125; www.railay.com. Reputable outfit with many years experience. Has even published the well-regarded *Kings Climbers Route Guide Book*.

Diving & Snorkelling

There are a number of outstanding dive sites close to Ao Nang and Railay beaches. Dive shops along the Ao Nang and Railay beachfronts offer day trips to these sites plus live-aboards to those further afield in the Andaman Sea. Snorkelling trips to nearby islands (like Ko Poda and Ko Kai) can be booked with any one of several tour agents along the beachfront.

Ao Nang Divers: 143 Moo 2, Ao Nang, tel: 0-7563 7242; www.aonang-divers.com. Modern dive centre with its base at the Krabi Seaview Resort. Full range of PADI courses plus the Bubble Makers programme for children 8 years and younger, and the Junior Open Water for those 10 years and older.

Scuba Addicts: 245/5 Moo 2, Ao Nang, tel: 0-7533 7705; www.scuba-addicts.com. Reputable operator offering PADI courses as well as day trips and live-aboards.

Ko Phi Phi Tour: 80 Th. Pisapon Road, Krabi Town, tel: 0-7562 0506. In addition to kayaking and rainforest trips, it also offers snorkelling trips that combine some sightseeing. The "Krabi 4 Islands" visits Phra Nang Cave, Ko Poda, Ko Tup and Ko Kai islands.

Thai Boxing

Krabi Thai Boxing Stadium: Ao Nang. One of the largest stadiums in the south, with seating for over 2,000 people. Matches are held on Friday evenings. Bookings can be made at any travel agent in the town or at the beaches.

SPAS

Rayavadee Spa: Rayavadee Resort, Hat Tham Phra Nang, tel: 0-7562 0740; www.rayavadee.com. Exclusive spa mainly for hotel guests, so expect to pay through your nose. The spa menu includes massages, scrubs, facials, wraps and baths as well as a range of pampering packages in a truly indulgent setting. Appointments are advised.

Villa Spa: Ao Nang Villa Resort, Ao Nang, tel: 0-7563 7270; www.aonangvilla.com. Opened in 2005 in a Thai-style house, the Villa Spa has specialised treatments such as a "face lift" massage to tone skin and increase elasticity, and a hot sand compress to relieve tired and stressed muscles.

Wanalee Health Spa: 325 Moo 2, Ao Nang, tel: 0-7563 7805; www.krabidir.com/wanaleespa. Located in a forest on the Ao Nang hillside. Therapists are trained at Bangkok's renowned Wat Pho massage school and use plant-based products. Offers reasonably priced packages to revive and detoxify.

KO PHI PHI

TRANSPORT

GETTING THERE

Although Ko Phi Phi is, administratively speaking, within the Krabi Province, it is located about the same distance from both mainland Krabi and Phuket over sea, roughly 2 hours by boat from either. It is not possible to fly to Ko Phi Phi; you need to get to either Phuket *(see page 230)* or Krabi *(see page 260)* and then make the crossing by sea.

Ferries from Krabi depart from the new **Passenger Ferry Terminal** on Th. Tharua in Krabi Town; those in Phuket leave from Phuket Town's **Rassada Pier**. All boats land on Ao Ton Sai on the larger island of Ko Phi Phi Don. Tickets can be purchased at travel agents in both Phuket and Krabi. It is best to ask around on arrival at the respective piers as different agents charge vastly different fees for the same boats. If you've booked accomodation on Ko Phi Phi, get your hotel to arrange the boat transfers for you.

Note: many people do Ko Phi Phi as a day trip from Phuket or Krabi; packages with roundtrip transfers, lunch and snorkelling cost anything from B1,200 to B1,600, depending on the type of boat used.

Between the months of May and October, ferries may not run due to bad weather, in which case private transfers can be arranged through travel agents.

GETTING AROUND

Transportation on Ko Phi Phi is non-existent. There are no roads, and therefore no motorbikes or cars. The only way to get around is by foot, although distances between some of the main beaches are short and pathways flat, so this is quick and easy to do. During the day, longtail boats will make the journey from the Laem Thong beach at the north of the island to Ton Sai in the south for about B400 or more, but may be reluctant to make the 1-hour journey back once darkness falls. Shorter rides to closer beaches will cost from B50 to B100.

RESTAURANTS

AO TON SAI

Only restaurants at this beach are listed here. Eating out at the other beaches is largely confined to the hotel restaurants.

Thai & Western

Restaurant H.C.Andersen
Ton Sai Village, mobile tel: 0-1894 5287. Open: daily, B L & D. $$. www.phiphisteakhouse.com
Long-standing steak house with choice cut meats and delicious sauces. One of the island's better restaurants, it has a casual and welcoming feel, no doubt aided by the cheerful Matts from Denmark who runs it. Offers a massive choice of breakfasts, everything from Scandinavian to English and American styles.

JJ's Pub
Ton Sai Village. Open: daily B, L & D. $$.
Strictly for homesick Brits. Few restaurants claiming to serve English food can pull it off, but this one does with its authentic bangers and mash, pies, and the obligatory English breakfast with baked beans.

Patcharee Bakery and Boulengerie
Ton Sai Village. Open: daily B, L & D. $.
Less popular than the Phi Phi bakery situated directly opposite yet just as good, this café serves Thai dishes and baked goods. Service is not as quick, but the atmosphere far less hectic and there is a greater chance of getting a table.

Phi Phi Bakery
Ton Sai Village. Open: daily B, L & D. $.
British-style café with food that comes quickly and in large portions. Given its popularity, the restaurant could do with a facelift but the food is undeniably tasty. The "Phi Phi Bakery Combination", of sausages, sauerkraut, garlic bread, potatoes and salad, is guaranteed to cure hangovers.

Thai

Pums Restaurant
Ton Sai Village. $$.
Stylish eatery, unlike most of the casual set-ups on the island. A large selection of well presented Thai dishes, including the "Green Lipstick" and "Red Lipstick" (green and red curries).

PRICE CATEGORIES

Price per person for a three-course meal without drinks:
$ = under US$10
$$ = US$10–$25

ACCOMMODATION

AO TON SAI

Moderate

Phi Phi Banyan Villa
Ao Ton Sai, tel: 0-7561 1233.
www.phiphi-hotel.com
If location is everything, then this place, right in the centre of Ao Ton Sai, wins hands down. The beach, restaurants, shops and pier are just 5 minutes' walk away. Rooms are comfortable (the ones in the garden wing are slightly pricier) and have air-condition-ing, cable TV and hot water. (40 rooms)

Budget

Chao Ko Phi Phi Lodge
Ao Ton Sai. Tel: 0-7562 0800.
www.chaokohphiphi.com
Set on the beachfront just a 2-minute walk from the busiest part of Ao Ton Sai. Rooms are comfortable, with air-conditioning and satel-lite TV. Facilities include a mini-mart and a small sea-facing swimming pool. (44 rooms)

Phi Phi Hotel
Ao Ton Sai. Tel: 0-7561 1233.
www.phiphi-hotel.com
Smaller and not quite as upmarket as its sister property, Phi Phi Banyan Villa, but sharing the same prime location, this low-rise property has rooms with either sea or mountain views. (64 rooms)

HAT HIN KHOM

Moderate

Bayview Resort
Hat Hin Khom. Tel: 0-2677 6240. www.phiphibayview.com
Split-level bungalows set on a hillside and encircled by a thick tree-filled grove. Restaurant and small pool on site. Rooms enjoy panoramic views across the sea towards Ko Phi Phi Ley. (70 rooms)

Budget

Phi Phi Andaman Resort
1 Moo 7, Hat Khin Khom.
Tel: 0-7560 1111.
www.krabidir.com/ppandamanresort
Located a 10-minute walk from Ton Sai pier and set in a tropical gar-den backing the beach. Mix of bungalows with fan or air-conditioning and basic white walls and tiled floors. All pleasant, bright and spotlessly clean. One of the better options for accommodation in this price range. (50 rooms)

HAT YAO

Moderate

Paradise Resort
Hat Yao. Mobile tel: 0-1968 3982. www.paradiseresort.co.th
Set on relatively quiet Hat Yao beach, this place

is accessed by a 10-minute boat ride from Ao Ton Sai. Variety of rooms, from cheaper fan-cooled ones to more expensive air-conditioned options. Restaurant, bar and internet access.

HAT LAEM THONG

Luxury

Zeavola Resort
Hat Laem Thong. Tel: 0-7562 7000. www.zeavola.com
One of Ko Phi Phi Don's newest all-suite resorts and situated on the island's far northern tip. The oversized suites – ranging from the cheaper Village Suites to the mid-range Garden and Hillside ones to the more expensive Beachfront Suites – are in the style of thatched bungalows, each with separate bed-room and living room. Completely made of wood, they would fit well on a snowy mountain-side but it were not for the air-conditioning. Two restaurants, a spa and pool. (52 rooms)

Expensive

Holiday Inn Resort
Hat Laem Thong.
Tel: 0-7562 1334.
www.phiphi-palmbeach.com
The former Phi Phi Palm Beach has been rebranded into a Holiday Inn. Nice resort, albeit a

little isolated from the island's thriving centre at Ao Ton Sai. Its seclusion, however, makes it a popular location for honeymooners. If a quiet island resort is what you are after, then this is the perfect hideaway. All the usual facilities expected from a high-end resort, including a large free-form pool and a good selection of restaurants and bars on site. (80 rooms)

AO LO BAKAO

Expensive

Phi Phi Island Village Resort & Spa
Ao Lo Bakao. Tel: 0-7623 6616.
www.ppisland.com
This attractive resort is situated on 800 metres (2,500 ft) of private beach, making it a popu-lar location for those looking to get away from it all. Rooms are taste-fully appointed but it is the idyllic location above all else that keeps guests coming back. Good range of facilities – three restaurants, two bars and a spa. (104 rooms)

PRICE CATEGORIES

Price categories are for a double room without breakfast and taxes:
Luxury = over US$200
Expensive = US$100–200
Moderate = US$50–100
Budget = under US$50

NIGHTLIFE

Ao Ton Sai

Nightlife on Ko Phi Phi is predictably all concentrated on Ao Ton Sai, with mainly small open-air bars making up the scene.
Apache: This huge sea-facing bar is a popular place to relax and chat. Features one-for-one deals on "buckets" of whiskey, gin, vodka and cocktails all night long.
Carlitos: Small but very popular bar that goes quite insane after midnight, with crowds spilling onto the beach. Great party atmosphere.
Reggae Bar: The island's biggest, and many would argue best, party venue with a huge Thai boxing ring on the ground floor and a dance floor on the open-air upper level.

Rolling Stoned Bar: Tucked away behind the Reggae Bar is this two-tiered bar with pool tables, hammocks swinging from beams and a selection of modern dance tunes that gets crowds up and dancing every night.

OUTDOOR ACTIVITIES

Diving & Snorkelling

Ko Phi Phi seems to have a dive shop at every turn, all offering pretty much the same trips at very similar prices. The only obvious difference is in the attitude of the staff. With so much competition, there is a lot of pressure from street touts who do a hard sell. Generally, the ones who don't try so hard for business are those

who have better reputations. The following are recommended.
Aquanauts Scuba: mobile tel: 0-1898 1838; www.aquanauts-scuba.com. One of the first dive centres on the island, with friendly and experienced staff. Strong emphasis is placed on personal instruction, with a maximum of four divers per instructor.
Barakuda Diving Center: tel: 0-7560 1006; www.barakuda.com. Friendly and informative dive shop, although sometimes a little pushy.
Island Divers: mobile tel: 0-9873 2205; www.islanddiverspp.com. Friendly and professional staff offer PADI dive courses, day trips and live-aboard diving, as well as snorkelling and kayaking tours.
Viking Divers: mobile tel: 0-1970 3644; www.vikingdiversthailand.com. Offers training for all PADI courses, as well as trips to local dive sites.

KO LANTA

GETTING THERE

It is not possible to fly directly to Ko Lanta. You will have to get to Krabi (see page 260) first and then make the transfer by boat. Ferries from Krabi depart from the new **Passenger Ferry Terminal**, located 3 km (2 miles) west of the town centre on Th. Tharua. Boats leave at 10.30am and 1.30pm daily and dock at Ban Sala Dan pier on the northern tip of Ko Lanta. The journey takes around 2 hours, but note that boats do not operate during the May–Oct monsoon season. Alternatively, if you

have booked accomodation on Ko Lanta, get your hotel to arrange the land and boat transfers.

There is no direct ferry from Phuket to Ko Lanta, but there are twice-daily boats from Phuket Town's Rassada Pier to Ko Phi Phi, where a connecting ferry will make the journey to Ko Lanta.

GETTING AROUND

There is only one road that runs through the west coast of Ko Lanta. Island transportation is difficult as there are no taxis or tuk-tuks. Some guesthouses and

higher-end resorts offer transfer services to the beaches and to Sala Dan village where there is a motorcycle taxi service.

Jeeps can be hired from rental agencies in Ban Sala Dan, and the majority of guesthouses can arrange motorbike rental. Be aware though that neither of these options are likely to include adequate, or in the case of motorbikes, any insurance. Safety helmets are advised.

Some of the more upmarket resorts on Ko Lanta will arrange boat transfers directly to the beach they are located on, dispensing with the need for any (bumpy) road travel.

RESTAURANTS

BAN SALA DAN

Thai & Western

Lanta Seafood
73 Moo 1, Ban Sala Dan. Tel: 0-7568 4106. Open: daily L & D. $$.
The seafood eateries along Sala Dan pier have dishes that look much the same. Locals, however, seem to favour this place, with its snapper, prawns and squid, all served on tables directly overlooking the sea.

AO PHRA AE

Thai & Western

The Brit Café
Ao Phra Ae. Tel: 0-6946 8702. Open: daily B, L & D. $–$$.
Blatantly British and proud of it, with Union Jacks on signs everywhere. This basic little café manages to pull in the crowds regularly with its traditional English breakfasts and pies. Packed during English football season as beer-swilling Brits gather around television sets.

Faim De Loup
255 Moo 2, Ao Prae Ae. Tel: 0-7568 4525. Open: daily B, L & D. $.
Undeniably French in character, with glass cabinets containing pastries and sugar-laden buns served on blue-and-white checked tablecloths. A great central location, and spoilt only slightly by its roadside location and lack of a view.

Red Snapper
Ao Phra Ae. Tel: 0-7885 6965. Open: daily L & D. $$.
www.redsnapper-lanta.com
Al fresco-style restaurant with direct beach access from its leafy garden location. Blends European dishes with Thai herbs for an interesting East-West fusion effect. The menu changes every 6 to 8 weeks, but the seven entrees and eight main courses on offer are always delicious.

HAT KHLONG NIN

Thai & Western

The Hut Restaurant
168 Moo 6, Hat Khlong Nin. Open: daily 8am–late. $.
If the food doesn't captivate you, owner Dang will with her beaming smile. Trained by a Brit, the Thai staff are adept at cooking up Western dishes, and if the extensive menu is not enough, they are happy to cook whatever you fancy.

AO KAN TIANG

Thai

Same Same But Different
85 Moo 5, Ao Kan Tiang. Mobile tel: 0-1787 8670. Open: daily B, L & D. $–$$.
Location is key to the popularity of this laid-back beach restaurant, with many customers strolling in from the neighbouring Pimalai resort. Menu contains a few sandwiches and salads but is predominantly Thai. A good range of dishes.

PRICE CATEGORIES

Price per person for a three-course meal without drinks:
$ = under US$10
$$ = US$10–$25

ACCOMMODATION

HAT KHLONG DAO

Expensive

Twin Lotus Resort & Spa
Hat Khlong Dao. Tel: 0-7560 7000. www.twinlotusresort.com
Minimalist and ultra-modern both inside and out, this resort uses clever lighting and solid blocks of colour to achieve a strikingly bold yet elegant ambience throughout the guest rooms, spa and reception. (78 rooms)

Budget

Southern Lanta Resort
Hat Khlong Dao. Tel: 0-7568 4174/7. www.southernlanta.com
Largest of the resorts on Hat Khlong Dao. Each bungalow has its own private balcony and garden area. Not the most modern compared to some of the island's other developments, but prices are a steal and there is a good range of facilities. (100 rooms)

AO PHRA AE

Luxury

Layana Resort and Spa
Ao Phra Ae. Tel: 0-7560 7100.
www.layanaresort.com
Warm and welcoming boutique resort more suited to couples than families. Both the swimming pool and oversized jacuzzi have the sea in front and a backdrop of forested hills behind. All

PRICE CATEGORIES

Price categories are for a double room without breakfast and taxes:
Luxury = over US$200
Expensive = US$100–200
Moderate = US$50–100
Budget = under US$50

rooms are equipped with broadband and internet connections. (50 rooms)

Expensive

Lanta Sand Resort & Spa
Ao Phra Ae. Tel: 0-7568 4633. www.lantasand.com
Everything spells tropical at this lovely resort, with its swimming pool, spa and guest rooms tucked in between luscious greenery and coconut palms. All rooms have open-air, natural garden bathrooms. (48 rooms)

Moderate

Lanta Garden Hill Resort
38/2 Moo 2, Ao Phra Ae. Tel: 0-2673 0966. www.lantagardenhill.com
There is a variety of accommodation options available at this resort, from standard to deluxe bungalows, many of which look like suburban homes with their long driveways and classic design. Situated on a hillside about 300 metres (900 ft) from the beach, it has nice views at sunset. (60 rooms)

HAT KHLONG NIN

Luxury

Rawiwarin Resort & Spa
Hat Khlong Nin. Tel: 0-7560 7400. www.rawiwarin.com
Ko Lanta's newest five-star resort opened in 2006. Situated at the foot of a series of hills and overlooking a lovely beach, it has four swimming pools (including one that is built into the sea). Complete range of facilities and even a mini cinema. (163 rooms)

Expensive

Sri Lanta
Hat Khlong Nin. Tel: 0-7569 7288. www.srilanta.com
Well regarded beachside property with charming thatched-roofed bungalows that are simple yet stylish. Its eclectic restaurant, scattered with floor cushions, is built almost completely from wood and grass and supported by tree trunks. (49 rooms)

Budget

The Narima
99 Moo 5, Hat Khlong Nin. Tel: 0-7560 7700. www.narima-lanta.com
Three rows of sea-facing wooden huts, all with air-conditioning, as well as fans and mosquito nets should you choose to open the windows and listen to the sound of the ocean during the night. Good value for money in this price range. (32 rooms)

AO KAN TIANG

Luxury

Pimalai Resort and Spa
Ao Kan Tiang. Tel: 0-7560 7999. www.pimalai.com
A luxurious five-star resort that cleverly mixes Thai and contemporary styling. Highy-rated spa, plus restaurants, dive centre, infinity-edge pool and direct access to a stunning 900-metre (2,950 ft) beachfront. Undeniably exclusive but a bit far out if you like to be close to the busier beaches. If it's isolation you crave, this is the perfect place to chill out. (79 rooms and 39 villas)

ACTIVITIES

NIGHTLIFE

Most of the action takes place on Ao Phra Ae, centred around bars set up along the beach.
Funky Fish: Ao Phra Ae. Nice ambience and a beachfront setting tucked away from the road behind a cluster of dense trees.
Opium: Ao Phra Ae. Popular British-owned bar. Stylish with a chilled-out ambience but only open in the high season.
The Laughing Leprechaun: Hat Khlong Dao. Irish Bar on the main road fronting Khlong Dao. Serves Guinness and cider and shows live premiership football.
Rasta Baby Bar: Hat Khlong Nin. Reggae bar with a relaxed island vibe. Has straw mats and low wooden tables inside, although many sit on the sand outside – under the stars.

OUTDOOR ACTIVITIES

Diving & Snorkelling

The waters around **Mu Ko Lanta Marine National Park** is home to some of Thailand's best snorkelling and diving sites (see page 258). Most dive operators are found at Ban Sala Dan, while upmarket resorts usually have a dive centre on their premises. The following are recommended:
Blue Planet Divers: Ban Sala Dan, tel: 0-7568 4165; www.blueplanet divers.net. Qualified instructors offer extensive courses and dive trips aboard a modern air-conditioned boat. Multilingual staff.
Lanta Diver Co Ltd: Ban Sala Dan, mobile tel: 0-1271 9050; www.lantadiver.com. A five-star IDC dive centre in operation since 1998. Keeps diver numbers limited on visits to nearby sites, with a maximum of four per instructor.

TRANG, SATUN AND SONGKHLA

Thailand's deep **south** is where you will find picture-perfect beaches **and** get a taste of Thai-Muslim culture and cuisine. While Trang and Satun provinces shelter pristine isolated islands, Hat Yai in Songkhla province is infamous for its sleazy massage parlours and bars

Bangkok

Misconceptions abound when it comes to Thailand's southernmost provinces. Among Thais, the predominantly Muslim residents are regarded as rough and prone to violence. To make things worse, the region is one of the poorest in Thailand, with scant tourist infrastructure. So relatively few people, foreign or domestic, visit the area. Although there are some areas that should be expressly avoided – Narathiwat, Yala and Pattani – which are in the midst of a violent insurgency, the provinces covered in this chapter, Trang, Satun and Songkhla, are perfectly safe to travel in. While the population in the countryside is mainly Muslim, you will find large Chinese communities in the cities.

A vibrant melting pot

Sampling Thai-Muslim culture and cuisine is a particular attraction. Some of the most fascinating highlights of the entire southern region are found in the deep south. These include the pristine islands of Ko Tarutao Marine National Park (where one season of the TV series *Survivor* was filmed), the vibrant cultural melting pot that is Songkhla, and Trang's diverse island life. If you want to avoid the crowds and sample some of Thailand's un-adulterated nature and culture, head for the deep south.

TRANG PROVINCE

Trang Province holds what is probably the greatest variety of attractions of any of the provinces in the deep south, as well as an interesting urban centre in Trang Town. North of the province, there are picture-perfect beaches and islands with ample accommodation, a wealth of outdoor activities and good food. To the south of Trang, the beaches and islands are more isolated but they offer some fascinating wildlife and the chance to observe everyday life on an island.

Map on page 272

LEFT: the village of Hua Laem on Ko Muk. **BELOW:** a coffee shop in Trang Town.

Trang Town

Trang Town ❶ is a pleasant place with a predominantly Chinese population and enough attractions to warrant at least an overnight stay. While Trang is well known among Thais as the birthplace of Chuan Leekpai, a former prime minister, travellers will be more taken by another legacy – its food. From Chinese-style coffee shops to one of Thailand's best night markets – located along Thanon Ruenrom – the food in Trang is one of its highlights. Trang Town also has a very colourful morning market. Every morning, vendors sell a plethora of fresh produce on Thanon Ratchadamnoen and Thanon Sathani while copious amounts of seafood line the streets behind the Ko Teng Hotel.

Thanks to its Chinese inhabitants, every October Trang plays host to a Vegetarian Festival that rivals the one celebrated in Phuket *(see page 43)*. During the week-long festival,

Shadow puppetry, common in Thailand's deep south region, is an art form that has its roots in nearby Malaysia.

the frenzied faithful, after having abstained from meat, alcohol and sex for a week, walk over red-hot coals and skewer themselves with all sorts of sharp instruments.

Trang's beaches

A string of secluded beaches along the Trang coast and several islands off the coast are worth seeking out. Trang's formidably long 119-km (74-mile) long coastline from Hat Pak Meng to Hat Chao Mai plus a number of lovely islands nearby are part of the **Hat Chao Mai National Park**.

Some 40 km (25 miles) west of Trang Town is **Hat Pak Meng**, a rather shallow beach that gets quite muddy at low tide. There are a few places to stay here, a string of seafood restaurants and a pier at the northern end where boats depart for trips to nearby islands. But apart from these, Pak Meng doesn't have much going for it. It's very much a local scene with Thais picnicking

Trang, Satun and Songkhla

0   50 km
0   50 miles

Gulf of Thailand

Andaman Sea

MALAYSIA

and having a good time on its shores on the weekends.

South of Hat Pak Meng is **Hat Chang Lang ❷**, a lovely and isolated beach with greyish white sands and backed by soaring casuarina trees. The beach is only swimmable at high tide; when the tide is low it exposes large sand banks which are great to walk on. The only hotel of note is here is the stylish **Amari Trang Beach Resort**, right on the beach and unexpectedly luxurious for such a remote area. When the conditions are right, the sunsets can be truly spectacular here, bathing the horizon studded with islands and limestone crags in an orange glow.

Beyong Hat Chang Lang are more beaches – **Hat Yong Ling**, **Hat Yao** and **Hat Chao Mai** – but both facilities and accommodation becomes very sparse. Nearby Ban Chao Mai is where the harbour is located, a jump-off point for tours of various islands off the coast.

Inland of Hat Yao are the caves at **Tham Lod**, which makes for an interesting daytrip. Reached by kayak, the journey winds it way past mangrove forests and enters a cave through a tiny gap. A 10-minute paddle in darkness follows until you emerge into a scenic hidden lagoon surrounded by mangroves and towering limestone walls.

Trang's islands

About 16 km (10 miles) southeast of Hat Pak Meng, is **Ko Hai ❸** (also known as Ko Ngai). It actually lies in Krabi Province, but is more accessible from Trang. Ringed by clear water and coral reefs, it has several low-key resorts and a near-perfect swimming beach on its eastern side.

Approximately 8 km (5 miles) south of Ko Hai (and facing Hat Chang Lang) is **Ko Muk ❹**. Boats to Ko Muk usually arrive at the small fishing village of Hua Laem, on the east side of the island, which is home to hundreds of permanent inhabitants and numerous rubber plantations, giving it a rural atmosphere. Ko Muk's finest beach is the secluded **Hat Farang** on the west coast, a cove-like inlet ringed by limestone cliffs not unlike Railay Bay in Krabi. The highlight of Ko Muk is the amaz-

Map on page 272

The streets of many towns in the region are lined with elaborate wooden birdcages holding doves. These birds are renowned for their cooing, with contests organised and awards given out.

BELOW: Amari Trang Beach Resort on Hat Chang Lang.

The National Museum in Satun is housed in the former Kuden Mansion.

ing and popular **Tham Morakot**, "Emerald Cave", in the northern part of the island. During low-tide, it's possible to swim through this partially submerged cave, the last few metres of which is done in complete darkness, to emerge in a hidden beach surrounded by towering limestone cliffs and lush greenery.

Another must-see island is **Ko Kradan** ❺, about 6 km (4 miles) southwest of Ko Muk, which some consider the most beautiful island in the area. The beaches are blinding white and there are some nice reefs offshore but, unfortunately, the accommodation on the island is rather ramshackle. The island is mainly visited by daytrippers who come to laze on its beaches, or to snorkel and dive. The Amari resort on mainland Trang runs the **Amari Beach Club** on Ko Kradan's stunning **Hat Na Ko**, with deck chairs, watersports facilities and a restaurant, but unfortunately, only hotel guests are allowed access.

Southwest of Ko Kradan are two less frequently visited islands. The first is **Ko Libong** ❻, the largest

island in the group and known for its wildlife. The waters around the island is one of Thailand's remaining habitats of the dugong, a marine mammal also known as the manatee. **Libong Nature Beach Resort** (one of only two resorts on the island) offers snorkelling trips which takes visitors into the waters populated by the dugongs.

Southeast of Ko Libong is **Ko Sukorn** ❼, home to nearly 3,000 people, and at last count, only four cars. The island's beaches are concentrated on the western shore, the most attractive of these being **Hat Talo Yai**, which is also home to one of the island's two decidedly low-key resorts.

SATUN PROVINCE

Sharing a border with Malaysia in the far south of Thailand, remote **Satun Province** is a mountainous area, and is in many ways more Malay than Thai in terms of culture. Despite this, Satun has successfully managed to avoid the conflicts of its neighbouring provinces to the east, and is a safe area to travel to. Satun Town offers no

BELOW:
Hat Na Ko on the island of Ko Kradan.

Map on page 272

real attractions, but nearby lies what is possibly the highlight of the entire deep south region, the pristine islands of Ko Tarutao Marine National Park.

Satun Town

Set in a lovely green valley walled by towering limestone cliffs, **Satun Town ❽** is a pleasant enough place, but in all aspects is more of a transit point than a destination in itself. The town's only real tourist attraction is the elegant Sino-Portuguese **Kuden Mansion**, a house originally built to accommodate King Rama V for a visit that never materialised. In 1902, the building become the governor's mansion before it was turned into Satun's **National Museum** (Wed– Sun 9am–4pm; free). The restored building features mainly exhibits on southern Thai life.

Ko Tarutao Marine N P

The **Ko Tarutao Marine National Park ❾** (open mid-Nov–mid-May; admission charge) encompasses more than 1,400 sq km (541 sq miles) of the Andaman Sea and comprises 51 islands. Only three of the islands are inhabited, mainly by *chao lay* (sea gypsies). Established as a national park in 1974, the forests and seas that comprise Tarutao are home to Thailand's most pristine coral reefs – said to harbour 25 percent of the world's tropical fish species – and an incredible variety of fauna. The islands support creatures such as langurs, crab-eating macaques and wild pigs, as well as aquatic mammals such as whales, dolphins and dugongs (manatees). Several kinds of turtle lay their eggs on the largest island, Ko Tarutao, especially on Ao Sone beach on the west coast. This spectacle can be witnessed every January.

The marine park is divided into two distinct parts: **Tarutao Archipelago** located 45 km (28 miles) off the coast of mainland Satun, and the **Adang-Rawi Archipelago**, about 50 km (30 miles) west of Ko Tarutao itself. The islands of the latter group are known for their excellent dive spots, and include the park's most popular island, Ko Lipe. The park is only open during the dry season, typically mid-November to mid-May. Boat trips to the islands set off from the fishing town of **Pak Bara**, 60 km (40 miles) north of Satun Town.

Ko Tarutao

Imposing **Ko Tarutao ❿**, the largest of the park's islands, is an excellent place for hiking and exploring caves, or simply relaxing on the wide beach. The 152-sq km (59-sq mile) island is home to the park headquarters (tel: 0-7478 3485), located behind the vast stretch of powdery white sand on the western shore known as **Ao Phante Malacca**. Behind the park office, at the end of a short path is **Toe Boo Cliff**, which provides great views over the bay from its craggy summit after a 30-minute climb.

Daily longtail boat trips depart from the park headquarters for

Hornbills on the island of Ko Tarutao.

BELOW: view from Toe Boo Cliff, Ko Tarutao.

BELOW:
arriving by boat at Hat
Na Ko on Ko Lipe.

Tham Jarakhe (Crocodile Cave).
Only accessible during low tide, the
cave was once supposedly home to
saltwater crocodiles. To the south of
Ao Phante Malacca are two scenic
beaches, **Ao Jak** and **Ao Molae**. To
get to the next beach, **Ao Sone**, an
important nesting ground for endangered turtles from September to
May (and especially January)
requires a good 2-hour walk.

On the island's eastern side is **Ao
Taloh Wow**. During the 1930s and
40s, this was a place of exile for Thai
prisoners, both criminal and political;
at one point in 1941, more than 3,000
prisoners were held here. Ko Tarutao
made the news again in 2002 when
Ao Rusi, located on the northeast
coast of the island, was used as a setting for the American reality television show *Survivor*. It gave rise to
some controversy as Thai environ-
mentalists feared that the virgin environment would be irrevocably
harmed. In the end, hard business
won out. But to its credit, CBS, the
show's producers, left the area more
or less in the pristine condition it was
in when the film crew first arrived.

Ko Lipe and Ko Adang

Tiny **Ko Lipe** ⓫, 40 km (25 miles)
from Ko Tarutao, is the most popular
and also the most developed island
in the park. Unlike on Ko Tarutao,
some of the accommodation on Ko
Lipe is open year-round, but access
to the island greatly depends upon
the state of the weather, which is
generally best from October to May.
Despite the fact that Ko Lipe lies
within the national park boundaries,
the approximately 1,000 *chao lay*, or
sea gypsies, who inhabit the island
have gained the right to develop sections of it. This accounts for the
largely disorganised and often unattractive development that has taken
root. Fortunately, there isn't enough
of it to detract from the natural
beauty of the island.

Boats from Pak Bara arrive at **Hat
Na Ko** ("front of the island") in the
north, where there is some accommodation. A short walk from Na Ko
via a dirt path is **Sunset Beach**,
probably the most beautiful of Ko
Lipe's beaches. It plays host to only
two small-scale resorts and offers a
wonderful view of the neighbouring
islands. On the south side of Ko Lipe
is **Ao Pattaya**, with its long sandy
coastline and clear water, making it
the most popular beach and home to
most of the island's accommodation.

For those interested in diving and
or snorkelling, Ko Lipe's prime
position in the middle of the Adang-
Rawi Archipelago makes for easy
access to nearby dive sites. Popular
spots in this area include the reefs
surrounding **Ko Rawi**, **Ko Yang**
and **Ko Hin Sorn**.

Visible from the shores of Sunset
Beach and less than 2 km (1 mile)
away is towering **Ko Adang** ⓬,
which has a densely-forested interior, lovely white sand beaches and
basic national park accommodation.
Popular with daytripping snorkellers,
jungle trails inland lead to waterfalls
and scenic viewpoints.

SONGKHLA PROVINCE

Songkhla Province is an oft over-looked destination. Although the flashy border city of Hat Yai draws thousands of Malaysian and Singaporean tourists each year, Western tourists typically give the entire province a wide berth. This is unfortunate as Hat Yai isn't nearly as seedy as it's thought to be, and offers great food and copious bargain shopping, as well as a chance to witness the particularly southern Thai pastime of bullfighting. Directly east of Hat Yai, the tiny provincial capital, Songkhla Town, is a fascinating melting pot of southern Thai culture, with decent enough beaches, interesting temples and what is probably the best night market in the entire deep south region.

Songkhla Town

Little-visited **Songkhla Town** ⑬, 25 km (16 miles) east of Hat Yai, is one of the deep south's most memorable towns. Essentially a Chinese town, but with a visible Muslim minority, Songkhla Town is located on a finger of land separating the Gulf of Thailand from the Thale Sap Songkhla, a large brackish lake. On the north coast of this promontory is **Hat Samila**, a long white sand beach marked by a bronze mermaid statue, a popular photo spot. While not great for swimming, the beach is nice enough for a stroll to watch the sun set or for a meal at one of the many beachside restaurants.

Songkhla Town's charming old enclave, located between Thanon Nakhorn Nok and Thanon Nang Ngaam, still possesses a number of Sino-Portuguese buildings and numerous Chinese-style restaurants and old coffee shops that haven't changed in decades.

Songkhla National Museum (Wed–Sun 9am–4pm; admission charge), housed in an elegant Sino-Portuguese mansion that was also at one time the city's poorhouse, is a good place to while away an hour or so if you're passing through town. Inside are exhibits of art, sculpture, pottery, ceramics and furniture from all the major periods of Thai history.

Songkhla's most famous temple, **Wat Matchimawat** (daily 8am–

Map on page 272

Yaksha statue outside Wat Matchimawat.

LEFT: Songkhla nightmarket.
BELOW: Songkhla National Museum.

Map
on page
272

*Songkhla Town's
Sino-Portuguese
architecture.*

BELOW: the view from
Khao Tang Kuan.

6pm; free), is located directly west of the old town. Its highlights are the beautiful temple paintings, probably executed in the early Rattanakosin period more than 200 years ago.

Another worthwhile temple to visit is the hilltop compound of **Khao Tang Kuan** (daily 8am–7pm; admission charge). Accessible by air-conditioned tram, construction of the quasi European-style temple complex was originally commissioned by King Rama V. It offers great views over Songkhla Town and Ko Yo island.

Around Songkhla

Directly east of Songkhla, in the salty waters of the Thale Sap, is the island of **Ko Yo** ⑭, an excellent day trip from Songkhla or Hat Yai. In recent years the island has become something of a cultural tourism spot. The island is famous for its hand-loomed cotton weaving called *phaa kaw yaw*. The best place to buy this fabric, either in lengths or as clothing, is at the central market.

Also on Ko Yo is the interesting **Thaksin Folklore Museum** (daily 8.30am–5pm; admission charge; tel: 0-7433 1185), which highlights the history, architecture, traditions and handicrafts of the people of South Thailand. One exhibit is dedicated to the display of coconut milk scrapers, de-huskers and grinders, emphasising the importance of coconuts as a cash crop in the south.

Another worthwhile destination in the environs of Songkhla is the Muslim fishing village of **Khao Saen**, located about 5 km (3 miles) from Songkhla Town. Look out for the rows of colourful prawn-fishing boats that are docked each evening along the beach. The intricately decorated boats, embellished with dragon prows, make for a interesting photo subject.

Hat Yai

The sprawling and featureless **Hat Yai** ⑮ is one of the largest cities in the south, and predominantly Chinese in character. Unfortunately, it has become a tourist destination for all the wrong reasons – it attracts busloads of Malaysians and Singaporeans who travel across the border from Malaysia to frequent the numerous sleazy massage parlours and nightclubs that seem to line every street in Hat Yai. There are no real draws in Hat Yai, but the shopping and great food plus ample accommodation options will appeal to those who have just come from an island.

If in Hat Yai during the first Saturday of the month, make sure to catch the particularly colourful southern Thai spectacle of **bullfighting**. This is held on the first Saturday of the month at the **Noen Khum Thong Stadium** (admission charge; tel: 0-7438 8753), located about 10 km (6 miles) west of Hat Yai. Unlike the Western version of the sport, Thai bullfights involve two bulls locking horns with each other and trying to force the opponent into submission. ❏

T RANG, SATUN AND SONGKHLA

TRANG TOWN AND BEACHES

TRANSPORT

GETTING THERE

By Air

Trang Airport (tel: 0-7521 8224) is located about 4 km (2 miles) south of Trang Town. There are daily flights between Bangkok and Trang on **Thai Airways**. At the airport, World Travel (tel: 0-7521 4010/1) operates minivans to Trang Town (B500) or to Trang's beaches (B1,000). Alternatively, resorts also arrange airport transportation for guests.

It is also possible to fly to Krabi, where there are more air connections (see page 260) and then take the taxi to either Trang Town or directly to its beaches for B1,800–2,000. The ride will take about 75 minutes.

By Train, Bus & Taxi

There are two overnight trains daily between Bangkok's **Hualamphong Station** and Trang, taking about 15 hours. Buses leave Bangkok's **Southern Bus Terminal** for Trang daily, taking about 12 hours. The bus terminal in Trang is at Th. Huay Yot. Ticket prices vary, depending on type of bus.

In addition, there are bus connections from nearby destinations like Phuket (4 hours), Krabi (2½ hours) and Hat Yai (4 hours).

GETTING AROUND

Motorcycle taxi and *tuk-tuk* trips within Trang Town cost between B10 and B20 for short rides. Taxis and minivans to Trang's beaches will cost between B300 and B400.

The jump-off point for Ko Hai and Ko Muk is Pak Meng pier, while the pier at Ban Chao Mai serves Ko Kradan, Ko Libong and Ko Sukorn; from these piers daily boats serve the islands. Or you can charter a longtail boat; be sure to negotiate the price (B200–400, depending on distance). Most island resorts will arrange transfers if you have booked a room with them.

RESTAURANTS

TRANG TOWN

Thai/Chinese

Trang is particularly well known for its old-world Chinese-style coffee shops, known locally as *raan kopi*. At these places, typically open from morning until afternoon, locally produced coffee (*kopi*) can be enjoyed on marble-topped tables along with Chinese steamed buns or Trang's famous barbecued pork. Try the long-standing **Yuchiang** on Th. Phraram VI (daily 7am–5pm; $), or the restaurant located below the **Ko Teng Hotel** (daily 8am–5pm; tel: 0-7521 9622; $), just a few blocks north.

Raan Khao Tom Phui
Th. Phraram IV. Tel: 0-7521 0127. Open daily 5pm–2am. $. This unpretentious restaurant, popular with locals and open only in the evenings, is an excellent place to fill up on spicy Chinese-Thai favourites such as *khanaa fai daeng*, Chinese kale flash fried with chillies and garlic, or *hoi lay phat phrik phao*, fresh clams fried with hot chilli paste.

Trang Night Market

Cnr Th. Ratchadamnoen and Th. Phraram VI. Open daily 5pm–midnight. $.

Trang's night market is one of the culinary highlights of the deep south region. Every evening, the small street at the corner of Ratchadamnoen and Phraram VI becomes an endless parade of *raan khao kaeng*, or rice and curry vendors, many of whom have roadside seating. It looks daunting but the food is mostly fresh. Try the local favourite, *khanom jeen*, rice noodles eaten with curry sauce and veggies.

Thai & Western

Trang Thana

Thumrin Thana Hotel, 69/8 Th.
Trang Thana. Tel: 0-7521 1211.
Open daily 6am–midnight. $$.
www.thumrin.co.th
Basic hotel coffee shop that serves a good selection of Thai dishes as well as some Western ones. The breakfast and lunchtime buffets which mainly cater to large tour groups are good value for money, but the a la carte selections are all very reasonably priced too.

HAT PAK MENG

This sleepy beach by the Pak Meng pier is very much a local scene, swarming with mainly Thai picnickers on the weekends. There are a string of seafood restaurants that come alive in the evenings, but most of them are quite basic and there is nothing that stands out except perhaps the restaurant at **Lay Trang Resort** (tel: 0-7527 4027). Seafood cooked Thai-style is well prepared here.

HAT CHANG LANG

Acqua Restaurant, and **Crabs & Co**

Amari Trang Beach Resort, Hat Chang Lang. Tel: 0-7520 5888. $$$. www.amari.com/trangbeach
If staying at the Amari Beach Resort at Hat Chang Lang, you are literally forced to eat at its restaurants as there are hardly any good eateries within walking distance of the hotel. So it's a good thing that the Amari makes great efforts to serve some fine food (and at prices that won't break your wallet). **Acqua** on the first floor serves Italian fare in elegant and stylish surroundings (reservations advised). On the lower level is the **Crabs & Co** restaurant. All done up in bright orange and a marine theme, there's excellent Thai food, both a la carte and some good-value sets.

PRICE CATEGORIES

Price per person for a three-course meal without drinks:
$ = under US$10
$$ = US$10–25
$$$ = US$25–50

ACCOMMODATION

TRANG TOWN

Moderate

Thumrin Thana Hotel

69/8 Th. Trang Thana. Tel: 0-7521 1211. www.thumrin.co.th
Largely oriented towards business travellers, this is Trang's poshest hotel. It has a convenient downtown location and all the amenities one would expect from a hotel of this size. Room rates for bookings on the Internet are a steal and can dip into the budget range. (289 rooms)

HAT CHANG LANG

Expensive

Amari Trang Beach Resort

Hat Chang Lang. Tel: 0-7520 5888. www.amari.com/trangbeach
The only international-class hotel on Hat Chang Lang. Large, tastefully furnished rooms, excellent Sivara Spa and fine restaurants (see above). The beach, unfortunately, is shallow even at high tide and is better for long walks rather than swimming. To make up for this, the hotel has a private beach club on Ko Kradan island for its guests. (138 rooms).

TRANG'S ISLANDS

The island hotels, except on Ko Hai, are simple budget affairs with basic facilities (the ones on Ko Hai are in the moderate range). So if it's luxury you want, forget it. The Amari group owns a large tract of land on Ko Kradan and may develop a luxury resort there in the near future.

Ko Hai

CoCo Cottage

Ko Hai. Tel: 0-7521 2375. www.coco-cottage.com
Features Balinese-style wooden bungalows with open-air bathrooms, only a few steps from the beach. Rooms with air-conditioning or just fan available. (28 rooms)

PRICE CATEGORIES

Price categories are for a double room without breakfast and taxes:
Expensive = US$100–200
Moderate = US$50–100
Budget = under US$50

Fantasy Resort
Ko Hai. Tel: 0-7521 5923.
www.kohhai.com
Features spacious air-conditioned bungalows and suites at a range of prices. The resort also provides a decent variety of services, including a pool, internet access, a spa and movie nights on weekends. (40 rooms)

Ko Muk

Koh Mook Charlie Beach Resort
Ko Mook. Tel: 0-7520 3281. $.
www.kohmook.com

This immensely popular resort, the largest on Hat Farang, has nice rooms at a range of prices, internet access, movie screenings, and a wonderful location among the cliffs and coconuts. Good restaurant on site. (80 rooms)

Ko Kradan

Koh Kradan Paradise Beach
Ko Kradan. Tel: 0-7521 1391.
www.kradanisland.com
This resort, as of now the only accommodation on

Ko Kradan, is rather basic and not known for the quality of its service or rooms. Its setting, however, on Hat Na Ko beach is idyllic. (100 rooms)

Ko Libong

Libong Nature Beach Resort
Ko Libong. Mobile tel: 0-1915 7537.
e-mail: natureresorts@thailand.com
Located on the secluded western shore of Ko Libong, it offers no-frills accommodation and dining on an attractive,

palm-lined beach. The resort is perhaps best known for its highly praised nature-oriented tours. (15 rooms)

Ko Sukorn

Sukorn Beach Bungalows
Tel: 0-7521 1457.
www.sukorn-island-trang.com
A low-key resort with a family atmosphere. Offers fan-cooled as well as air-conditioned rooms. Known for its efforts to work with the local community. (20 rooms)

ACTIVITIES

OUTDOOR ACTIVITIES

Diving & Snorkelling

Princess Divers: tel: 0-7520 3281. Located at Charlie Beach Resort on Ko Muk, it offers PADI courses and diving and snorkelling tours.

Rainbow Blub Club Divers: tel: 0-7520 6923; www.rainbow-diver.com. Based at Ko Hai's Fantasy Resort, this is a reputable and German-run operation.
Sea Breeze Sport: tel: 0-7521 7460; www.seabreeze.co.th. With offices at Trang Town and Ko Ngai Resort on Ko Hai, it offers diving and snorkelling trips.

UNDERWATER WEDDINGS

Every Valentine's Day, the waters off Trang play host to the Underwater Wedding Ceremony, a unique way to tie the knot and a popular tourist draw. For more information, check: www.underwaterwedding.com.

SATUN & KO TARUTAO NATIONAL PARK

TRANSPORT

GETTING THERE

Getting to Satun isn't easy. The closest airport to Satun Town is in Hat Yai *(see page 283)*, 130 km (80 miles) away on the east coast. From Hat Yai, there are buses and taxis that make the trip to Satun Town. Or travel by road from Trang, 140 km (87 miles) away.

From Bangkok's **Hualamphong Station**, there are five trains a day to Hat Yai, from where you can travel by road to Satun. The train journey alone will take 14 to 18 hours, so it is best to book the overnight service. From Bangkok's **Southern Bus Terminal** there is one air-conditioned bus every evening bound for Satun, taking approximately 15 hours to cover the 973 km (605 miles).

GETTING AROUND

Downtown Satun Town is compact enough to walk to most destinations. Motorcycle taxis and *tuk-tuks* are also available, and should cost no more than B20 for any point in town. For information on getting to Ko Tarutao National Park, see next page.

Ko Tarutao N P

Boats to Ko Tarutao National Park leave from Pak Bara, 60 km (40 miles) north of Satun Town. Although in Satun Province, Pak Bara is more easily accessible from Hat Yai and Trang than from Satun Town; both Hat Yai and Trang have direct bus services to the pier. From Satun Town you can hire a *songthaew* to take you to Pak Bara. At Pak Bara pier are numerous touts and agencies selling tickets to the islands. A round-trip ticket costs B900 and allows one to disembark at any of the islands. There are twice-daily boats leaving Pak Bara, at noon and at 3.30pm. The trip to Ko Tarutao takes 1 hour and Ko Adang or Ko Lipe 3 to 4 hours.

RESTAURANTS

Food options for the tourist are predictably meagre in Satun Town. On the islands of Ko Tarutao National Park, eating out is largely confined to the guest houses there.

Thai & Western

Satun Night Market
Th. Satun Thani. Open: daily
5pm–midnight. $.
Satun's night market is one of the best in southern Thailand. The quality of the food is good, and the emphasis here is on rich curries. As Muslims are a majority in Satun, most of the food is *halal*.

Time
43 Th. Satun Thani.
Tel: 0-7471 2286. Open daily 11am–11pm. $.
Features very good Thai and decent Western-style food. Highlights include the sea bass, and the excellent but intimidating sounding "fish-head noodles".

ACCOMMODATION

SATUN TOWN

Pinnacle Tarutao Hotel
43 Th. Satun Thani.
Tel: 0-7471 1607/8.
www.pinnaclehotels.com
Satun's only "upmarket" hotel lies slightly outside the town centre, but is a comfortable place to stay. The downtown hotels are really not worth considering. (108 rooms)

KO TARUTAO NP

Ko Tarutao

Very basic lodgings on **Ao Phante Malacca** and **Ao Taloh Wow** are available from Nov to May. Book with the park authorities on the island (tel: 0-7478 3485). Electricity is only available from 6pm to 6am.

Ko Lipe

Porn Resort
Sunset Beach, Ko Lipe.
Tel: 0-7472 8032.
Bare-bones establishment with rustic wooden bungalows, friendly, staff and a wonderful location right on the beach. (20 rooms)

Lee Pae Resort
Ao Pattaya, Ko Lipe.
Tel: 0-7472 4336.
Located in the middle of Pattaya beach, this operation is one of the biggest on the island and offers several comfy bungalows in a shady wooded area. (70 rooms)

Mountain Resort
Hat Na Ko, Ko Lipe.
Tel: 0-7472 8131.
New resort located at Na Ko has wooden bungalows on a hilltop. The highlight is the view from the restaurant over blue waters. (43 rooms)

ACTIVITIES

OUTDOOR ACTIVITIES

Diving & Snorkelling

Scuba diving and snorkelling are the main reason many choose to visit Ko Tarutao National Park. Several dive operators can be found at Pak Bara pier and on Ko Lipe. In addition, many of the bungalows on Ko Lipe can arrange snorkelling trips.

Adang Sea Tour: Pak Bara, tel:
0-7478 3338; www.adangseatour.com.
Provides boat services for sightseeing as well as scuba diving and snorkelling.

Chaolay Diving: 142 Moo 7, Satun Town, mobile tel: 0-6957 2911. Offers a typical range of PADI courses as well as diving and snorkelling tours, particularly oriented toward first-time divers.

Sabye Sports: Ao Pattaya, Ko Lipe, mobile tel: 0-1897 8725; www.sabye-sports.com. Based on Ko Lipe, it offers equipment rental and a variety of PADI dive courses.

SONGKHLA AND HAT YAI

TRANSPORT

GETTING THERE

Hat Yai Airport (tel: 0-7425 1007/12), located 12 km (8 miles) from the city, is a major hub for both international and domestic flights. It is serviced by several airlines, including AirAsia, Nok Air, Tiger Airways, Malaysia Airlines, Orient Thai and Thai Airways.

From Bangkok, there are five trains a day to Hat Yai, 900 km (560 miles) away. Travel time is 14 to 18 hours, depending on the type of train, so it is best to book a sleeper on the overnight train. Several air-conditioned buses depart daily from Bangkok's Southern Bus Terminal on the 14-hour trip to Hat Yai.

Hat Yai is less than 50 km (30 miles) from the Malaysian border, and it's possible to travel between the two countries. There are countless tourist buses that run between Hat Yai and major cities in Malaysia, including Penang and Kuala Lumpur, and even as far as Singapore. Contact any of the travel agents in downtown Hat Yai for details and tickets. There are also local buses, taxis and a daily train that make the hour-long trip to Padang Besar, the nearest town on the Malaysian side.

GETTING AROUND

There are plenty of motorcycle taxis and *songthaews* within Hat Yai and Songkhla. The latter is about 25 km (16 miles) east of Hat Yai, and can easily be reached by either bus, minivan or taxi.

RESTAURANTS

SONGKHLA

Thai

Raan Tae Hiang Iw
85 Th. Nang Ngam. Tel: 0-7431 1505. Open: daily 11am–8pm. $.
Located in the heart of Songkhla's old district, this Chinese-Thai eatery, known to locals as "Tae", is a local legend. Highly recommended are the *yam mamuang*, a spicy salad of sour mangoes and dried shrimp, and *tom yam haeng*, a delicious "dry" version of the famous *tom yam* soup.

Songkhla Night Market
Th. Wachira. Open: daily 5pm–midnight. $.
Songkhla's night market, probably the largest in the region, has Chinese, Thai and Muslim food, all at very low prices. To get there, tell the minivan or motorcycle driver to go to "Wachira", the name of the road where the market is held.

HAT YAI

The lively strip downtown known as Th. Thammanoonvithi has a wide variety of restaurants.

Western & Thai

The Swan
129-131 Th. Thammanoonvithi. Tel: 0-7435 4310. Open: daily 11am–midnight. $$.
This gregarious English-style pub is a great place to relax with a draught beer. Features a diverse selection of Thai and English dishes.

Thai

Hat Yai Night Market
Th. Montri 1 (near the Pakistan Mosque). Open daily 5pm–midnight. $.
Hat Yai's night market has a mix of Muslim and seafood dishes. Though not as diverse as the offerings at Songkhla's night market, it is still a great place to sample local food, such as the Muslim-influenced *khao mok kai*, or rice cooked with chicken and spices.

Sky Buffet
Lee Gardens Plaza Hotel, 29 Th. Prachatipat. Tel: 0-7426 1111. Open: daily L & D. $.
www.leeplaza.com
This hotel, the tallest building in Hat Yai, offers a Thai-style buffet lunch and dinner at its 33rd-storey restaurant with panoramic views. Enjoy all-you-can-eat Thai favourites such as *kaeng khiao waan*, or green curry, as well as the view over downtown Hat Yai.

Sor Heung
79/16 Th. Thammanoonvithi. Mobile tel: 0-1896 3455. Open: daily L & D. $.
Expect good Thai-Chinese food at this restaurant, which has branches all over Hat Yai. Choose from a variety of fresh ingredients to be flash-fried or made into a Thai spicy salad called *yam*, or simply pick from the diverse pre-cooked Chinese-style dishes.

PRICE CATEGORIES

Price per person for a three-course meal without drinks:
$ = under US$10
$$ = US$10–25

ACCOMMODATION

SONGKHLA

Expensive

Pavilion Songkhla Hotel
17 Th. Platha. Tel: 0-7444
1850/9. www.pavilionhotels.com
One of the taller buildings in Songkhla, the Pavilion is one of only two higher-end hotels in the town. Features the amenities one would expect in a hotel of this category, as well as a snooker room and Thai massage. (179 rooms)

Moderate

BP Samila Beach Hotel & Resort
8 Th. Ratchadamnoen.
Tel: 0-7444 0222.
www.bphotelsgroup.com
This grand-looking hotel is located at the end of Hat Samila, near the famous mermaid statue. It offers clean, comfy rooms, the more expensive of which have views over the Gulf of Thailand. Range of facilities such as a pool, fitness centre, spa, coffee shop and restaurants. (228 rooms)

HAT YAI

Moderate

Novotel Central Sukhontha Hat Yai
3 Th. Sanehanusorn.
Tel: 0-7435 2222.
www.centralhotelsresorts.com
Located in the heart of Hat Yai, above the Central Department Store, this imposing hotel, easily the best in town, offers comfortable rooms plus the usual four-star facilities. (200 rooms)

Budget

New Season Hotel
106 Th. Prachathipat.
Tel: 0-7435 2888.
Relatively small but clean and well-designed budget hotel. Excellent location in downtown Hat Yai. (119 rooms)

PRICE CATEGORIES

Price categories are for a double room without breakfast and taxes:
Expensive = US$100–200
Moderate = US$50–100
Budget = under US$50

ACTIVITIES

NIGHTLIFE

In **Songkhla**, Th. Sisuda, near the Indonesian Consulate, is home to many of the bars frequented by expats. The more popular ones are **Auntie** and **Corner Bier**. A block north, along Th. Sadao, are a group of raucous but friendly bars with Thai hostesses and catering mostly to expat oil workers.

Much of the nightlife in **Hat Yai** is sleazy, fuelled by thousands of Malaysians and Singaporeans looking for a good time. But there are some places worth checking out.
Post Laser Disc: 82/83 Th. Thammanoonvithi, tel: 0-7423 2027. This popular restaurant-bar is an expat hangout of sorts, and has live music every Friday night.
Sugar Rock: 114 Th. Thammanoonvithi. Laid-back bar and cafe that has been a Hat Yai fixture for some time.

SHOPPING

Much of downtown **Hat Yai** resembles a large market, with products from knock-off brand-name T-shirts to cashew nuts, all sold on the streets. Popular shopping areas include the maze-like **Kim Yong Market** and **Santisuk Market**. Be prepared to bargain. For more formal, air-conditioned shopping, visit **Central** department store, or **Lee Gardens Plaza** opposite.

OUTDOOR ACTIVITIES

Diving

Starfish Scuba: 166 Th. Phat-Talung, Songkhla, tel: 0-7444 2170; www.starfishscuba.com. This reputable outfit can organise diving trips to Ko Losin, just off Songkhla.

SPAS

The streets of central **Hat Yai** are virtually lined with massage parlours and spas, many of which, despite appearances, do in fact offer legitimate massages. Below are some of the better ones.
C-Spa: 68 Th. Jooti-Uthit 3, tel: 0-7434 6156/8. Provides various massage services, including hot-stone massage.
Centara Spa: Novotel Central Sukhontha, 3 Th. Sanehanusorn, tel: 0-7435 2222. Offers massage and treatments that use indigenous Thai products.
Garabuning Spa: 50/6 Th. Sripoowanat, tel: 0-7435 4140. Has an herbal steam sauna as well as herbal and salt-based body scrubs.
Sittara Spa: 78 Radyindee Soi 7, tel: 0-7423 8594. Offers treatment packages with an emphasis on aromatherapy.

A HANDY SUMMARY OF PRACTICAL INFORMATION, ARRANGED ALPHABETICALLY

A ddresses

Since most of Bangkok developed with little central planning, finding your way around can be a bit confusing at first, given the size of the city and its many twisting alleyways. The city is mostly laid out using the *soi* system – smaller streets leading off a main road of the same name, with each *soi* having a number after the name. For example, Sukhumvit Road (or Thanon Sukhumvit) has numerous streets branching from it in sequence such as Sukhumvit Soi 33, Sukhumvit Soi 55, etc. Most hotels provide business cards with the address written in Thai to show to taxi drivers. Fortunately, taxis are very inexpensive in Bangkok, so if you do get lost, it won't cost you too much to find your destination.

Thailand's island and beach destinations are a lot easier to work out. There are fewer roads, many of which are recent additions to the landscape. A typical address might be preceded by the word Moo (referring to the residential estate) before the name of the road or *soi*, as in 23/3 Moo 1. But many places don't even have complete addresses and will just state the beach or general area they are located in.

B udgeting your Trip

By Western standards Bangkok is a bargain. Five-star hotels cost half or a third of what they would in New York or London, and at the other end, budget (if a bit dingy) accommodation can be as cheap as B100 per night. Street food can be excellent and you can have a filling and tasty meal for B30 to B40. Transport is cheap with bus fares priced from B4 to B16, a ride on the Skytrain and metro from B15 to B40. Taxis are inexpensive as well *(see page 102)*. Drinks in bars cost from B60 to B100 and in clubs from

B180 to B300. If you live frugally, you can get by with B1,000 a day, but the sky is the limit here if you want to live it up at luxury hotels and eat at fine restaurants.

As a general rule of thumb, prices are generally higher outside the capital. In fact, destinations that attract a lot of tourists will have higher costs of living. Phuket and Ko Samui, for instance, are the most expensive islands, while Ko Phangan, Ko Lanta and Ko Chang are gradually moving up the cost of living scale. On the other hand, largely untouched places like Trang and Satun offer the best bargains.

Business Hours

Government offices in Thailand operate from 8.30am–4.30pm Mon–Fri. Most businesses are open 8am–5.30pm Mon–Fri while some are open 8.30am–noon on Sat. Banks are open 9.30am–3.30pm Mon–Sat.

Department stores are open 10.30am–9pm daily, though larger stores are open as late as 10pm. Ordinary shops open at 8.30am or 9am and close between 6pm and 8pm, depending on location and type of business.

Small open-air coffee shops and restaurants open at 7am and close at 8.30pm, though some stay open past midnight. Large restaurants generally close by 10pm. In Bangkok, most hotel coffee shops close at midnight; some stay open 24 hours, and the city has several outdoor restaurants that are open as late as 4am for post-bar hopping suppers.

Bangkok's nightlife venues generally close by 2am, but at some places like Phuket, Ko Phangan and Ko Tao, they don't close till much much later.

Generally, outside of Bangkok, opening times are more flexible at small family-run shops, eateries and bars. Knowing that most people are out having fun, businesses located near beaches tend to open later in the afternoon and stay open all evening.

Business Travellers

As Thailand strives to become a regional business hub, the capital hosts an increasing number of business travellers from all over the world. Most Bangkok hotels have business centres with communications and secretarial services. Outside of the capital such services are scarce, limited only to places like Pattaya, Phuket and Ko Samui, all of which are popular as venues for business conferences and seminars.

A good starting point for overseas business people wanting to start a company in Thailand is the **Board of Investment** (BOI), tel: 0-2537 8111; www.boi.go.th. The BOI is authorised to grant tax holidays and other incentives to promote certain key industries.

C limate

There are three official seasons in Thailand: hot, rainy and cool. But to the tourist winging in from more temperate regions, Thailand has only one temperature: hot. To make things worse, the temperature drops only a few degrees during the night, and is accompanied 24 hours by humidity above 70 percent. Nights, however, during the cool season can be pleasant. Here is what you can expect:
• Hot season (Mar to May): 27–35°C (80–95°F)
• Rainy season (June to Oct): 24–32°C (75–90°F)
• Cool season (Nov to Feb): 22–30°C (72–86°F) but with less humidity.

There are regional variations along Thailand's coastline, but generally the Eastern Seaboard and northern Gulf of Thailand is similar to Bangkok. The southern Gulf of Thailand around Ko Samui has intermittent rain from May through November, which is heaviest around November. The Andaman coast is generally wetter, with a longer and unpredictable rainy season starting in May.

Children

Travelling with children is not especially difficult in Thailand. Thais love kids, and those with blonde hair will receive special attention. It can be a bit overwhelming, but people are just being friendly and it is part of the Thai sense of community.

Footpaths in Bangkok are not pedestrian friendly. They are often in disrepair and inevitably, something or somebody obstructs them: leave the baby stroller at home and bring back- or chest-mounted baby carriers. Children should never approach dogs, monkeys or other small animals; those wandering the streets are more feral than back at home, and rabies is still a risk.

The tropical sun is intense, so high SPF sun block lotion and hats are important. Make sure the kids keep their hands clean as well, since kids frequently suck their fingers or thumbs and can easily pick up stomach bugs.

Clothing

Clothes should be light and loose; fabrics made from natural fibres are definitely more com-

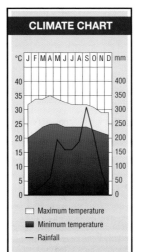

CLIMATE CHART

°C J F M A M J J A S O N D mm

Maximum temperature
Minimum temperature
— Rainfall

fortable than synthetics. During the height of the rainy season, sandals are preferable to shoes. Sunglasses, hats and sunscreen are recommended for protection from the tropical sun.

Suits are sometimes worn for business in Bangkok but, in general, Thailand does not have the formal dress code of Hong Kong or Tokyo. A shirt and tie is expected for business appointments.

Shorts are taboo for women and men who wish to enter some of the more revered temples. Women wearing sleeveless dresses and short skirts may also be barred from some temples and mosques.

In some parts of south Thailand, Muslims are in the majority so dress properly in deference to the religion and to Thai sensitivities. Although topless sunbathing is common at some beaches in Pattaya, Phuket and Ko Samui, it makes locals uncomfortable and should be avoided.

Crime & Security

Thailand is a relatively safe country in terms of violent crime. The biggest risk to travellers is from scams and con artists. If you do run into trouble, there are **Tourist Police** (TP) units at the major destinations which are specially assigned to assist travellers. However, much of the time, there is little they are able to do but record the details of the crime and provide a report (for insurance purposes). Most members of the force speak some English.

Tourist Police

TP National Hotline: 1155; www.tourist.police.go.th.
Bangkok Tourist Assistance Centre: 4 Th. Rachadamnern Nok, tel: 0-2281 5051. In Bangkok TP booths can also be found in tourist areas, including Lumphini Park (near the intersection of Th. Rama IV and Th. Silom) and Patpong (at the Th. Silom intersection).
Hat Yai TP: tel: 0-7424 6733

Hua Hin TP: tel: 0-3251 5995
Krabi TP: tel: 0-7563 7208
Ko Chang TP: tel: 0-1982 8381
Ko Samui TP: tel: 0-7742 1281
Pattaya TP: tel: 0-3842 9371
Phuket TP: tel: 0-7622 5361

Drugs

Both hard and soft drugs are easy to procure in Thailand but it is illegal to possess, consume or trade in them. If caught, the penalties are harsh and the death sentence can apply. Stay clear of drug dealers. Police raids are common at tourist destinations and at the infamous full moon parties at Ko Phangan *(see page 176)*, both plainclothed and uniformed police will be on the prowl.

Insurgent Activity

Over the past three decades, a low-level insurgency has been brewing in the southern provinces closest to the Malaysian border, i.e. Pattani, Yala and Narathiwat. Fuelled by foreign Muslim fundamentalists, this has given rise to violent separatist movements and sporadic unrest. You are advised to stay clear of these provinces.

Common Scams

• Touts at Bangkok's Patpong who offer live sex shows upstairs. Once inside, you are handed an exorbitant bill and threatened if you protest. Pay, take the receipt, and go immediately to the Tourist Police, who will usually take you back and demand a refund.
• Don't follow touts who offer to take you to a gem factory for a "special deal". The gems are usually synthetic or of substandard quality and there is no way to get your money back.
• Tuk tuk drivers who offer to take you on a free tour and then stop at every gem, silver and tailor shop along the way where he will collect a commission for wasting your day. A common ruse they use to lure you is by pretending that the attraction you want to visit is closed for a special ceremony. Don't believe them.

Keep in mind that in Thai culture, strangers rarely approach and engage foreigners in conversation, so if you find yourself on the receiving end, be on guard no matter how polite and innocent they appear to be. Feel free to be rude and walk away, even if it goes against the rules of polite behaviour.

Women Travellers

Thailand is generally safe for women travellers, even those travelling alone. Thais tend to be non-confrontational, so violent and sexual crimes towards foreign women are not common. That said, like anywhere, it isn't a great idea to be walking alone on quiet streets or beaches late at night. Also, there is a perception (probably a by-product of Hollywood films) that Western women are "easy", so be careful in your associations with local men, because they may have the wrong idea about you. Reasonably modest dress will certainly help.

Customs Regulations

The Thai government prohibits the import or export of drugs, dangerous chemicals, pornography, firearms and ammunition. Attempting to smuggle heroin or other hard drugs in or out may be punishable by death. Scores of foreigners are serving very long prison terms for this offence.

Tourists may freely bring in foreign banknotes or other types of foreign exchange. For travellers leaving Thailand, the maximum amount permitted to be taken out in Thai currency without prior authorisation is B50,000. Foreign guests are allowed to bring in without tax 200 cigarettes and 1 litre of wine or spirits.

Buddha images, antiques and art objects cannot leave Thailand without a Department of Fine Arts permit *(see page 289)*.

For more details check the Thai **Customs Department** website at www.customs.go.th, or call the hotline: 1164.

EXPORT PERMITS

The Thai **Department of Fine Arts** prohibits the export of all Thai Buddha images, images of other deities and fragments (hands or heads) of images dating before the 18th century. All antiques must be registered with the department. The shop will usually do this for you. If you decide to handle it yourself, take the piece to the office at Thanon Na Prathat (tel: 0-2226 1661) together with two postcard-sized photos of it. The export fee ranges from B50 to B200 depending on the antiquity of the piece. Fake antiques do not require export permits, but airport customs officials are not art experts and may mistake it for a genuine piece. If it looks authentic, clear it at the Department of Fine Arts to avoid problems later.

D isabled Travellers

Thailand falls short on accommodating the disabled, though this is slowly improving. Pavements are often uneven, studded with obstructions and there are no ramps. Few buildings have wheelchair ramps. In Bangkok, some major roads have textured brickwork on the paths for the blind. A few Skytrain stations have lifts, but not nearly enough; the metro has lifts at every station. Getting to many of Thailand's smaller islands often entails taking small boats that are moored at poorly designed piers. It would be a challenge for a disabled traveller on his/her own to get around Thailand – a companion is essential.

E lectricity

Electrical outlets are rated at 220 volts, 50 cycles and accept flat-pronged or round-pronged plugs. Adaptors can be purchased at department or hardware stores.

Embassies & Consulates

Australia: 37 Th. Sathorn Tai, tel: 0-2287 2680.
Canada: 15/F, Abdulrahim Place, Th. Rama IV, tel: 0-2636 0540.
New Zealand: M Thai Tower, 14th Fl, All Seasons Place, 87 Th. Withayu, tel: 0-2254 2530.
Singapore: 129 Th. Sathorn Tai, tel: 0-2286 1434.
United Kingdom: 1031 Th. Ploenchit, tel: 0-2385 8333.
United States: 120-122 Th. Withayu, tel: 0-2205 4000.

Entry Requirements

Visas & Passports

Travellers should check visa regulations at a Thai embassy or consulate before starting their trip as visa rules vary for different nationalities. For an updated list, check the Thai **Ministry of Foreign Affairs** website at www.mfa.go.th.

All foreign nationals entering Thailand must have valid passports with at least six-month validity. At the airport, nationals from most countries will be granted a visa on arrival valid for up to 30 days. Officially you need an air ticket out of Thailand, but this is very rarely checked.

Longer tourist visas, obtained from the Thai consulate of your home country prior to arrival, allow for a 60-day stay. People seeking a work permit can apply for a non-immigrant visa which is good for 90 days. A letter of guarantee is needed from the Thai company you intend to work for and this visa can be obtained from a Thai consulate at home.

The on-arrival 30-day visa can be extended by 7–10 days for a fee of B1,900 in Bangkok or at the regional immigration offices, or you can leave the country (even for half an hour) and return to receive another free 30-day visa. The 60-day visa can be extended for another 30 more days for the same price.

Overstaying your visa can carry a daily fine of B200 to a maximum of B20,000. If the police catch you with an expired visa, life can get very complicated, and you can get thrown into the immigration prison.

In Bangkok, the Thai **Immigration Bureau** is at 507 Soi Puan Plu, Th.Sathorn Tai, tel: 0-2287 3101-10; www.immigration.go.th; (open Mon–Fri 8.30am–4.30pm).
Pattaya: Pattaya Klang Soi 8, tel: 0-3842 9409.
Phuket: Kalim Beach Rd, tel: 0-7634 0477.
Ko Samui: Route 4169 Nathon, tel: 0-7742 1069.
Satun: Th. Burivanich, Satun Town, tel: 0-7471 1080.
Songkhla: Th. Phetchkasem, Hat Yai, tel: 0-7424 3019 or 6333.

Etiquette

Thais are remarkably tolerant and forgiving of foreigners' eccentricities, but there are a few things that upset them (see also Clothing, page 287).

The Royal Family

Thais have a great reverence for the monarchy, and any disrespect directed towards members of the royal family will be taken very personally. At movies the King's Anthem is played before the movie starts and it is the height of bad manners not to stand up when the others do.

Buddhism

A similar degree of respect is accorded to the second pillar of Thai society, Buddhism. Disrespect towards Buddha images, temples or monks is not taken lightly and as with the monarchy, public expressions against the institution are actually illegal.

Monks observe vows of chastity that prohibit being touched by (or touching) women, even their mothers. When in the vicinity of a monk, a woman should try to stay clear to avoid accidental contact.

At temples, the scruffy and the underclad are frequently turned away, so dress appropriately.

Terms of Address

Thais are addressed by their first rather than their last names. The name is usually preceded by the word *khun*, a term of honour, a bit like Mr or Ms. Following this to its logical conclusion, Silpachai Krishnamra would be addressed as Khun Silpachai.

Thai Greetings

The common greeting and farewell in Thailand is *sawadee*, (followed by *khrap* when spoken by men and *kha* by women). In more formal settings this is accompanied by a *wai* – raising the hands in a prayer-like gesture, the fingertips touching the nose, and bowing the head slightly. However, don't make the mistake of giving a *wai* to all hotel staff, children or the people at the corner shop – it embarrasses them. In these cases, a nod is sufficient. Almost all Thais understand that this is not a part of Western cultures. In business meetings, the *wai* is often followed by a handshake.

Head and Feet

Thai Buddhism regards the head as the wellspring of wisdom and the feet as unclean. For this reason, it is insulting to touch another person on the head (children are an exception), point one's feet at anything or step over another person. In formal situations, when wishing to pass someone who is seated on the floor, bow slightly while walking and point an arm down to indicate the path to be taken, and a path will be cleared.

Public Behaviour

Two decades ago, Thai couples showed no intimacy in public. That has changed due to modernisation and foreign influence on the young, but even these days, intimacy rarely extends beyond holding hands. As in many traditional societies, displaying open affection in public, such as kissing and passionate cuddling, is a sign of bad manners.

F estivals & Events

Thailand practically heaves with festivals all year through. Some of these (like Songkhran in Apr and Loy Krathong in Nov) are celebrated throughout the country while others are confined to certain areas, like Phuket's Vegetarian Festival. For a full listing of annual festivals, check the website of the Tourism Authority of Thailand: www.tourismthailand.org.

G ay & Lesbian Travellers

Gays quickly discover that Thailand is one of the most tolerant countries in the world. The gay nightlife scene in Bangkok, Pattaya and Phuket is a thriving one. Bangkok also hosts the annual Bangkok Gay Pride Festival (www.bangkokpride.org/en) in November, with a similar one taking place in Pattaya in December (www.pattayagayfestival.com).

Utopia at 116/1 Soi 23 Sukhumvit; tel: 0-2259 9619; www.utopia–asia.com is Bangkok's centre for gays and lesbians. It's a good place to make contacts and to find out what's going on.

Utopia Tours in Bangkok is an affiliated travel agency that caters exclusively to gay travellers. It is located at Tarntawan Place Hotel, 119/5-10 Th. Surawong, tel: 0-2238 3227, www.utopia-tours.com.

H ealth & Medical Care

Visitors entering Thailand are not required to show evidence of vaccination for smallpox or cholera. Check that your tetanus boosters are up to date. Immunisation against cholera is a good idea as are hepatitis A and B innoculations. Malaria and dengue persist in remote and rural areas outside Bangkok. When in the countryside, especially in the monsoon season, apply mosquito repellent on exposed skin at all times – dengue mosquitoes are at their most active during the day.

Many first-time visitors take awhile to adjust to the heat. It is important to drink plenty of water, especially if you've drunk alcohol. Avoid too much sun when out and about and use sunblock with a high SPF – the sun is far more powerful at this latitude than in temperate regions.

Tap water in Bangkok has been certified as potable, but take no chances and drink bottled water instead, which is widely available throughout Thailand. In Bangkok and at reputable hotels and restaurants at Thailand's major tourist centres, ice is clean and presents no health problems.

Stomach upsets are usually caused by over indulgence and rarely by contaminated food. Many foreigners over-eat and their stomachs react negatively to a sudden switch to a different cuisine. Stick only to freshly cooked food.

Buy travel insurance before travelling to Bangkok. Evacuation insurance is not really necessary since hospitals listed below are of international standard.

Hospitals

The level of medical care in Bangkok and some of Thailand's regional centres is excellent, particularly at the hospitals listed here – all of which have specialised clinics as well as standard medical facilties. In fact, there has been a growing business in "medical tourism" over the past 10 years with people coming to Thailand to have procedures performed (including cosmetic surgery and sex changes) that would cost many times more at home or require waiting in a months-long queue. Equipment is up to date and the doctors are usually trained overseas and speak English. By Thai standards, these are considered expensive, but the fees are a fraction of what they are in most Western countries. Note: the hospitals listed here also have dental clinics.

Bangkok

BNH Hospital: 9/1 Th. Convent, Silom, tel: 0-2686 2700;

www.bnhhospital.com. This squeaky-clean hospital offers comfortable rooms, top-notch equipment and a large team of specialists. Service is efficient and English is widely spoken.

Bumrungrad Hospital: 33 Soi 3, Th. Sukhumvit, tel: 0-2667 1000; www.bumrungrad.com. This one is the top of the heap, and looks more like a five-star hotel than a hospital. Offers a huge range of specialised clinics, excellent staff, and a selection of rooms from basic four-bed to luxury suites.

Ko Samui

Samui International Hospital: 90/2 Moo 2, Chaweng, tel: 0-7742 2272; www.sih.co.th. The best on the island and on par with the best in Bangkok.

Pattaya

Bangkok Pattaya Hospital: 301 Moo 6, Th. Sukhumvit km 143, tel: 0-3825 9999; www.bph.co.th. Part of a network of well-equipped modern private hospitals that also has a branch in Phuket.

Pattaya International Hospital: Pattaya Soi 4, tel: 0-3842 8374-5; www.pih-inter.com. This hospital is equipped to deal with emergencies and elective surgical procedures, including sex changes.

Phuket

Bangkok Hospital Phuket: 21 Th. Hongyok Utis, Phuket Town, tel: 0-7625 4425; www.phuket hospital.com. Popular with foreign tourists who come for health checks and surgical procedures.

Phuket International Hospital: 44 Th. Chalermprakiat, tel: 0-7624 9400; www.phuket-inter-hospital.co.th. Probably the best healthcare facility on the island and familiar with the needs of international patients.

Medical Clinics

In Bangkok, for minor problems, head to the **British Dispensary**, 109 Th. Sukhumvit (between Soi 3 and 5), tel: 0-2252 8056. It has British doctors on its staff. All the major hotels in Bangkok

and on the major tourist centres also have doctors on call or clinics they can recommend.

Badalveda (www.badalveda.com) is a network of dive medicine centres, with branches in Phuket, Ko Tao, Surat Thani and Bangkok. As well as having hyperbaric chambers, they are experienced in treating other dive-related ailments.

Dental Clinics

Apart from the dental clinics at the international hospitals listed here, the **Dental Hospital** at 88/88 Soi 49 Th. Sukhumvit, tel: 0-2260 5000-15, is recommended. It looks more like a hotel than a dental hospital and has the latest equipment.

In the major tourist centres, head to the recommended hospitals, all of which offer dental services; otherwise grit your teeth if you can and get it fixed when you return to Bangkok.

Pharmacies

These are found everywhere in downtown Bangkok as well as most island and beach destinations. In recent years, official control on prescription drugs has been more strongly enforced and requires the presence of a licensed pharmacist on the premises, especially in Bangkok. Nonetheless, most antibiotics and many other drugs that would require a prescription in the West are still available without one in Thailand.

Check the expiry date on all drugs you buy, and wherever possible, purchase them from an air-conditioned pharmacy. There are several branches of **Boots** and **Watson's** pharmacies in central Bangkok.

Internet

Wireless surf zones (WiFi), at Bangkok airport, and in some hotels and some branches of Starbucks in Bangkok, are a growing trend.

All major hotels in Thailand offer broadband internet services,

including in the rooms, though these are generally more expensive than the public internet cafés. These days, even the smallest bungalow outfits on relatively remote beaches have internet terminals for guests to use. Connection speeds at such places, however, can be painfully slow.

In Bangkok, internet cafés usually charge B30 per hour for broadband services. Be warned though that – in Bangkok at least – they tend to be full of teenagers playing violent games online and can be quite noisy. The Khao San area has more internet cafés than any other area in Bangkok, but the Silom and Ploenchit areas have some internet cafés as well. Ask at your hotel reception for advice.

Left Luggage

There are two left-luggage facilities at Bangkok International Airport. One is on the 1st floor of the Arrival Hall, and the second is on the 3rd floor of the Departure Hall near the currency exchange counter. The fee is B20 per bag per day. The airports at Phuket and Ko Samui also have left-luggage facilities; enquire at the information desks at the respective airports.

All hotels and guesthouses offer a left-luggage service; usually it is free but some may levy a small daily fee.

Lost Property

If you lose any valuable property, report it as soon as possible to the **Tourist Police** (see page 288) to get an insurance statement.
Airport: For property lost at Bangkok airport, contact tel: 0-2535 1254.
Public Transit: BMTA **city bus** service, tel: 0-2246 0973; BTS **Skytrain**, tel: 0-2617 6000; MRTA **subway**, tel: 0-2690 8200, **Hualamphong Railway Station**, tel: 1690.
Taxis: Bangkok taxi drivers frequently listen to two radio

stations that have set up lost property hotlines and it is surprising how often forgetful passengers get their lost items back: **JS100 Radio 100FM** hotline: 1137 and **Community Radio 96FM** hotline: 1677.

M aps

Basic maps of Bangkok are available free at the offices of the **Tourism Authority of Thailand** (TAT) offices *(see page 295)* and at big hotels. More detailed ones can be found at bookshops. The *Insight Fleximap* and *Nelles Map* of Bangkok are probably the best. Other more useful and off-beat insights to Bangkok's attractions can be found in Nancy Chandler's *Map of Bangkok* and Groovy Map's *Bangkok by Day* and *Bangkok by Night*. In addition, Groovy Map also publishes a *Phuket Day & Night*, and *Pattaya Day & Night*. At the larger islands like Phuket, Ko Samui and Ko Chang, free maps are available at hotels and tour agencies.

Media

Newspapers

Thailand has two longstanding English-language dailies, the *Bangkok Post* and *The Nation*. The *Bangkok Post* is more conservative than *The Nation*, which is more maverick and has had a few run-ins with the current government for their often biting coverage. Many big hotels furnish one or the other for free in the room, or they can be purchased at newsstands for B20.

Regional, advertisement-driven newspapers include the weekly *Phuket Gazette* (www.phuketgazette. net), *Pattaya Mail* (www.pattayamail. com) and *Pattaya Today* (www.pattaya toay.net) and the monthly *Hua Hin Today* (www.huahintoday.net).

Magazines

There are several "what's on in Bangkok" type publications in English, covering events, nightlife,

art galleries, restaurants, etc. though most of the free ones are advertisement-riddled and out of date. The best two of the paid glossies are *Untamed Travel* (www.farangonline.com), a monthly that provides listings and well-written stories about Thailand, Cambodia and Laos, with a comprehensive Bangkok section, and *Metro Magazine* (www.bkkmetro. com), aimed more at residents than visitors and focusing more exclusively on Bangkok. Both cost B100 each.

New regional magazines geared toward the tourist market are constantly appearing on the scene. Recommended are the monthly *Hua Hin Observer* (www.observergroup.net), Ko Samui's *Community* (www.samuicommunity. com) and Phuket's *Benjarong* (www.travel-phuket.com).

Radio

AM radio is devoted entirely to Thai-language programmes. FM frequencies include several English-language stations with the latest pop hits. Some frequencies have bilingual DJs and play a mixture of Thai and English songs in the same programme.
• **97 MHz:** Radio Thailand has 4 hours of English-language broadcasts each day.
• **105.5 MHz:** Tourism Authority of Thailand offers useful tips to tourists every hour.
• **Fat FM 104.5:** Has the latest on Thailand's thriving indie music scene.
• **Eazy FM 105.5 FM:** As the name suggests, mostly easy listening middle-of-the-road music.
• **FMX 95.5 FM:** Contemporary dance and pop hits.

Television

Thailand has six Thai-language television channels. ITV or Independent Television specialises in news and documentaries. The rest mainly air soaps and game shows with a sprinkling of mostly domestically-orientated news. There is also UBC, a cable television network that provides

subscribers with a choice of about 24 international channels, including BBC, CNN and CNA.

Money Matters

The baht is the principal Thai monetary unit. Though it is divided into 100 units called satang, this is becoming outdated; only 50 and 25 satang pieces are used.

Banknote denominations include 1,000 (light brown), 500 (purple), 100 (red), 50 (blue) and 20 (green). There is a 10-baht coin (brass centre with silver rim), a 5-baht coin (silver with copper edge), a 1-baht coin (silver), and two small coins of 50 and 25 satang (both brass-coloured).

At the time of press US$1 was trading at B39.

Changing Money

Banking hours are from Mon–Fri 9.30am–3.30pm, but nearly every bank maintains money-changing kiosks in the tourist areas of Thailand. Better hotels almost always have exchange facilities at their reception desks, but generally give poor exchange rates when compared to banks.

Credit Cards

American Express, Diner's Club, MasterCard, JCB and Visa are widely accepted throughout Bangkok and major resort towns like Phuket, Ko Samui, Hua Hin and Pattaya. Smaller establishments, however, may impose a 3 percent surcharge on card transactions. Credit cards can be used to draw emergency cash at most banks. If you lose your credit card, contact your card company as soon as possible so that your card can be cancelled.
American Express: tel: 0-2273 0022/44.
Diner's Club: tel: 0-2238 3600.
Visa: tel: 0-2273 7449.
Mastercard: tel: 0-2260 8572.

Warning: Credit card fraud is a major problem in Thailand. Don't leave your credit card in safe-deposit boxes. When making a purchase, make sure that you get the carbon slips and dispose of them. When your card is swipped through the machine, make sure it is done in your presence.

Travellers' Cheques

Travellers' cheques can be cashed at all exchange kiosks and banks, and generally receive better exchange rates compared to cash. There is nominal charge of B25 for each travellers' cheque cashed.

P hotography

With more than 10 million visitors per year, Thailand gets its photos taken an awful lot. The country and its people are very photogenic, and everything the photographer may need is readily available. Camera shops and photo development outlets are commonly found in the tourist areas, and most now offer digital transfers onto CD and hard copy photos from digital memory cards. Prices are cheaper than in many other countries at B3–4 per print, with bigger enlargements working out to be a real bargain.

Population

Thailand has a population of over 60 million. The official population of Bangkok is about 6 million but given the huge migrant population from upcountry (as well as illegals), it's generally acknowledged to be closer to 9 to 10 million. The population of regional tourist centres can fluctuate greatly according to the number of migrant workers, but rough estimates put the number of inhabitants on Phuket at 288,000, Ko Samui at 50,000, Pattaya at 95,000 and Hua Hin at 42,000.

Postal Services

The Thai postal service is reasonably reliable, though mail seems to go more astray outside

Bangkok and at Christmas time. The odds for domestic mail can be improved by registering or sending items by **EMS** for a fee of B20 for a business-sized letter. EMS is supposed to guarantee that a letter reaches a domestic destination in one day, and it generally does, particularly in Bangkok. If you wish to send valuable parcels or bulky documents overseas, it is better to use a courier service.

In Bangkok, the **General Post Office** at Th. Charoen Krung, tel: 0-2233 1050, is open from Mon to Fri 8am to 8pm, and Sat, Sun and holidays 8am to 1pm.

Post offices elsewhere in Bangkok and Thailand usually open at 8am and close at 4pm on weekdays. Postal services are found at all tourist centres, even on small islands like Ko Samet.

In Bangkok, you can find mini post offices in some office buildings and hotels. Look for a red sign in English. These outlets offer basic mail services and accept small packages, but have no telecommunications services.

Courier Services

The usual global courier services are available in Bangkok. You can call direct or book online.
DHL: www.dhl.co.th; **Bangkok**, tel: 0-2345 5000; **Phuket**, tel: 0-7625 8500; **Hat Yai**, tel: 0-7423 4799.
Fedex: www.fedex.com/th; **Bangkok**, tel: 0-2229 8800, or hotline: 1782; **Pattaya**, tel: 1800-236-236 (toll free).
UPS: www.ups.com/th; **Bangkok**, tel: 0-2712 3300; **Pattaya**, tel: 0-3841 3440; **Phuket**, tel: 0-7626 3987; **Hat Yai**, tel: 0-7436 5596.

Public Holidays

1 Jan: New Year's Day
Jan/Feb: (full moon) Magha Puja. Note: Chinese New Year is not an official holiday but many businesses close for several days.
6 Apr: Chakri Day
13–15 Apr: Songkran
1 May: Labour Day
5 May: Coronation Day

May: (full moon) Visakha Puja
July: (full moon) Asanha Puja and Khao Pansa
12 Aug: Queen's Birthday
23 Oct: Chulalongkorn Day
5 Dec: King's Birthday
10 Dec: Constitution Day

Public Toilets

There are few public toilets in Thailand, though Bangkok is beginning to address this in tourist areas. Public restrooms are usually dirty and sometimes of the squat toilet variety, a tricky experience for the uninitiated. Your best bet is usually to sneak into fast food outlets, which are very easy to find. Shopping malls usually have clean toilets as well, particularly near the food courts. Sometimes a small fee of a few baht applies.

R eligious Services

Though it is predominantly Buddhist, Thailand has historically been tolerant of other religions. According to government census, 94 percent are Theravada Buddhists, 3.9 percent are Muslims, 1.7 percent Confucians, and 0.6 percent Christians (mostly hill-tribe people living in the north).

Buddhist people will find no lack of temples to worship at. The further south you venture the more mosques you will find. There is a handful of Christian churches, one major Hindu temple and at least one synagogue in Bangkok.

Christian

Bangkok: International Church of Bangkok, 67 Soi 19, Th. Sukhumvit, tel: 0-2258 5821. Services at 8am; and **International Christian Assembly**: 196 Soi Yasoop 1, Th. Ekamai, tel: 0-2391 4387. Services at 10.30am and 6pm.
Phuket: Phuket Christian Centre, 74/123 Th. Phunphon, Phuket Town, tel: 0-7624 6380.
Pattaya: Victory Family Church, Pattaya Marriott Hotel, Th. Hat Pattaya, tel: 0-3830 0612.

Catholic

Bangkok: Holy Redeemer Church, 123/19 Soi Ruam Rudi, Th. Withayu, tel: 0-2256 6305. Sunday mass at 8.30am, 9.45am, 11am and 5.30pm; and **St Louis Church:** 215/2 Th. Sathorn Tai, tel: 0-2211 0220. Sunday mass at 6am, 8am, 10am and 5.30pm.
Ko Samui: St. Anna Catholic Church, Na Thon, tel: 0-7742 1149.
Pattaya: St Nikolaus Church, Th. Sukhumvit, tel: 0-3842 2290.
Phuket: Phuket Catholic Church, Le Meridien Hotel, Phuket, tel: 0-7621 1788.

T axes

Thailand has a Value-Added Tax (VAT) of 7 percent. This is added on to most goods and services (but not goods sold by street vendors and markets). You can get the VAT refunded if you purchase at least B5,000 worth of goods *(see text box)*.

All major hotels add 10 percent tax plus 8 percent service charge to the room rate. At top-class restaurants, 10 percent service charge is added to the bill.

When leaving the country from Bangkok International Airport, there is an airport departure tax of B500. There is no departure tax for domestic flights.

Telephones

Public Phones

Even though Thais are heavy users of mobile phones, there are still plenty of coin and card operated telephone booths in the city. Public telephones accept B1, B5 and B10 coins. Phone cards for local calls in denominations of B50, B100 and B200 can be purchased at 7-11 convenience shops throughout the city.

Local Calls

In 2002, area codes were merged with phone numbers and in theory do not exist anymore.

VAT REFUNDS

It is possible to get the 7 percent VAT refunded from your shopping if you purchase goods from stores displaying the "VAT Refund for Tourists" sign. Refunds can only be claimed on single purchases of B2,000 or more, with a minimum overall expenditure of B5,000. At the time of purchase, present your passport and ask the sales assistant to complete the VAT refund form. Before departure at the airport, present your goods together with the VAT refund form and sales invoice to the Customs officers for inspection. After approval, present your claim to the Revenue officers at the airport's VAT Refund Counter.

Refunds not exceeding B30,000 will be made in cash (in Thai baht) or by bank draft or credit to your credit card account. Refunds over B30,000 cannot be made in cash. In addition, there is an administrative fee of B100 for cash refunds; bank drafts and credit card refunds will incur extra charges. See www.rd.go.th for more details.

The prefix 0 must be dialled for all calls made within Thailand, even when calling local numbers within the same city. Therefore when in Bangkok, dial 0 first, followed by the local 8-digit number; if you need local directory assistance, dial 1133.

International Calls

The country code for Thailand is 66. When calling Thailand from overseas, dial your local international access code, followed by 66 and the 8-digit number (without the preceding 0) in Thailand.

To make an international call from Thailand, dial 001 before the country and area codes followed by the telephone number. If you need international call assistance,

dial 100. Peak-hour calls made from 7am–9pm are the most expensive, so it pays to call during non-peak hours from 5–7am and 9pm–midnight. The lowest call rates are from midnight to 5am.

Prepaid international phone cards (called Thaicard) of B300, B500 and B1,000 value can be used to make international calls. These can be bought at post offices, certain shops that carry the Thaicard sign or the office of the **Communications Authority of Thailand** in Bangkok, tel: 0-2950 3712; www.cat.or.th.

Mobile Phones

Any local telephone number that begins with the prefix 01, 04, 06 or 09 denotes a mobile phone. Just like fixed-line phones, dial the prefix 0 for all calls made within Thailand but drop the zero when calling from overseas.

Only users of GSM 900 OR GSM 1800 mobile phones with international roaming facility can hook up automatically to the local Thai network. Check with your service provider if you're not sure, especially if coming from US, Korea and Japan. Your phone will automatically select a local service provider and this enables you to make calls within Thailand at local rates. However if someone calls your number, international call rates will apply. Charges will be billed to your account in your home country.

If you're planning to travel in Thailand for any length of time, it's more economical to buy a local SIM card with a stored value from a mobile phone shop. You will be assigned a local number and local calls to and from the phone will be at local rates. International rates will apply to overseas calls.

Time Zones

Thailand is 8 hours ahead of GMT. Since it gets dark between 6 to 7pm uniformly throughout the year, Thailand does not observe daylight savings time.

Tipping

Tipping is not a custom in Thailand, although it is becoming more prevalent. A service charge of 10 percent is included in the more expensive restaurants and is usually, though not always, divided among the staff. Do leave a small tip when service charge has not been included. Do not tip taxi or tuk-tuk drivers unless the traffic has been particularly bad and he has been especially patient. Porters are becoming used to being tipped but will not hover with their hand extended.

Tourist Offices

The **Tourism Authority of Thailand** (TAT) spends billions of baht every year to promote tourism domestically and abroad. They have information outlets in several countries and service kiosks within Thailand that offer maps and other promotional materials as well as advice on things to do and places to see. The main website www.tourismthailand.org has dozens of pages of information.

Bangkok

TAT Call Centre: tel: 1672. Open daily 8am–8pm.
Tourism Authority of Thailand Main Office: 1600 Th. Phetchaburi, Makkasan, Bangkok 10400, tel: 0-2250 5500. Open daily 8.30am–4.30pm.
TAT Tourist Information Counter (Airport Terminal 1): Arrival Hall, Bangkok International Airport, tel: 0-2504 2701. Open daily 8am–midnight.
TAT Tourist Information Counter (Airport Terminal 2): Arrival Hall, Bangkok International Airport, tel: 0-2504 2703. Open daily 8am–midnight.
TAT Tourist Information Counter (Ratchadamnoen): 4 Th. Ratchadamnoen Nok. Open daily 8.30am–4.30pm.

Regional Offices

TAT Central Region office: 500/51 Th. Phetchkasem, Cha-am,

Phetchaburi, tel: 0-3247 1005/6.
TAT Central Region office: 609 Th. Phra Tamnak, Pattaya. Chonburi, tel: 0-3842 8990.
TAT Central Region office: 153/4 Th. Sukhumvit, Rayong, tel: 0-3865 5420/1.
TAT Central Region office: 100 Moo 1 Th. Trat-Laem Ngop, Laem-Ngop, Trat, tel: 0-3959 7259/60.
TAT Southern office: 1/1 Soi 2 Th. Niphatuthit 3, Hat Yai, Songkhla, tel: 0-7424 3747.
TAT Southern office: 73–75 Th. Phuket, Phuket Town, tel: 0-7621 2213.
TAT Southern office: 5 Th. Thalad Mai, Surat Thani, tel: 0-7728 8818/9.

Overseas Offices

UK: 3rd Floor, Brook House, 98–99 Jermyn Street, London SW1 6EE, tel: 44-20 7925 2511, fax: 44-20 7925 2512.
USA: 61 Broadway, Suite 2810, New York, NY 10006, tel: 1-212 432 0433, fax: 1-212 269 2588; and 611 North Larchmont Blvd, 1st Floor, Los Angeles, CA 90004, tel: 1-323 461 9814, fax: 1-323 461 9834.
Australia & New Zealand: Level 2, 75 Pitt Street, Sydney 2000, tel: 61-2 9247 7549, fax: 61-2 9251 2465.

W ebsites

Thailand

www.tourismthailand.org
The official website of the Tourism Authority of Thailand.
www.dininginthailand.com
A guide to the hundreds of restaurants and bars in Bangkok, plus also Phuket and Pattaya.
www.bangkokpost.com
Daily news from the *Bangkok Post* daily newspaper.
www.nationmultimedia.com
Daily news clips from *The Nation* newspaper.
www.farangonline.com
Listings and articles on Southeast Asia and beyond.
www.circleofasia.com
Reliable hotel and tour bookings

with lots of feature stories and guides on activities and culture.

Bangkok

www.bkkmetro.com
What's on and what's hot in Bangkok, plus nightlife and restaurant listings from one of the city's best lifestyle mags.
www.stickmanbangkok.com
An often humorous and insightful look at Bangkok through the eyes of a somewhat embittered expat.
www.EnglishThai.com
Interpreter and translation services in Bangkok.
www.bangkoktourist.com
Information on Bangkok from the Bangkok Tourist Bureau.

Regional

Hua Hin
www.huahintoday.com
www.huahinafterdark.com
Ko Chang
www.koh-chang.com
Ko Phangan
www.kohphangan.com
www.phanganinfo.com
Ko Samui
www.kosamui.com
www.samui.org
www.samui.sawasdee.com
Ko Si Chang
www.ko-sichang.com
Ko Tao
www.kohtao.com
www.on-koh-tao.com
Krabi
www.krabi-hotels.com
www.phi-phi.com
www.kolanta.net
Pattaya
www.pattaya-at-night.com
www.pattayainformation.com
Phuket
www.phuket.com
www.phuketgazette.net
www.phuket.net
Trang
www.trangonline.com

Weights & Measures

Thailand uses the metric system, except for their traditional system of land measurement (1 rai = 1,600 sq km) and the weight of gold (1 baht = 15.2 grammes).

LANGUAGE

UNDERSTANDING THE LANGUAGE

Origins & Intonation

For centuries the Thai language, rather than tripping from foreigners' tongues, has been tripping them up. Its roots go back to the place Thais originated from in the hills of southern China, but these are overlaid by Indian influences. From the original settlers come the five tones that seem designed to frustrate visitors. One sound can have five different tones: high (h), low (l), mid (m), rising (r) and falling (f), and each of these means a different thing from the other *(see text box below)*.

Therefore, when you mispronounce a word, you don't simply say a word incorrectly, you say another word entirely. It is not unusual to see a semi-fluent

THE FIVE TONES

Mid tone: Voiced at the speaker's normal, even pitch.
High tone: Pitched slightly higher than the mid tone.
Low tone: Pitched slightly lower than the mid tone.
Rising tone: Sounds like a questioning pitch, starting low and rising.
Falling tone: Sounds like an English speaker suddenly understanding something: "Oh, I see!"

foreigner standing before a Thai and running through the scale of tones until suddenly a light of recognition dawns on his companion's face. There are misinformed visitors who will tell you that tones are not important. These people are not communicating with Thais – they talk at them in a one-sided exchange that frustrates both parties.

Phonology

The way Thai consonants are written in English often confuses foreigners. An "*h*" following a letter like "*p*" and "*t*" gives the letter a soft sound; without the "*h*", the sound is more explosive. Thus, "*ph*" is not pronounced "*f*" but as a soft "*p*"; without the "*h*", the "*p*" has the sound of a very hard "*b*". The word *thanon* (street) is pronounced "*tanon*" in the same way "Thailand" is not meant to sound like "*Thighland*". Similarly, final letters are often not pronounced as they look. A "*j*" on the end of a word is pronounced "*t*"; "*l*" is pronounced as an "*n*". To complicate matters further, many words end with "*se*" or "*r*", which are not pronounced at all.

Vowels are pronounced as follows: **i** as in *sip*, **ii** as in *seep*, **e** as in *bet*, **a** as in *pun*, **aa** as in *pal*, **u** as in *pool*, **o** as in *so*, **ai** as

in *pie*, **ow** as in *cow*, **aw** as in *paw*, **iw** as in *you*, **oy** as in *toy*.

In Thai, the pronouns "*I*" and "*me*" are the same word, but it is different for males and females. Men use the word *phom* when referring to themselves, while women say *chan* or *diichan*. Men use *khrap* at the end of a sentence when addressing either a male or a female to add politeness, or in a similar manner as please (the word for please, *karuna*, is seldom used directly) i.e. *pai* (f) *nai*, *khrap* (h) (where are you going sir?). Women add the word *kha* to their statements, as in *pai* (f) *nai*, *kha* (h).

To ask a question, add a high tone *mai* to the end of the phrase i.e. *rao pai* (we go) or *rao pai mai* (h) (shall we go?). To negate a statement, insert a falling tone *mai* between the subject and the verb i.e. *rao pai* (we go), *rao mai pai* (we don't go). "Very" or "much" are indicated by adding *maak* to the end of a phrase i.e. *ron* (hot), *ron maak* (very hot), or *phaeng* (expensive), *phaeng maak* (very expensive), and the opposite *mai phaeng* (not expensive).

Thai Names

From the languages of India have come polysyllabic names and words, the lexicon of literature.

Thai names are among the longest in the world. Every Thai person's first and surname has a meaning. Thus, by learning the meaning of the name of everyone you meet, you would acquire a formal, but quite extensive vocabulary.

There is no universal transliteration system from Thai into English, which is why names and street names can be spelled in three different ways. For example, the surname Chumsai is written Chumsai, Jumsai and Xoomsai depending on the family. This confuses even the Thais. If you ask a Thai how they spell something, they may well reply, "how do you want to spell it?" So, Bangkok's thoroughfare of Ratchadamnoen is also spelled Ratchadamnern. Ko Samui can be spelled Koh Samui. The spellings will differ from map to map, and from book to book.

To address a person one has never met, the title *khun* is used for both male and female. Having long and complicated surnames, Thais typically address one another by their first name only and preceded by the title *khun* for formality, i.e. Hataichanok Phrommayon becomes *Khun Hataichanok*. Thais usually adopt nicknames from birth, often accorded to their physical or behavioural attributes as a baby i.e. *Lek* (small), *Yai* (big), *Daeng* (red), *Moo* (pig), etc. If the person is familiar – a friend, relative or close colleague – then according to the senior age relationship between both persons, they are addressed *Pii* (if older), or *Nong* (if younger). So an older friend would be addressed *Pii Lek*, or if younger *Nong Lek*.

Numbers

0 soon (m)
1 nung (m)
2 song (r)
3 sam (r)
4 sii (m)
5 haa (f)
6 hok (m)
7 jet (m)
8 bet (m)
9 kow (f)
10 sip (m)
11 sip et (m, m)
12 sip song (m, r)
13 sip sam (m, r) and so on
20 yii sip (m, m)
30 sam sip (f, m) and so on
100 nung roi (m, m)
1,000 nung phan (m, m)

Useful Words & Phrases

Days of the Week

Monday Wan Jan
Tuesday Wan Angkan
Wednesday Wan Phoot
Thursday Wan Pharuhat
Friday Wan Sook
Saturday Wan Sao
Sunday Wan Athit
Today Wan nii (h)
Yesterday Meua wan nii (h)
Tomorrow Prung nii (h)

Colour sii

White sii kao
Black sii dum
Red sii daeng
Yellow sii leung
Blue sii num ngern
Green sii keeow
Orange sii som
Pink sii chompoo

Short Phrases

Hello, goodbye Sawadee (a man then says khrap; a woman says kha: thus sawadee khrap or sawadee kha)
How are you? Khun sabai dii, mai (h)
Well, thank you Sabai dii, khopkhun
Thank you very much Khopkhun maak
May I take a photo? Thai roop (f) noi, dai (f) mai (h)
Never mind Mai (f) pen rai
I cannot speak Thai Phuut Thai mai (f) dai (f)
I can speak a little Thai Phuut Thai dai (f) nit (h) diew
Where do you live? Khun yoo thii (f) nai (r)
What is this called in Thai? An nii (h), kaw riak aray phasa Thai
How much? Thao (f) rai

Directions & Travel

Go Pai
Come Maa
Where Thii (f) nai (r)
Right Khwaa (r)
Left Sai (h)
Turn Leo
Straight ahead Trong pai
Please slow down Cha cha noi
Stop here Yood thii (f) nii (f)
Fast Raew
Slow Cha
Hotel Rong raem
Street Thanon
Lane Soi
Bridge Saphan
Police Station Sathanii Dtam Ruat
Ferry Reua
Longtail boat Reua haang yao
Train Rot fai
Bus Rot may
Skytrain Rot fai faa
Metro/subway Rot fai tai din
Pier Tha Reua
Bus stop Pai rot may
Station Sathanii (rot may), (rot fai), (rot fai faa)

Other Handy Phrases

Yes Chai (f)
No Mai (f) chai (f)
Do you have...? Mii...mai (h)
Expensive Phaeng
Do you have something cheaper? Mii arai thii thook (l) kwa, mai (h)
Can you lower the price a bit? Kaw lot noi dai (f) mai (h)
Do you have another colour? Mii sii uhn mai (h)
Too big Yai kern pai
Too small Lek kern pai
Do you have any in a bigger size? Mii arai thii yai kwa mai (h)
Do you have any in a smaller size? Mii arai thii lek kwa mai (h)
Do you have a girlfriend/ boyfriend? Mii faen mai (h)
I don't want it Mai ao
Hot (heat hot) Ron (h)
Hot (spicy) Phet
Cold Yen
Sweet Waan (r)
Sour Prio (f)
Delicious Aroy
I do not feel well Mai (f) sabai

FURTHER READING

Travel & Culture

Culture Shock: Thailand by Robert Cooper and Nanthapa. Graphic Arts Centre, 2003. Very useful look at Thai customs and how to avoid major faux pas.

Mai Pen Rai Means Never Mind by Carol Hollinger. Asia Books, 1995. A very personal book that describes hilarious experiences in Thailand half a century ago. Both amusing and informative.

Travellers' Tales Thailand edited by James O'Reilly and Larry Habegger. Travelers' Tales Inc., 2002. A stimulating collection of observations and true stories by at least 50 writers.

Very Thai: Everyday Popular Culture by Philip Cornwel-Smith. River Books, 2005. If you've ever wondered why every compound in Thailand has a spirit house or why insect treats are such a hit, this book is for you. A must-read for tourists and residents.

Fiction

Bangkok 8 by John Burdett. Vintage, 2004. A best-selling story about a half-Thai, half-American policeman who avenges his partner's death.

The Beach by Alex Garland. Riverhead Trade, 1998. The beach read that inspired the movie staring Leonardo Dicaprio about a group of backpackers trying to find their own paradise.

The Big Mango by Jake Needham. Asia Books, 1999. An action-adventure story about a search for millions of dollars in cash that went missing during the fall of Saigon in 1975.

Sightseeing by Rattawut Lapcharoensap. Grove Press, 2005. Colourful debut novel from

young Thai-American writer that paints a real face of modern cross-cultural Thailand.

Sleepless in Bangkok by Ian Quartermaine. IQ Inc., 2002. A funny thriller about an ex-SAS security consultant on a covert assignment to Siam.

History & Society

Thaksin: the Business of Politics in Thailand by Dr Pasuk Phongpaichit and Chris Baker. Silkworm Books, 2004. Carefully researched study of PM Thaksin Shinawatra and his impact on the economy, society and democracy.

Jim Thompson: The Legendary American by William Warren. Asia Books, 1979. The intriguing story of the American Thai silk magnate, Jim Thompson.

The Revolutionary King: The True-Life Sequel to The King and I by William Stevenson. Robinson, 2001. An intimate portrait of the current King Bhumibol Adulyadej. As monarchy matters are taken very seriously here, the book is unavailable in Thailand.

Bangkok Then & Now by Steve Van Beek. AB Publications, 2000. Hardcover book with photos both old and new showing how the city has changed in many ways, but also remained the same in others.

The Balancing Act: A History of Modern Thailand by Joseph Wright. Pacific Rim Press, 1991. Accessible and detailed history of modern Thailand from 1932 to 1991.

Art

Architecture of Thailand by Nithi Sthapitanonda and Brian Mertens. Editions Didier Millet,

2005. Explores Thailand's unique architectural lineage, from the simple bamboo hut to teak mansions and magnificent religious edifices.

Flavours: Thai Contemporary Art by Steven Pettifor. Thavibu Gallery, 2005. Full of colourful illustrations, it offers insights into Thailand's burgeoning contemporary visual arts scene.

The Arts of Thailand by Steve Van Beek and Luca Tettoni. Periplus Editions, 1999. Beautifully illustrated and includes the minor arts.

Things Thai by Tanistha Dansilp and Michael Freeman. Periplus Editions, 2002. Coffeetable book that presents quintessential Thai objects and artefacts.

The Grand Palace by Nngnoi Saksi, Naengnoi Suksri, and Michael Freeman. River Books, 1998. Beautifully illustrated and detailed account of Bangkok's Grand Palace and its surroundings.

Religion

A History of Buddhism in Siam by Prince Dhani Nivat. Bangkok: Siam Society, 1965. Written by one of Thailand's most respected scholars.

What the Buddha Taught by Walpola Rahula. Grove Press, 1974. Comprehensive account of Buddhist doctrine.

Cookery

Green Mangoes and Lemongrass: Southeast Asia's Best Recipes From Bangkok To Bali by Wendy Hutton. Tuttle Publishing, 2003. Well researched book on the rich diversity of Southeast Asian cuisine, accompanied by many striking photographs.

ART & PHOTO CREDITS

Aleenta 3, 4T, 155
Amari Trang Beach Resort 144, 273
Andrew Woodley/Alamy 46, 64/65
Austin Bush/APA 48, 270, 271, 272M, 273M, 274M, 275, 275M, 276, 277L/R, 278, 278M
Banyan Tree Bangkok 110
Baron/Getty Images 22
Chris McLennan/Alamy 12/13, 176
Chris McGrath/Getty Images 25
Christian Kober/Alamy 56
Craig Lovell/Alamy 28/29
D. Saulnier/HBL 170
David Bowden 31
David Henley/CPA 19R, 21, 26, 40, 81, 167, 169, 221, 225, 245
David Sanger/Alamy 229
Derrick Lim/APA 222M
Devarana Spa 139
E-Sarn Cultural Center 23R
Francis Dorai/APA 74R, 80M, 82, 83M, 86, 227, 274
George Brewin/Alamy 215
Gerald Cubitt/NHPA 150
Hanan Isachar/Jon Arnold Images 212
Ingolf Pompe 6B, 8/9, 249, 253
Jason Lang/APA 33, 41R, 49, 52, 73, 75M, 76, 77, 77M, 85L/R, 85M, 86M, 89, 90, 91L/R, 92L/R, 95R, 97, 97M, 114, 128, 129, 129M, 146, 147, 149M, 150M, 151, 153
Jock Montgomery 38, 50, 53, 62/63, 88, 156, 165, 168, 171, 173, 177, 178M, 204, 204M, 242, 248
Jochem Wijnands/Alamy 118
Joe Louis Puppet Theatre 93
Joerg Kohler/Old Maps & Prints Co. Ltd 17
Johan Furusjö/Alamy 175

John W. Ishii/APA 1, 2/3, 4C, 4B, 5, 6L, 7L, 7C, 7R, 8R, 9T, 30, 32, 34R, 35, 44, 57, 66, 120M, 121L/R, 123L, 123M, 124M, 125, 126R, 127, 130, 130M, 132M, 151M, 152L/R, 153M, 155M, 166M, 169M, 170MT, 170MB, 172, 172M, 174M, 177M, 180, 180M, 181, 182, 182M, 195, 196, 196M, 197L/R, 198, 198M, 199, 200, 200M, 201, 202, 202M, 203M, 205, 213, 215M, 219M, 222, 224M, 226, 227M, 241, 243, 244, 244M, 246, 247M, 248M, 250, 250M, 251L/R, 251M, 252, 253M, 254, 254M, 255, 256, 257M, 258, 259, 259M, 285
Jon Hicks/Alamy 10/11
JW Marriott Resort & Spa 220
Kate Noble/Alamy 223
Lauren Jane Smith 51R, 60, 246M
Livio Bourbon/Archivio White Star 19L
Luca Invernizzi Tettoni 76M, 79, 83R
Marcus Gortz 96
Marcus Wilson Smith/APA 39, 41L, 47, 51L, 58, 74L, 78, 79M, 80, 83L, 84, 84M, 87L/R, 88M, 89M, 90M, 93M, 95L, 95M, 124, 126M, 128M, 171M, 216, 217M, 218R, 219, 228M, 277M
Matthew Burns/Asia Images 218L
Mary Evans Picture Library 16
Michael Aw 8C, 61
Nicholas Pitt/Alamy 164
Oliver Hargreave/CPA 119, 123R, 132
Oriental Hotel 94, 94M
Paula Bronstein/Getty Images 179
Paul Chesley/Getty Images 203
Peter Horree/Alamy 126L

Photobank 18
Pimalai Resort & Spa 257
Pornchai Kittiwongsakul/Getty Images 6R, 20, 24, 43
Private collection 45
Purestock/Alamy 14
Rainer Krack/CPA 42, 217
Rungroj Yongrit/Corbis 27
SIME/Giovanni Simeone/4 Corners Images 224
Stephen Frink/Getty Images 178
Steve Jones/Alamy 194
Steven John Pettifor 7T, 34L, 59, 131, 149, 154, 154M
The Racha 9BR, 228
Travis Rowan/Alamy 72
US National Archives 23L

PICTURE SPREADS

Pages 36/37: Top row from left to right: Steven John Pettifor, David Henley/CPA, Saeed Khan/Getty Images. Bottom row from left to right: David Henley/CPA, Joe Cummings/CPA, AFP/Getty Images, Rainer Krack/CPA
Pages 54/55: All by Michael Aw
Pages 98/99: Top row from left to right: Marcus Wilson Smith/APA, Marcus Wilson Smith/APA. Bottom row from left to right: Marcus Wilson Smith/APA, Marcus Wilson Smith/APA, Francis Dorai/APA, Marcus Wilson Smith/APA, Derrick/APA

Map Production: Mike Adams
@2006 Apa Publications GmbH & Co. Verlag KG (Singapore Branch)

GENERAL INDEX